Commission of the European Communities

ZZ
EM 112
G 26
1990

XXIVth General Report
on the Activities of
the European Communities
1990

Brussels • Luxembourg • 1991

Cataloguing data can be found at the end of this publication

Luxembourg: Office for Official Publications of the European Communities, 1991

ISBN 92-826-2176-6

Catalogue number: CM-60-90-086-EN-C

Printed in Belgium

The President and the Members of the Commission of the European Communities to the President of the European Parliament

Sir,

We have the honour to present the General Report on the Activities of the Communities, which the Commission is required to publish by Article 18 of the Treaty establishing a Single Council and a Single Commission of the European Communities.

This report, for 1990, is the twenty-fourth since the merger of the executives.

In accordance with the procedure described in the Declaration on the system for fixing Community farm prices contained in the Accession Documents of 22 January 1972, the Commission has already sent Parliament the 1990 Report on the Agricultural Situation in the Community.

Under Article 122 of the Treaty establishing the European Economic Community, the Commission is also preparing a Report on Social Developments in the Community in 1990.

And, in accordance with an undertaking given to Parliament on 7 June 1971, the Commission is preparing its twentieth annual Report on Competition Policy.

Please accept, Sir, the expression of our highest consideration.

Brussels, 11 February 1991

Jacques DELORS President	António CARDOSO E CUNHA
Frans M.J.J. ANDRIESSEN Vice-president	Abel MATUTES
Henning CHRISTOPHERSEN Vice-president	Peter M. SCHMIDHUBER
	Christiane SCRIVENER
Manuel MARÍN Vice-president	Bruce MILLAN
Filippo Maria PANDOLFI Vice-president	Jean DONDELINGER
Martin BANGEMANN Vice-president	Ray MAC SHARRY
Leon BRITTAN Vice-president	Karel VAN MIERT
Carlo RIPA DI MEANA	Vasso PAPANDREOU

The following currency abbreviations are being used in all language versions of the General Report and of the other reports published in conjunction with it.

ECU	=	European currency unit
BFR	=	Belgische frank/franc belge
DKR	=	Dansk krone
DM	=	Deutsche Mark
DR	=	Drachma
ESC	=	Escudo
FF	=	Franc français
HFL	=	Nederlandse gulden (Hollandse florijn)
IRL	=	Irish pound
LFR	=	Franc luxembourgeois
LIT	=	Lira italiana
PTA	=	Peseta
UKL	=	Pound sterling
USD	=	United States dollar

Summary

Contents

Contents 23

The Community in 1990

'History has speeded up but the Community, too, has quickened
its pace'
(Speech by the President of the Commission to the European
Parliament, 23 October 1990)

*In view of the changes in the international situation, including the end of East-West
confrontation, German unification and the uncertainty created by the Gulf crisis, the
Community has been concerned neither to limit its horizons nor to ignore its responsibilities. It has drawn on its inner strength (implementation of the Single Act, economic
and social advances in anticipation of the single market, first phase of economic and
monetary union) to give a positive response to the demands made on Europe throughout
the world. With the opening of the two intergovernmental conferences in December the
Community began to give form and substance to European union — the ideal to which
public opinion has rallied in the last few years. The necessary steps were also taken to
ensure that the five new German Länder were smoothly incorporated into the Community.*

*The Community made a valuable contribution towards the establishment of a trade and
cooperation area extending all across Europe, a process which culminated in Paris in
November when a Charter for a New Europe was approved by the Heads of State or
Government of the countries attending the CSCE and was signed by both the President
of the European Council and the President of the Commission. The endeavours of the
countries of Central and Eastern Europe to introduce political and economic reforms were
given encouragement by the conclusion of a full range of trade and cooperation agreements, by the opening of negotiations on a new generation of agreements (known as
'European agreements') which would bring the two sides into closer partnership, and by
the provision of further aid and assistance coordinated by the Group of 24. The Community was particularly anxious to ensure the success of the reforms undertaken in the
Soviet Union with a view to establishing a democratic system and a market economy: on
the basis of proposals drawn up by the Commission in accordance with the instructions
it had received in April, the European Council, meeting in Rome in December, adopted
a number of measures to help meet that country's urgent needs and to help reorganize
and revitalize its economy.*

*As agreed in late December 1989, negotiations with the EFTA countries were opened
during the first half of 1990, with a view to creating a European economic area. These*

negotiations received fresh impetus from the ministerial-level meeting held in December.

Relations between the Community and the United States have been constructive: taking the view that their partnership was an important factor for political stability in a changing world, the two parties reaffirmed their commitment to further cooperation by adopting, in November, a joint transatlantic declaration the scope of which was widened by the signing of a similar document with Canada.

In the Uruguay Round of trade negotiations the Community did all it could to bring about agreement on more liberal arrangements for multilateral trade, which are needed for the growth of the world economy and to safeguard the legitimate interests of the developing countries. Although it proved impossible to reach a positive conclusion within the time available, the European Council nevertheless reaffirmed the determination of the Community and its Member States to reach a balanced agreement on all sectors as soon as possible.

The Community's reaction to the crisis rising from the Iraqi invasion of Kuwait was rapid and effective: from the outset it played a key role in applying the economic sanctions imposed by the international community; it made generous provision for the reception and repatriation of those fleeing from Iraq and Kuwait; it also made the first moves to provide financial assistance to the countries most directly affected by the crisis.

This reaction showed that the Community could mobilize itself to meet an exceptional challenge, while the Twelve now had an extra incentive to speak with a single voice on the world stage. These major international upsets obliged the Member States to work out the beginnings of a common foreign policy, anticipating possible developments in the process of revising the Treaties. The successful action taken in this area lent greater credibility to the plans for political union, to which the common foreign policy had given the kiss of life, so to speak.

On several occasions the Community showed that it was not only ready to shoulder its full responsibilities but was keen to enter into broader commitments vis-à-vis *other parts of the world.*

For example, the Council's adoption of the Commission proposals for a new Mediterranean policy should encourage the framing of a policy on regional cooperation and thus make a useful contribution towards the solution of the structural problems affecting the Mediterranean area and the Middle East, making for greater stability and better economic and social conditions. Similarly, under the new guidelines proposed by the Commission for cooperation with the developing countries of Latin America and Asia, not only would increased funds be made available but the instruments of cooperation would be adapted to suit the needs of the 40 developing countries concerned (with a total population of 2 300 million) and to reflect the extremely wide economic, social and cultural diversity of these countries. In 1989 the Lomé Convention was renewed for the third time, again reaffirming Community solidarity with the ACP countries. A frank dialogue ended with agreement on the programming of Community aid, the cornerstone of the new Convention. Another indication of the Community's readiness to make a real contribution to resolving all aspects of development problems was the Commission's proposal for forgiving the ACP countries' debts.

Although the success of the Community has placed it under an obligation to help others, it has also strengthened itself internally to guard against dilution and to remain the guiding influence which it has become.

Further significant progress has been made towards achieving a major common objective, namely the successful implementation of the Single Act in its entirety. All the measures proposed in the White Paper on completing the internal market have now been sent to the Council: substantial advances have been made in all areas of economic activity, including company taxation, and it is now for the Council to take the awaited decisions as soon as possible, giving special priority to the measures needed for the total removal of internal frontiers.

In the favourable context created by renewed economic growth, the promotion of social progress received a new impetus at Community level with the adoption, in 1989, of the Community Charter of Fundamental Social Rights for Workers by 11 Member States and of the Commission's action programme for its implementation. Without usurping the role of the Member States or the two sides of industry, the Commission laid the basis for a common approach by submitting a first set of proposals covering those areas of the Charter which were considered most urgent. Reiterating the need to give social and economic aspects equal importance in the construction of Europe, the European Council stressed the importance which it attached to the implementation of the Commission's programme.

Future guidelines for environmental policy, a prerequisite for viable economic growth, were set forth in a declaration issued by the European Council when it met in Dublin in June: the Heads of State or Government undertook to intensify their efforts to protect and make better use of the natural environment not only throughout the Community but also in the context of increasing worldwide interdependence.

The Commission's approval of the 15 specific programmes proposed in the new framework programme plotted the course of the research and technology policy which will help to sustain balanced economic growth in the Community over the period 1990-94. Improving the viability of Community industry in an open and competitive environment was also a central theme of the guidelines for industrial policy which the Commission presented to the Council in October. The Merger Control Regulation, which came into force in September, will also help to keep markets competitive.

Further Community integration must keep pace with progress towards economic and monetary union, the natural complement to the full implementation of the Single Act and the completion of the single market in 1992. From the economic and social point of view, neither the Member States nor the citizens of the Community can reap the full benefits of a unified trade and cooperation area unless they can use a single currency (the ecu) and unless the Member States can increase the convergence of their macroeconomic policies. The Community was thus anxious to make a success of Stage I of economic and monetary union, which began on 1 July, and the intergovernmental conference which was called to discuss the arrangements for the subsequent stages. The preparations for this conference were completed when the European Council met in Rome in October, and the conference itself opened in December, broad agreement having been reached on the main points, namely that 1 January 1994 should be the date for launching Stage II and that the ecu should be the sole currency of EMU.

Now that the Member States have acknowledged essential common interests, the institutions must make a quantum leap to bring the Community closer to political union. The results achieved thanks to 'Project 1992', the implementation of common policies under the Single Act and the agreement reached in February 1988 have shown the need to widen the Community's powers and to reinforce its decision-making processes so that it is in a better position to fulfil the hopes placed in the construction of Europe over the past 40 years. The very scale of these achievements raises the question whether the citizens of Europe should not play a real part in this collective venture, and calls for positive action to meet the need for greater democracy. Such is the new frontier towards which the Community now strives, while taking care to strengthen its capacity for effective action in the fields of foreign policy and security.

It was with these considerations in mind that the European Council, having set the ball rolling in April, agreed in Dublin in June that a second intergovernmental conference on political union should be held in December. This conference was to discuss ways of achieving greater democratic legitimacy, developing a common policy on external relations and security, promoting the idea of European citizenship, extending and strengthening the Community and improving the effectiveness of its institutions.

Lastly, the Community successfully met the challenge set by German unification in 1990. At the Strasbourg European Council in December 1989 the Twelve had made a clear commitment to the process whereby the German people were to exercise their right of self-determination and become reunited. The support of the Member States and the action taken by the Community institutions in response to Commission proposals enabled the newly united Germany to integrate immediately and harmoniously into the Community. Full advantage was thus taken of the opportunities which this historic event presented for the development of Europe as a whole and the Community in particular.

Chapter I

Towards European union

Section 1

Economic and monetary union

1. The Strasbourg European Council, held in December 1989,[1] established that the requisite majority existed for the convening of an intergovernmental conference to consider what steps should be taken in relation to the next stages of economic and monetary union (EMU).

Work continued throughout the year[2] in the various Community forums involved on devising an overall plan for EMU and defining ways of achieving it. The Commission put forward a working document[3] as a contribution to the discussions between the Ministers for Finance and central bank governors meeting in Ashford Castle, Ireland, on 31 March and 1 April.[4]

At its meeting in Dublin on 25 and 26 June the European Council took the view that the main issues surrounding the intergovernmental conference had been clarified and decided that it would open in December.[5]

2. The European Parliament adopted two resolutions on economic and monetary union. In May it emphasized the urgent need to complete the single market and to complement it by establishing EMU with a view to introducing a single currency, the

---

[1]   Twenty-third General Report, point 129.
[2]   Bull. EC 1/2-1990, point 1.1.1; Bull. EC 6-1990, point 1.3.2; Bull. EC 7/8-1990, point 1.3.1; Bull. EC 10-1990, points 1.1.2 and 1.1.9 to 1.1.13; Bull. EC 11-1990, point 1.1.2; Bull. EC 12-1990.
[3]   Bull. EC 3-1990, point 1.1.2
[4]   Bull. EC 4-1990, point 1.1.1.
[5]   Bull. EC 4-1990, point I.10.

ecu, as soon as possible.[1] In October it also stressed the need for a rapid transition towards the final stage of economic and monetary union and the introduction of the ecu as the single currency of the Community by the end of 1995.[2] Hand in hand with the latter resolution came another on economic and monetary cohesion, in which Parliament stated its view on the regional impact of EMU.[2]

On 21 August the Commission delivered its opinion on economic and monetary union under Article 236 of the Treaty.[3] It proposed a comprehensive overview of EMU as a means of securing the widest possible agreement, and advocated the adoption of a single currency, the ecu, as swiftly as possible and the establishment of a European system of central banks (Eurofed) which would be independent but democratically accountable and whose basic object would be price stability. The Commission believed there was a clear case for a short transitional period and made a number of suggestions for containing the potential threat to monetary stability from excessive budget deficits.

At its meeting in Rome on 27 and 28 October, the European Council took note of the results of the preparatory deliberations which would form the basis for the intergovernmental conference.[4] Eleven of the Member States laid down a number of guidelines for the conference, including setting the date for the beginning of the second stage, the date on which Eurofed would actually be set up, at 1 January 1994, and providing for the ecu to be adopted as the single currency when the final stage was carried into effect.

3.   The second interinstitutional meeting, which took place in Luxembourg on 8 October,[5] gave Parliament an opportunity to set out its basic requirements in terms of the content and operation of EMU, and on 22 November it gave a favourable opinion under Article 236 of the Treaty on the convening of the two intergovernmental conferences on economic and monetary union and political union, subject to the Council's agreeing to give a number of commitments.[6]

4.   After the Council had given a favourable opinion under Article 236 on 5 December,[7] the intergovernmental conference opened in Rome on 15 December with Mr Carli, Italian Minister for the Treasury and President of the Council, in the chair and in the presence of Mr Delors and Mr Christophersen, President and Vice-President respectively of the Commission.[7] The purpose of the conference is to draft the requisite amendments to the Treaty with a view to making progress towards EMU, in time for their ratification by the Member States by 1 January 1993. The Commission, having

---

[1]   OJ C 149, 18.6.1990; Bull. EC 5-1990, point 1.2.1.
[2]   OJ C 284, 12.11.1990; Bull. EC 10-1990, point 1.1.12.
[3]   Bull. EC 7/8-1990, point 1.3.2; available from the Office for Official Publications of the European Communities.
[4]   Bull. EC 10-1990, point I.5.
[5]   Bull. EC 10-1990, point 1.1.11.
[6]   OJ C 324, 24.12.1990; Bull. EC 11-1990, point 1.1.2.
[7]   Bull. EC 12-1990.

regard to the main contributions to the debate on EMU, took the opportunity to submit a preliminary draft treaty revising the Treaty establishing the Community.[1] A broad consensus had already emerged on many of the principles and rules governing the operation of EMU, many of which were based on the conclusions of the report submitted by the committee chaired by Mr Delors in 1989.[2] Certain options, however, remained open and would have to be decided on at the intergovernmental conference, whose proceedings would move ahead in parallel with those of the intergovernmental conference on political union, which opened at the same time.[3]

---

[1]   Bull. EC 12-1990.
[2]   Twenty-third General Report, point 137.
[3]   Point 5 of this Report.

Section 2

Political union

5.   Intensive preparations took place within the Community institutions for the convening of the intergovernmental conference on political union.

Following the line traced out by the Single European Act, the Dublin European Council of 28 April, having discussed a paper from the Belgian Government and a Franco-German initiative, agreed to take new and decisive steps towards European union.[1] With this object in view, it mandated the Ministers for Foreign Affairs to examine the need for possible Treaty changes with the aim of strengthening the democratic legitimacy of the union while making it more efficient and ensuring unity and coherence in the Community's international action.

Discussions in the Council had started at its meeting of 7 May.[2] At an informal meeting on 19 and 20 May the Ministers for Foreign Affairs agreed that they and the President of the Commission would each appoint personal representatives to prepare the work of the European Council.

In a resolution adopted on 14 June, Parliament said that it could not agree to any unilateral strengthening of the intergovernmental institutions of the Community which would diminish its role as the legitimate representative of the citizens of Europe, and hoped that interinstitutional agreement would be reached on the close involvement of Parliament with the intergovernmental conferences.[3] In a separate resolution it also came out in favour of integrating European political cooperation fully into the Community's activities.[4]

6.   On the basis of the report by the personal representatives and the proposals submitted by the Member States and the Commission, the European Council meeting in Dublin on 25 and 26 June reached agreement on the convening of an intergovernmental conference on political union under Article 236 of the EEC Treaty.[5] The European

---

[1]   Bull. EC 4-1990, point I.12.
[2]   Bull. EC 5-1990, point 1.1.1.
[3]   OJ C 175, 16.7.1990; Bull. EC 6-1990, point 1.1.3.
[4]   OJ C 175, 16.7.1990; Bull. EC 6-1990, point 1.1.4.
[5]   Bull. EC 6-1990, points I.11 and I.35.

Council said that the conference, like the one on EMU, should conclude its work rapidly so that the results could be ratified by Member States by the end of 1992. The two conferences should proceed in parallel, and more detailed arrangements were laid down at the special European Council meeting in Rome in October.[1] The Commission agreed that work should proceed in parallel and undertook to play its part in ensuring that this happened.

7.   Parliament gave its views in a number of resolutions on 11 July.[2] It set out the changes which it wished to see in the foreign policy field and in the areas of social policy, the environment, research and culture, fundamental rights and freedoms and a people's Europe. It also spelled out the changes it would be seeking to achieve in relation to the enhancing of the Council's decision-making capacity, the strengthening of the Commission's executive powers, the strengthening of the Community's ability to enforce its law, the reform of Community finances, particularly the system of own resources, and recognition of the duality of Community legitimacy represented by the Council and Parliament. It announced that it had decided to draw up a draft constitution for the European union on the basis of the main points of the draft treaty adopted in 1984[3] and specific guidelines. Parliament went on to give its views on the principle of subsidiarity, which it hoped would be taken into consideration not only as a means of defining powers but also in determining how such powers were exercised; it considered that the principle should be enshrined in the Treaty and protected by political and judicial guarantees. Lastly, it spoke out in favour of a meeting with the national parliaments (the 'Assizes'), but considered that there was no point in setting up a 'chamber of national parliaments', which might further complicate the decision-making procedure.

On Parliament's initiative, four interinstitutional meetings were held on a number of topics raised in the run-up to the intergovernmental conferences.[4]

8.   A draft revision of the Treaty was submitted by the Italian Government on 13 July.

At its meeting of 16 and 17 July the Council took note of the timetable for preparations for the intergovernmental conference scheduled to open in December.[5] It said that the preparatory work should be based on the four points defined by the Dublin European Council: the overall objective of political union, including its scope; democratic legitimacy; the efficiency and effectiveness of the Community and its institutions; and unity and coherence in the Community's international action.

9.   In an opinion adopted on 21 October under Article 236 of the Treaty, the Commission gave its views on the following aims: integrating the new objectives into a single

---

[1]   Bull. EC 10-1990, point I.14.
[2]   OJ C 231, 17.9.1990; Bull. EC 7/8-1990, points 1.1.1 to 1.1.4.
[3]   OJ C 77, 19.3.1984; Eighteenth General Report, point 1.
[4]   Bull. EC 5-1990, point 1.1.2; Bull. EC 10-1990, points 1.1.6 and 1.1.11; Bull. EC 12-1990.
[5]   Bull. EC 7/8-1990, point 1.1.5.

Community, with the Commission recommending that the final outline of the European union should not be sketched out yet, while holding course towards a federal type of organization; a common foreign and security policy based on the sharing of vital common interests by the Member States; the strengthening of democratic legitimacy through the development of the concept of European citizenship and a strengthening of the role of Parliament; and improving the effectiveness of the Community by extending and broadening its powers and enshrining the principle of subsidiarity in the Treaty.[1]

10.   At a special meeting in Rome on 27 and 28 October, the European Council, to which the ministers' personal representatives had submitted a new report, confirmed, with reservations on the part of the United Kingdom, its will progressively to transform the Community into a European union by developing its political dimension, strengthening its capacity for action and extending its powers to other supplementary sectors of economic integration.[2] It declared that European citizenship needed to be defined and Parliament's legislative and monitoring role developed. It noted that there was consensus on the objective of a common foreign and security policy.

11.   The Economic and Social Committee, in a resolution on political union adopted on 20 November, called for the Committee to be confirmed in its role as an institution in its own right, with a consultative role, and for it to be given the means of expressing its point of view on political union.[3]

12.   At its November part-session Parliament adopted two resolutions on reports by Mr Martin (S/UK) and Mr Giscard d'Estaing (LDR/F) — on its own strategy for European union[4] and on the principle of subsidiarity[5] — translating its July resolutions[6] into legal terms. In December, acting on a report by Mr Colombo (EPP/I), it passed a resolution on the constitutional basis of European union.[7] The content of these three resolutions was largely endorsed by the President of the Commission, who also supported Parliament's being given a degree of joint decision-making power. Following assurances from the President of the European Council, particularly as regards its involvement in the work of the conferences, Parliament also delivered a favourable opinion on the holding of the conferences.[8]

---

[1]   Bull. EC 10-1990, point 1.1.5; available from the Office for Official Publications of the European Communities.
[2]   Bull. EC 10-1990, point I.4.
[3]   Bull. EC 11-1990, point 1.1.7.
[4]   OJ C 324, 24.12.1990; Bull. EC 11-1990, point 1.1.4.
[5]   OJ C 324, 24.12.1990; Bull. EC 11-1990, point 1.1.5.
[6]   Point 7 of this Report.
[7]   OJ C 19, 28.1.1991; Bull. EC 12-1990.
[8]   Point 1 of this Report.

13. The conference of Community parliaments took place in Rome from 27 to 30 November.[1] Its final declaration pleaded for greater cooperation between national parliaments and the European Parliament through regular meetings of specialist committees, exchanges of information and the holding of conferences between parliaments on important occasions, particularly when the intergovernmental conferences were being held.

14. Under the procedure laid down in Article 236 of the Treaty, the Council gave a favourable opinion on 5 December on the convening of the intergovernmental conferences scheduled for 15 December.[2]

15. At its meeting in Rome on 14 and 15 December, just before the opening of the intergovernmental conferences, the European Council discussed the transformation of the Community into a political union in detail.[2] It called on the conference to consider ways of strengthening democratic legitimacy by increasing the powers of the European Parliament, particularly through the development of joint decision-making procedures in relation to acts of a legislative character. It also recommended giving thought to the role of national parliaments in the Community.

As regards the development of a common foreign and security policy, through a process of evolution and on the basis of general objectives defined in the Treaty, it urged the setting-up of the following institutional framework: a single decision-making centre — the Council; the harmonization of preparatory work; a unified secretariat; a strengthening of the Commission's role through a non-exclusive right of initiative; proper procedures for consulting and informing Parliament; and arrangements whereby the union would be able to speak with one voice in the international arena. The decision-making process should be based on consensus for the purpose of defining general guidelines and the possibility of recourse to qualified majority voting for the implementation of agreed policies. It called for the union to have powers in the area of defence, within the Atlantic Alliance and without prejudice to the traditional positions of other Member States.

It looked forward to the concept of European citizenship being given practical form by enshrining in the Treaty such rights as the right to take part in European and local government elections in the country of residence, freedom of movement and freedom of residence for European citizens, and common protection for Community citizens outside its borders. It also recommended the institution of an office of Community ombudsman.

It acknowledged that the Conference should consider the question of extending or redefining the Community's powers in the social field and in the areas of the environment, health, research, energy and cultural and educational infrastructure. It saw a place

---

[1]   Bull. EC 11-1990, point 1.1.1.
[2]   Bull. EC 12-1990.

for the transfer within the scope of the union of certain key areas such as internal affairs and justice in relation to immigration, visas, the right of asylum and combating drugs and organized crime. It recognized the importance of the principle of subsidiarity and of allocating to the union the resources needed to attain the objectives which it had set itself.

As regards the effectiveness of the union, the European Council agreed to continue to act as a political driving force and asked the conference to consider whether that role should be strengthened. It envisaged the possibility of making majority voting the general rule in the Council, subject to a limited number of exceptions. It also recommended reinforcing the role of the Commission, particularly its executive powers.

16.   The intergovernmental conference, which was convened by the Italian Presidency on 4 December, opened in Rome on 15 December, with Mr De Michelis, President of the Council, in the chair, and in the presence of Mr Delors and Mr Andriessen, President and Vice-President respectively of the Commission.

Chapter II

German unification

17. On 3 October 1990 Germany was united once more and the German people thus regained their rightful place in Europe and the world. This marked the achievement of a fervent ambition consistently supported by the Community and its Member States. In a statement issued at the time, the Commission stressed the significance of this historic event, which would give a new impetus for a stronger and more united Community as it moved towards economic and monetary union and political union. [1]

The Community institutions had all done their utmost to help the integration of the former German Democratic Republic into the Community to proceed as smoothly as possible within the timescale set by the pace of unification. From the outset the Commission took the view that the process could be carried out in stages without any need to amend the Treaties, and it began considering the necessary practical arrangements immediately after the first free elections in March, which it warmly welcomed. [2] A blueprint for integration was submitted to the European Council and adopted at the special meeting in Dublin on 28 April, [3] where the Heads of State or Government agreed that, subject to the necessary transitional provisions, the integration of the territory of the German Democratic Republic would take effect without any revision of the Treaties as soon as unification was legally established. They also asked the Commission to submit proposals for transitional measures to the Council, as part of a comprehensive report.

18. Welcoming the European Council's wholehearted support for the unification process, [4] the European Parliament, and in particular its specially constituted temporary committee, [5] was closely involved from the outset [6] in the Commission's appraisal of the implications in consultation with the authorities of the two Germanys. It adopted a

---

[1] Bull. EC 10-1990.
[2] Bull. EC 3-1990, point 1.2.11.
[3] Bull. EC 4-1990, points I.5 and I.6.
[4] OJ C 149, 18.6.1990; Bull. EC 5-1990, point 1.7.1.
[5] OJ C 68, 19.3.1990; Bull. EC 1/2-1990, point 1.6.6.
[6] OJ C 113, 7.5.1990; Bull. EC 4-1990, point 1.6.1.

number of opinions on matters of concern to the House,[1] and in October it decided to amend its Rules of Procedure so as to allow the President to invite the Bundestag to nominate observers from the former German Democratic Republic.[2] The number of observers was set at 18.

19.   Having been involved in the discussions that led to the signing on 18 May of the Treaty (Staatsvertrag) establishing a monetary, economic and social union between the two Germanys with effect from 1 July, the Commission adopted a communication on 13 June spelling out the implications and setting out a timetable for making the necessary adjustments to Community law.[3] The assumption was that integration would proceed in stages, beginning with an interim phase prior to unification, followed by a transitional stage during which some waivers to Community law would be authorized, and culminating in the final stage when the legislation would be applied in full. The approach followed was centred on three main principles: that the integration of the German Democratic Republic should proceed swiftly, with waivers limited both in number and in terms of their scope and duration; that it should not affect the current allocation of budget appropriations nor the priorities defined for the Community policies; and that it should not require any amendments to the Treaties. In the event, the German authorities' use of Article 23 of the Basic Law (accession of the new German *Länder* to the Federal Republic by declaration) meant that Article 237 of the EEC Treaty, which deals with the accession of new Member States, did not apply.

20.   Still in June a series of measures were adopted to establish a *de facto* customs union between the Community and the German Democratic Republic prior to unification;[4] customs duties and charges having equivalent effect were suspended, as were quantitative and other restrictions imposed by Community policy instruments. A similar regulation for trade in agriculture and fishery products was adopted in July.[5]

At the same time provision was made for the measures needed to give the German Democratic Republic access to the Community financial instruments: finance from the European Investment Bank for capital investment,[6] ECSC loans,[7] and Euratom loans.[8] It also became eligible for aid under Operation Phare.[9]

---

[1]   OJ C 295, 26.11.1990; Bull. EC 10-1990, point 1.2.4; OJ C 324, 24.12.1990; Bull. EC 11-1990, point 1.2.3.
[2]   OJ C 295, 26.11.1990; Bull. EC 10-1990, point 1.8.7.
[3]   Bull. EC 6-1990, point 1.2.2.
[4]   OJ L 166, 29.6.1990; Bull. EC 6-1990, points 1.2.3 to 1.2.5.
[5]   OJ L 188, 20.7.1990; OJ L 203, 1.8.1990; Bull. EC 7/8-1990, points 1.2.6 and 1.2.7. Commission proposal: OJ C 165, 6.7.1990; Bull. EC 6-1990, point 1.2.6.
[6]   Bull. EC 6-1990, point 1.2.7.
[7]   Bull. EC 6-1990, point 1.2.9; Bull. EC 7/8-1990, point 1.2.8.
[8]   Bull. EC 10-1990, point 1.2.7. Commission proposal: Bull. EC 6-1990, point 1.2.8.
[9]   Point 669 of this Report.

21. With the date of unification brought forward to 3 October, the Commission's communication of 21 August[1] not only had to cover the transitional measures and essential technical derogations themselves but also had to deal with the delegation of the necessary powers to the Commission for their early application.

22. Thanks to excellent collaboration between the Community institutions underpinned by an interinstitutional agreement on the procedures and timetable to be followed in order to complete the legislative process in time, Directive 90/476/EEC[2] and Regulation (EEC) No 2684/90[2] laying down the interim measures were already on the statute book by 17 September, enabling the Commission to proceed with the rapid adoption of the appropriate regulations and decisions.[3] In October the Commission informed Parliament and the Council of the measures taken to monitor the application of these arrangements.[4]

23. The Commission's proposals on transitional measures were given their first reading in Parliament on 24 October[5] and some of them were modified by the Commission at the same time.[6] On 30 October the Council adopted a common position on the proposals coming under the cooperation procedure,[7] with a political agreement being reached on the agricultural proposals on 5 November.[8] After discussion by the Economic and Social Committee on 20 November[8] and the second reading in Parliament the day after,[9] following which the Commission accepted a number of amendments,[8] the entire package of measures was passed on 4 December.[10] They enter into force on 1 January, replacing the existing interim measures.

24. The transitional measures cover a number of areas. In foreign trade, the former German Democratic Republic's trading partners in Central and Eastern Europe have been granted a two-year period of protection during which the Community will allow the traditional volume of imports into the territory free of duty. Goods that do not satisfy Community standards may be authorized for import but will not be allowed to circulate freely within the Community.

Businesses in the territory of the former German Democratic Republic are exempted from compliance with Community technical regulations and may continue producing goods destined solely for the market there under their old technical regulations. This

---

[1] OJ C 230, 15.9.1990; Bull. EC 7/8-1990, points 1.2.1 to 1.2.3; Supplement 4/90 — Bull. EC.
[2] OJ L 263, 26.9.1990; OJ L 266, 28.9.1990; Bull. EC 9-1990, point 1.1.2.
[3] OJ L 267, 29.9.1990; Bull. EC 9-1990, point 1.1.3.
[4] Bull. EC 10-1990, point 1.2.1.
[5] OJ C 295, 26.11.1990; Bull. EC 10-1990, points 1.2.3 and 1.2.6.
[6] Bull. EC 10-1990, point 1.2.3.
[7] OJ C 295, 26.11.1990; Bull. EC 10-1990, point 1.2.3.
[8] Bull. EC 11-1990, point 1.2.1.
[9] OJ C 324, 24.12.1990; Bull. EC 11-1990, point 1.2.1.
[10] OJ L 353, 17.12.1990; Bull. EC 12-1990.

arrangement, which will apply until the end of 1992, recognizes the excessive burden on industry and society in general which withdrawing these goods would involve. The reverse side of the coin is that goods which do not meet Community standards are not allowed to enter into free circulation. The same also applies to the packaging and labelling of dangerous substances: firms in the new territory have been given two years in which to comply with Community rules.

In the case of agriculture it was decided to integrate the new territory into the market organizations immediately. In view of the uncertainty connected with the conversion of its agriculture and the fact that the guarantee threshold system is due to be reviewed in 1991-92, it was decided to leave the maximum guaranteed quantities broadly unchanged but to apply the current price rules to production in the five new *Länder* in the event of Community production overshooting the limits. Ceilings were set for milk and sugar production. To avoid imbalances on the agricultural markets, the Commission may adopt safeguard measures on its own initiative or at the request of a Member State.

In veterinary matters and in the sphere of plant and animal health, the new territory is exempt from the Community rules until the end of 1992 and the Federal Republic may, with Commission approval, introduce a specific agricultural aid scheme there.

To accommodate Spain and Portugal, where transitional accession measures still apply for some products, the Council decided that their agricultural exports to the former German Democratic Republic would be exempt from the normal duty on imports into the Community until 31 December 1992.

Few exceptions were necessary in the field of transport and were mainly limited to legislation on access to the road haulage business, introduction of the tachograph, driving licences, and adjustments to maritime freight agreements.

A close watch is being kept on developments in the energy sector as it undergoes a radical transformation and on their environmental impact. As regards nuclear safety, no exceptions were made to the Euratom Treaty rules on monitoring nuclear installations.

As far as the structural policies are concerned, the inadequacy of the data available and the need to act swiftly and flexibly led the Community to agree to waive the rules whereby eligible regions have to be determined in advance in accordance with given criteria. On the basis of a Community support framework the Commission will identify specific areas eligible for assistance. So as not to upset the delicate balance in the Funds' allocation of resources and their breakdown by objectives and regions, finance for structural assistance granted in the five new *Länder* will be added to the resources already budgeted. Extra commitment appropriations of ECU 3 000 million will be entered for 1991-93, of which ECU 900 million will be available in 1991.

In the social field, the Community rules will apply straight away. Since 3 October the new *Länder* have been fully included in the training and education programmes. In some cases, however, full involvement may be delayed because of financial commitments already made for 1991.

The current Directives on health and safety at work (except those on exposure to chemical, physical and biological agents) came into effect immediately. The Directives which have to be incorporated into national law by the end of 1992 will also become effective in the whole of Germany by then.

The environment poses one of the most serious problems facing the five new *Länder*, and cleaning up calls for rapid and drastic action. As far as legislative and administrative measures, product standards (except in the case of certain dangerous substances) and new installations and projects are concerned, no exceptions whatsoever will be made. Similarly, nuclear installations immediately became subject to the rules on safeguards and controls. However, transitional measures are warranted for quality standards and discharges by existing installations. Longer deadlines have therefore been granted for compliance with the rules on surface water (end of 1995), bathing water (end of 1993), fish-farming waters (end of 1992), dangerous discharges (end of 1992), groundwater and drinking water quality, the sulphur and nitrogen dioxide content of air (end of 1995), lead in the air (1 July 1994) and asbestos pollution (1 July 1993). Most of these extensions go hand in hand with the provision that strict cleaning-up plans must be drawn up. The Directives on the packaging and labelling of dangerous substances will have to be applied by the end of 1992. In the mean time these products will not be allowed to circulate freely inside the Community. The Directive on waste will have to be applied by the end of 1995.

25.   At the beginning of the year, when the merger of the two Germanys was still expected to take much longer, work on a cooperation agreement between the Community and the German Democratic Republic, begun in 1989,[1] continued, and it was initialled in March[2] and signed in May.[3] However, the agreement was never ratified as it was soon overtaken by the rapid pace of the unification process.

---

[1]   Twenty-third General Report, point 794.
[2]   Bull. EC 3-1990, point 1.2.9.
[3]   Bull. EC 5-1990, point 1.3.10.

Chapter III

Building the Community

Section 1

Economic and monetary policy

Priority activities and objectives

26. In accordance with the objective set by the European Council in Madrid in June 1989, Stage I of economic and monetary union (EMU) began on 1 July. In March the Council had adopted the two Decisions on convergence and cooperation between Member States' central banks that are designed to facilitate implementation of this stage. At its meeting in Dublin on 25 and 26 June the European Council noted that the main issues concerning the intergovernmental conference which — as it had confirmed in Strasbourg in December 1989 — was to be convened to discuss the arrangements for the next stages of EMU were being clarified. In October, in Rome, the European Council reached agreement among 11 Member States on the overall design of the union, involving the adoption of a single currency (the ecu), the setting of 1 January 1994 as the date for transition to Stage II and of the general conditions for the transition from Stage I to Stage III. The aim of the intergovernmental conference, which opened in Rome on 15 December, was to prepare the necessary amendments to the Treaty with a view to their ratification by the Member States by 1 January 1993.[1]

---

[1] Point 1 of this Report.

The economic situation

27.   Despite slackening slightly, growth in the Community contined at a steady pace, with GDP expanding by 2.9% in real terms compared with 3.3% in 1989. The maintenance of such a rate of growth was made possible by the sound structure of the determinants of growth, reinforced by industry's positive expectations regarding completion of the single market in 1992. The slowdown noted was due mainly to the adjustment of certain economies to the counter-inflationary policies resolutely pursued in recent years and to rise in oil prices triggered by the Gulf crisis in the second half of the year. Once again, exports and investment were the most dynamic components of demand, although private consumption played an increasingly important part.

28.   Investment rose at an annual rate of 4.4% compared with 6.8% in 1989, mirroring the slowdown in growth.

29.   Despite a slight decline, exports of goods and services continued to grow strongly at an annual rate of 7.2% compared with 8% in 1989. The Community's external position remained virtually in equilibrium. The divergences in Member States' external positions narrowed as a result of a reduced surplus in Germany (expressed as a percentage of GDP) and lower balance-of-payments deficits in the United Kingdom and Denmark.

30.   Once again, the Community's steady growth performance led to an increase in the number of jobs. Total employment has expanded at an average annual rate of 1.6% since 1988. As a result, there was a further reduction in the number of unemployed, particularly in the under-25 age group. The best performances were recorded in Belgium, Spain, the Netherlands and the United Kingdom. However, the unemployment rate is still too high at 8.5% about two percentage points above its 1980 level.

31.   Inflation in the Community accelerated to 5.1% in 1990, primarily under the impact of the more buoyant trend of wage costs. The rise in oil prices in the second half of the year contributed to this trend.

Economic and monetary union

Start of Stage I

32.   As decided by the European Council at its meeting in Madrid in June 1989[1] and confirmed at its meeting in Strasbourg in December,[2] Stage I of EMU, which involves strengthening economic and monetary policy coordination within the existing institutional framework, began on 1 July. Along with the complete liberalization of capital movements in eight Community countries,[3] the launching of Stage I was facilitated by the Council's adoption on 12 March of two Decisions: one on the attainment of progressive convergence of economic policies and performance and the other on cooperation between Member States' central banks.[4]

33.   On 11 June the Council conducted the first multilateral surveillance exercise in accordance with the procedures laid down in the 'convergence' Decision.[5]

34.   Pursuant to the Decision of 12 March on the convergence of economic policies and performance, the Commission, in December, drew up the annual economic report 1990/91.[6] The Council has been invited to adopt the report, after consulting Parliament and the Economic and Social Committee, and the economic policy guidelines to be followed by the Community in 1991.

Thrust of economic policy in 1990 and 1991

35.   The two economic policy challenges that the Community has had to face in recent years — namely, to reinforce the determinants of growth and to improve convergence — still apply following the latest developments in the Gulf region. The imbalances which have arisen in some countries in the last two years must be corrected if there are not to be disastrous consequences for the basic conditions of growth. Furthermore, nominal economic convergence in the Community must be reinforced in order to ensure that Stage I of EMU is successful.

36.   The uncertainties surrounding, on the one hand, the outcome of the Gulf crisis and its impact on oil prices and, on the other, the United States economy will have a

---

[1]   Twenty-third General Report, point 138.
[2]   Twenty-third General Report, point 129.
[3]   Point 140 of this Report.
[4]   OJ L 78, 24.3.1990; Bull. EC 3-1990, point 1.1.1; Commission proposals: OJ C 283, 9.11.1989; Twenty-third General Report, point 139; OJ C 100, 20.4.1990; Bull. EC 3-1990, point 1.1.1.
[5]   Bull. EC 6-1990, points 1.3.3.
[6]   Bull. EC 12-1990.

considerable influence on the world economy, and in particular the Community economy, in the short and medium term. Economic policy should therefore aim to cushion
the impact of the rise in oil prices on economic growth as much as possible. It should
have two prime objectives: first, to prevent a price-wage-price spiral and the emergence
of further price disparities between the Member States and, second, to lay the
foundations for future growth. In addition, policies should be closely coordinated so as
to avoid any divergence between them and any adverse knock-on effects.

The emergence of an inflationary spiral can be averted by implementing a rigorous
counter-inflationary monetary policy: it must be made clear to those involved in the
economic process that no inflationary tendency will be tolerated so as to quash immediately any expectations in that direction.

Fiscal policy should continue to pursue the aim of medium-term consolidation. While
some initial deterioration in net budget positions is to be expected given the slackening
pace of growth and the possible rise in interest rates, the necessary adjustments must
be made on the revenue and expenditure sides to boost spending that will safeguard
medium-term growth, such as that on public investment, vocational training and
measures to promote research and development.

As the two previous oil-price shocks showed, control over wages and indirect wage costs
will play a key role in containing the negative effects of the rise in oil prices on growth.
The burden imposed on the economy by income losses must be shared fairly in order
to limit the damage to growth. While the precise share-out of that burden between
central government, households and firms will depend on the specific situation in each
Member State, it must be borne in mind that the less firms' capacity to invest is affected,
the more quickly economic growth will tend to pick up again.

Medium-term economic development in the Community

37.   The efforts made and the policies pursued since the beginning of the 1980s have
borne fruit. Not only have growth rates recovered, but growth itself has become more
employment-creating. The proportion of GDP devoted to investment now amounts to
some 20%, while the rate of growth of the capital stock is of the order of 3%. This
performance in the investment sphere suggests that sustained growth can be maintained
in the medium term.

The continued high rate of growth, underpinned by investment, has finally reversed the
employment trend, with increases of 1.6 and 1.7% being recorded in 1989 and 1990.
The improvement has already led to a slight reduction in umemployment, although this
is still too high at around 8.5%, when compared with a figure of 6% in the 1970s and
one of 3% in the 1960s. The Community's growth performance can be enhanced by

strengthening further the economic conditions underlying the current investment-led expansion. Completion of the internal market will improve economic performances further by reducing the administrative cost of trade, by promoting competition between firms and by increasing economies of scale in the productive sector. On present trends, growth rates of 3 to 3.5% suggest that employment will grow by between 1 and 1.5% a year. If this steady growth continues, and given an increase in the labour force of some 0.6% a year, and appreciable reduction in unemployment looks possible.

Operation and strengthening of the EMS

38.   At Italy's request, the fluctuation margin for the lira was reduced on 5 January from 6 to 2.25% on either side of the central rates in such a way as to leave the floor rates for the lira unchanged against the narrow-band currencies.[1] As a result, the lira had to be devalued by 3.677% against the previous central rates. This was the first realignment since January 1987.[2]

39.   Sterling joined the EMS exchange-rate mechanism on 8 October, with a central rate of ECU 1.4349.[3] For a transitional period, it will have a wide fluctuation margin of 6% on either side of the bilateral central rates fixed in relation to the other currencies participating in the EMS. This decision was welcomed by Parliament in a resolution adopted a few days later.[4]

40.   The EMS remained a zone of monetary stability despite marked fluctuations in the rates of other currencies, despite the liberalization of capital movements in the Community, which has the potential significantly to destabilize exchange-rate markets, and despite the Gulf crisis and its immediate and expected consequences.

Wider use of the ecu

41.   One of the measures that will need to be taken during Stage I of EMU is the removal of all obstacles to the private use of the ecu.[5]

42.   The ecu was much more widely used on markets. The number of ecu-denominated issues increased significantly. This was due in large part to the continuing programme

---

[1]   Bull. EC 1/2-1990, point 1.1.3.
[2]   Twenty-first General Report, point 132.
[3]   Bull. EC 10-1990, point 1.3.1.
[4]   OJ C 284, 12.11.1990; Bull. EC 10-1990, point 1.3.2.
[5]   Twenty-third General Report, point 137.

of domestic issues in the United Kingdom, Italy, France and Greece, with Spain too launching its first ecu issue.

43.   As regards use of the ecu by the Community institutions, the Commission adopted the Regulation on the use of the ecu in the structural Funds,[1] which stipulates that payments by the Commission will be made in ecus to the authorities designated by the Member States to receive them. In addition, the protocol signed on 5 July between the Commission and the trade unions and staff associations provides for the transmission to the Council of a proposal concerning use of the ecu in paying Community staff salaries.[2]

44.   The prominent role played by the ecu was accentuated by the decisions to use it for denominating the capital of the European Bank for Reconstruction and Development[3] and for paying the loan granted to Hungary as medium-term financial assistance.[4] In addition, the Norwegian authorities' decision to base their exchange-rate policy on the ecu confirmed the importance of the latter and the area of monetary stability created by economic and monetary union.[5]

The Community and the international monetary system

45.   The annual meeting of the International Monetary Fund was held in Washington at the end of September. The Community was represented by Mr Carli, President of the Council, and by Mr Christophersen, Commission Vice-President. Among international monetary and financial issues, particular attention was paid to the implications of the oil-price rise triggered by the Gulf crisis, the developments in Central and Eastern Europe and the Soviet Union, and the efforts being made to alleviate the debt burden of the poorest countries.

46.   The IMF Interim Committee's 34th meeting, held in Washington in April, focused on the developments in Central and Eastern Europe and on German unification. Special emphasis was placed on the need for major efforts to raise national saving in order to lessen pressure on interest rates and thereby promote investment and alleviate debt burdens.

At its 35th meeting, held in Washington immediately prior to the annual meeting of the IMF, the Interim Committee examined the international economic situation against the

---

[1]   Point 330 of this Report.
[2]   Point 952 of this Report.
[3]   Point 54 of this Report.
[4]   Point 50 of this Report.
[5]   Bull. EC 10-1990, point 1.3.3.

background of the rapid increase in oil prices brought about by the Gulf crisis and the role of the IMF under those circumstances. It underscored the need for a stability-oriented monetary policy and a balanced fiscal policy in order to avoid the risks of inflation and slower growth. It also expressed concern at the slow pace of the Uruguay Round trade negotiations.[1] It appealed to commercial banks and debtor nations to expedite negotiations and to find a solution to the problems linked to outstanding arrears. It called on the Paris Club to study the new proposals for improving the situation of the poorest countries and of the lower middle-income countries.

Community initiatives and financial activities

Development of financing techniques

47.   With a view to promoting venture capital, the Commission conferred the first three 'Eurotech Capital' labels[2] on three financing agencies which agreed to commit a total of ECU 38 million to finance transnational high-technology projects. Negotiations on expanding the capacity for financing such projects in the Community are under way with other financial institutions. In the same connection, initiatives involving 'Eurotech Projects' (creation of a database on transnational high-technology projects seeking finance) and 'Eurotech Data' (technical and economic documentation for appraising such projects) were launched.

Under the Venture Consort pilot scheme for promoting European risk capital activity to assist small and medium-sized firms, finance was provided towards eight acquisitions of holdings in innovative small businesses by transnational consortia.

Community borrowing and lending

Raising Euratom's borrowing ceiling

48.   Euratom's borrowing mechanism was set up in 1977.[3] The initial borrowing ceiling of 500 million EUA was raised to 1 000 million EUA in 1979,[4] ECU 2 000 million in 1982[5] and ECU 3 000 million in 1985.[6] On 23 April the Council decided to raise the

---

[1]   Points 817 to 824 of this Report.
[2]   Twenty-second General Report, point 167.
[3]   OJ L 88, 6.4.1977; Eleventh General Report, point 78.
[4]   OJ L 12, 17.1.1980; Thirteenth General Report, point 63.
[5]   OJ L 78, 24.3.1982; Sixteenth General Report, point 111.
[6]   OJ L 334, 12.12.1985; Nineteenth General Report, point 123.

ceiling to ECU 4 000 million, with a new ceiling to be fixed by it, acting unanimously on a proposal from the Commission, when the level of borrowing reached ECU 3 800 million.[1]

Financial assistance for the countries of Central and Eastern Europe

49.   By decision of 12 February the Council granted a Community guarantee to the European Investment Bank against losses under loans for projects in Hungary and Poland.[2] On 1 August the Commission proposed that the guarantee be extended to loans for projects in Czechoslovakia, Bulgaria and Romania.[3]

50.   On 22 February the Council decided to provide medium-term financial assistance for Hungary totalling not more than ECU 870 million in principle over a maximum period of five years in order to permit it to overcome the structural adjustment difficulties facing its economy.[4] The Commission was empowered to borrow, on behalf of the Community, an initial tranche of ECU 350 million in principle.[5] The grant of a second tranche of ECU 260 million was decided by the Council in December.[6]

51.   The geographical range of ECSC loans was extended to Poland and Hungary, where ECU 200 million was used chiefly to finance projects promoting the sale of Community steel and industrial projects which could be run as joint ventures.[7] In December the Commission adopted a draft decision that would enable ECSC loans to be made also in Czechoslovakia, Bulgaria and Yugoslavia.[6]

52.   As its meeting in Rome in December the European Council agreed that steps would be taken, in particular within the framework of the Group of 24, to meet the financing needs of the countries of Central and Eastern Europe not yet met by public and private aid.[6] It also confirmed the Community's willingness to support, within the same framework, the programme launched by Czechoslovakia with a view to stabilizing and modernizing its economy and making its currency convertible.

---

[1]   OJ L 112, 3.5.1990; Bull. EC 4-1990, point 1.4.14. Commission proposal: Twenty-second General Report, point 128.
[2]   OJ L 42, 16.2.1990; Bull. EC 1/2-1990, point 1.2.9. Commission proposal: OJ C 283, 9.11.1989; Twenty-third General Report, point 145.
[3]   OJ C 242, 27.9.1990; Bull. EC 7/8-1990, point 1.4.4.
[4]   OJ L 58, 7.3.1990; Bull. EC 1/2-1990, point 1.2.12. Commission proposal: OJ C 20, 27.1.1990; Twenty-third General Report, point 45; OJ C 51, 2.3.1990; Bull. EC 1/2-1990, point 1.2.12.
[5]   Bull. EC 3-1990, point 1.2.7.
[6]   Bull. EC 12-1990.
[7]   Bull. EC 3-1990, pont 1.2.5; OJ C 122, 18.5.1990; Bull. EC 5-1990, point 1.3.6.

Borrowing and lending

53.   On 1 February and 7 June the Commission adopted for transmission to Parliament and the Council the twelfth [1] and thirteenth [2] six-monthly reports on the rate of utilization of NCI tranches.

European Bank for Reconstruction and Development (EBRD)

54.   The initiative of establishing a bank to facilitate the transition towards a market economy in the countries of Central and Eastern Europe was discussed at the informal meeting of members of the European Council in Strasbourg on 18 November 1989 [3] following Mr Mitterrand's address to Parliament in October and was approved by the European Council in Strasbourg in December. [2] The first steps towards giving practical shape to the intiative were taken on 15 and 16 January at the inaugural meeting of an intergovernmental conference. [4] As future shareholders, the Community, represented by the Commission, and the EIB met again in March [5] and April [6] to pave the way for the signing of the Agreement establishing the EBRD in Paris on 29 May. [7]

According to Article 1 of the Agreement, 'In contributing to economic progress and reconstruction, the purpose of the Bank shall be to foster the transition towards open market-oriented economies and to promote private and entrepreneurial initiative in the Central and Eastern European countries committed to and applying the principles of multiparty democracy, pluralism and market economics'. The Bank will help finance the considerable investment necessitated by this transition. It will have the right to grant or guarantee loans primarily to firms in the private sector but also to State-run infrastructures and firms that are being privatized or are managed according to the principles of free competition, and to acquire or finance acquisitions of holdings in such firms. The Bank's capital, which will be ECU 10 000 million, will be contributed initially by 41 shareholders (39 countries, the European Economic Community in its own right and the European Investment Bank). The bulk (over 75%) of the capital will come from Europe (51% from the Community and its Member States, some 12% from the countries of Central and Eastern Europe, which are the potential beneficiaries, and around 12% from other European countries). The balance will be contributed by non-European countries, in particular the United States of America and Japan. Apart from the

---

[1]   Bull. EC 1/2-1990, point 1.1.4.
[2]   Bull. EC 6-1990, point 1.3.5.
[3]   Twenty-third General Report, point 786.
[4]   Bull. EC 1/2-1990, point 1.2.7.
[5]   Bull. EC 3-1990; point 1.2.2.
[6]   Bull. EC 4-1990, point 1.2.2.
[7]   Bull. EC 5-1990, point 1.3.1.

resources made up of the 30% of capital that will be paid in, the Bank will have the right to grant loans or acquire holdings using funds raised on capital markets.

On 19 November the Council adopted the Decision on the conclusion of the Bank's Articles of Agreement.[1]

SPES activities

55.   The European stimulation plan for economic science (SPES)[2] generated a considerable amount of interest in university circles during its first year of operation. This prompted the Commission to transmit to the Council a proposal for raising the initial budget from ECU 6 million to ECU 10 million.[3] The proposal was endorsed by the Economic and Social Committee in September.[4] In addition, cooperation agreements between the Community and the EFTA countries aimed at extending the geographical coverage of the SPES programme are in the process of being approved: proposals from the Commission[5] were endorsed by Parliament[6] and the Economic and Social Committee[7] in October, the Council adopting a common position in November.[8] Financing for 20 projects and the allocation of 13 grants were approved under the programme. As part of Operation Phare,[9] measures were taken to foster cooperation with Poland and Hungary in the field of economic science. The operational procedures and activities envisaged, for which a budget of ECU 1.5 million was set for 1990, are similar to those of the SPES programme.

---

[1]   OJ L 372, 31.12.1990; Bull. EC 11-1990, point 1.4.5. Commission proposal: OJ C 241, 26.9.1990; Bull. EC 5-1990, point 1.3.1.
[2]   OJ L 44, 16.2.1989; Twenty-third General Report, point 148.
[3]   OJ C 155, 26.6.1990; Bull. EC 5-1990, point 1.2.92.
[4]   Bull. EC 9-1990, point 1.2.75.
[5]   OJ C 148, 16.6.1990; Bull. EC 5-1990, point 1.2.110.
[6]   OJ C 284, 12.11.1990; Bull. EC 11-1990, point 1.3.74.
[7]   OJ C 321, 21.12.1990; Bull. EC 11-1990, point 1.3.74.
[8]   Bull. EC 11-1990, point 1.3.81.
[9]   Point 668 of this Report.

Section 2

Completing the internal market

Priority activities and objectives

56.   Progress towards completion of the internal market programme set out in the Commission's White Paper[1] is an irreversible process. All of the measures planned have been presented to the Council by the Commission; furthermore, the Council has already adopted more than two-thirds of the programme, a considerably faster rate of progress than originally thought possible. It is now for the Council to take the outstanding decisions as quickly as possible, giving special priority to the measures necessary for ensuring the complete removal of internal frontiers. This is because the legislative process will have to be completed by the end of 1991 to allow all the relevant legislation to be transposed into national law during 1992.

57.   Substantial progress has been made in all areas of economic activity. Important decisions taken in 1990 include those relating to the extension of the right of residence to all Community citizens, a series of measures designed to eliminate double taxation in transfrontier operations in the Community and a second series of measures liberalizing air transport;[2] there was also a marked increase in the number of decisions relating to veterinary and plant health checks. In the public procurement field, two Directives were adopted: one on the transport, energy, water and telecommunications sectors and the other on review procedures in connection with the earlier Directives on public works and public supply contracts. As regards standardization, decisions have been taken concerning gas appliances, non-automatic weighing machines, and assessment and conformity procedures. In the financial services field, particular progress has been made in the insurance sector; the Directive liberalizing capital movements came into force in July. As indicated in the document adopted by the Commission in March on the programme's impact with three years to go to the deadline set, both Community and non-Community companies are preparing for completion of the internal market and are making the European dimension an integral part of their strategies. This is reflected particularly in the growth of investment and in the ever-growing number of transfrontier mergers, takeovers and acquisitions.

---

[1]   Nineteenth General Report, points 162 to 166.
[2]   Point 556 of this Report.

58.   *Despite the progress made in the decision-making process, the Commission systema-tically drew attention, both in its fifth report on the implementation of the White Paper[1] and in its communication on implementation of the legal acts required to build the single market,[2] to those parts of the programme which still pose problems. It did so again in November in the report it is required to present to the Council under Article 8b of the Treaty.[3] It identified two main difficulties. Firstly, the rate of decision-making in the case of measures for which the Single Act does not impose any cooperation procedure is still too slow, especially as regards the total removal of internal frontier controls, intellectual property and transport. Secondly, despite the real progress made in the legislative process, some Member States still fail to implement decisions on time. In the light of that report, the Council adopted[4] in December conclusions committing Member States to speed up the rate of transposition of Community legislation so that all the current leeway can be fully made up by the end of 1991. Parliament also expressed its view[5] in November on the progress made towards completing the internal market.*

59.   *The Commission is endeavouring to ensure that the internal market functions smoothly and is aiming to achieve three major objectives in that regard: to establish efficient and transparent procedures for administering Community legislation, to extend the principle of mutual recognition by direct application of the Treaty and by implementing the principles set out in the 'new approach', and to monitor compliance with Community obligations.[6] Transparency with regard to implementation of Community law calls for the regular publication of reports, the reinforcement of contacts with the authorities in the Member States and the use of computerized databases allowing cross-monitoring by Member States and by economic agents and organizations.*

60.   *In parallel with this legislative process to eliminate obstacles to trade, the Com-mission, in consultation with the Member States and other parties concerned, has con-tinued to examine ways of improving the infrastructures essential to the proper functioning of the internal market in line with its December 1989 communication on trans-European networks and the ensuing Council resolution.[7] The four fields covered by this work are transport, telecommunications, energy and training. The Commission submitted an in-terim report[8] to the Council in July and laid before it, in December, an action programme[9] comprising three closely linked parts: priority projects in each of the fields in question;*

---

[1]   Bull. EC 3-1990, point 1.1.4.
[2]   Bull. EC 10-1990, point 1.3.6.
[3]   Bull. EC 11-1990, point 1.3.2.
[4]   Bull. EC 12-1990.
[5]   OJ C 324, 24.12.1990; Bull. EC 11-1990, point 1.3.3.
[6]   Further information is contained in the eighth annual report to Parliament on Commission monitoring of
       the application of Community law (1990).
[7]   OJ C 27, 6.2.1990; Twenty-third General Report, point 154.
[8]   Bull. EC 7/8-1990, point 1.3.5.
[9]   Bull. EC 12-1990.

horizontal measures relating to working methods, regulation or standardization; and financial arrangements.

61.   With regard to the removal of tax frontiers, the entire package of proposals for the temporary VAT arrangements, which are due to come into force on 1 January 1993, is now before the Council, and proposals for the new structure of excise duties and the movement of goods subject to such duties have also been made. The Council made a major step forward in this sensitive area when it reached agreement on the basic features of the new VAT arrangements, namely the chargeable event and controls. It also agreed on general arrangements for the holding and movement of dutiable goods. Despite such advances, the Council has not so far been able to agree on the proposal for changing over to the definitive system in 1996 or on raising travellers' allowances.

62.   In the customs field, priorities have been dictated by the proximity of the 1992 deadline. A number of customs procedures have thus been amended to adapt them to the future single market without internal frontiers, particularly in connection with the movement of goods. With the same aim in view, the Commission has endeavoured to ensure that the Member States apply Community legislation more uniformly, mainly by continuing work on the proposal for a Community customs code, which is before the Council, and by stepping up its activities relating to the training of Member States' customs officers, which include the 'Matthaeus' programme of exchanges of national officials.

BUSINESS ENVIRONMENT

Removal of physical frontiers

Checks on goods

Movement of goods within the Community

Simplification of checks and formalities in trade

Single Administrative Document

63.   On 30 July[1] the Commission amended Regulation (EEC) No 2793/86 laying down the codes to be used in the Single Administrative Document[2] following the modification

---

[1]   OJ L 202, 31.7.1990; Bull. EC 7/8-1990, point 1.3.8.
[2]   OJ L 263, 15.9.1986; Twentieth General Report, point 283.

by the International Chamber of Commerce of the Incoterm codes for delivery terms. In order to take account of the removal of frontiers, a proposal was also put to the Council for another regulation eliminating use of the document in trade in Community goods within the Community from 1 January 1993.[1] This proposal was examined by Parliament[2] and the Economic and Social Committee[3] in December.

Simplification of transit procedures

64. On 22 February the Council adopted an amendment[4] to Regulation (EEC) No 222/77 on Community transit,[5] abolishing from 1 July the requirement for traders to lodge a transit advice note at each crossing of an internal Community frontier. On 29 May the Community accordingly amended[6] Regulation (EEC) No 1062/87[7] with effect from 1 July, to provide for implementation of the Regulation abolishing the transit advice note rule, and also to extend the general waiver of guarantee under the internal Community transit system. Regulation (EEC) No 1062/87[7] was amended again on 10 October, this time to enable traders to establish the Community status of goods in intra-Community trade by production of an invoice or transport document, thus removing the need for administrative forms.[8]

65. On 17 September the Council adopted Regulation (EEC) No 2726/90 modifying the customs provisions applying to the Community transit procedure in readiness for the completion of the internal market and the concomitant abolition of internal frontiers on 1 January 1993.[9] On 16 May the Commission adopted a proposal for a regulation designed to ensure that the application in the Community of the TIR and ATA transit arrangements is adapted to reflect the abolition of internal frontiers.[10] This proposal had its first reading in Parliament[11] and was examined by the Economic and Social Committee[12] in November, and the Council adopted a common position in December.[2]

---

[1]   OJ C 214, 29.8.1990; Bull. EC 7/8-1990, point 1.3.7.
[2]   Bull. EC 12-1990.
[3]   OJ C 19, 28.1.1991; Bull. EC 12-1990.
[4]   OJ L 51, 27.2.1990; Bull. EC 1/2-1990, point 1.1.8; Commission proposal: OJ C 245, 26.9.1989;
       Twenty-third General Report, point 374.
[5]   OJ L 38, 9.2.1977; Eleventh General Report, point 167.
[6]   OJ L 137, 30.5.1990; Bull. EC 5-1990, point 1.2.9.
[7]   OJ L 107, 22.4.1987; Twenty-first General Report, point 179.
[8]   OJ L 279, 11.10.1990; Bull. EC 10-1990, point 1.3.7.
[9]   OJ L 262, 26.9.1990; Bull. EC 9-1990, point 1.2.8; Commission proposal: OJ C 307, 6.12.1989;
       Twenty-third General Report, point 174.
[10]   OJ C 142, 12.6.1990; Bull. EC 5-1990, point 1.2.19.
[11]   OJ C 324, 24.12.1990; Bull. EC 11-1990, point 1.3.10.
[12]   Bull. EC 11-1990, point 1.3.10.

Other simplifications

66. In late July the Commission adopted a set of proposals for: a Regulation concerning the elimination of controls and formalities applicable to the cabin and checked baggage of passengers taking an intra-Community flight and the baggage of passengers making an intra-Community sea crossing, to ensure that such passengers enjoy the freedom of movement conferred by Article 8a of the Treaty;[1] Directive[2] amending Directive 83/643/EEC in the facilitation of physical inspections and administrative formalities in respect of the carriage of goods between Member States,[3] introducing further simplifications for the period prior to completion of the internal market; and a Regulation[4] amending Regulation (EEC) No 3/84 introducing arrangements for movement within the Community of goods sent from one Member State for temporary use in one or more Member States,[5] to extend its scope pending its repeal on 1 January 1993. In December the Council adopted a common position[6] on the latter proposal, on which Parliament[7] and the Economic and Social Committee[8] had delivered opinions in November. In December Parliament delivered its opinion on the proposal for an amendment to Directive 83/643/EEC[9] and the proposal for a regulation on baggage;[9] the Economic and Social Committee also delivered an opinion on the latter.[6]

67. A Council decision[10] adopted on 23 April approved on behalf of the Community the Agreement with Switzerland on the simplification of inspections and formalities in respect of the carriage of goods, initialled on 20 December 1989.[11] The Agreement was signed on 21 November.[12]

68. In September the Council authorized the Commission to participate on behalf of the Community in the Customs Cooperation Council negotiations for a Convention on the Single Goods Declaration.[13]

---

[1]   OJ C 212, 25.8.1990; Bull. EC 7/8-1990, point 1.3.9.
[2]   OJ C 204, 15.8.1990; Bull. EC 7/8-1990, point 1.3.6.
[3]   OJ L 359, 22.12.1983.
[4]   OJ C 212, 25.8.1990; Bull. EC 7/8-1990, point 1.3.10.
[5]   OJ L 2, 4.1.1984; Seventeenth General Report, point 221.
[6]   Bull. EC 12-1990.
[7]   OJ C 324, 24.12.1990; Bull. EC 11-1990, point 1.3.7.
[8]   Bull. EC 11-1990, point 1.3.7.
[9]   OJ C 19, 28.1.1991; Bull. EC 12-1990.
[10]   OJ L 116, 8.5.1990; Bull. EC 4-1990, point 1.1.4.
[11]   Twenty-third General Report, point 178.
[12]   Bull. EC 11-1990, point 1.3.6.
[13]   Bull. EC 9-1990, point 1.2.11; Commission proposal: Bull. EC 3-1990, point 1.1.14.

Coordinated development of computerized administrative procedures

69.   In order to modernize certain customs procedures central management functions need to be computerized. The Taric interface (electronic transfer to Member States of updatings of the Community's integrated tariff) and the Quota system for automatic tariff quota and ceiling management are now in place. The electronic transfer of requests for drawings is operational for Ireland and Denmark and trials are under way in Belgium, France, Luxembourg and the Netherlands. Specifications were drawn up for a pilot project on transit procedures, which is now in preparation. Specifications are also being worked out for a databank to store binding tariff information issued by Member States, and arrangements were finalized for Stage II of the Taric and Scent (system for a customs enforcement network) projects. Electronic messages representing the customs declaration and the response to it, drawn up in accordance with the Edifact standard, were given UN status 1 approval in September.

Mutual assistance, administrative cooperation and fraud control

70.   In accordance with the mandate it received from the Council in October 1989,[1] the Commission started negotiations with the EFTA countries for an agreement on mutual administrative assistance in the customs field. Such an agreement is of capital importance, not only for the smooth functioning of the customs union, but also for the European Economic Area being formed between the Community and EFTA.[2] The measures proposed by the Commission in May in connection with the abolition of tax frontiers include provision for administrative cooperation in the field of indirect taxation so that a satisfactory level of control can be maintained.[3]

71.   On 12 November the Commission adopted a proposal[4] for the amendment of Council Directive 76/308/EEC on mutual assistance for the recovery of claims in respect of import duties and VAT.[5] The proposed amendment would extend the provisions in force to excise duties and put all claims on the same footing.

72.   On 8 October the representatives of the governments of the Member States, meeting within the Council, adopted a declaration concerning the continuing role of customs after the completion of the internal market.[6]

---

[1]   Twenty-third General Report, point 171.
[2]   Point 688 of this Report.
[3]   Point 156 of this Report.
[4]   OJ C 306, 6.12.1990; Bull. EC 11-1990, point 1.3.18.
[5]   OJ L 73, 19.3.1976; Tenth General Report, point 78.
[6]   OJ C 262, 17.10.1990.

Training: the Matthaeus programme

73. The exchange programme for national customs officials (the Matthaeus programme)[1] got under way; 578 officials from the Member States participated. The programme is organized around the twinning of customs offices from different Member States and is aimed at officials concerned with the day-to-day implementation of Community law or with fraud control. In the light of this experience the Commission adopted, in December, a draft decision for a Community customs training programme to come into force in 1991.[2]

Customs union: the external dimension

Harmonization of customs rules on trade with non-member countries

Common Customs Tariff, Combined Nomenclature and Taric

74. With a view to establishing a system of information valid Community-wide, on 20 June the Council adopted Regulation (EEC) No 1715/90 on the information provided by the customs authorities of the Member States concerning the classification of goods in the customs nomenclature.[3]

75. By virtue of the powers of delegation contained in Regulation (EEC) No 2658/87,[4] the Commission adopted the Combined Nomenclature (CN) applicable in 1991[5] and a number of regulations intended to ensure uniform application of the CN.

At international level, the Commission represented the Community in the Customs Cooperation Council in discussions relating to the administration of the Harmonized Commodity Description and Coding System (HS) and in preparatory work on revision of the HS nomenclature.

76. The new edition of Taric, the integrated Community tariff, which was published in April, incorporates all Community measures applicable to trade with non-member countries, product by product. Taric database updates are transmitted electronically to

---

[1]   Twenty-third General Report, point 180.
[2]   Bull. EC 12-1990.
[3]   OJ L 160, 26.6.1990; Bull. EC 6-1990, point 1.3.9; Commission proposal: OJ C 256, 8.10.1981; Fifteenth General Report, point 198; OJ C 81, 22.3.1984; OJ C 28, 3.2.1989; Twenty-third General Report, point 157; OJ C 142, 12.6.1990; Bull. EC 5-1990, point 1.2.13.
[4]   OJ L 256, 7.9.1987; Twenty-first General Report, point 157.
[5]   OJ L 247, 10.9.1990; Bull. EC 7/8-1990, point 1.3.13.

the Member States.[1] Taric codes are used in Community regulations whose application requires the use of subdivisions of the CN codes. The Commission and the Member States began work on the incorporation of new measures in Taric in preparation for 1992.

Economic tariff matters

77.   In many instances tariff measures, whether required under agreements or introduced unilaterally, and generally adopted by Council regulation, involve reductions in CCT duties or zero-rating for all or some imports of the products concerned. They take the form of Community tariff quotas, tariff ceilings or total or partial suspension of duties.

78.   In 1990, 236 tariff quotas or ceilings were opened pursuant to commitments entered into by the Community during GATT negotiations, under bilateral agreements with non-member countries or on a unilateral basis, in order to secure the Community supply situation for certain products on favourable terms.

79.   For the same reason, and also in many cases to encourage Community industry to use or introduce new technology, the Council temporarily suspended duties on about 1 600 products or groups of products, mainly chemicals and products of the electronics or aircraft industries. Tariffs were also suspended on a number of agricultural and fishery products, to improve the supply of certain types of food and honour commitments entered into with certain preferential non-member countries.

80.   The Regulations giving effect to generalized tariff preferences for imports from certain countries were renewed as part of the Community's development aid policy. Preferences were also granted for a limited period to Czechoslovakia and Bulgaria as well as Poland and Hungary.[2] The process of updating the quotas and widening the differential in preferential treatment for the benefit of less competitive countries was continued.

Customs valuation

81.   On 27 September, in preparation for the unification of Germany,[3] the Commission amended[4] the rules on the place of introduction to be taken into consideration for the calculation of customs value.[5] The incorporation into the Community's customs territory

---

[1]   Point 69 of this Report.
[2]   Point 795 of this Report.
[3]   Point 22 of this Report.
[4]   OJ L 267, 29.9.1990; Bull. EC 9-1990, point 1.1.6.
[5]   OJ L 335, 12.12.1980; Fourteenth General Report, point 167.

of the territory of the former German Democratic Republic also made it necessary to amend[1] the rules on air transport costs to be included in customs value.[2]

82. The Commission also amended[3] the list of goods covered by the system of simplified procedures[4] and the list of marketing centres used for the purposes of that system, in order to take account of trends in the importation of perishable goods.

Customs procedures with economic impact

83. On 26 March, in order to ensure equality of treatment for all traders, the Commission amended[5] Regulation (EEC) No 3677/86 on inward processing relief arrangements,[6] simplifying the procedure for granting authorization and providing for the application of compensatory interest to offset windfall gains arising from the postponement of customs debt when goods previously entered for the arrangements are released for free circulation. On the basis of the new provision the Commission then adopted Regulation (EEC) No 1415/90 laying down rates of compensatory interest applicable during the second half of 1990;[7] to ensure that the rules are applied in a uniform manner, it published specimen interest rate calculations.[8] On 31 October it adopted Regulation (EEC) No 3185/90 introducing the possibility of using a document checking system to establish that the compensating products have been made from temporarily exported goods and specifying the precise conditions subject to which the standard exchange system may be used.[9] On 13 November the Commission adopted a proposal[10] for an amendment to Regulation (EEC) No 3677/86 laying down rules for the application of the economic conditions and consolidating the existing provisions.

84. On 14 March the Commission adopted a proposal[11] for a Regulation amending Regulation (EEC) No 2763/83 on arrangements permitting goods to be processed under customs control before being put into free circulation.[12]

85. In order to facilitate transit traffic and clarify the rules on storage of goods, the Commission adopted Regulations (EEC) Nos 2561/90 and 2562/90 laying down pro-

---

[1]   OJ L 273, 3.10.1990; Bull. EC 9-1990, point 1.1.7.
[2]   OJ L 347, 23.12.1985; Nineteenth General Report, point 176.
[3]   OJ L 321, 21.11.1990; Bull. EC 11-1990, point 1.3.9.
[4]   OJ L 154, 13.6.1981; Fifteenth General Report, point 190.
[5]   OJ L 81, 28.3.1990; Bull. EC 3-1990, point 1.1.8.
[6]   OJ L 351, 12.12.1986; Twentieth General Report, point 174.
[7]   OJ L 136, 29.5.1990; Bull. EC 5-1990, point 1.2.11.
[8]   OJ C 161, 30.6.1990.
[9]   OJ L 304, 1.11.1990; Bull. EC 10-1990, point 1.3.9.
[10] Bull. EC 11-1990, point 1.3.8.
[11] Bull. EC 3-1990, point 1.1.6.
[12] OJ L 272, 5.10.1983; Seventeenth General Report, point 211.

visions for the implementation of the customs warehousing arrangements and those for free zones and free warehouses.[1]

86. In June the Commission, on behalf of the Community, signed the Customs Cooperation Council's Convention on Temporary Admission.[2] It was also authorized by the Council to take part in the negotiations for a convention on the customs arrangements applicable to containers used within an international pool, under the aegis of the UN's Economic Commission for Europe.[3]

Origin of goods

87. Transitional measures were adopted in March pending the entry into force of the new ACP-EEC Convention.[4] On 8 October the Council adopted a proposal for a decision establishing a procedure for derogations from the origin rules in Protocol 1 to the Lomé Convention.[5] Derogations from the ACP/OCT origin rules were granted by the Council to St Pierre and Miquelon (fishery products)[6] and the Netherlands Antilles (protective clothing[7] and cigarettes[8]). A new procedure was introduced allowing Mauritius automatic derogations for its canned tuna.[9]

88. The Council adopted a series of Regulations implementing decisions of the Association/Cooperation Councils modifying amounts expressed in ecus in the 'origin' Protocols to the Agreements with Egypt, Jordan, Lebanon, Morocco and Yugoslavia.[10] It also adopted two Regulations amending these Protocols to the Cyprus and Malta Agreements to take account of the accession of Spain and Portugal.[11]

89. The Council and the Commission adopted various Regulations implementing decisions[12] of the Joint Committees under the Agreements with the EFTA countries (Austria, Finland, Iceland, Norway, Sweden and Switzerland) concerning revisions to the transposition of the origin rules of those Agreements into the Harmonized System.[13]

---

[1]   OJ L 246, 10.9.1990; Bull. EC 7/8-1990, points 1.3.11 and 1.3.12.
[2]   Bull. EC 6-1990, point 1.3.14.
[3]   Bull. EC 5-1990, point 1.2.18; Commission proposal: Bull. EC 3-1990, point 1.2.18.
[4]   Point 766 of this Report.
[5]   OJ L 290, 23.10.1990; Bull. EC 10-1990, point 1.3.11; Commission proposal: Bull. EC 6-1990, point 1.3.12.
[6]   OJ L 202, 31.7.1990; Bull. EC 7/8-1990, point 1.3.21; Commission proposal: Bull. EC 6-1990, point 1.3.13.
[7]   OJ L 174, 7.7.1990; Bull. EC 6-1990, point 1.3.10; Commission proposal: Bull. EC 3-1990, point 1.1.12.
[8]   OJ L 279, 11.10.1990; Bull. EC 10-1990, point 1.3.10; Commission proposal: Bull. EC 3-1990, point 1.1.12.
[9]   OJ L 206, 4.8.1990.
[10] OJ L 198, 28.7.1990; Bull. EC 7/8-1990, point 1.3.20; OJ L 295, 26.10.1990; Bull. EC 10-1990, point 1.3.14; OJ L 307, 7.11.1990; Bull. EC 10-1990, point 1.3.13; Bull. EC 12-1990.
[11] OJ L 198, 28.7.1990; Bull. EC 7/8-1990, point 1.3.19; OJ L 307, 7.11.1990; Bull. EC 10-1990, point 1.3.12; Commission proposals: Bull. EC 4-1990, point 1.1.9.
[12] OJ L 108, 28.4.1990; Bull. EC 4-1990, point 1.1.5; OJ L 176, 10.7.1990; Bull. EC 6-1990, point 1.3.12; OJ L 187, 19.7.1990; OJ L 199, 30.7.1990; OJ L 210, 8.8.1990; Bull. EC 7/8-1990, points 1.3.14 to 1.3.17.
[13] OJ L 198, 20.7.1987; Twenty-first General Report, point 157.

90.   The Commission adopted a number of Regulations on the transposition of the non-preferential origin rules for ceramics,[1] certain goods made from eggs,[2] grape juice,[2] ball bearings[3] and meat and offal[4] into the Harmonized System.

General legislation

91.   On 28 February the Commission adopted a proposal for a Regulation establishing a Community customs code.[5] The Economic and Social Committee examined the proposal in December.[6] The Code consolidates the corpus of customs rules in a single text and, together with the appropriate implementing regulations, will ensure greater legal transparency from 1993 onwards, in the interests of business, the administration and those concerned in the fight against fraud.

92.   On 9 October the Council amended[7] Directive 79/695/EEC on the harmonization of procedures for the release of goods for free circulation,[8] with the aim of securing greater uniformity in the use of simplified procedures. Henceforth, Community traders will automatically be entitled to use those procedures provided certain conditions are satisfied.

93.   In preparation for the unification of Germany the Council and the Commission adopted various provisions establishing a customs union with the German Democratic Republic from 1 July.[9]

94.   On 20 June the Council amended[10] Regulation (EEC) No 1031/88 determining the persons liable for payment of a customs debt,[11] to include provsions concerning debtors in free zones.

---

[1]   OJ L 347, 12.12.1990.
[2]   OJ L 276, 6.10.1990.
[3]   OJ L 356, 19.12.1990; Bull. EC 12-1990.
[4]   OJ L 351, 15.12.1990; Bull. EC 12-1990.
[5]   OJ C 128, 23.5.1990; Bull. EC 1/2-1990, point 1.1.5.
[6]   Bull. EC 12-1990.
[7]   OJ L 281, 12.10.1990; Bull. EC 10-1990, point 1.3.8; Commission proposal: OJ C 235, 13.9.1989; Twenty-third General Report, point 170; OJ C 54, 6.3.1990; Bull. EC 1/2-1990, point 1.1.11.
[8]   OJ L 205, 13.8.1979; Thirteenth General Report, point 149.
[9]   Point 2 of this Report.
[10] OJ L 160, 26.6.1990; Bull. EC 6-1990, point 1.3.8; Commission proposal: OJ C 142, 8.6.1989; Twenty-third General Report, point 169.
[11] OJ L 102, 21.4.1988; Twenty-second General Report, point 194.

Monitoring the implementation of Community customs law[1]

95.   Although the conversion of directives into regulations resulted in more uniform and binding application of Community customs law, and certainly made users more aware of their rights and obligations, it is still necessary to monitor implementation of the law. In this connection, proceedings were taken under Article 169 of the Treaty *inter alia* in the matter of charges having equivalent effect to import duties, with reference to Directive 83/643/EEC,[2] while the Commission kept up pressure on the Council to speed the adoption of provisions needed to settle difficult questions of interpretation under Community law. One such provision concerns duty-free imports of military equipment, the subject of a proposal for a Regulation which the Commission sent to the Council in October 1988.[3] Infringement proceedings have been suspended pending the outcome of discussions in the Council.

Harmonization of animal health and plant health rules

Animal health and plant health legislation

96.   The Council introduced financial aid from the Community for the eradication of African swine fever in Sardinia,[4] brucellosis in sheep and goats,[5] and infectious haemo-poietic necrosis of salmonids.[6] On 26 June the Council adopted Decision 90/424/EEC on expenditure in the veterinary field,[7] which covers various veterinary measures for the rational development of livestock farming and improved productivity.

97.   Various parts of the Community were recognized as being either officially swine-fever free or swine-fever free for trade purposes.[8]

98.   The Council harmonized measures for the control of foot-and-mouth disease, adopting a non-vaccination policy.[9] It amended Directive 64/432/EEC[10] as regards

---

[1]   For more detailed information see the eighth annual report to Parliament on Commission monitoring of the application of Community law (1990).
[2]   OJ L 359, 22.12.1983.
[3]   OJ C 265, 13.10.1988; Twenty-second General Report, point 184.
[4]   OJ L 116, 8.5.1990; Bull. EC 4-1990, point 1.1.117; Commission proposal: OJ C 327, 30.12.1989; Bull. EC 10-1989, point 2.1.155.
[5]   OJ L 140, 1.6.1990; Bull. EC 4-1990, point 1.1.122; Commission proposal: OJ C 327, 30.12.1989; Bull. EC 10-1989, point 2.1.157.
[6]   OJ L 276, 6.10.1990; Bull. EC 4-1990, point 1.1.125; Comission proposal: OJ C 327; 30.12.1989; Bull. EC 10-1989, point 2.1.156.
[7]   OJ L 224, 18.8.1990; Bull. EC 6-1990, point 1.3.141; Commission proposal: OJ C 84, 2.4.1990; Bull. EC 12-1989, point 2.1.197.
[8]   OJ L 43, 17.2.1990; Bull. EC 1/2-1990, point 1.1.217; OJ L 143, 6.6.1990; Bull. EC 5-1990, point 1.2.183; OJ L 328, 28.11.1990; Bull. EC 11-1990, point 1.3.153.
[9]   OJ L 224, 18.8.1990; Bull. EC 6-1990, point 1.3.139; Commission proposal: OJ C 327, 30.12.1989; Bull. EC 10-1989, point 2.1.163.
[10]   OJ L 121, 29.7.1964.

enzootic bovine leukosis.[1] It also laid down animal health conditions govering the movement and import from third countries of *equidae*,[2] intra-Community trade in and imports of semen of domestic animals of the porcine species,[3] and poultry and hatching eggs.[4]

99. In the zootechnical field, the Council laid down the conditions for the acceptance of pure-bred[5] and hybrid[6] breeding pigs for breeding, the zootechnical and genealogical conditions governing intra-Community trade in *equidae*,[7] and the rules on trade in *equidae* intended for competitions and the conditions for participation therein.[8]

The Council adopted Directive 90/425/EEC concerning veterinary and zootechnical checks applicable in intra-Community trade in certain live animals and plants.[9] This particularly important Directive will facilitate the movement of live animals and products and eliminate veterinary checks at frontiers, such checks being carried out before departure.

100. In the area of public health, the conditions for the administration of bovine somatotrophin were laid down.[10] The Council also laid down rules for the placing on the market of rabbit and reared game birds,[11] and for the disposal and processing of animal waste.[12] The Commission continued its work on residues and the ban on the use of hormonal substances. Proposals for regulations laying down the health rules for the production and placing on the market of fresh meat,[13] meat products,[14] minced meat, meat preparations and comminuted meat,[15] fresh poultrymeat,[16] live bivalve molluscs

---

[1]   OJ L 224, 18.8.1990; Bull. EC 6-1990, point 1.3.196; Commission proposal: OJ C 17, 24.1.1990; Bull. EC 12-1989, point 2.1.198.
[2]   OJ L 224, 18.8.1990; Bull. EC 6-1990, point 1.3.197; Commission proposal: OJ C 327, 30.12.1989; Bull. EC 10-1989, point 2.1.164.
[3]   OJ L 224, 18.8.1990; Bull. EC 6-1990, point 1.3.195; Commission proposal: OJ C 267, 6.10.1983; Bull. EC 9-1983, point 2.1.103.
[4]   OJ L 303, 31.10.1990; Bull. EC 10-1990, point 1.3.141; Commission proposal: OJ C 89, 10.4.1989; Bull. EC 5-1989, point 2.1.200.
[5]   OJ L 71, 17.3.1990; Bull. EC 3-1990, point 1.1.143; Commission proposal: Bull. EC 10-1989, point 2.1.153.
[6]   OJ L 71, 17.3.1990; Bull. EC 3-1990, point 1.1.144; Commission proposal: Bull. EC 10-1989, point 2.1.153.
[7]   OJ L 224, 18.8.1990; Bull. EC 6-1990, point 1.3.199; Commission proposal: OJ C 327, 30.12.1989; Bull. EC 10-1989, point 2.1.164.
[8]   OJ L 224, 18.8.1990; Bull. EC 6-1990, point 1.3.198; Commission proposal: OJ C 327, 30.12.1989; Bull. EC 10-1989, point 2.1.164.
[9]   OJ L 224, 18.8.1990; Bull. EC 6-1990, point 1.3.140; Commission proposal: OJ C 225, 31.8.1988; Bull. EC 7/8-1988, point 2.1.185.
[10] OJ L 116, 8.5.1990; Bull. EC 4-1990, point 1.1.116; Commission proposal; OJ C 272, 25.10.1989; Bull. EC 9-1989, point 2.1.113.
[11] Bull. EC 11-1990, point 1.3.158; Commission proposal: OJ C 327, 30.12.1989; Bull. EC 10-1989, point 2.1.162.
[12] Bull. EC 11-1990, point 1.3.159.
[13] OJ C 84, 2.4.1990; Bull. EC 1/2-1990, point 1.1.126.
[14] OJ C 84, 2.4.1990; Bull. EC 1/2-1990, point 1.1.228.
[15] OJ C 84, 2.4.1990; Bull. EC 1/2-1990, point 1.1.229.
[16] OJ C 84, 2.4.1990; Bull. EC 1/2-1990, point 1.1.231.

and fishery products,[1] raw milk and milk for the manufacture of milk-based products,[2] and heat-treated drinking milk[3] were laid before the Council. The conditions for granting temporary and limited derogations were the subject of a further proposal.[4]

101.   Both in non-member countries and in the Community animal health inspections continued at the same rate as last year and the Commission made known its intention to increase the number of inspections in the Member States.

102.   The Commission is responsible for administering the general rules adopted by the Council and adopting the necessary implementing provisions. It adopted many such decisions concerning *inter alia* the notification of animal diseases,[5] African swine-fever,[6] rabies,[7] contagious pleuropneumonia,[8] catarrhal fever,[9] residues,[10] and zootechnical standards for pure-bred breeding sheep and goats.[11]

Legislation on plant health, seeds and propagating material and feedingstuffs

103.   The Council adopted an amendment[12] to Directive 77/93/EEC on harmful organisms,[13] approving the principle of the total elimination of plant health checks on intra-Community trade, and an amendment[14] to Directive 79/117/EEC on the prohibition of certain plant protection products.[15] It also adopted a Directive on pesticide residues[16] and a Directive[17] amending Directive 79/373/EEC on the marketing of feedingstuffs.[18]

---

[1]   OJ C 84, 2.4.1990; Bull. EC 1/2-1990, point 1.1.233.
[2]   OJ C 84, 2.4.1990; Bull. EC 1/2-1990, point 1.1.232.
[3]   OJ C 84, 2.4.1990; Bull. EC 3-1990, point 1.1.147.
[4]   OJ C 84, 2.4.1990; Bull. EC 1/2-1990, point 1.1.230.
[5]   OJ L 227, 21.8.1990.
[6]   OJ L 170, 3.7.1990; Bull. EC 6-1990, point 1.3.204.
[7]   OJ L 161, 27.6.1990; Bull. EC 5-1990, point 1.2.175.
[8]   OJ L 108, 28.4.1990; Bull. EC 4-1990, point 1.1.120.
[9]   OJ L 93; 10.4.1990; Bull. EC 3-1990, point 1.1.147.
[10] OJ L 76, 22.3.1990; OJ L 91, 6.4.1990.
[11] OJ L 145, 8.6.1990; Bull. EC 5-1990, point 1.2.188.
[12] OJ L 92, 7.4.1990; Bull. EC 3-1990, point 1.1.159; Commission proposal: OJ C 117, 4.5.1988; Bull. EC 3-1988, point 2.1.169.
[13] OJ L 26, 31.1.1977.
[14] OJ L 296, 27.10.1990; Bull. EC 10-1990, point 1.3.148; Commission proposal: Bull. EC 6-1990, point 1.3.206.
[15] OJ L 33, 8.2.1979.
[16] OJ L 350, 14.12.1990; Bull. EC 11-1990, point 1.3.161; Commission proposal: OJ C 46, 25.2.1989; Bull. EC 12-1988, point 2.1.291.
[17] OJ L 27, 31.1.1990; Bull. EC 1/2-1990, point 1.1.238; Commission proposal: OJ C 178, 7.7.1988; Bull. EC 5-1988, point 2.1.164.
[18] OJ L 86, 6.4.1979; Thirteenth General Report, point 310.

104. The Commission sent the Council three proposals for regulations on the marketing of various plants and seeds,[1] two proposals for directives on protective measures against the introduction into the Member States of organisms harmful to plants or plant products[2] and a new proposal on Community plant variety rights.[3]

Application of Article 115

105. Completing the internal market will require the removal by 1992 both of disparities in import arrangements and the protective measures under Article 115 of the Treaty to which they give rise.

The Commission has undertaken a systematic study of the industries producing the products concerned. The study concluded that in most cases the provisions adopted under Article 115 could be eliminated without the need for back-up measures; indeed, the number of cases in which Article 115 is applied is already falling as a result of a fall in the number of applications from the Member States and greater selectivity by the Commission is dealing with such applications. Proposals relating to various aspects of the policies to be adopted at Community level on motor vehicles,[4] textiles,[5] and footwear[6] are under discussion at the Council, as are proposals on consumer electronics[4] and iron and steel products covered by the third paragraph of Article 71 of the ECSC Treaty.[7] The Commission is also preparing measures on bananas which take account of the interests of Community producers and the international commitments entered into by the Community.[8]

Checks on individuals

106. Commission proposals and Council decisions that are of direct concern to individuals (tax-free allowances, easing of intra-Community controls) are reported in the second part of this Section ('A people's Europe').[9]

---

[1] OJ C 46, 27.2.1990; OJ C 52, 3.3.1990; OJ C 54, 6.3.1990.
[2] OJ C 29, 8.2.1990; Bull. EC 1/2-1990, point 1.1.236; OJ C 31, 9.2.1990; Bull. EC 1/2-1990, point 1.1.237.
[3] OJ C 244, 28.9.1990; Bull. EC 7/8-1990, point 1.3.166.
[4] Point 220 of this Report.
[5] Point 223 of this Report.
[6] Point 227 of this Report.
[7] Point 216 of this Report.
[8] Point 426 of this Report.
[9] Point 162 *et seq.* of this Report.

Removal of technical and legal frontiers

Free movement of goods

Removal of non-tariff barriers[1]

General aspects — Article 30 et seq.

107.   The Commission intensified its efforts[2] to set aside non-tariff barriers to intra-Community trade during the year. In carrying out this task, it can rely on the articles of the Treaties relating to the free movement of goods, in particular Articles 30, 34 and 36 of the EEC Treaty, whose implementation by the Member States it monitors. In all, 1 326 cases were examined this year. This increase is due to the fact that business has become more conscious of the moves under way to develop a Community-wide market and, hence, of the barriers which still obstruct its completion. Faced with a growing number of complaints, the Commission introduced more systematic arrangements for handling them. Firstly, in the infringement proceedings it initiated, it looked for general solutions based on the principle of mutual recognition, and not simply individual solutions tailored to specific cases. Secondly, it continued the practice of holding meetings with Member States at which all complaints and infringements concerning a particular Member State are examined, thus making it possible to settle many of the cases prior to litigation by reaching pragmatic solutions consistent with Community law. Such meetings also keep Member States informed of what the Commission is doing to remove the barriers erected their products by other Member States. They thus provide a means of ensuring transparency in disputes. Thirdly, the Commission persisted in its efforts to disseminate information by publishing, in the monthly *Bulletin of the European Communities,* summaries of its reasoned opinions delivered pursuant to Article 169 of the Treaty and by issuing press releases concerning leading cases.

Prevention of further barriers

108.   Directive 83/189/EEC laying down a procedure for the provision of information in the field of technical standards and regulations[3] constitutes a particularly valuable means of removing new technical barriers to intra-Community trade. The number of draft technical regulations notified pursuant to the Directive went up by more than 21%, from 319 in 1989 to 386 in 1990. Since the above procedure came into force, the

---

[1]   Further information is contained in the eighth annual report to Parliament on Commission monitoring of the application of Community law (1990).
[2]   Twenty-third General Report, point 191.
[3]   OJ L 109, 26.4.1983; Seventeenth General Report, point 150.

Commission has received 1 321 notifications. It requested that the regulations be amended in 123 of the new cases, on account of the barriers they were likely to create. Similar requests were made by Member States in 76 cases.

The agreement between the Community and the EFTA countries establishing a system for exchanging information on draft technical regulations[1] was concluded by the Council in September[2] and came into force on 1 November.

Harmonization of laws

109.   With regard to the technical harmonization of industrial products, the efforts begun in previous years continued at all levels of the Community institutions. They focused not only on the preparation of new proposals but also on the follow-up to Community instruments.

110.   As regards motor vehicles, the proposals for Directives on the establishment of a complete procedure for type-approval of motor vehicles[3] were endorsed by the Economic and Social Committee in July[4] and by Parliament in October.[5] The Commission also adopted proposals on the restriction of the emission of pollutants from motor vehicles powered by a positive-ignition engine with a capacity of more than 1.4 litres or by a diesel engine.[6] On 30 October the Commission also adapted to technical progress[7] the Directives on safety belts and restraint systems,[8] safety-belt anchorages[9] and the field of vision of motor vehicle drivers.[10]

On 13 December the Council adopted the common position[11] on the proposal for a Directive on spray-suppression devices,[12] which had been amended by the Commission in July[13] following Parliament's first reading in March.[14]

---

[1]   Twenty-third General Report, point 193.
[2]   OJ L 291, 23.10.1990; Bull. EC 9-1990, point 1.3.11.
[3]   OJ C 95, 12.4.1990; Bull. EC 1/2-1990, point 1.1.19.
[4]   OJ C 225, 10.9.1990; Bull. EC 7/8-1990, points 1.3.23 to 1.3.25.
[5]   OJ C 284, 12.11.1990; Bull. EC 10-1990, points 1.3.18 to 1.3.20.
[6]   Point 520 of this Report.
[7]   OJ L 341, 6.12.1990; Bull. EC 10-1990, points 1.3.15 to 1.3.17.
[8]   OJ L 220, 29.8.1977; Eleventh General Report, point 159.
[9]   OJ L 24, 30.1.1976; Ninth General Report, point 91.
[10]   OJ L 267, 19.10.1977; Eleventh General Report, point 159.
[11]   Bull. EC 12-1990.
[12]   OJ C 263, 16.10.1989; Twenty-third General Report, point 194.
[13]   OJ C 203, 14.8.1990; Bull. EC 7/8-1990, point 1.3.26.
[14]   OJ C 96, 17.4.1990; Bull. EC 3-1990, point 1.1.15.

111.   Action in the area of foodstuffs concentrated on strengthening and implementing existing Community legislation. A Directive on the nutrition labelling of foodstuffs[1] was adopted by the Council in September. It will enable consumers to choose products on the basis of their nutritional properties.

The Commission adopted a Directive on plastic materials in contact with foodstuffs.[2] The Directive, which is based on framework Directive 89/109/EEC concerning materials and articles intended to come into contact with foodstuffs,[3] lays down an overall migration limit and establishes a positive list of the monomers and other starting materials that can be used in plastic materials. Pursuant to framework Directive 89/107/EEC on food additives,[2] the Commission adopted in August a proposal for a Directive on sweeteners for use in foodstuffs.[4] The proposal, which constitutes a stage in the preparation of a future comprehensive directive on additives, provides for the compilation of a positive list of sweeteners and their conditions of use. In September the Commission also proposed an amendment,[5] in respect of ice-cream, to the Directive of June 1989 on the identification of the lot to which a foodstuff belongs;[6] this proposal was examined by Parliament (at first reading) in November[7] and by the Economic and Social Committee in December[8] and was the subject of a Council common position also in December.[8] In October it adopted two proposals amending[9, 10] the 1979 Directive on labelling[11] and the 1988 Directive on flavourings[12] with a view in particular to clarifying the designation of flavouring substances and determining the circumstances in which the term 'natural' can be used. Also in October it adapted to technical progress[13] the 1978 Directive on emulsifiers, stabilizers, thickeners and gelling agents.[14] In addition, implementation of the Directive of June 1989 on the official control of foodstuffs[15] was the subject of a communication in September.[16]

---

[1]   OJ L 276, 6.10.1990; Bull. EC 9-1990, point 1.2.19; Community proposal: OJ C 282, 5.11.1988; Twenty-second General Report, point 218; OJ C 296, 24.11.1989; Twenty-third General Report, point 195; OJ C 204, 15.8.1990; Bull. EC 7/8-1990, point 1.3.28.
[2]   OJ L 75, 21.3.1990; Bull. EC 1/2-1990, point 1.1.22.
[3]   OJ L 40, 11.2.1989; Twenty-second General Report, point 218.
[4]   OJ C 242, 27.9.1989; Bull. EC 7/8-1990, point 1.3.27.
[5]   OJ C 267, 23.10.1990; Bull. EC 9-1990, point 1.2.20.
[6]   OJ L 186, 30.6.1989; Twenty-third General Report, point 195.
[7]   OJ C 324, 24.12.1990; Bull. EC 11-1990, point 1.3.13.
[8]   Bull. EC 12-1990.
[9]   Bull. EC 10-1990, point 1.3.25.
[10] Bull. EC 10-1990, point 1.3.24.
[11] OJ L 33, 8.2.1979; Twelfth General Report, point 274.
[12] OJ L 184, 15.7.1988; Twenty-second General Report, point 218.
[13] OJ L 326, 24.11.1990; Bull. EC 10-1990, point 1.3.23.
[14] OJ L 223, 14.8.1978; Twelfth General Report, point 104.
[15] OJ L 186, 30.6.1989; Twenty-third General Report, point 195.
[16] Bull. EC 9-1990, point 1.2.22.

Continuing its policy of international cooperation, the Commission also adopted a proposal for a regulation on Community acceptance of the *Codex alimentarius* standards.[1]

112.   Major progress was made in the pharmaceuticals sector. In January the Commission formally adopted the three proposals for Directives concerning the rational use of medicinal products[2] approved by it in December 1989.[3] To these were added in March two proposals for Directives extending the scope of Community pharmaceuticals legislation to homeopathic medicinal products for human and veterinary use[4] and in May a proposal for a Directive on the advertising of medicinal products for human use,[5] on which the Economic and Social Committee delivered its opinion in December.[6] In November the Commission adopted a proposal for a Regulation and three proposals for Directives on the future system for the free movement of medicinal products for human or veterinary use, including in particular the establishment of a European agency for the evaluation of medicinal products.[7]

In June the Council adopted a Regulation laying down a Community procedure for the establishment of maximum residue limits for veterinary medicinal products,[8] and, on 13 December, two Directives[9] amending the 1981 Directive on the approximation of the laws of the Member States relating to such products,[10] with a view to progressively abolishing formalities in trade between Member States.

113.   With regard to chemicals, the Commission adopted in January a proposal amending for the 11th time[11] Directive 76/769/EEC relating to restrictions on the marketing and use of certain dangerous substances and preparations,[12] with a view to extending its scope to include certain substitutes for polychlorinated biphenyls (PCBs). With regard to this proposal, on which the Economic and Social Committee[13] and Parliament (at first reading)[14] delivered their opinons in April and October respectively, the Council adopted a common position[6] on 13 December, following amendment[15] of the proposal

---

[1]   Bull. EC 5-1990, point 1.2.25.
[2]   OJ C 58, 8.3.1990; Bull. EC 1/2-1990, point 1.1.24.
[3]   Twenty-third General Report, point 197.
[4]   OJ C 108, 1.5.1990; Bull. EC 3-1990, point 1.1.16.
[5]   OJ C 163, 4.7.1990; Bull. EC 5-1990, point 1.2.7.
[6]   Bull. EC 12-1990.
[7]   OJ C 330, 31.12.1990; Bull. EC 11-1990, point 1.3.1.
[8]   OJ L 224, 18.8.1990; Bull. EC 6-1990, point 1.3.26; Commission proposal: OJ C 61, 10.3.1989; Twenty-second General Report, point 220; OJ C 131, 30.5.1990; Bull. EC 4-1990, point 1.1.17.
[9]   OJ L 373, 31.12.1990; Bull. EC 12-1990; Commission proposals: OJ C 61, 10.3.1989; Twenty-third General Report, point 220.
[10] OJ L 317, 6.11.1981; Fifteenth General Report, point 138.
[11] OJ C 24, 1.2.1990; Bull. EC 1/2-1990, point 1.1.20.
[12] OJ L 262, 27.9.1976.
[13] OJ L 168, 10.7.1990; Bull. EC 4-1990, point 1.1.11.
[14] OJ L 284, 12.11.1990; Bull. EC 10-1990, point 1.3.22.
[15] Bull. EC 11-1990, point 1.3.12.

by the Commission in November. On the same date the Council also adopted a common position[1] on the proposal amending Directive 76/769/EEC for the 10th time,[2] as amended[3] by the Commission in November in response to the opinions of the Economic and Social Committee[4] and Parliament.[5] The Council had adopted a common position[6] in October on the proposal amending the Directive for the ninth time.[7] In September the Commission adapted to technical progress[8] Directive 88/379/EEC relating to the classification, packaging and labelling of dangerous preparations.[9]

Implementation of the new approach to technical harmonization and standards

Technical harmonization

114. Under the new approach to technical harmonization and standards, as defined in its resolution of 7 May 1985,[10] the Council adopted the Directives on active implantable medical devices,[11] non-automatic weighing instruments[12] and appliances burning gaseous fuels,[13] electrically operated lifts,[14] electrical equipment for use in potentially explosive atmospheres employing certain types of protection[15] and simple pressure vessels.[16]

On 13 December the Council also adopted a common position[1] on the proposal[17] extending the Directive on the safety of machinery[18] to further types of equipment

---

[1] Bull. EC 12-1990.
[2] OJ C 309, 8.12.1989.
[3] Bull. EC 11-1990, point 1.3.11.
[4] OJ C 124, 21.5.1990; Bull EC 3-1990, point 1.1.19.
[5] OJ C 260, 15.10.1990; Bull. EC 9-1990, point 1.2.18.
[6] Bull. EC 10-1990, point 1.3.21.
[7] OJ C 117, 4.5.1988, Twenty-second General Report, point 219.
[8] OJ L 275, 5.10.1990; Bull. EC 9-1990, point 1.2.17.
[9] OJ L 187, 16.7.1988; Twenty-second General Report, point 219.
[10] OJ C 346, 3.4.1985; Nineteenth General Report, point 210.
[11] OJ L 189, 20.7.1990; Bull. EC 6-1990, point 1.3.16; Commission proposal: OJ C 14, 18.1.1989; Twenty-second General Report, point 217; Twenty-third General Report, point 199; OJ C 165, 6.7.1990; Bull. EC 6-1990, point 1.3.16.
[12] OJ L 189, 20.7.1990; Bull. EC 6-1990, point 1.3.17; Commission proposal: OJ C 55, 4.3.1989; Twenty-second General Report, point 217; OJ C 297, 25.11.1989; Twenty-third General Report, point 199; OJ C 167, 10.7.1990; Bull. EC 6-1990, point 1.3.17.
[13] OJ L 196, 26.7.1990; Bull. EC 6-1990, point 1.3.22; Commission proposal: OJ C 42, 21.2.1989; Twenty-second General Report, point 217; OJ C 260, 13.10.1989; Twenty-third General Report, point 199; OJ C 192, 1.8.1990; Bull. EC 6-1990, point 1.3.22.
[14] OJ L 270, 2.10.1990; Bull. EC 9-1990, point 1.2.12; Commission proposal: OJ C 17, 24.1.1990; OJ C 170, 12.7.1990; Bull. EC 6-1990, point 1.3.18.
[15] OJ L 270, 2.10.1990; Bull. EC 9-1990, point 1.2.14; Commission proposal: OJ C 111, 5.5.1990; Bull. EC 1/2-1990, point 1.1.18.
[16] OJ L 270, 2.10.1990; Bull. EC 9-1990, point 1.2.13; Commission proposal: OJ C 13, 19.1.1990.
[17] OJ C 37, 17.2.1990; Twenty-third General Report, point 199.
[18] OJ L 183, 29.6.1989; Twenty-third General Report, point 199.

(lifting equipment). The proposal was amended[1] by the Commission in September, in response to the opinions of the Economic and Social Committee[2] and Parliament (first reading).[3]

European standardization

115.   Adoption of the two Directives on active implantable medical devices and non-automatic weighing instruments[4] made it possible to assign standardization remits to two European standardization agencies, CEN (European Committee for Standardization) and Cenelec (European Committee for Electrotechnical Standardization). Other remits were assigned, notably in the fields of personal protective equipment, construction products, advanced ceramics and information technology. The work on Eurocodes, previously carried out by the Commission, was transferred to CEN. In the field of telecommunications, remits were assigned to the European Telecommunications Standards Institute (ETSI).[5]

116.   These three agencies continued to reinforce their structures and procedures so as to cope with growing demand. As well as increasing the number of its technical committees, CEN decided to carry out a general review of its priorities, to introduce an early-warning system for standards production deadlines and to provide its technical committees with up-to-date information. Cenelec, for its part, developed procedures for speeding up public inquiries and for transferring national work to European level. ETSI continued to align its rules of procedure on the basic principles of standardization. The three agencies concluded a general cooperation agreement, the CEN/Cenelec chairmanship group being expanded to include ETSI representatives.

117.   Despite these efforts, fewer European standards were issued than requested, and the Commission was obliged to make a thorough review of the current situation. On 3 October it adopted a Green Paper on the development of European standardization,[6] which sets out a series of recommendations for all interested parties: industry, standardization agencies and public authorities.

118.   On 3 May the Commission amended[7] the lists of national standards institutions annexed to Directive 83/189/EEC.[8]

---

[1]   OJ C 268, 24.10.1990; Bull. EC 9-1990, point 1.2.16.
[2]   OJ C 168, 10.7.1990; Bull. EC 4-1990, point 1.1.15.
[3]   OJ C 175, 16.7.1990; Bull. EC 6-1990, point 1.3.21.
[4]   Point 114 of this Report.
[5]   Point 324 of this Report.
[6]   Bull. EC 10-1990, point 1.3.4.
[7]   Bull. EC 5-1990, point 1.2.26.
[8]   OJ L 109, 26.4.1983; Seventeenth General Report, point 150.

Recognition of tests and certificates

119. On 13 December the Council adopted the Decision concerning the modules for the various phases of the conformity assessment procedures which are intended to be used in the technical harmonization Directives.[1]

120. In accordance with the Council resolution of December 1989,[2] the Commission expedited the setting-up of the European Organization for Testing and Certification (EOTC), whose memorandum of understanding was signed on 25 April by the Commission, EFTA, CEN and Cenelec. The purpose of the organization is to ensure that measures taken in the field of testing and certification are consistent. The organization officially became operational in November, when its council met for the first time.

Government procurement

121. On 17 September the Council adopted Directive 90/531/EEC on the procurement procedures of entities operating in the water, energy, transport and telecommunications sectors.[3]

122. On 23 July the Commission adopted a proposal for a Directive coordinating the provisions relating to the application of Community rules on procurement procedures in those same sectors.[4] In December the Economic and Social Committee delivered its opinion[5] on the proposal, which is designed to extend to those sectors the remedies and review procedures covered by Directive 89/665/EEC.[6]

123. On 19 September the Commission adopted a proposal for a Directive relating to the coordination of procedures for the award of public service contracts.[7] This proposal covers the larger contracts in the service sector which firms from other Member States are likely to consider worthwhile. It also contains measures aimed at promoting the Community's interests in the commercial policy field.

---

[1] Bull. EC 12-1990; Commission proposal: OJ C 231, 8.9.1989; Twenty-third General Report, point 201; OJ C 179, 19.7.1990; Bull. EC 7/8-1990, point 1.3.34.
[2] OJ C 10, 16.1.1990; Twenty-third General Report, point 201.
[3] OJ L 297, 29.10.1990; Bull. EC 9-1990, point 1.2.6; Commission proposal: OJ C 319, 12.12.1988; OJ C 40, 17.2.1989; Twenty-second General Report, point 177; Supplement 6/88 — Bull. EC; OJ C 264, 16.10.1989; Twenty-third General Report, point 204; Bull. EC 7/8-1990, point 1.3.36.
[4] OJ C 216, 31.8.1990; Bull. EC 7/8-1990, point 1.3.35; Supplement 3/90 — Bull. EC.
[5] Bull. EC 12-1990.
[6] OJ L 395, 30.12.1989; Twenty-third General Report, point 203.
[7] Bull. EC 9-1990, point 1.2.7.

124.   On 13 July the Commission updated[1] Annex I to Council Directive 89/440/EEC concerning coordination of procedures for the award of public works contracts.[2] The Annex lists the bodies and categories of bodies governed by public law which are deemed to be contracting authorities within the meaning of the Directive.

125.   The Commission continued its efforts to open up government procurement through tighter monitoring of the application of Community law.[3]

Free movement of workers and of members of the professions

126.   The details of the Commission proposals and Council decisions directly affecting individuals (removal of restrictions, mutual recognition of diplomas, access to economic activity, special rights of individuals and passport) are given in the second part of this section, 'A people's Europe'.[4]

Common market in services

Financial services

Banks and other financial institutions

127.   The Commission continued its efforts to bring about mutual recognition of the systems of prudential supervision in the light of the second banking Directive (89/646/EEC).[5] On 3 October it adopted a proposal for a Directive relating to the supervision of credit institutions on a consolidated basis[6] which, in order to take account of groups with a complex structure, would replace Directive 83/350/EEC,[7] which applies only to banking groups whose parent company is a credit institution.

128.   On 21 March the Council adopted a proposal for a Directive on prevention of the use of the financial system for the purposes of money laundering which would require the reporting of transactions suspected of arising out of drug trafficking, terrorism or other crimes and would make money laundering a criminal offence in all Member

---

[1]   OJ L 187, 19.7.1990; Bull. EC 7/8-1990, point 1.3.37.
[2]   OJ L 210, 21.7.1989; Twenty-third General Report, point 203.
[3]   Further information is contained in the eighth annual report to Parliament on Commission monitoring of the application of Community law (1990).
[4]   Point 162 *et seq.* of this Report.
[5]   OJ L 386, 30.12.1989; Twenty-third General Report, point 210.
[6]   OJ C 315, 14.12.1990; Bull. EC 10-1990, point 1.3.5.
[7]   OJ L 193, 18.7.1983; Seventeenth General Report, point 261.

States.[1] The proposal was endorsed by the Economic and Social Committee in September;[2] the Commission amended it[3] to take account of the opinon delivered by Parliament on first reading in November.[4] With a view to arriving at a common position, the Council in December reached agreement in principle on a number of unresolved matters, including the definitions of money laundering and of crime (with an undertaking to adapt the definitons to shifts in opinion), the prohibition of money laundering, and the measures Member States will have to take to ensure that all the provisions of the Directive are applied in full.[5]

129. To help facilitate transfers of funds from one Member State to another, the Commission adopted on 14 February a recommendation on the transparency of bank charges relating to cross-border transactions.[6] In a discussion paper on making payments in the internal market which it adopted on 26 September, the Commission examined the problems posed by cash payments, transfers, and operations conducted using cheques or payment cards.[7] It noted that these systems could be improved, e.g. by linking together automated clearing houses in order to facilitate cross-border transfers. It proposed that those concerned, including the banking community, should join with it in conducting studies in this field.

130. On 14 February Parliament delivered its opinion at first reading[8] on the proposal for a Regulation on guarantees issued by credit institutions or insurance undertakings.[9]

131. The Banking Advisory Committee met three times, under the chairmanship of Mr Padoa-Schioppa, Deputy Director-General of the Banca d'Italia.

Insurance

132. On 14 May the Council adopted the third Directive relating to insurance against civil liability in respect of the use of motor vehicles.[10] The Directive is intended to provide better protection for accident victims and insured persons. It imposes compulsory cover for all passengers of the vehicle, including where the passenger is the owner,

---

[1] OJ C 106, 28.4.1990; Bull. EC 3-1990, point 1.1.24.
[2] Bull. EC 9-1990, point 1.2.25.
[3] OJ C 319, 19.12.1990; Bull. EC 11-1990, point 1.3.17.
[4] OJ C 324, 24.12.1990; Bull. EC 11-1990, point 1.3.17.
[5] Bull. EC 12-1990.
[6] OJ L 67, 15.3.1990; Bull. EC 1/2-1990, point 1.1.7.
[7] Bull. EC 9-1990, point 1.2.26.
[8] OJ C 68, 19.3.1990; Bull. EC 1/2-1990, point 1.1.26.
[9] OJ C 51, 28.2.1989; Twenty-second General Report, point 235.
[10] OJ L 129, 19.5.1990; Bull. EC 5-1990, point 1.2.8; Commission proposal: OJ C 16, 20.1.1989; Twenty-second General Report, point 240; OJ C 11, 17.1.1990; Twenty-third General Report, point 219; OJ C 134, 1.6.1990; Bull. EC 5-1990, point 1.2.8.

the holder of the vehicle or the insured person himself. It stipulates that each liability insurance policy, in addition to covering the entire territory of the Community, must guarantee in each Member State the cover imposed in the Member State where the vehicle is norally based or that imposed by the Member State in which the vehicle is travelling, whichever is the greater. Lastly, it harmonizes national provisions concerning the guarantee funds which compensate victims where the vehicle which has caused the accident was not insured or was not identified; the victim will thus no longer be responsible for establishing that the person liable is unable or refuses to compensate him.

133. On 8 November the Council adopted the second Directive on direct life assurance. Member States are required to implement the Directive by the end of 1992; it lays down specific provisions relating to freedom to provide services in the life-assurance field which offer policy-holders the choice between all the different types of contract available in the Community.[1] With regard to the establishment of life-assurance companies from third countries, not including branches, it establishes a Community mechanism similar to that found in the second banking Directive of December 1989[2] and in the proposal for a Directive on investment services.[3]

134. Also on 8 November the Council adopted the Directive aimed at facilitating effective exercise of freedom to provide services in the field of compulsory motor vehicle liability insurance.[4] The Directive brings compulsory third-party motor insurance within the framework of the freedom to provide services established by the second non-life insurance Directive of June 1988.[5] It reproduces the same criteria as appear in that Directive for distinguishing between large risks and mass risks according to the policy-holder's need for protection. The arrangements for large risks, i.e. mainly car or lorry fleets, is based on control by the country of the insured person, whereas those for mass risks are based on control by the country in which the relevant activity is carried on. However, in order to provide appropriate protection for the persons concerned, the arrangements for large risks will be introduced gradually, in the light of progress in adopting the proposals for a Directive on the annual accounts of insurance companies[6] and for a third non-life insurance Directive.[7]

[1] OJ L 330, 29.11.1990; Bull. EC 11-1990, point 1.3.4; Commission proposal: OJ C 38, 15.2.1989; Twenty-second General Report, point 242; OJ C 72, 22.3.1990; Bull. EC 3-1990, point 1.1.22; OJ C 179, 19.7.1990; Bull. EC 6-1990, point 1.3.29; Bull. EC 11-1990, point 1.3.4.
[2] OJ L 386, 30.12.1989; Twenty-third General Report, point 210.
[3] Point 127 of this Report.
[4] OJ L 330, 29.11.1990; Bull. EC 11-1990, point 1.3.5; Commission proposal: OJ C 65, 15.3.1989; Twenty-second General Report, point 241; OJ C 180, 20.7.1990; Bull. EC 6-1990, point 1.3.30.
[5] OJ L 172, 4.7.1988; Twenty-second General Report, point 238.
[6] OJ C 131, 18.4.1987; Twentieth General Report, point 233.
[7] Point 135 of this Report.

135.   On 18 July the Commission adopted a proposal for a third Directive on direct insurance other than life assurance.[1] The proposal would extend to mass risks the arrangements for control by the country of the insurer. It would introduce a single licence to be issued by the supervisory authority of the Member State in which the insurance company had its head office. The licence would be valid for all activities carried on by the insurance company, both as regards establishment in branch form and as regards the provision of services. Lastly, the proposal contains provisions on insurance conditions and technical reserves.

136.   On 18 July the Commission adopted a proposal for a Directive setting up an Insurance Committee that would assist the Commission in the exercise of the implementing powers conferred on it by the Council and would examine any matter relating to application of the existing directives and the preparation of new proposals for directives in the insurance field.[2]

Stock exchanges and other institutions in the securities field

137.   On 23 April the Council amended[3] Directive 80/390/EEC[4] in respect of the mutual recognition of public-offer prospectuses as stock-exchange listing particulars.

138.   On 25 April the Commission adopted a proposal for a Directive on the capital adequacy of investment firms and credit institutions aimed essentially at laying down minimum amounts of initial capital and defining a common framework for supervising market risks.[5] The Economic and Social Committee considered the proposal in December.[6]

139.   On 23 January, following the opinion given by Parliament on second reading,[7] the Commission amended[8] its proposal for a Directive on investment services in the securities field.[9]

[1]   OJ C 244, 28.9.1990; Bull. EC 7/8-1990, point 1.3.4.
[2]   OJ C 230, 15.9.1990; Bull. EC 7/8-1990, point 1.3.38.
[3]   OJ L 112, 3.5.1990; Bull. EC 4-1990, point 1.1.19; Commission proposal: OJ C 101, 22.4.1989; Twenty-third General Report, point 223; OJ C 70, 20.3.1990; Bull. EC 1/2-1990, point 1.1.28.
[4]   OJ L 100, 17.4.1980; Fourteenth General Report, point 207.
[5]   OJ C 152, 21.6.1990; Bull. EC 4-1990, point 1.1.3.
[6]   Bull. EC 12-1990.
[7]   OJ C 38, 19.2.1990; Bull. EC 1/2-1990, point 1.1.29.
[8]   OJ C 42, 22.2.1990; Bull. EC 1/2-1990, point 1.1.29.
[9]   OJ C 43, 22.2.1989; Twenty-second General Report, point 247.

Creation of a financial area

Liberalization of capital movements and removal of exchange controls

140. In the first half of the year, the remaining restrictions on capital movements were dismantled in France and Italy. As a result, the deadline of 1 July 1990 set by Directive 88/361/EEC[1] for the complete liberalization of capital movements in eight Member States was met. Considerable headway was also made, often before expiry of the deadlines set, in the four countries (Greece, Spain, Ireland, Portugal) that had been authorized by the Directive to retain temporarily certain restrictions, most of which concerned short-term capital movements. On 28 June the Commission decided to extend[2] until 31 December the authorization for Greece to apply certain protective measures, the scope of which was further reduced.

These positive developments represent major progress towards establishing the internal market. The free movement of capital allows firms and individuals in Europe to take full advantage of the investment and financing opportunities opened up by a Community-wide market and thus helps to strengthen economic and financial integration in Europe. At macroeconomic level, it increases the degree of integration of national financial systems and paves the way for closer economic and monetary policy coordination and ultimately for economic and monetary union, Stage I of which began on 1 July.[3]

141. On 15 February Parliament adopted a resolution on taxation of interest.[4]

Tax provisions conducive to the development of a common market in financial services

142. On 23 March the Commission adopted[5] a proposal for a Directive amending Directive 69/335/EEC concerning indirect taxes on the raising of capital.[6] The proposal is designed to enable Member States to exempt contributions of capital to collective investment undertakings established in the form of investment companies. The Economic and Social Committee and Parliament endorsed the proposal in May[7] and June[8] respectively.

---

1   OJ L 178, 8.7.1988; Twenty-second General Report, point 180.
2   OJ L 170, 3.7.1990; Bull. EC 6-1990, point 1.3.32.
3   Points 32 to 34 of this Report.
4   OJ C 68, 19.3.1990; Bull. EC 1/2-1990, point 1.1.30.
5   OJ C 111, 5.5.1990; Bull. EC 3-1990, point 1.1.23.
6   OJ L 249, 3.10.1969.
7   OJ C 182, 23.7.1990; Bull. EC 5-1990, point 1.2.29.
8   OJ C 175, 16.7.1990; Bull. EC 6-1990, point 1.3.31.

A propitious legal and tax environment for businesses

Company law

143. On 8 November the Council amended Directives 78/660/EEC[1] and 83/349/EEC[2] on annual accounts and consolidated accounts as regards their scope[3] and as regards exemptions for small and medium-sized companies and the publication of accounts in ecus.[4]

144. On 10 September the Commission amended[5] its proposal for a 13th company law Directive concerning takeover and other general bids,[6] on which Parliament had given its views in January.[7] Further to its communication of 8 May on the measures it proposed should be taken with a view to removing certain legal obstacles to takeover and other general bids,[8] the Commission proposed in December amending[9] the second company law Directive (77/91/EEC)[10] and amending[11] the proposal for a fifth Directive[12] concerning the structure of public limited companies.

145. In March the Economic and Social Committee gave its view[13] on the proposals for a Regulation on the Statute for a European company and for a Directive supplementing that Statute with regard to the involvement of workers.[14]

Economic and commercial law

Jurisdiction and the enforcement of judgments

146. A codified version of the Brussels Convention on jurisdiction and the enforcement of judgments in civil and commercial matters and the Protocol on its interpretation by the Court of Justice[15] were published in July.[16]

---

[1]   OJ L 222, 14.8.1978; Twelfth General Report, point 108.
[2]   OJ L 193, 18.7.1983; Seventeenth General Report, point 160.
[3]   OJ L 317, 16.11.1990; Bull. EC 11-1990, point 1.3.106.
[4]   OJ L 317, 16.11.1990; Bull. EC 11-1990, point 1.3.105.
[5]   OJ C 240, 26.9.1990; Bull. EC 9-1990, point 1.2.101.
[6]   OJ C 64, 14.3.1989; Twenty-second General Report, point 261; Supplement 3/89 — Bull. EC.
[7]   OJ C 38, 19.2.1990; Bull. EC 1/2-1990, point 1.1.141.
[8]   Bull. EC 5-1990, point 1.2.28.
[9]   OJ C 8, 12.1.1991; Bull. EC 12-1990.
[10] OJ L 26, 31.1.1977; Tenth General Report, point 139.
[11] OJ C 7, 11.1.1991; Bull. EC 12-1990.
[12] OJ C 131, 13.12.1972; Sixth General Report, point 117; Supplement 10/72 — Bull. EC; OJ C 240, 9.9.1983; Seventeenth General Report, point 162; Supplement 6/83 — Bull. EC.
[13] OJ C 124, 21.5.1990; Bull. EC 3-1990, point 1.1.100.
[14] OJ C 263, 16.10.1989; Twenty-third General Report, point 232; Supplement 5/89 — Bull. EC.
[15] OJ L 299, 31.12.1972.
[16] OJ C 189, 28.7.1990.

Intellectual and industrial property

Legal protection of topographies of semi-conductor products

147. On 10 May the Commission announced[1] that it had decided not to sign the Treaty on the protection of intellectual property in respect of integrated circuits (Washington Treaty)[2] but not to rule out the possibility of acceding to the Treaty at some future date.

148. On 9 October the Council adopted two decisions on the extension of legal protection of topographies in respect of persons from certain countries and territories.[3] The first decision extends, on a permanent basis and unconditionally, the protection afforded to natural and legal persons of countries which themselves apply similar protection arrangements to all Member States, while the second grants limited protection over time and subject to a number of conditions of reciprocity. The countries satisfying those conditions were identified in a Commission decision dated 26 October.[4]

Copyright and neighbouring rights

149. On 17 October the Commission amended[5] its proposal for a Directive on the legal protection of computer programs,[6] on which Parliament had delivered an opinion on first reading on 11 July.[7] The Council adopted a common position on this proposal on 13 December.[8]

150. On 5 December the Commission agreed a work programme in the field of copyright and neighbouring rights[8] comprising a package of measures to be taken before 31 December 1992 based on the Green Paper on copyright adopted in June 1988.[9] On the same date it also approved two proposals, one concerning accession by the Member States to the Berne Convention for the Protection of Literary and Artistic Works and to the Rome Convention for the Protection of Performers, Producers of Phonograms and Broadcasting Organizations,[8] and the other concerning the rules governing rental, lending and certain neighbouring rights,[8] in order in particular to offer more appropriate legal means of combating piracy.

---

[1]   Bull. EC 5-1990, point 1.2.127.
[2]   Twenty-third General Report, point 241.
[3]   OJ L 285, 17.10.1990; Bull. EC 10-1990, point 1.3.102; Commission proposal: Bull. EC 5-1990, point 1.2.128; Bull. EC 9-1990, point 1.2.102; Bull. EC 10-1990, point 1.3.102.
[4]   OJ L 307, 7.11.1990; Bull. EC 10-1990, point 1.3.103.
[5]   OJ C 320, 20.12.1990; Bull. EC 10-1990, point 1.3.104.
[6]   OJ C 91, 12.4.1989; Twenty-second General Report, point 332.
[7]   OJ C 231, 17.9.1990; Bull. EC 7/8-1990, point 1.3.158.
[8]   Bull. EC 12-1990.
[9]   Twenty-second General Report, point 182.

Pharmaceutical patents

151. On 28 March the Commission adopted a proposal for a Regulation concerning the creation of a supplementary protection certificate for medicinal products.[1] The proposal is designed to improve protection of innovation in the pharmaceutical field by affording extra protection to innovative medicinal products through the creation of a supplementary protection certificate that would take effect immediately on expiry of the corresponding patent. Parliament delivered its opinion on the proposal at first reading in December.[2]

Trade marks

152. The Council authorized[3] the Community to participate in work under the auspices of the World Intellectual Property Organization (WIPO) aimed at drawing up the rules for implementing the 1989 Protocol[4] relating to the Madrid Arrangement on the international registration of marks.

Plant variety rights

153. The Commission adopted a proposal for a Regulation on Community protection of plant variety rights.[5]

Company taxation

154. On 18 April the Commission adopted a communication on the guidelines it intended to apply in the field of company taxation and the tax measures which, in its view, needed to be taken in conjunction with the moves to complete and deepen the internal market.[6] Accordingly, it withdrew the proposal for a Directive concerning the harmonization of company taxation and of withholding taxes on dividends.[7] As announced in the communication, the Commission adopted on 28 November two proposals for Directives on arrangements for the taking into account by undertakings

---

[1] OJ C 114, 8.5.1990; Bull. EC 3-1990, point 1.1.95.
[2] OJ C 19, 28.1.1991; Bull. EC 12-1990.
[3] Bull. EC 3-1990, point 1.1.101.
[4] Twenty-third General Report, point 240.
[5] Point 436 of this Report.
[6] Bull. EC 4-1990, point 1.1.87.
[7] OJ C 253, 5.11.1975; Nineteenth General Report, point 155.

of the losses of their permanent establishments and subsidiaries situated in other Member States and on a common system of taxation applicable to interest and royalty payments made between parent companies and subsidiaries in different Member States.[1]

155.   As urged by the Commission in its April communication, the Council adopted on 23 July two Directives, one on the common system of taxation applicable to mergers, divisions, transfers of assets and exchanges of shares concerning companies of different Member States and the other on the common system of taxation applicable in the case of parent companies and subsidiaries of different Member States.[2] On that same date, the representatives of the Member States' Governments signed in Brussels a Convention on the elimination of double taxation in connection with the adjustment of profits of associated enterprises. The Convention replaces the Directive on the same subject proposed by the Commission in 1976.[3] Based on Article 220 of the Treaty, it will enter into force following its ratification by all Member States and preferably before 1 January 1992, the deadline for incorporating the abovementioned two Directives into national law.

Removal of tax frontiers

Indirect taxation

Value-added tax (VAT)

156.   On 8 May the Commission adopted[4] a series of proposals that were consistent with the guidelines[5] laid down by the Council in November 1989 regarding the broad lines of the VAT arrangements to be applied after 1992 and that formed part of the process of completely abolishing tax frontiers initiated by the Commission in 1987.[6] In addition to a proposal for a Regulation on the statistics relating to the trading of goods between Member States,[7] it adopted two proposals for a Directive supplementing the common system of VAT and amending Directive 77/388/EEC[8] and for a Regulation on administrative cooperation in the field of indirect taxation, which serve a dual purpose:

---

[1]   Bull. EC 11-1990, points 1.3.102 and 1.3.103.
[2]   OJ L 225, 20.8.1990; Bull. EC 7/8-1990, points 1.3.155 and 1.3.156; Commission proposals: OJ C 39, 22.3.1969.
[3]   OJ C 301, 21.12.1976; Tenth General Report, point 191.
[4]   OJ C 177, 18.7.1990; OJ C 187, 27.7.1990; Bull. EC 5-1990, points 1.2.2 to 1.2.5.
[5]   Twenty-third General Report, point 245.
[6]   OJ C 250, 18.9.1987; OJ C 251, 19.9.1987; OJ C 252, 22.9.1987; OJ C 262, 1.10.1987; Twenty-first General Report, point 153.
[7]   Point 973 of this Report.
[8]   OJ L 145, 13.6.1977; Eleventh General Report, point 219.

first, they set out transitional VAT arrangements to be applied from 1 January 1993 to 31 December 1996 under which all tax checks and formalities at intra-Community frontiers would be abolished, with VAT continuing to be paid temporarily in the country of destination only; second, they provide for the changeover to the definitive VAT system, which, at the end of the transitional period, i.e. from 1 January 1997, will be based on payment of VAT in the Member State in which the goods originate. The proposals were endorsed by the Economic and Social Committee in September[1] and Parliament in November.[2] In December the Council adopted conclusions[3] on the transitional VAT arrangements in which it states its position on the main aspects of the arrangements, in particular the chargeable event and the procedures which are to replace frontier checks after 1 January 1993.

157.   On 4 May the Commission amended[4] Directive 85/362/EEC (exemption from VAT on the temporary importation of goods other than means of transport)[5] following the entry into force of the combined nomenclature.[6]

158.   In accordance with Directive 77/388/EEC,[7] the Council authorized the United Kingdom to apply measures derogating from that Directive.[8] In December the Council granted[9] Germany's request concerning the tax status of the Soviet troops still stationed on its territory. On 29 November the Commission adopted a proposal for a Directive[10] determining the scope of Article 14(1)(d) of Directive 77/388/EEC as regards the exemption from VAT of certain permanent imports.

Excise duties and other indirect taxes

159.   On 19 September the Commission adopted a communication together with four proposals for Directives on the general arrangements for products subject to excise duty and the holding and movement of such products; the harmonization of the structures of excise duties on alcoholic beverages and on the alcohol contained in other products; taxes other than turnover taxes which are levied on the consumption of manufactured tobacco; and the harmonization of the structures of excise duty on mineral oils.[11] These

---

[1]   Bull. EC 9-1990, points 1.2.28 to 1.2.30.
[2]   OJ C 324, 24.12.1990; Bull. EC 11-1990, points 1.3.21 and 1.3.22.
[3]   Bull. EC 12-1990.
[4]   OJ L 133, 24.5.1990; Bull. EC 5-1990, point 1.2.30.
[5]   OJ L 192, 24.7.1985; Nineteenth General Report, point 260.
[6]   OJ L 256, 7.9.1987; Twenty-first General Report, point 457.
[7]   OJ L 145, 13.6.1977; Eleventh General Report, point 219.
[8]   OJ L 73, 20.3.1990; Bull. EC 3-1990, point 1.1.25; OJ L 276, 6.10.1990; Bull. EC 9-1990, point 1.2.27.
[9]   OJ L 349, 13.12.1990; Bull. EC 12-1990.
[10] Bull. EC 11-1990, point 1.3.20.
[11] OJ C 322, 21.12.1990; Bull. EC 9-1990, points 1.2.1 to 1.2.5.

proposals supplement those put forward in 1989 on the approximation of rates of excise duty, [1] on which the Economic and Social Committee delivered its opinion in July. [2] The proposals now tabled deal with the general arrangements for and the structure of excise duties in the internal market and establish the definitive excise duty arrangements applicable from 1 January 1993.

As regards the general arrangements for the holding and movement of products subject to excise duty, the general principle underlying the movement of such products within the Community is payment of duty in the Member State of consumption. In the case of individuals, free movement will be achieved through abolition of travellers' allowances in the Community and through the arrangements for mail-order sales. Movements between traders will take place under duty-suspension arrangements on the basis of the interconnected warehouses procedure. The detailed rules proposed for ensuring compliance with those provisions in the various Member States rest on the principle of subsidiarity.

The proposal on the structure of excise duty on mineral oils given definitions of the dutiable products and the different stages in the production process and specifies the end-uses which qualify for exemption or application of a reduced rate. The proposal relating to alcoholic beverages lays down definitions of dutiable products, specifies the cases where products are or may be exempted and establishes the rules for granting special arrangements to certain small producers.

As far as manufactured tobacco is concerned, the Commission proposes withdrawing, in the case of cigarettes, the timetable for harmonizing the ratio between the overall tax charge and the specific excise component; updating the specific concepts of manufacture and importation; calculating VAT on the basis of the maximum retail selling price; and designating a number of exempted uses.

160.   On the basis of these proposals the Council reached, on 17 December, an agreement on the principal rules to govern the movement and supervision of products subject to excise duty and traded between professional traders in different Member States. [3] In the conclusions adopted on that date a number of guidelines were laid down relating to movement under duty suspension arrangements between authorized traders and to the reception of dutiable products by professional traders without authorized trader status.

---

[1]   OJ C 12, 18.1.1990; OJ C 16, 23.1.1990; Twenty-third General Report, point 247.
[2]   OJ C 225, 10.9.1990; Bull. EC 7/8-1990, points 1.3.40 to 1.3.43.
[3]   Bull. EC 12-1990.

*Monitoring the application of Community provisions
in the field of indirect taxation*[1]

161.   The Commission continued its monitoring of the application of Community
provisions by initiating proceedings under Article 169 of the Treaty in a number of cases,
in particular for failure to comply with Article 95 of the Treaty or failure properly to
implement Community regulations and harmonization directives. In addition, proceedings were initiated in several instances on the basis of Article 171 of the Treaty as a result
of the increase in the number of cases in which some Member States failed to comply
with judgments given by the Court of Justice in tax matters.

A PEOPLE'S EUROPE

External frontier controls

162.   The Commission continued to play an active part in the work of the ministers
responsible for immigration,[2] who discussed the right of asylum, the crossing of the
Community's external frontiers and policy on visas, and in that of the Coordinators
Group on the free movement of persons,[3] which was overseeing progress on the various
measures that are essential for achieving the aim, laid down in Article 8a of the Treaty,
of freedom of movement for individuals.

Removal of intra-Community physical frontiers

163.   The Coordinators Group dealing with the free movement of persons, which was
set up following the decision of the European Council in Rhodes in December 1988,[4]
continued its work and in June submitted a progress report to the European Council
in Dublin. That report took stock of the results achieved;[5] it welcomed in particular
the conclusion and signing by 11 Member States of the Convention determining the

---

[1]   Further information is contained in the eighth annual report to Parliament on Commission monitoring of
      the application of Community law (1990).
[2]   Point 896 of this Report.
[3]   Point 163 of this Report.
[4]   Twenty-second General Report, point 284.
[5]   Bull. EC 6-1990, point I.14.

Member State responsible for examining applications for asylum.[1] Another progress report was submitted in December to the European Council in Rome,[2] which regretted the failure to adhere to the timetable for conclusion of the agreement on crossing external borders and asked that all the decisions needed to ensure that the deadline of 1 January 1993 was met be taken without delay.

Legislation on weapons and drugs

164. On 11 July Parliament approved,[3] at its first reading, the proposal for a Directive on control of the acquisition and possession of weapons,[4] subject to a number of amendments designed to make the proposal more stringent. Some of these amendments have been accepted by the Commission,[5] the Council reached in December a political agreement on a common position.[2]

Possession of narcotic drugs

165. Drugs have become a major problem in the Community, especially during the past five years. In view of ever-increasing demand in the West, in particular the United States of America and Europe, and the disappearance of frontiers both within the Community and, more recently, in dealings with the countries of Central and Eastern Europe, an organized response by the Community to this scourge is needed as a matter of urgency. Parliament paved the way in 1986 when it adopted a resolution on drug abuse.[6] This year the European Council meetings in Dublin[7] and the meetings of the Western Economic Summit[8] and the United Nations[9] ushered in an era of closer cooperation in this field at both European and world level. The formation of the Coordinators Group on Drugs in December 1989[10] (now known as the European Committee to Combat Drugs (ECCD)) marked the beginning of a drive to coordinate the anti-drugs policies of the Community and its Member States.

166. At the request of the European Council meeting in Dublin on 25 and 26 June,[11] ECCD prepared, in close consultation with the Commission, a European programme

---

[1] Point 896 of this Report.
[2] Bull. EC 12-1990.
[3] OJ C 231, 17.9.1990; Bull. EC 7/8-1990, point 1.3.22.
[4] OJ C 235, 2.9.1987; Twenty-first General Report, point 261.
[5] OJ C 265, 20.10.1990; Bull. EC 9-1990, point 1.2.15.
[6] OJ C 283, 10.11.1986; Twentieth General Report, point 505.
[7] Bull. EC 4-1990, point I.13; Bull. EC 6-1990, point I.16.
[8] Point 691 of this Report.
[9] Point 852 of this Report.
[10] Twenty-third General Report, point 254.
[11] Bull. EC 6-1990, point I.16.

to combat drugs, covering measures on prevention, on demand reduction programmes, on health and social policy with regard to drug addicts and on the suppression of drugs trafficking and providing for an active European role in international action, both bilaterally and in multilateral forums. At its meeting in Rome in December,[1] the European Council called upon the competent authorities to ensure speedy implementation of the programme. Machinery has also been set up, at the request of the United States of America, for consultations between ECCD, the United States and other industrialized countries (Sweden, Japan, Canada and Australia). In addition to a political forum, this system provides for six regional groups to be responsible for coordinating the strategies to be implemented in the countries of production and transit.

167.   While national efforts continue to provide the main response in certain areas, for example health and the suppression of trafficking, Community initiatives have been launched successfully. This is the case with the ratification by the Community of the United Nations Convention against Illicit Traffic in Narcotic Drugs and Psychotropic Substances,[2] adopted in Vienna in December 1988,[3] the adoption of an integrated programme of cooperation with Colombia[4] and a proposal for a Directive aimed at preventing the financial system from being used for money laundering.[5] Moreover, on 13 December the Council adopted a Regulation laying down measures to be taken to discourage the diversion of certain substances to the illicit manufacture of narcotic drugs and psychotropic substances.[6] The Regulation is designed to set up, on a Community basis, a system for monitoring international trade in the substances in question in accordance with the abovementioned United Nations Convention. In December, the Commission sent the Council a proposal for a Directive to set up a similar system for the manufacture and marketing of these substances in the Community.[2]

Free movement of persons

Right of entry and of residence

168.   The Council adopted on 28 June the three Directives concerning the right of residence for students, for employees and self-employed persons who have ceased their occupational activity, and for other Community nationals.[7]

---

[1]   Bull. EC 12-1990.
[2]   Point 806 of this Report.
[3]   Twenty-second General Report, point 986.
[4]   Point 758 of this Report.
[5]   Point 128 of this Report.
[6]   OJ L 357, 20.12.1990; Bull. EC 12-1990; Commission proposal: Bull. EC 5-1990, point 1.2.6.
[7]   OJ L 180, 13.7.1990; Bull. EC 6-1990, points 1.3.261 to 1.3.264; Commission proposals: OJ C 191; 28.7.1989; Twenty-third General Report, point 257; OJ C 26, 3.1.1990.

169.   On 14 February Parliament delivered,[1] at its first reading, an opinion on the proposals[2] for amending Regulation (EEC) No 1612/68 and Directive 68/360/EEC[3] on freedom of movement and residence within the Community for workers of Member States and their families. It also adopted, on 15 March, a resolution on the free movement of persons in the internal market.[4]

Right of establishment

Recognition of diplomas

170.   The proposal for a Directive[5] on a second general system for the recognition of professional education and training which complements Directive 89/48/EEC[6] was the subject of opinons by the Economic and Social Committee[7] in January and Parliament (first reading)[8] in May. In August the Commission amended[9] its proposal in the light of these opinions.

Special rights

Right of petition

171.   In accordance with Parliament's Rules of Procedure and the Interinstitutional Agreement signed in 1989,[10] the Commission sent 400 communications concerning petitions to Parliament in 1990. This reflects the ever-increasing use made of this right by Community citizens. Among the subjects raised most frequently there were, as in previous years, social security, the environment, taxation, right of residence, recognition of diplomas and free movement of persons and goods. Moreover, on 15 June Parliament adopted[11] a resolution on the deliberations of the Committee on Petitions in 1989-90 in which it makes a number of suggestions regarding procedure.

---

[1]   OJ C 68, 19.3.1990; Bull. EC 1/2-1990, point 1.1.92.
[2]   OJ C 100, 21.4.1989; Twenty-second General Report, point 286.
[3]   OJ L 257, 19.10.1968.
[4]   OJ C 96, 17.4.1990; Bull. EC 3-1990, point 1.1.198.
[5]   OJ C 263, 16.10.1989; Twenty-third General Report, point 259.
[6]   OJ L 19, 24.1.1989; Twenty-second General Report, point 289.
[7]   OJ C 75, 26.3.1990; Bull. EC 1/2-1990, point 1.1.95.
[8]   OJ C 149, 18.6.1990; Bull. EC 5-1990, point 1.2.66.
[9]   OJ C 217, 1.9.1990; Bull. EC 7/8-1990, point 1.3.89.
[10] Twenty-third General Report, point 935.
[11] OJ C 175, 16.7.1990; Bull. EC 6-1990, point 1.3.269.

Recognition of driving licences

172. On 12 June Parliament adopted[1] a favourable opinion on the proposal for a Directive on the European driving licence.[2]

Taxation

Tax-paid allowances

173. On 22 February the Commission amended[3] its proposal[4] for amending Directive 69/169/EEC[5] to increase in real terms the tax-paid allowances in intra-Community travel.

Health

174. On 17 May the Council and the representatives of the governments meeting within the Council adopted[6] Decision 90/238/EEC concerning the 1990-94 action plan in the context of the 'Europe against cancer' programme. Allocated a budget of ECU 50 million, this plan follows on from the 1987-89 action plan,[7] which was the subject of a Commission report[8] presented to the Council on the same date.

175. On 17 May the Council adopted Directive 90/239/EEC on the maximum tar yield of cigarettes.[9]

176. In the light of Parliament's opinion,[10] the Commission amended,[11] on 19 April, its proposal for a Directive on the advertising of tobacco products in the press and by

---

[1] OJ C 175, 16.7.1990; Bull. EC 6-1990, point 1.3.267.
[2] OJ C 48, 27.2.1989; Twenty-second General Report, point 291.
[3] OJ C 70, 20.3.1990; Bull. EC 1/2-1990, point 1.1.16.
[4] OJ C 245, 26.9.1989; Twenty-third General Report, point 264.
[5] OJ L 133, 4.6.1969.
[6] OJ L 137, 30.5.1990; Bull. EC 5-1990, point 1.2.235; Commission proposal: OJ C 164, 1.7.1989; Twenty-third General Report, point 423; Bull. EC 4-1990, point 1.1.163.
[7] OJ C 50, 26.2.1987; Twentieth General Report, point 317.
[8] Bull. EC 5-1990, point 1.2.234.
[9] OJ L 137, 30.5.1990; Bull. EC 5-1990, point 1.2.236; Commission proposal: OJ C 48, 20.2.1988; Twenty-second General Report, point 496; OJ C 228, 5.9.1988; Twenty-third General Report, point 423.
[10] OJ C 96, 17.4.1990; Bull. EC 3-1990, point 1.1.193.
[11] OJ C 116, 11.5.1990; Bull. EC 4-1990, point 1.1.162.

means of bills and posters.[1] Following the Council's discussion of the proposal on 3 December, the Commission announced that it would re-examine it in the light of the opposition to any partial harmonization.

177. On 14 November the Commission adopted a proposal[2] for a Directive supplementing the 1989 Directive on the labelling of tobacco products[3] and specifying the position with regard to products other than cigarettes.

Audiovisual policy

178. In its communication[4] of 21 February, the Commission set out the broad lines of its audiovisual policy embracing three areas: the technological aspects,[5] the regulatory framework and the programme-making industry.

179. On 10 April the Commission adopted[6] a communication on an action programme to promote the development of the European audiovisual industry — Media (1991-95) — which was accompanied by a report drawn up by a committee of experts and two proposals for decisions, one of which concerns the implementation of a Community vocational training measure in the audiovisual sector. With its pilot phase completed, Media[7] is set in 1991 to become a well-established Community programme with all the concomitant qualitative and quantitative developments. The programme will also ensure that the necessary synergies are estabished with Audiovisual Eureka, which was launched by 26 countries and the Commission in October 1989.[8] This initiative, which was welcomed by the Economic and Social Committee in September[9] and by Parliament in November,[10] was approved by the Council in December.[11]

180. On 15 February Parliament adopted a resolution on media takeovers and mergers.[12]

---

[1]   OJ C 124, 19.5.1989; Twenty-third General Report, point 423.
[2]   Bull. 11-1990, point 1.3.205.
[3]   OJ L 359, 8.12.1989; Twenty-third General Report, point 423.
[4]   Bull. EC 1/2-1990, point 1.1.270.
[5]   Point 312 of this Report.
[6]   OJ C 127, 23.5.1990; Bull. EC 4-1990, point 1.1.157.
[7]   Twentieth General Report, point 242.
[8]   Twenty-third General Report, point 58.
[9]   Bull. EC 9-1990, point 1.2.188.
[10] OJ C 324, 24.12.1990; Bull. EC 11-1990, point 1.3.189.
[11] Bull. EC 12-1990.
[12] OJ C 68, 19.3.1990; Bull. EC 1/2-1990, point 1.2.172.

Culture

181.   In October the Commission adopted a communication setting out a plan of action for vocational training in the arts.[1] It proposes during an initial stage (1991 and 1992) to work with the Member States on pinpointing the specific requirements for vocational training in the arts and then, in a second stage, to take priority measures accordingly. It also intends to launch immediate experimental projects in two priority areas: conservation and restoration; and translation. On 19 November the Council and the Ministers responsible for Cultural Affairs meeting within the Council adopted conclusions in which they said that they shared the approach of the Commission and invited it to associate the Member States with the evaluation of the actions proposed.[2]

182.   The Commission carried on with the work outlined in the communication it adopted in April 1989 — Books and reading: a cultural challenge for Europe.[3] It supported efforts to provide reliable and comparable statistics on publishing as a means of obtaining a better view of the situation of the book sector in Europe. In November the European literary prize and the European translation prize were awarded for the first time in Glasgow, European City of Culture for 1990.[4] Under the pilot scheme to provide financial aid for translations of contemporary literary works, the Community financed a first batch of 39 translations.

183.   Under the annual scheme to protect and conserve the architectural heritage, the Commission granted a total of ECU 2.6 million to 26 projects selected from the 1 120 submitted. It also supported a growing number of training scholarships and cultural and artistic projects.

184.   The Commission continued examining, together with the Member States, measures to ensure the protection of national treasures of artistic, historical or archaeological value in connection with the abolition of internal frontiers in 1992.[5] The Community will have to reconcile the objectives linked with completing the single market with those relating to protection of the national heritage. In their conclusions of 19 November the Council and the Ministers meeting within the Council approved three major guidelines, relating to the exchange of information and more effective cooperation between Member States and with the Commission; the need for firmer, harmonized control measures at the Community's external frontiers; and the principle of restitution of cultural objects ranking as national treasures in the event of their unlawful expor-

---

[1]   Bull. EC 10-1990, point 1.3.217.
[2]   Bull. EC 11-1990, point 1.3.188.
[3]   Twenty-third General Report, point 708.
[4]   Bull. EC 11-1990, point 1.3.192.
[5]   See also Twenty-third General Report, point 711.

tation.[1] In December Parliament also adopted a resolution on the movement of cultural assets in the run-up to the single market.[2]

185. In their conclusions of 18 May on the manner in which the European City of Culture will be chosen in future and on a special event for European Cultural Month, the Council and the Ministers for Cultural Affairs meeting within the Council noted that designations had been made for the years up to and including 1996 and that by then a first round of Member States would have been completed.[3] They agreed that after that date the event should be open to cities not only in the Member States but also in other European countries. With this in view, they decided on 19 November that the European Cultural Months should be held in Cracow in 1992 and Graz in 1993.[4] Parliament expressed its approval of these new guidelines.[5]

Protection of personal data

186. On 18 July the Commission adopted a communication incorporating a package of proposals on the protection of personal data and information security.[6] Since measures in this field are necessary for the completion of the internal market and for the expansion of the computer industry and of new telecommunications services, the Commission has proposed a set of measures to establish a data-protection system within the Community and has adopted a declaration on how this will apply to the Community institutions. In view of the diversity of national approaches, the Commission suggests a single overall approach to ensure an equivalent, high degree of protection throughout the Member States and to develop an active policy on the security of data systems. This approach is based on a range of additional internal and external measures which start from the same general principles and form a homogeneous and consistent whole. The package includes: a proposal for a Directive covering data in the public and private sectors, laying down *inter alia* general principles relating to the lawfulness of processing, the rights of data subjects and data quality; a draft resolution of the Representatives of the Governments of the Member States designed to extend these principles to cover files held by public authorities whose activities are not governed by Community law; a resolution on the opening of negotiations with a view to the accession of the European Community to the Council of Europe Convention for the Protection of Individuals with regard to the Automatic Processing of Personal Data; a proposal for a Directive

---

[1] Bull. EC 11-1990, point 1.3.187.
[2] OJ C 19, 28.1.1991, Bull. EC 12-1990.
[3] Bull. EC 5-1990, point 1.2.233.
[4] Bull. EC 11-1990, point 1.3.193.
[5] OJ C 324, 24.12.1990; Bull. EC 11-1990, point 1.3.194.
[6] OJ C 277, 5.11.1990; Bull. EC 7/8-1990, point 1.3.309.

concerning the protection of personal data and privacy in the context of public digital telecommunications networks, in particular the Integrated Services Digital Network (ISDN) and public digital mobile networks; and a proposal for a Decision in the field of information security.

Civil protection

187. On 23 November the Council and the Representatives of the Governments of the Member States meeting within the Council approved two resolutions. The first of these, on Community cooperation on civil protection, relates mainly to the various possibilities for meeting the requirements of civil protection offered by advanced telecommunications systems.[1] The Council and the Ministers also agreed to carry out a coordinated campaign to inform, educate and raise the awareness of Community citizens, and declared the period from June 1993 to May 1994 a European Year of Civil Protection. They called on the Commission to investigate the scope for enhancing the training of young people doing civilian or voluntary service who are engaged in civil-protection-related activities and to take action to improve intra-Community cooperation in preventing and combating forest fires. In the second resolution, the Council and the Ministers agreed to examine, together with the Commission, how common objectves in relation to improving mutual aid between Member States in the event of a natural or technological disaster should be implemented.[2] At the same meeting, agreement was reached on the proposal for a Decision concerning the introduction of a single European emergency telephone number.[3]

---

[1]   OJ C 315, 14.12.1990; Bull. EC 11-1990, point 1.3.195.
[2]   OJ C 315, 14.12.1990; Bull. EC 11-1990, point 1.3.196.
[3]   Point 312 of this Report.

Section 3

Competition[1]

Priority activities and objectives

188.   The Commission adopted an implementing regulation and a set of guidelines to ensure smooth implementation of the Merger Control Regulation, which entered into force on 21 September. These measures will be useful to firms contemplating a merger or takeover which requires vetting and clearance by the Commission.

The Commission continued to develop new ways of strengthening competition in the services sector. To help establish a single market in air transport, the Commission proposed an amendment to the 1987 Regulation on measures to liberalize air transport which would enable it to take interim measures against airlines using unfair practices to eliminate competition. In the field of liner shipping, the Commission asked the Council to approve a regulation empowering it to grant block exemption to joint service ('consortium') agreements between shipping companies. Such a block exemption regulation should rapidly end the legal uncertainty currently surrounding the compatibility of this type of agreement with competition law.

In the run-up to German unification the Commission, in consultation with the Government of the German Democratic Republic, drew up a set of basic principles to govern certain aspects of competition policy of mutual interest during the transitional period following German monetary union. Consideration was given to questions relating to mergers, takeovers and joint ventures which might have wider repercussions at Community level.

The judgment delivered by the Court of Justice in Case C-301/87 France v Commission goes a long way towards meeting the Commission's concern at the growing number of aid measures introduced in violation of Article 93(3) of the Treaty. The Court built on its existing case-law to provide an effective bar to infringements of the procedural rules laid down in Article 93(3), which might otherwise have been deprived of its preventive effect.[2]

---

[1]   For further details see the *Twentieth Report on Competition Policy (1990),* to be published by the Office for Official Publications of the European Communities in 1991, in conjunction with this General Report.
[2]   Point 1047 of this Report.

General rules applying to businesses

189.   To ensure application of the principle of compulsory notification on which the Merger Control Regulation[1] is based, the Commission, in July, adopted a Regulation on the time-limits and hearings provided for therein and the form, content and other procedural aspects of notification.[2] A standard format for notifications is laid down in an annex to the Regulation, which is further supplemented by two notices, one on restrictions ancillary to concentrations and the other dealing with the definition of the concentrative and cooperative operations caught by the Merger Control Regulation, with particular reference to joint ventures.[3] The Economic and Social Committee delivered a separate opinion on these measures in July.[4]

190.   On 24 July the Council amended[5] Regulation (EEC) No 3976/87 on the application of Article 85(3) of the Treaty to certain categories of agreements and concerted practices in the air transport sector.[6] The purpose of the amendment was to make it possible to extend until 31 December 1992 the block exemptions granted by the Regulation, which were originally to apply for a limited period only. Pursuant to this provision, the Commission, on 5 December, renewed three exempting regulations on stopover assistance services, computer reservation systems and the joint planning and coordination of capacity, and consultations on tariffs and slot allocation.[7] The Economic and Social Committee[8] and Parliament[9] delivered opinions on the three proposals for regulations attached to the Commission's memorandum of September 1989 on the application of the competition rules to air transport.[10]

On 2 May the Commission adopted a proposal[11] for an amendment to Council Regulation No 3975/87 on competition in the air transport sector,[6] in order to facilitate the operation of the current system by allowing the Commission to require suspension of certain unfair practices. The Economic and Social Committee delivered an opinion on the proposal in November.[12]

---

[1]   OJ L 395, 30.12.1989; OJ L 257, 21.9.1990; Twenty-third General Report, point 376; Supplement 2/90 - Bull. EC.
[2]   OJ L 219, 14.8.1990; Bull. EC 7/8-1990, point 1.3.46; Supplement 2/90 - Bull. EC.
[3]   OJ L 203, 14.8.1990; Bull. EC 7/8-1990, point 1.3.47; Supplement 2/90 - Bull. EC.
[4]   OJ L 225, 10.9.1990; Bull. EC 7/8-1990, point 1.3.48.
[5]   OJ L 217, 11.8.1990; Bull. EC 7/8-1990, point 1.3.45; Commission proposal: OJ C 258, 11.10.1987; Twenty-third General Report, point 377; OJ C 159, 29.6.1990; Bull. EC 6-1990, point 1.3.33.
[6]   OJ L 374, 31.12.1987; Twenty-first General Report, point 369.
[7]   OJ L 10, 15.1.1991; Bull. EC 12-1990.
[8]   OJ C 112, 7.5.1990; Bull. EC 3-1990, point 1.1.26.
[9]   OJ C 175, 16.7.1990; Bull. EC 6-1990, point 1.3.35.
[10]   OJ C 248, 29.9.1989; Twenty-third General Report, point 377.
[11]   OJ C 155, 26.6.1990; Bull. EC 5-1990, point 1.2.31.
[12]   Bull. EC 11-1990, point 1.3.23.

191.   As regards shipping, growing containerization has led to an increase in the number of consortium agreements, and on 18 June the Commission adopted a proposal which would allow block exemptions to be granted to certain categories of agreements of this kind under Article 85(3) of the EEC Treaty. The proposal also covers consortia for the joint operation of combined maritime/land transport services.

192.   The proposal for a regulation which would allow a block exemption to be granted to certain categories of agreements in the insurance sector[1] obtained the Council's agreement in principle in June[2] and was the subject of favourable opinions by the Economic and Social Committee[3] and Parliament.[4]

193.   In *Tetra Pak Rausing* v *Commission*[5] the Court of First Instance held that the acquisition of an exclusive patent licence could constitute an abuse of a dominant position even though the licence was covered by a Commission block exemption regulation under Article 85(3) of the Treaty.[6] The judgment illustrates once again the fact that the competition rules apply with greater severity to businesses occupying a dominant position.

Application of the competition rules: specific cases

194.   In 1990 the Commission adopted 14 decisions applying Articles 85 and 86 of the EEC Treaty, including five decisions formally rejecting complaints, and 33 decisions applying Articles 65 and 66 of the ECSC Treaty. A further 171 cases were settled by comfort letter and 547 cases disposed of informally. At 31 December there were 2 734 cases pending, of which 2 145 were applications for negative clearance or notifications for exemptions (201 received in 1990), 345 complaints (97 received in 1990) and 244 cases in which the Commission had started proceedings on its own initiative (77 of them in 1990).

195.   On 19 December the Commission adopted a decision under Articles 85 and 86 fining the main European producers of soda ash for infringing those Articles. The Commission also addressed a decision under Article 85 to an association of soda ash producers in the United States, and to the members of the association individually, prohibiting the application of their joint export sales agreement in the Community.[7]

---

1   OJ C 16, 23.1.1990; Twenty-third General Report, point 378.
2   Bull. EC 6-1990, point 1.3.36.
3   OJ C 182, 23.7.1990; Bull. EC 5-1990, point 1.2.33.
4   OJ C 260, 15.10.1990; Bull. EC 9-1990, point 1.2.32.
5   Point 1049 of this Report.
6   OJ L 219, 16.8.1984; Eighteenth General Report, point 210.
7   Bull. EC 12-1990.

196.   An Article 85(1) case involving the European Conference of Postal and Telecommunications Administrations (CEPT) was resolved without a formal decision.[1] Following this intervention, the CEPT withdrew a recommendation to its member organizations concerning the terms for leasing out international telecommunications' circuits. The Commission took action under the same Article in the farm machinery sector, and terminated proceedings after the freedom to engage in parallel imports was restored.[2]

197.   As regards admissible forms of cooperation, the Commission adopted three decisions granting exemptions under Article 85(3) of the EEC Treaty. The Commission granted negative clearance in the *Elopak/Metal Box/Odin* case, which concerned a joint venture being set up by parties who were not competitors, actual or potential, and involving no territorial restrictions. The Commission's Decision established the principle that, where the creation of a joint venture is not itself caught by Article 85(1), ancillary restrictions which are necessary to ensure the starting-up and proper functioning of the joint venture are not caught either.[3] The Commission gave negative clearance to ECR 900, a consortium set up under a cooperation agreement for the development of a pan-European mobile telephone system.[4] In *Moosehead/Whitbread* the Commission decided that the block exemption regulation for know-how agreements[5] did not apply where the main interest of the parties lay in the exploitation of a trade mark rather than of know-how, but it granted individual exemption under Article 85(3).[6] The Commission also granted individual exemption to a research and development agreement between Alcatel Espace SA and ANT Nachrichtentechnik GmbH.[7]

198.   The Commission took action under Article 86 of the Treaty against the Belgian Régie des télégraphes et téléphones in response to a complaint that it was abusing its dominant position.[8] The matter was closed without the adoption of a formal decision after the Régie undertook not to impose on third parties any restrictions other than a requirement that they were not to use circuits for the simple transfer of data.

199.   Since the Merger Control Regulation entered into force on 21 September[9] the Commission has examined 12 notifications submitted under Article 4(1) of the Regulation and adopted six decisions under Article 6(1) within the time allowed. It concluded that the Regulation did not apply to certain aspects of one case (Renault/Volvo, cars)[10]

---

[1]   Bull. EC 1/2-1990, point 1.1.35.
[2]   Bull. EC 6-1990, point 1.3.40.
[3]   OJ L 209, 8.8.1990; Bull. EC 7/8-1990, point 1.3.53.
[4]   OJ L 228, 22.8.1990; Bull. EC 7/8-1990, point 1.3.51.
[5]   OJ L 61, 4.3.1989.
[6]   OJ L 100, 20.4.1990.
[7]   OJ L 32, 3.2.1990; Bull. EC 1/2-1990, point 1.1.36.
[8]   Bull. EC 1/2-1990, point 1.1.34.
[9]   Point 189 of this Report.
[10] OJ C 281, 9.11.1990; Bull. EC 11-1990, point 1.3.25.

or to a second case in its entirety (Arjomari/Wiggins Teape). [1] Elsewhere (Renault/Volvo, lorries and buses; AG/Amev; ICI/Tioxide; Promodes/Dirsa; and Cargill/Unilever) [2] the Commission decided not to oppose the concentrations notified, on the grounds that they did not raise serious doubts as to their compatibility with the common market. The initial experience gained here with the application of the Regulation is confined to the first procedural stage, but it tends to indicate that the internal procedures which the Commission has adopted do provide an adequate response to the demands made by the Regulation. While none of the decisions adopted actually initiated proceedings, they did provide an opportunity to establish the Commission's position on various questions of principle arising out of the Regulation and on other technical mechanisms which will be important to businesses.

200.   On the basis of Article 65(1) of the ECSC Treaty the Commission prohibited a market-sharing and price-fixing agreement between the seven major Community producers of cold-rolled stainless steel flat products, and imposed fines on the companies concerned. [3]

201.   Thirty favourable decisions were adopted under Article 66(2) of the ECSC Treaty, concerning *inter alia* the setting-up of a joint venture called Société monterelaise de broyage, [4] the formation of a joint enterprise by BHP-Utah International Exploration Inc., United States, and Meekatharra (NI) Ltd, Northern Ireland, [5] the setting-up of a joint venture called AP Steel UK Ltd and the merging of the ferrous and non-ferrous scrap processing interests of Sheerness Steel Co. and Mayer Newman Ltd. [6]

The rules of competition applied to forms of State intervention

General schemes

202.   Most aid awards are made under schemes which in many cases were approved some years ago; the Commission therefore embarked upon a systematic review of all systems of aid existing in the Member States. The review, which is being carried out under Article 93(1) of the EEC Treaty, should enable changes in the economic and industrial situation due to the completion of the internal market to be taken into account. Those aid measures whose effect on intra-Community trade and competition is the most

---

[1]   Bull. EC 12-1990.
[2]   Bull. EC 11-1990, point 1.3.26; Bull. EC 12-1990.
[3]   OJ L 220, 15.8.1990; Bull. EC 7/8-1990, point 1.3.50.
[4]   Bull. EC 1/2-1990, point 1.1.40.
[5]   Bull. EC 1/2-1990, point 1.1.41.
[6]   Bull. EC 7/8-1990, point 1.3.54.

damaging will be examined first. The Commission considers that general investment aid schemes clearly fall into this category inasmuch as the award of such aid, without any specific reference to a sectoral or regional plan, may run counter to the objectives of the Community's regional development policy and ultimately distort competition.

203.   The Commission adopted a second report on State aid to manufacturing industry and certain other sectors. Covering the period 1986-88, it updates and supplements the first report,[1] which dealt with the period 1981-86, by including data on Spain and Portugal. Its findings confirm the need for even greater transparency in the aid sphere. The Commission drew up proposals for discussion with the Member States on standardizing the information to be supplied to it on aid schemes.

Industry schemes

204.   The Commission defined its position on a large number of investment aid proposals in the motor industry, applying the restrictive criteria laid down in the guidelines for that industry, which have been in force since 1 January 1989.[2]

205.   Following the unification of Germany, it was decided,[3] in the context of the sixth Directive on aid to shipbuilding,[4] to provide for the possibility that operating aid may be granted, under certain conditions, in the territory of the former German Democratic Republic in excess of the common ceiling set by the Commission for 1990. In view of the impending expiry of that Directive on 31 December, the Council, in December, adopted a seventh Directive renewing the basic aid strategy followed so far for a further three years.[5] In December, the Commission, in consultation with the Member States, set a ceiling on aid for shipbuilding of 13% for 1991, and of 9% for the building of small vessels costing less than ECU 10 million and for conversion aid.[6]

206.   The scope of the rules on aid to the steel industry[7] was extended to include the eastern parts of Germany,[3] enabling aid to be awarded for investments there, provided it does not lead to any increase in capacity.

---

[1]   Twenty-second General Report, point 431.
[2]   OJ C 123, 18.5.1989; Twenty-third General Report, point 386.
[3]   Point 24 of this Report.
[4]   OJ L 69, 12.3.1987; Twentieth General Report, point 446.
[5]   Bull. EC 12-1990; Commission proposal: OJ C 223, 7.9.1990; Bull. EC 5-1990, point 1.2.38.
[6]   Bull. EC 12-1990.
[7]   OJ L 38, 10.2.1989; Twenty-third General Report, point 387.

Regional aid schemes

207.   In its ongoing work of assessing the Member States' regional aid schemes, the Commission presented a proposal concerning the French scheme.[1] It continued its review of the German scheme,[1] which has become more complex as a result of unification, and undertook an examination of the Belgian and Dutch schemes. A new Greek scheme was notified and was approved in December.[2]

State monopolies

208.   Information on infringement proceedings in respect of State monopolies of a commercial character will be provided in the eighth annual report to Parliament on Commission monitoring of the application of Community law (covering action taken in 1990). The report will be presented in the course of 1991.

Public enterprises

209.   Following its approval in June 1989,[3] Directive 90/388/EEC on competition in the markets for telecommunications services was formally adopted by the Commission on 28 June.[4] As was decided when it was approved, the date by which Member States are to have taken the necessary implementing measures is the same as that in the Council Directive on the establishment of the internal market for telecommunications services through the implementation of open network provision, which was likewise adopted on 28 June and was published in the same Official Journal.[5]

210.   After the Greek Government had taken steps to ensure that its scheme of insurance for public property complied with the Decision adopted by the Commission in 1985[6] and the judgment delivered by the Court of Justice in 1988,[7] the Commission terminated the infringement proceedings it had initiated in respect of the scheme.[8]

---

[1]   Twenty-third General Report, point 390.
[2]   Bull. EC 12-1990.
[3]   OJ L 192, 24.7.1990.
[4]   Twenty-third General Report, point 392.
[5]   Point 312 of this Report.
[6]   OJ L 152, 11.6.1985; Nineteenth General Report, point 403.
[7]   OJ C 199, 29.7.1988; Twenty-second General Report, point 444.
[8]   Bull. EC 6-1990, point 1.3.69.

211.   On 1 August the Commission adopted a decision concerning the Spanish legislation governing postal services, in which it called upon the Spanish Government to take steps to liberalize the international express letter delivery service.[1]

---

[1]   OJ L 233, 28.8.1990; Bull. EC 7/8-1990, point 1.3.73.

Section 4

Industrial strategy and services

Priority activities and objectives

212.   *Despite the slowdown in the economy at the end of the year, particularly as a result of the Gulf crisis, 1990 was a good year for industry in the Community, during which it continued the restructuring processes necessary for the establishment of the single market, mobilized the investment required to keep pace with technological advance and stiffer international competition, and concluded further international cooperation agreements made essential by the internationalization of markets and industry. These trends were highlighted in the 1990 edition of* Panorama of EC industry *(second report on the state of European industry)* [1] *compiled by the Commission together with all the professional associations representing industry at Community level, which contains 170 detailed profiles of the main manufacturing and service industries in the Community. The Commission draws particular attention in the report to the increased importance of services in the economy and to the expansion of international investment. It also underlines the greater scope offered to industry by the efforts to improve environmental protection.*

In its communication to the Council on industrial policy in an open and competitive environment, [2] *the Commission set out the approach it believes the Community should follow in the field of industrial policy, namely a strategy of continuous adaptation based on the principle of free trade and on the action of competitive forces on the markets. The aim of the guidelines set out in this communication is to strengthen the disciplines which ensure continued competition on markets, to frame policies of positive adaptation, in particular in order to promote cooperation between SMEs and large firms and to monitor industrial development closely so as to anticipate problems instead of reacting to them. This communication was favourably received by the Council, which asked the Commission to continue its work in order to define a common industrial policy.* [3]

The Commission also adopted a communication in July in which it advocates more cooperation with the countries of Central and Eastern Europe with a view to developing

---

[1]   Bull. EC 7/8-1990, point 1.3.153.
[2]   Bull. EC 11-1990, point 1.3.109.
[3]   Bull. EC 11-1990, point 1.3.110.

industrial activity there.[1] The specific measures proposed in order to consolidate those already in place concentrate on three main themes: greater legal and economic transparency; horizontal measures to create an environment conducive to business activity, support SMEs and to develop areas such as standardization and product certification; and, thirdly, sectoral measures, particularly in the steel industry.[2]

The Commission also decided[3] in November to transmit to the ECSC Consultative Committee a working document on the future of the ECSC Treaty, which, under Article 97, is due to expire in the year 2002. Three options are put forward, namely maintenance beyond this expiry date of the rules governing coal and steel, early expiry of the Treaty and expiry on schedule, subject to gradual inclusion in the EEC Treaty of the two sectors in question. A preference is expressed for the second scenario, which in particular would make it possible to establish a stable legal framework for undertakings and examine how the provisions of the ECSC Treaty regarded as the most useful might be incorporated into the EEC Treaty.

Steel

213.   Crude steel production in the Community (excluding the former German Democratic Republic) fell back slightly from its peak of 139.6 million tonnes[4] in 1989 to just over 136 million tonnes in 1990. The main reason for this decline was the running down of stocks which had been a feature of 1989, and the uncertainty affecting the markets during the latter months of 1990 following events in the Gulf. However, Community demand remained buoyant virtually throughout the year owing to vigorous activity in the capital goods and construction industries and, to a lesser extent, in the motor industry. On the export markets, on the other hand, there was a sharp decline not only in the level of demand but also in prices.

214.   The market surveillance arrangements introduced in 1988 when the quota system expired,[5] and the publication of production guidelines for certain products in the forward programmes, ended in June. However, the steel market continued to be closely monitored in the quarterly forward programmes[6] which look at market developments and future

---

[1]   Bull. EC 7/8-1990, point 1.4.6.
[2]   Point 215 of this Report.
[3]   Bull. EC 11-1990, point 1.3.101.
[4]   Bull. EC 1/2-1990, point 1.1.143.
[5]   Twenty-second General Report, point 302.
[6]   OJ C 19, 21.1.1990; Bull. EC 1/2-1990, point 1.1.142; OJ L 103, 25.4.1990; Bull. EC 4-1990, point 1.1.90; OJ C 185, 26.7.1990; Bull. EC 7/8-1990, point 1.3.161; OJ C 264, 19.10.1990; Bull. EC 10-1990, point 1.3.107.

prospects. As part of its policy to clamp down on firms which fail to meet their obligations arising from Community rules, the Commission imposed five penalties.[1]

This was the last year of the five-year transition period for the Portuguese steel industry under Protocol No 20 to the Act of Accession.[2] On 30 October the Commission,[3] with the Council's assent,[4] set the ceiling for deliveries of steel products from Portugal to the rest of the Community market, excluding Spain, at 150 000 tonnes compared with 110 000 in 1989.[5]

215.   On 2 May the Commission adopted the document 'General objectives for steel 1995'.[6] Forecasts of Community steel consumption based on macroeconomic trends are favourable, although they may be invalidated by the economic effects of the Gulf crisis which are impossible to evaluate at present. This document assumes that consumption will stabilize at the 1988 level, which was regarded as very good. On the basis of this scenario the Commission defines the main lines of its medium-term economic policy for the steel industry: continuing liberalization of economic policies, greater commitment by the Commission to securing compliance with competition rules and continuation of the Commission's policy of supporting corporate initiatives.

216.   As the disappearance of certain barriers to free trade in the Community by the end of 1992 will also affect steel products, the Commission is studying the implications for industry of the removal of certain barriers preventing the free movement of steel products from State-trading countries, although this sector will be only moderately affected.

217.   The aim of cooperation with the steel industries of the countries of Central and Eastern Europe[7] is to help these industries, which in technical and organizational terms are in a very poor state, to become competitive but without increasing their capacity. This offer of assistance is extended under the Phare programme.[8] The Commission is currently preparing a status report based on visits to Poland, Hungary and Czechoslovakia, which contains a monograph on each country.

---

[1]   OJ C 98, 18.4.1990; Bull. EC 3/1990, point 1.1.103; OJ C 104, 26.4.1990; Bull. EC 4-1990, point 1.1.91.
[2]   OJ L 302, 15.11.1985; Nineteenth General Report, points 717 to 744.
[3]   OJ L 313, 13.11.1990; Bull. EC 10-1990, point 1.3.108.
[4]   OJ C 269, 25.10.1990; Bull. EC 10-1990, point 1.3.108.
[5]   OJ L 321, 4.11.1989; Twenty-third General Report, point 279.
[6]   Bull. EC 5-1990, point 1.2.135.
[7]   For the various aspects of the external sector, see the heading 'Individual sectors' in Section 10 (Commercial policy) of Chapter IV of this Report.
[8]   Point 668 of this Report.

Transport

Motor industry

218. Provisional figures indicate that the trend followed on the Community's private car market in 1989 continued in 1990.[1] Overall Community production stabilized at a level slightly below last year's figure at 12.5 million vehicles, matched by a similar trend in demand, which reached 12.2 million units. There was a marked increase in demand in the Federal Republic of Germany and France, contrasting with a downward trend in Spain and the United Kingdom. The continuing increase in new registrations, combined with the positive effects of the restructuring of this industry, should mean that all manufacturers achieve positive results for the fifth consecutive year.[2]

Sales of Japanese cars increased significantly, reaching nearly 1.2 million units or 10% of the Community market, which is a 9% increase on 1989.[1]

219. However, although the Community motor industry would appear to be in good health, there is uncertainty about the future for various reasons already identified in previous years,[3] but compounded in 1990 by events in the Gulf, even though their effects could be partially offset by new opportunities as a result of the changes taking place in the countries of Central and Eastern Europe.

220. The Commission continued its activities on the basis of the guidelines set out in the 1989 communication on the single market for motor vehicles.[4] The aim of the measures in question, which include technical harmonization, approximation of indirect taxation, managing State intervention, coordination of research and technological development, promotion of training and retraining schemes, is gradually to put in place a set of incentives designed to enable the European motor industry as a whole to cope with the gradual disappearance of the protection from Japanese competition which it enjoys in certain Member States. Recognizing the increasingly international nature of the factors that determine competitiveness, the Commission also conducted an in-depth study of the component manufacturing industry and looked at ways of promoting an efficient distribution network which provided the best possible service to the consumer. Furthermore, now that the financial reorganization of firms has been largely completed, if manufacturers' cash flow stays at current levels it should be possible, during a transitional period prior to the full opening up of the market, for them to increase capital expenditure and spending on research and technological development so as to sustain the improvement in this industry's competitive position.

---

[1]   Twenty-third General Report, point 276.
[2]   Twentieth General Report, point 337; Twenty-first General Report, point 281; Twenty-second General Report, point 309; Twenty-third General Report, point 276.
[3]   Twenty-third General Report, point 277.
[4]   Twenty-third General Report, point 278.

Railway equipment

221.   The Commission carried out a study of the competitiveness of the Community rail industry which identified high-speed trains, combined transport and urban transport as the three growth markets of the future. These trends form part of a context marked by the entry into force of the directive on the opening up of markets in the excluded sectors, of which transport is one,[1] and the current merger activity in this sector at European level is another.

Shipbuilding

222.   In view of the outcome of the exploratory talks on restoring normal conditions of competition in the shipbuilding industry, the Council authorized the Commission, in July, to participate in formal negotiations initiated on this matter in the OECD.[2]

In October, in line with the 1978 Council Resolution on the reconstruction of the shipbuilding industry,[3] the Commission adopted a report on the state of the industry in the Community in 1989.[4] As far as the situation in 1990 is concerned there were some positive signs, particularly with regard to the volume of new orders. However, as prices are not yet at a profitable level and as the sixth Directive on shipbuilding aid expired at the end of this year, the Council adopted a seventh Directive which, apart from a few changes, is modelled very largely on the previous directive.[5]

Textiles

223.   In its conclusions of 13 March the Council stressed the importance, in its view, of supporting the modernization of the European textile and clothing industry through consistent and coordinated use of Community resources.[6] The Commission, in its annual report on the situation in the industry,[7] which was formally adopted in May, emphasized that consumption of textiles and clothing had picked up again in 1989 after faltering slightly during the previous year. However, this increase in consumption had not

---

[1]   Point 121 of this Report.
[2]   Point 844 of this Report.
[3]   OJ C 229, 27.9.1978; Twelfth General Report, point 126.
[4]   Bull. EC 10-1990, point 1.3.109.
[5]   Point 205 of this Report.
[6]   Bull. EC 3-1990, point 1.1.98.
[7]   Bull. EC 5-1990, point 1.2.134.

prevented a fresh decline in production, mainly of clothing articles, because non-Community producers had benefited more from the upturn in the Community market. The report also indicated that this industry, whose situation varied considerably from one Member State to another, was still vulnerable, in spite of the radical change taking place in terms of its competitive position. Firms were therefore invited to press ahead with the changes they were introducing in order to maintain their long-term chances of survival. This effort had to be underpinned, in particular, by technological innovation, concentration on certain quality areas of the market and the establishment of closer links between production and distribution. Although the continuing growth of firms bears witness to a return to competitiveness, at least for certain types of production, the fact remains that the future of this sector may be under threat from the closure of markets and illicit commercial practices. The Commission therefore endeavoured to address these various needs providing for appropriate measures under the programmes for research and technological development and regional assistance, and initiating a series of studies which may contribute to the development of appropriate strategies.

Biotechnology

224.   The Commission began evaluating methods of promoting the competitiveness of industrial activities which exploit biotechnology. It examined in particular the economic situation of the industries concerned and the impact of Community intiatives on them, as well as the effects of ethical public debates on the development of this sector. On the regulatory front the Commission started drawing up legislation on new food ingredients and processes. In addition, research and development activities were given a particular boost with the start of the Bridge programme[1] and the adoption by the Commission of a proposal for a new specific programme (Biotech).[2]

Services

225.   The new edition of the *Panorama of EC industry*[3] reveals that services are acquiring increasing prominence in the Community, with the greatest expansion in the area of business services. The Commission completed its analysis of the business services sector's contribution to industrial performance[4] and forwarded its conclusions to the

---

[1]   Point 271 of this Report.
[2]   Point 273 of this Report.
[3]   Point 212 of this Report.
[4]   Twenty-third General Report, point 285.

Member States. In conjunction with the trade associations it undertook a survey of the obstacles to the completion on the internal market to supplement its action in this sector. It also forwarded to the Council a draft decision implementing a multiannual programme for the compilation of Community statistics on services.[1]

Aerospace

226. In its communication on a competitive European aeronautical industry,[2] the Commission emphasizes this industry's major contribution to Europe's economic and technological development. While the adjustment of industrial structures is the responsibility of managers, it is appropriate to establish, at Community level, a reference framework accepted by all concerned, so as to enable the Community to create the general conditions to facilitate the industrial operations involved. Following a preliminary examination of this communication in October, the Council asked the Commission for a more detailed analysis of competitiveness in various segments of the industry, namely business jets, regional transport aircraft and helicopters.

Other activities

227. On the basis of a communication from the Commission[3] the Council expressed its views on the guidelines for action to be taken by firms and by national and Community bodies to facilitate the restructuring of the footwear industry. These guidelines deal in particular with the promotion of research and development and technology transfer, the development of training and retraining schemes, the protection of intellectual property, the opening up of markets in non-Community countries and the dismantling of obstacles to access to raw materials on those markets, and measures to ensure easier access for small and medium-sized undertakings to programmes adopted and implemented at Community level. In addition, given the harm caused by the rapid growth of imports from certain non-Community countries, the Commission felt it advisable to take certain steps[4] in order to avoid further excessive growth in such imports jeopardizing the restructuring exercise up to the end of 1992.

---

1   Point 970 of this Report.
2   Bull. EC 7/8-1990, point 1.3.154.
3   Bull. EC 3-1990, point 1.1.99.
4   Point 831 of this Report.

228.   In order to ensure the implementation of the Council Resolution of July 1989 on the development of the Community mining industry,[1] the Commission, in consultation with the Member States, began to examine the issues of access to and dissemination of geological and mining data, vocational training, taxation and social arrangements, regulatory aspects and external aspects of mining policy. The results of this work should enable the Commission to draw up specific measures designed to integrate the mining industry into the internal market by the 1992 deadline.

229.   The Commission conducted a study of the competitiveness of the consumer electronics industry in the Community which enabled it to make an accurate assessment of the completion of the internal market in an industry which, though dynamic, is up against tough international competition. On the basis of the findings of this study the Commission began, in consultation with all the parties concerned, to draw up proposals which will be finalized in 1991.

230.   On 13 July the European Parliament adopted a resolution on disarmament, the conversion of defence industries and arms' exports.[2]

Specific development programme for Portuguese industry (Pedip)

231.   All the operational programmes approved under the Pedip[3] are now being implemented. The necessary steps were taken to launch and implement a system for evaluating the impact of Pedip on the structure of Portuguese industry. Another specific study was initiated to assess the impact of the programme on business practices. According to the interim report on the implementation of the programme adopted[4] by the Commission on 16 May and the annual report by the Portuguese authorities on the implementation of the individual operational programmes, the Pedip programme is proceeding as planned. Utilization of the resources from the additional budget heading proceeded according to schedule; commitment appropriations of ECU 108.8 million and payment appropriations of ECU 101 million entered in the 1990 budget[5] were fully utilized. Consequently, for the third consecutive year since Pedip was launched, all the budget appropriations were used. For 1991,[6] commitment appropriations of ECU 119.8 million and payment appropriations of ECU 104.4 million are entered against the additional budget heading.

---

[1]   OJ C 207, 12.8.1989; Twenty-third General Report, point 286.
[2]   OJ C 231, 17.9.1990; Bull. EC 7/8-1990, point 1.3.162.
[3]   OJ L 185, 15.7.1988; Twenty-second General Report, point 536.
[4]   Bull. EC 5-1990, point 1.2.136.
[5]   OJ L 24, 29.1.1990; Twenty-third General Report, points 79 to 82.
[6]   Point 988 *et seq.* of this Report.

Section 5

Enterprise

Priority activities and objectives

232. The Commission pressed ahead with its programme for the improvement of the business environment and the promotion of the development of enterprises, in particular small and medium-sized enterprises (SMEs), as set out in the Council Decision of July 1989.[1] In November it laid before the Council a proposal for a review of the programme.[2]

The Council adopted a recommendation on policies for administrative simplification in the Member States. It also gave a favourable response to the Commission documents concerning improvements in the business environment and participation by small firms in public procurement and in Community research and technological development programmes.

The expansionary phase of the two major networks providing direct assistance to small business (the Euro-Info-Centres and BC-Net) was completed. Further measures were taken to promote business cooperation, particularly through subcontracting. Work commenced on a proposal for facilitating mergers and joint ventures between cooperatives and on an action programme for the distributive sector in preparation for the internal market. A wide range of projects was supported as part of European Tourism Year.

Promotion of enterprises and the business environment

233. On 28 May the Council adopted a recommendation relating to the implementation of a policy of administrative simplification in favour of SMEs in the Member States.[3] The recommendation calls on the Member States to adopt programmes for lightening the administrative burden on businesses. In addition, the Commission is asked to facilitate access for small firms to the structural Funds and other programmes, to

---

[1]   OJ L 239, 16.8.1989; Twenty-third General Report, point 290.
[2]   Bull. EC 11-1990, point 1.3.104.
[3]   OJ L 141. 2.6.1990; Bull. EC 5-1990, point 1.2.129. Commission proposal: OJ C 189, 26.7.1989; Twenty-third General Report, point 291; OJ C 101, 21.4.1990; Bull. EC 3-1990, point 1.1.102.

improve further its system for assessing the impact of Community legislation on businesses[1] and to submit a regular report on Community and national measures relating to administrative simplification.

234.   The same day, the Council examined a Commission report on the improvement of the business environment.[2] After examining the report, it called on the Member States to take more systematic account of the business environment when adopting specific proposals in the administrative, legal and tax fields.

Supply of business services — Improving the adaptability of firms to the internal market

Improving the flow of information

235.   The extension of the Euro-Info-Centre (EIC) network[3] was completed in 1990,[4] bringing the total number of centres to 188, together with a further 16 regional subcentres, almost all of which are now operational. Following German unification, it was decided to set up between eight and 10 centres in the five new *Länder*:[5] four of the new centres were operational by the end of the year, with the others due to be opened in 1991. The centres provide small firms with a customized information and advice service. They seek to motivate local businesses to take an interest in Community policy and provide the Commission with feedback on matters of concern to businesses. The first annual conference of the EICs took place in September in Sophia-Antipolis, France.[6]

Fostering cooperation

236.   Pursuant to the Council resolution of September 1989 on the development of subcontracting,[7] the second part of the practical guide on the legal aspects of subcontracting was completed. Other multilingual sectoral glossaries were prepared and further consideration was given to the plan for establishing a European centre for information on subcontracting. The scope of the Business Cooperation Centre (BCC) was extended and now covers 35 countries in five continents.

---

[1]   Twenty-third General Report, point 292.
[2]   Bull. EC 5-1990, point 1.2.130.
[3]   Twenty-first General Report, point 290.
[4]   Twenty-third General Report, point 293.
[5]   Bull. EC 11-1990, point 1.3.108.
[6]   Bull. EC 9-1990, point 1.2.103.
[7]   OJ C 254, 7.10.1989; Twenty-third General Report, point 294.

237.   In June, a successful business cooperation initiative, 'Europartenariat', took place
in Cardiff, Wales, and the 2 500 contacts established there suggest that the number of
cooperation projects could surpass the 70 that resulted from the Europartenariat event
held in Spain in 1989.[1]

238.   The experimental phase of the Business Cooperation Network (BC-Net) was
completed in July and a new phase of consolidation and development was launched. The
network now has some 460 members and work is continuing with a view to expanding
its use and improving its effectiveness. The intention is to extend it to non-member
countries, with priority being given to the countries of Eastern Europe and the EFTA
countries.

Preparing small businesses for 1992

239.   In April the Commission adopted a communication on promoting small business
participation in public procurement[2] and a working paper on small business and
Community activities in the field of research and technological development.[3] Both
documents were examined by the Council on 28 May.

In its conclusions regarding public procurement, the Council called on the Member
States to take the measures advocated by the Commission so as to facilitate access by
small firms, to reduce the cost of such access and to prepare firms for effective
participation in public procurement.[4] As regards participation in Community research
and technological development programmes,[5] the Council asked the Commission to
intensify its efforts by improving access to information and by simplifying application
procedures. It also asked that particular consideration should be given to the development of research infrastructures in the peripheral regions and that the Commission
should increase cooperation with Member States with a view to drawing up new
proposals.

Seed capital

240.   The Community pilot project that was started in October 1988[6] is well under way
and most of the funds receiving support are operating smoothly. The Commission

---

[1]   Twenty-third General Report, point 295.
[2]   Bull. EC 4-1990, point 1.1.88.
[3]   Bull. EC 4-1990, point 1.1.89.
[4]   Bull. EC 5-1990, point 1.2.131.
[5]   Bull. EC 5-1990, point 1.2.132.
[6]   Twenty-second General Report, point 339.

provided assistance for the setting-up, within the European Venture Capital Association, of a unit responsible for monitoring the funds, helping them to find and select investment opportunities, and acting as an intermediary in the possible syndication of investments by two or more funds.

Other measures to assist small businesses

241.   The Commission completed an initial study entitled 'Enterprises in Europe' on the size of businesses in the Community by industry and by country. A pilot project was also launched in Germany with a view to providing craft training for young persons from the peripheral regions of the Community, the objective being to increase awareness of the dual system whereby formal vocational training is combined with on-the-job training.

242.   In November the Council amended the Directives on annual and consolidated accounts as regards the exemptions for small firms and the publication of accounts in ecus. [1]

The cooperative, mutual and non-profit sector

243.   In September the Economic and Social Committee endorsed[2] the Commission communication of December 1989 on the cooperative, mutual and non-profit sector.[3] It suggested, among other things, that the Commission should draft a specific European statute capable of facilitating mergers and joint ventures in this sector. To that end, the Commission is preparing proposals for a regulation and a directive and is endeavouring to give greater consideration in its legislative programme for the internal market to the specific nature of businesses in this sector.

The distributive trades

244.   Further to the Council resolution of November 1989,[4] the Commission is preparing an action programme for the distributive trades in preparation for the internal market. The programme, which will be drawn up in conjunction with the Member States

---

[1]   Point 143 of this Report.
[2]   Bull. EC 9-1990, point 1.2.104.
[3]   Twenty-third General Report, point 300.
[4]   OJ C 297, 25.11.1989; Twenty-third General Report, point 301.

and trade interests concerned, will take account of the diversity of commercial practice and consumer behaviour.

Tourism

245.   As part of European Tourism Year,[1] which was the subject of a Parliament resolution in December,[2] financial assistance was provided for a wide range of both national and pan-European projects contributing to attainment of the two objectives set, namely to demonstrate the economic and social importance of tourism and to illustrate its role in the integration of a frontier-free Europe. The projects, some of which involve EFTA countries, are concerned in particular with encouraging the staggering of holidays, creating new forms of tourism, promoting new tourist destinations and developing intra-Community tourism. In a resolution adopted in July, Parliament gave its views on the measures that should be taken as part of European Tourism Year to protect the environment against any damage that tourism might cause.[3] This issue is also being looked into closely by the Commission, particularly with regard to the protection of coastal areas.[4]

246.   In December the Council adopted a decision on the development of Community statistics on tourism designed to lay the foundations for a Community system capable of providing the information needed for the conduct of tourism policy and regional policy.[5] In November it had called on the Commission to present a multiannual programme of measures in the field of tourism. In September the Commission adopted a communication on rural tourism that underscored the need to assist the development and promotion of high-quality tourism products as the alternative to mass tourism.[6] The same month, the Economic and Social Committee adopted an own-initiative opinion on tourism and regional development.[7]

---

[1]   OJ L 17, 21.1.1989; Twenty-second General Report, point 294; Twenty-third General Report, point 302.
[2]   OJ C 19, 28.1.1991; Bull. EC 12-1990.
[3]   Point 500 of this Report.
[4]   Point 518 of this Report.
[5]   OJ L 358, 21.12.1990; Bull. EC 12-1990. Commission proposal: OJ C 150, 19.6.1990; Bull. EC 5-1990, point 1.6.3.
[6]   Bull. EC 9-1990, point 1.2.100.
[7]   Bull. EC 9-1990, point 1.2.106.

Section 6

Research and technology

Priority activities and objectives

247.   *The main feature of 1990 in the research and technological development field was the implementation of the new framework programme (1990-94)* [1] *on which the Council had reached a political agreement on 15 December 1989.* [2] *Starting in April, the Commission adopted for transmission to the Council and Parliament virtually all of the new proposals for specific programmes envisaged in the new framework programme, the last two proposals being adopted in July and September, respectively. The Council adopted common positions on three of these proposals in December.*

The preparation of the new programmes was characterized by a very clear desire for simplification and harmonization of form. All the proposals are based on the same model in order to streamline the approval process and, ultimately, to make it easier for the bodies concerned, especially small and medium-sized businesses (SMEs), to gain access to and manage the programmes.

An examination of the various proposals reveals an evolution in Community priorities. There was a significant increase in the proportion of resources allocated to the environment (ECU 414 million), biotechnology (ECU 164 million) and agro-industrial research (ECU 343 million), and to the mobility of research scientists (ECU 518 million). However, the importance of information technologies (ECU 1 352 million) and industrial technologies (ECU 748 million) remained undiminished in absolute terms.

This set of 15 specific programmes is characterized by a number of new features. The first of these is the special research effort to be devoted to telematic systems in areas of general interest, [3] *with a view to interconnecting the various existing networks in the Member States to create a genuine 'European nervous system'. This system, which is essential to the successful completion of the single market, will ensure the efficient management of information flows after frontiers have been eliminated, particularly in the areas of customs, transport and social security.*

---

[1]   OJ L 117, 8.5.1990; Bull. EC 4-1990, point 1.1.54; Commission proposal: OJ C 243, 23.9.1989; Twenty-third General Report, point 309.
[2]   Twenty-third General Report, point 303.
[3]   Point 317 of this Report.

Another area which has received particular attention is the utilization of human capital and mobility. The aim of the specific programme in this field is to encourage researchers — particularly young researchers — to participate in high-level research in centres of excellence, networks of such centres or specialized facilities through the granting of fellowships. The objective is to provide training and increased mobility for about 5 000 researchers over the five years of the programme.

The importance attached to the environment is another aspect worthy of note. This sector has now expanded beyond the confines of a specific programme to become an integral part of the Community's overall research effort.

The role of pre-normative research carried out within the Community, particularly in the fields of biotechnology and the environment, is also emphasized. The aim is to build up, through effective research activities, the basic scientific and technical knowledge that is essential for the framing of common legislation.

A fifth and last new feature concerns programme management. Alongside the conventional method of choosing participants through a public call for proposals, the option of using a 'special' procedure in exceptional cases was proposed. The purpose of this procedure, which would operate within precisely defined limits and be backed by effective safeguards to prevent any abuse, is to provide a workable means of addressing the specific research requirements which arise as a result of ever more rapid advances and often unforeseeable innovations.

Community R&TD policy

Framework programme 1987-91

248. Implementation of the framework programme (1987-91)[1] continued and was virtually completed during 1990 with the adoption by the Council of four specific programmes: agricultural research,[2] human genome analysis,[3] transport (Euret),[4] and machine translation (Eurotra).[5] In addition, a review of the stimulation plan for economic science (SPES) (1989-92) is under way.[6]

---

[1]   OJ L 302, 24.10.1987; Twenty-first General Report, point 307.
[2]   Point 276 of this Report.
[3]   Point 279 of this Report.
[4]   Point 599 of this Report.
[5]   Point 322 of this Report.
[6]   Point 55 of this Report.

Joint Research Centre

249.   The reform of the Joint Research Centre (JRC), approved[1] in 1988 and set in train[2] in 1989, continued during the year. The new JRC structure was strengthened by the merging of two institutes whose fields of interest were clearly complementary, namely the Institute for Systems Engineering and the Centre for Information Technologies and Electronics. The eight institutes constituting this new structure saw an increase in their operational and budgetary independence in four areas of their activity during the year: framework programme, support for Commission departments, exploratory research and work for outside bodies. The demand for work in support of the Commission was particularly heavy in 1990: a number of multiannual contracts were signed for the supply of continuous and long-term services in support of Community policies. Although work for outside bodies increased as a proportion of the JRC's activities as a whole, the level was not as high as anticipated. However, the JRC has a reputation among its clients as a body capable of high-quality work and it established a series of formal links with associated laboratories in the Member States which will provide a basis for carrying out work for outside bodies. During the year, all the institutes also contributed to an in-depth debate on the future strategy of the JRC with a view to the adoption of an action plan in 1991.

International cooperation

250.   On 13 June the Commission adopted a communication on cooperation in science and technology with third countries.[3] In it, the Commission describes the current forms of scientific and technical cooperation with the various groups of countries and sets out options for a reference framework for future activities in this field. It highlights three principles which apply independently of the form of cooperation or the location of the country concerned: support for global initiatives to tackle problems common to all countries, the Community's contribution towards the development of the international scientific community and participation in selective cooperation activities in the field of science and technology at international level. These three principles should be applied in conjunction with criteria that relate to the specific characteristics and geographical location of the countries concerned. These fall into three main categories: neighbouring European countries (distinguishing between EFTA member countries and the countries of Central and Eastern Europe), developed countries outside Europe, and the newly-industrializing or developing countries.

---

[1]   OJ L 286, 20.10.1988; Twenty-second General Report, point 345.
[2]   Twenty-third General Report, point 305.
[3]   Bull. EC 6-1990, point 1.3.92.

In its conclusions[1] of 20 November the Council examined all the aspects of scientific and technological cooperation with non-Community countries, recommending that it be gradually developed, on the basis of the principles of subsidiarity and mutual benefit, within the context of the framework programme.

251. Also on 13 June the Commission adopted a communication on the Community's scientific and technical cooperation with the countries of Central and Eastern Europe.[2] In it the Commission lists the areas in which this type of cooperation could be undertaken between the Community and these countries to their mutual benefit. Having regard to the specific needs of the countries of Central and Eastern Europe, three types of activities are envisaged: development of research concentrating on the introduction and adaptation of technologies, rather than on technological advance, strengthening of the already established cooperation between centres of excellence and scientists in the Community and in the countries concerned, and promotion of cooperation in the field of human resources. The document outlines the available and possible new instruments which can be used: COST cooperation, participation in Community programmes, and activities under bilateral and multilateral agreements. This communication was supplemented by another document dealing more particularly with the role of telecommunications.[3] Scientific and technological cooperation with the countries of Central and Eastern Europe was also the subject of a Parliament resolution in July.[4]

252. European cooperation in the field of scientific and technical research (COST) continued with the entry into force of memoranda of understanding in respect of the following projects: COST 14 (Cooperation technology), 92 (Metabolic and physiological aspects of dietary fibre), 94 (Post-harvest treatment of fruit and vegetables), 227 (Integrated space/terrestrial mobile networks), 229 (Applications of digital signal processing in communications), 232 (Speech recognition over the telephone line), 508 (Wood mechanics) and 813 (Diseases and disorders in forestry nurseries). On 29 June, the Council adopted[5] a resolution in which it acknowledged the advantages of the gradual integration into the COST cooperation framework of the countries of Central and Eastern Europe in the process of implementing democratic reforms.

253. Alongside the ongoing negotiations between the Community and the EFTA countries for the conclusion of a treaty on the establishment of a European economic area,[6] bilateral cooperation with these countries in the field of science and technology also continued. The following agreements have already entered into force: the agree-

---

[1]   Bull. EC 11-1990, point 1.3.65.
[2]   Bull. EC 6-1990, point 1.3.93.
[3]   Point 312 of this Report.
[4]   OJ C 231, 17.9.1990; Bull. EC 7/8-1990, point 1.3.129.
[5]   OJ C 172, 13.7.1990; Bull. EC 6-1990, point 1.3.95.
[6]   Point 688 of this Report.

ment with Finland on the protection of the environment[1] and the agreements on medical research[2] and on the international scientific cooperation and interchange needed by European research scientists (Science programme)[3] with Norway, Sweden, Switzerland, Austria and Finland. Extension of the European stimulation plan for economic science (SPES) to these countries was also proposed,[4] as was extension of the Science programme[5] to Iceland,[6] and extension of the programme on applied metrology (BCR)[7] to Sweden, Finland and Switzerland.[8] The latter two proposals were examined by the Economic and Social Committee in October[9] and by the Parliament in November[10] and October,[11] respectively. The Council adopted common positions on them in November[12] and December.[13] Cooperation agreements were also concluded between Euratom and Sweden[14] concerning research and training in the field of radiation protection[15] and between Euratom and a Swiss body[16] concerning research on radioactive waste storage.

254.   Cooperation between the Community and Eureka was continued and reinforced. The need for synergy between Eureka and Community programmes was explicitly mentioned in the Council Decision adopting the framework programme of Community activities in the field of research and technological development (1990-94).[17] The Commission continued to contribute to the management and funding of Eureka projects, and the JRC likewise continued to take part in certain of them. The Commission also continued to encourage support measures, particularly in the standardization field, and also participated in the organization of the overall evaluation of the Eureka initiative, and of each of the technological fields covered and their relationship with Community programmes.

255.   International cooperation with the industrialized countries was strengthened and extended. Several new areas of cooperation with the United States were identified:[18]

---

[1]   OJ L 304, 20.10.1989; Twenty-second General Report, point 308.
[2]   OJ L 74, 20.3.1990; Bull. EC 1/2-1990, point 1.1.119; Commission proposal: OJ C 223, 30.8.1989; Twenty-third General Report, point 308.
[3]   OJ L 50, 26.2.1990; Bull. EC 1/2-1990, point 1.1.118; Commission proposal: OJ C 154, 22.6.1989, OJ C 197, 2.8.1989; Twenty-third General Report, point 308.
[4]   Point 55 of this Report.
[5]   OJ L 206, 30.7.1988; Twenty-second General Report, point 395.
[6]   OJ C 181, 21.7.1990; Bull. EC 6-1990, point 1.3.110.
[7]   OJ L 206, 30.7.1988; Twenty-second General Report, point 371.
[8]   OJ C 148, 16.6.1990; Bull. EC 5-1990, point 1.2.111.
[9]   OJ C 284, 12.11.1990; Bull. EC 10-1990, points 1.3.75 and 1.3.76.
[10]   OJ C 324, 24.12.1990; Bull. EC 11-1990, point 1.3.84.
[11]   OJ C 284, 12.11.1990; Bull. EC 10-1990, point 1.3.75.
[12]   Bull. EC 11-1990, point 1.3.82.
[13]   Bull. EC 12-1990.
[14]   OJ L 228, 22.8.1990; Bull. EC 7/8-1990, point 1.3.130.
[15]   OJ L 200, 13.7.1989; Twenty-third General Report, point 3.1.6.
[16]   Bull. EC 7/8-1990, point 1.3.131.
[17]   Point 247 of this Report.
[18]   Bull. EC 9-1990, point 1.2.83; Bull. EC 11-1990, point 1.3.86.

in the field of biotechnology for example, a scientific and technological cooperation committee and a joint task force were set up. The Commission also decided to participate in the pilot phase of the international human frontier science programme proposed by Japan[1] on basic research on living organisms. An agreement was also signed with the Japanese government body responsible for nuclear safeguards research.[2]

256.   Scientific cooperation with countries in Latin America, Asia and the Mediterranean expanded considerably in 1990. Agreements which included a scientific cooperation component were prepared with Chile, Argentina and Paraguay, and there was increased cooperation with India, Pakistan, Yugoslavia, Brazil and Mexico. During the year, 166 research fellowships, over 70 joint research projects and three workshops were funded, the overall budget for these activities amounting to ECU 17.6 million.

Information technologies and telecommunications

257.   Information on research and technological development activities in the field of information technologies and telecommunications is to be found in Section 7 'Telecommunications, information industries and innovation' of Chapter III of this Report.

Industrial technologies and materials

258.   The Commission continued to implement the programme of research and technological development in the field of industrial technologies and materials (Brite/Euram) (1989-92).[3] Work started on the 194 projects selected in 1989 and 1990 following a first call for proposals in the first four sectors of the programme, as did the work covered by the 78 'feasibility awards' granted in total. Of the 651 new proposals received in response to a second call for proposals in the field of advanced materials and production technologies,[4] 146 were selected for funding by the Commission. On 21 and 22 May, the Brite/Euram days,[5] attended by some 1 300 university and industry representatives, provided an opportunity for existing and potential participants in the programme to meet. A group of independent experts, in a report assessing Community aerospace research activities published in July, considered that the current exploratory phase represented an important stage towards a more ambitious initiative.

---

[1]   Bull. EC 9-1990, point 1.2.84.
[2]   Bull. EC 5-1990, point 1.2.112.
[3]   OJ L 98, 11.4.1989; Twenty-third General Report, point 323.
[4]   OJ C 36, 16.2.1990; Bull. EC 1/2-1990, point 1.1.107.
[5]   Bull. EC 5-1990, point 1.2.88.

259. One hundred and sixty-two proposals were received in response to the call for proposals published under the programme of research and technological development in the field of raw materials and recycling (1990-92):[1] 133 of these were for the sub-programme on primary raw materials and 29 for the sub-programme on the recycling of non-ferrous metals. Fifty-four proposals totalling ECU 18 million were selected under the first sub-programme, and 15 proposals totalling ECU 5.3 million under the second sub-programme.

260. On 30 May the Commission adopted a proposal for a new programme of research and technological development in the field of industrial materials and technologies (1990-94).[2] This programme will cover materials and raw materials, on the one hand, and design and manufacturing on the other. The proposed budget is ECU 748 million, of which ECU 78 million are to be allocated to the part of the programme to be undertaken by the JRC. This proposal was examined by the Economic and Social Committee[3] in November and by Parliament[4] (first reading) in December.

261. The JRC's Institute for Advanced Materials set up an international consortium involving a number of major European research organizations engaged in materials research and technological development. The main aim of this consortium, called 'E-Marc', is to provide a framework for European industry to undertake large-scale projects in the materials field. The Institute also undertook some pre-standardization research as part of a project on the standardization of advanced ceramics carried out in cooperation with the European standards organizations CEN and Cenelec.

Measurement and testing

262. Under the programme for applied metrology and chemical analysis (1988-92),[5] seven new metrology projects designed to perfect methods of calibrating measuring instruments used in automated machining processes were launched following the publication, in February, of an invitation to submit proposals.[6] Methods were developed for determining aflatoxin in animal feedingstuffs, glucosinolates in oilseed rape and gluten in wheat. Efforts were made to encourage collaboration between the national systems for quality assurance in medical analyses with a view to harmonizing the reference values adopted in the Member States for the most common parameters.

---

[1]   OJ L 359, 8.12.1989; Twenty-third General Report, point 324.
[2]   OJ C 174, 16.7.1990; Bull. EC 5-1990, point 1.2.96.
[3]   Bull. EC 11-1990, point 1.3.71.
[4]   OJ C 19, 28.1.1991; Bull. EC 12-1990.
[5]   OJ L 206, 30.7.1988; Twenty-second General Report, point 371.
[6]   OJ C 31, 9.2.1990; Bull. EC 1/2-1990, point 1.1.109.

263.   On 30 May the Commission adopted a new proposal for a programme of research and technological development in the field of measurements and testing (1990-94).[1] This programme is divided into four parts: support to regulations and directives, sectoral testing problems, common methods of calibration for the Community, and development of new methods of measurement. The proposed budget is ECU 140 million, of which ECU 90 million are to cover work undertaken by the JRC. This proposal was endorsed by the Economic and Social Committee in November.[2]

264.   The JRC Central Bureau for Nuclear Measurements continued its work in the field of nuclear measurements and standards. Work was completed on the probability of the emission of X-rays and gamma rays from 23 radionuclides, to be applied to calibrating the effectiveness of sensors, and the results will be published by the IAEA. Work at Community level on the certification of plutonium oxide reference materials was also completed. The Bureau stepped up its activities in support of the Community Bureau of References programme in the field of non-nuclear materials.

Environment

Environment

265.   Fourteen new projects were launched, following the call for proposals published in 1989, thereby completing the implementation of the fourth programme of research in the field of the environment (1986-90).[3] Following two calls for proposals published in 1989, 98 projects were selected for funding by the Commission under the (1989-92) research programme[4] on the environment (STEP)[5] and 37 under the research programme on climatology and natural hazards (Epoch).[6] Ninety proposals were received in response to the publication of a call for proposals covering the specific fields of environment and human health and evaluation of the risks associated with chemical products.[7] The call for proposals published in 1989 covering the Reward programme for the recycling of waste[8] resulted in nine projects being selected.

---

[1]   OJ C 174, 16.7.1990; Bull. EC 5-1990, point 1.2.97.
[2]   Bull. EC 11-1990, point 1.3.72.
[3]   OJ L 159, 19.6.1986; Twentieth General Report, point 396.
[4]   OJ L 359, 8.12.1989; Twenty-third General Report, point 319.
[5]   Science and technology for environmental protection.
[6]   European programme on climatology and natural hazards.
[7]   OJ C 64, 14.3.1990; Bull. EC 3-1990, point 1.1.69.
[8]   OJ L 359, 8.12.1989; Twenty-third General Report, point 324.

266.   On 30 May the Commission adopted a new proposal for a programme of research and technological development in the field of environment (1990-94).[1] This programme is divided into four parts covering the Community's participation in international global change programmes (research on global climate change), technologies and engineering for the environment, research on economic and social aspects of environmental issues, and integrated research projects as part of large-scale transnational programmes requiring an interdisciplinary approach. Of the proposed budget of ECU 414 million, an amount of ECU 154 million is earmarked for work undertaken by the JRC. The Economic and Social Committee delivered an opinion on this proposal in September,[2] followed by Parliament (first reading) in November,[3] the Commission then changing[4] it to take account of certain amendments made by the latter. On 21 December the Council reached agreement in principle[5] on a common position on this subject.

267.   The JRC's Institute for the Environment carried out a study on a new spectrometric method of evaluating the characteristics and the concentration of a number of pollutants in atmospheric aerosols. On the subject of water quality, it completed a study on the environmental conditions of Lake Garda. In the field of industrial hazards, the Institute for Systems Engineering carried out a study of new methods for the mathematical modelling of decision-making processes and a study of a number of past accidents related to the shipment of hazardous materials. It also continued its activities in connection with the STAR projects, and the Formentor project under the Eureka programme. The Institute for Remote Sensing Applications undertook the development and construction of a European microwave signature laboratory and developed a neuron network for interpretation of remote sensing images which can be used for both marine and earth observation.

Marine science and technology

268.   The 42 projects selected in 1989 under the programme of research in the field of marine science and technology (1989-92) (MAST)[6] were implemented in 1990. A call for proposals concerning large-scale underwater acoustic calibration facilities was published in May.[7] A number of horizontal support measures were also taken in relation to the exchange of oceanographic data, coordination of research vessels and training.

---

[1]   OJ C 174, 16.7.1990; Bull. EC 5-1990, point 1.2.98.
[2]   Bull. EC 9-1990, point 1.2.71.
[3]   OJ C 324, 24.12.1990; Bull. EC 11-1990, point 1.3.73.
[4]   OJ C 327, 29.12.1990; Bull. EC 11-1990, point 1.3.73.
[5]   Bull. EC 12-1990.
[6]   OJ C 200, 13.7.1989; Twenty-third General Report, point 345.
[7]   OJ C 127, 23.5.1990; Bull. EC 5-1990, point 1.2.91.

269. A proposal for a decision adopting a specific programme of research and techno-logical development in the field of marine science and technology (1990-94) was adopted by the Commission on 30 May.[1] This programme covers marine science, coastal en-gineering and marine technology. The proposed budget is ECU 104 million. The Economic and Social Committee examined this proposal in September[2] and Parliament (first reading) in November.[3] It was adopted[4] by the Commission after taking account of amendments made by Parliament and was the subject of a common position by the Council on 21 December.[5]

Life sciences and technologies

Biotechnology

270. In September the final report containing an illustrated catalogue of the results of the cooperative projects under the Biotechnology action programme (1985-89)[6] was published following the completion of the programme in 1989.[7]

271. The 1990-94 programme[8] of research and development in the field of biotechnol-ogy (Bridge) began this year. Following a call for proposals covering all sectors of the programme, with the exception of the bio-safety area which was the subject of a separate call for proposals,[9] 404 proposals for transnational projects were received. sixty-one of these, involving 300 different partners, were selected and allocated a total budget of ECU 60 million. These projects include five major targeted projects ('T projects') integrating the activities of between 20 and 30 different laboratories. Over 100 new fellowships were also granted under the heading of training in biotechnology.

272. Concertation in the field of biotechnology continued with the development of the Biodoc database, the organization of an international US-Community seminar on the subject of biotechnology and food, and the continuation of activities related to public information and public attitudes to biotechnology.

---

[1]   OJ C 174, 16.7.1990; Bull. EC 5-1990, point 1.2.99.
[2]   Bull. EC 9-1990, point 1.2.72.
[3]   OJ C 324, 24.12.1990; Bull. EC 11-1990, point 1.3.74.
[4]   OJ C 321, 21.12.1990; Bull. EC 11-1990, point 1.3.74.
[5]   Bull. EC 12-1990.
[6]   OJ C 83, 25.3.1985; Nineteenth General Report, point 354.
[7]   Twenty-third General Report, point 330.
[8]   OJ C 360, 9.12.1989; Twenty-third General Report, point 331.
[9]   OJ C 118, 12.5.1990; Bull. EC 5-1990, point 1.2.89.

273.   On 30 May the Commission adopted a new proposal for a specific research and technological development programme in the field of biotechnology (1990-94) (Biotech). [1] This programme is divided into three parts: molecular approaches, cellular and organism approaches, and ecology and population biology. The proposed funding amounts to ECU 164 million. This proposal was examined by the Economic and Social Committee in October. [2]

Agricultural and agro-industrial research

274.   Under the 1988-93 programme [3] for biotechnology-based agro-industrial research and technological development (Eclair), [4] 48 additional projects involving some 360 different organizations were selected following a call for proposals published in 1989. The total Community contribution to these projects is ECU 60 million. More than 25 mobility grants were also awarded and three specialized studies were launched.

275.   On 30 May the Commission adopted a proposal for a new programme of research and technological development in the field of agriculture and agro-industry (1990-94). [5] The areas covered are primary production in agriculture, forestry, aquaculture and fishing, inputs to agriculture and forestry, processing of biological raw materials and end-use of the products. The budget proposed is ECU 333 million. The Economic and Social Committee delivered an opinion on this proposal in September. [6]

276.   On 26 February the Council adopted a specific Community programme in the field of competitiveness of agriculture and management of agricultural resources (1989-93). [7] This programme covers the following fields: conversion, diversification, including extensification of agricultural production; cost reduction and protection of the rural environment; product quality, new uses for traditional agricultural products, plant and animal health aspects; socio-economic aspects and specific activities for all regions lagging behind in development; dissemination of agricultural research information. The financial contribution committed in 1990 for the proposals adopted under the first two tranches of an invitation to tender issued in 1989 amounts to ECU 19 million. In addition, the results of the 1984-88 programme [8] were the subject of a final report adopted in May. [9]

---

[1]   OJ C 174, 16.7.1990; Bull. EC 5-1990, point 1.2.100.
[2]   Bull. EC 10-1990, point 1.3.65.
[3]   OJ L 60, 3.3.1989; Twenty-third General Report, point 333.
[4]   European collaborative linkage of agriculture and industry through research.
[5]   OJ C 174, 16.7.1990; Bull. EC 5-1990, point 1.2.101.
[6]   Bull. EC 9-1990, point 1.2.73.
[7]   OJ L 58, 7.3.1990; Bull. EC 1/2-1990, point 1.1.111; Commission proposal: OJ C 146, 13.6.1989; Twenty-second General Report, point 377; OJ C 269, 21.10.1989; Twenty-third General Report, point 335.
[8]   OJ L 358, 22.12.1983; Seventeenth General Report, point 592.
[9]   Bull. EC 5-1990, point 1.2.140.

277.   In March the Economic and Social Committee adopted[1] an own-initiative opinion on increasing the use of agricultural and forestry resources in the non-food industrial and energy sectors: prospects opened up by research and technological innovation.

Biomedicine and health

278.   The fourth Community coordination programme in the field of medical and health research (1987-91)[2] continued in 1990, during which time 52 new concerted-action projects selected in 1989 were launched.[3] The funding for the programme was increased by a further ECU 5 million contributed by the EFTA countries taking part in the programme (Austria, Finland, Norway, Sweden and Switzerland).[4]

279.   On 29 June the Council adopted the new programme of research in the field of human genome analysis (1990-92).[5] An initial call for proposals was published in October.[6]

280.   On 30 May the Commission adopted a proposal for a decision adopting a new programme of research and technological development in the field of biomedicine and health (1990-94).[7] This programme covers three areas: harmonization of methodologies and protocols in epidemiological, biological and clinical research; applications to diseases of great socio-economic impact; and human genome analysis. The proposed budget is ECU 133 million. Opinions were delivered on this proposal by the Economic and Social Committee in November[8] and by Parliament (first reading) in December.[9]

Life sciences and technologies for developing countries

281.   Following the call for proposals issued in 1987 for a two-year period, which closed on 31 December 1989, 13 new projects (eight in agriculture and five in medicine, health and nutrition) were chosen for funding under the second programme of research in the

---

[1]   OJ C 124, 21.5.1990; Bull. EC 3-1990, point 1.1.70.
[2]   OJ L 334, 24.11.1987; Twenty-first General Report, point 314.
[3]   Twenty-third General Report, point 313.
[4]   Point 253 of this Report.
[5]   OJ L 196, 26.7.1990; Bull. EC 6-1990, point 1.3.97; Commission proposal: OJ C 27, 2.2.1989; Twenty-second General Report, point 356; OJ C 303, 2.12.1989; Twenty-third General Report, point 314; Bull. EC 6-1990, point 1.3.97.
[6]   OJ C 250, 4.10.1990; Bull. EC 10-1990, point 1.3.62.
[7]   OJ C 174, 16.7.1990; Bull. EC 5-1990, point 1.2.102.
[8]   Bull. EC 11-1990, point 1.3.75.
[9]   OJ C 19, 28.1.1991; Bull. EC 12-1990.

field of science and technology for development (1987-91)[1] In conjunction with the additional funding allocated to certain pre-selected projects,[2] these new projects helped to restore the balance in the fields of research which have received less coverage hitherto: agriculture and nutrition, tropical forests, environment, production systems, malaria and AIDS.

282.   On 30 May the Commission adopted[3] a proposal for a new programme of research and technological development in the field of life sciences and technologies for developing countries (1990-94). This programme, with a proposed budget of ECU 111 million, covers agriculture, medicine, health and nutrition. The Economic and Social Committee delivered an opinion on the proposal in September[4] and Parliament delivered its opinion (first reading) in December.[5]

Energy

Non-nuclear energy

283.   The 200 projects selected following the call for proposals published in 1989 as part of the 1989-92 programme[6] in the field of non-nuclear energies (Joule)[7] started in 1990. In response to a call for proposals published in May limited to deep geology,[8] 12 projects were received. A number of large international conferences were held, notably the conference on wind energy, in September, in Madrid and the conference on oil and gas, in October, in Palermo.

284.   On 30 May the Commission adopted[9] a proposal for a new programme of research and technological development in the field of non-nuclear energies (1990-94). This programme covers four areas: analysis of strategies and modelling, improved used of fossil fuels, renewable energy sources and rational utilization of energy. The proposed budget amounts to ECU 157 million. The Economic and Social Committee delivered an opinion on this programme in October.[10]

---

[1]   OJ L 355, 17.12.1987; Twenty-first General Report, point 345.
[2]   Twenty-second General Report, point 391; Twenty-third General Report, point 344.
[3]   OJ C 174, 16.7.1990; Bull. EC 5-1990, point 1.2.103.
[4]   Bull. EC 9-1990, point 1.2.74.
[5]   OJ C 19, 28.1.1991; Bull. EC 12-1990.
[6]   OJ L 98, 11.4.1989; Twenty-third General Report, point 343.
[7]   Joint opportunities for unconventional or long-term energy supply.
[8]   OJ C 126, 22.5.1990; Bull. EC 5-1990, point 1.2.90.
[9]   OJ C 174, 16.7.1990; Bull. EC 5-1990, point 1.2.104.
[10]   Bull. EC 10-1990, point 1.3.66.

285. The JRC's Institute for Systems Engineering conducted a study on the degradation of photovoltaic modules made of amorphous silicon under the effect of light using solar simulation and extended the measurements and models of the solar spectrum to include low-insolation conditions.

Nuclear fission safety

286. Under the programme of research and training in the field of radiation protection (1990-91),[1] some 100 multinational research projects were selected for funding by the Commission in the various areas covered. In addition a number of radiation protection training courses were initiated. A report evaluating the 1980-84[2] and 1985-89[3] radiation protection programmes was published by an independent panel of experts, who described these programmes as relevant and well balanced.

287. In the field of reactor safety the JRC's Institute for Systems Engineering continued with the development of the Composant Event Data Bank. The Institute for Safety Technology continued the activities started under the Strike project for the 1:5 scale testing of reactor vessels, and began the first phase of the Artic project, an expert system for evaluating the residual life of damaged components. A call for expressions of interest was published in April[4] under the JRC action programme 1988-91[5] with a view to promoting activities in the field of source term analysis for LWR reactors.

288. The results of the third programme of research in the field of the management and storage of radioactive waste (1985-89)[6] were exhibited at a conference held in Luxembourg from 17 to 21 September. More than 300 proposals were received in response to a call for proposals published[7] on 7 March under the fourth programme 1990-94.[8] The JRC's Institute for Environmental Studies continued its work on the migratory behaviour of inorganic contaminants in groundwater due to possible seepage from material deposited in geological formations. Special efforts were made to develop non-invasive speciation methods and the quantitative description of retention mechanisms. In December the Council adopted conclusions on the basis of a communication on objectives, standards and criteria for radioactive waste disposal.[9]

---

1   OJ L 200, 13.7.1984; Twenty-third General Report, point 316.
2   OJ L 78, 25.3.1980, Fourteenth General Report, point 494.
3   OJ C 83, 25.3.1985; Nineteenth General Report, point 367.
4   OJ C 103, 25.4.1990; Bull. EC 4-1990, point 1.1.69.
5   OJ L 186, 20.10.1988; Twenty-second General Report, point 345.
6   OJ L 83, 25.3.1985; Nineteenth General Report, point 336.
7   OJ C 55, 7.3.1990; Bull. EC 3-1990, point 1.1.71.
8   OJ L 395, 30.12.1989; Twenty-third General Report, point 340.
9   Point 652 of this Report.

289.   Following an initial call for proposals published in September 1989, 16 multi-national research projects were selected under the research and training programme in the field of remote handling in hazardous or disordered nuclear environments (Teleman) (1989-93).[1] Work carried out under these projects will make it possible to develop components for the demonstration machines which are intended to be the subject of the second stage of the programme.

290.   Under the programme on the decommissioning of nuclear installations (1989-93),[2] 51 multinational research projects were selected following the call for proposals published in June 1989. A start was also made on four pilot projects on dismantling.

291.   As part of a project coordinated by the OECD, the JRC's Institute for Transuranium Elements analysed fuel fragments and debris from the Three Mile Island reactor, developed a new database for thermo-physical data on actinides and built a robotized sample preparation unit. With regard to the inspection of finished materials, the Institute for Systems Engineering prepared and carried out the installation of a series of ultrasonic seals at the Sellafield facility, and developed and tested a system for identifying the contents of fuel containers at the La Hague reprocessing plant.

292.   On 1 August the Commission adopted[3] a proposal for a new programme of research and technological development in the field of nuclear fission safety (1990-94). This programme will cover two areas: radiation protection and reactor safety. The proposed total budget is ECU 199 million, of which ECU 162 million are to be allocated to JRC activities under a separate proposal.

Controlled thermonuclear fusion

293.   Under the programme of research and training in the field of controlled thermo-nuclear fusion (1988-92)[4] the Community maintained its position as world leader in the field of fusion by magnetic confinement. The JET (Joint European Torus), which was shut down in order to reinforce its internal components, started up again in June at full heating power. The construction and placing in service of medium-sized devices continued in the associated laboratories. In August, the Asdex-Upgrade tokamak, specially designed for controlling plasma purity, went into service at Garching (Germany). The Next Step conceptual design activities, which form part of the Next European Torus and

---

[1]   OJ L 226, 3.8.1989; Twenty-third General Report, point 341.
[2]   OJ C 98, 11.4.1989; Twenty-third General Report, point 342.
[3]   OJ C 247, 2.10.1990; Bull. EC 7/8-1990, point 1.3.115.
[4]   OJ C 222, 12.8.1988; Twenty-second General Report, point 380.

international quadripartite collaboration under ITER (International thermonuclear experimental reactor), were completed.[1]

294. The JRC's Institute for Systems Engineering continued work on the design of components for the NET and their remote handling. The Institute for Advanced Materials intensified its studies of the behaviour under irradiation of components exposed to plasma and the thermal fatigue of such components. The Institute for Safety Technology continued with the construction of Ethel, a laboratory designed to study the safety of components in contact with tritium.

295. An evaluation report on the fusion programme, drawn up by a committee of independent experts, was published in July; it recommends that this topic be maintained as one the priorities of Community research policy. In line with this report's recommendations, the Commission adopted,[2] on 25 September, a proposal for a specific programme of research and technological development in the field of thermonuclear fusion (1990-94). The prime objective of this programme will be to establish the scientific and technological base and to prepare industry for the construction of a Next Step experimental fusion reactor. The preferred framework for the detailed study of the Next Step device will be ITER cooperation; and full account will be taken of safety and environmental considerations in the execution of the programme. The proposal covers the following four areas: Next Step design, long-term technical development, JET and the support programme. On the same date the Commission also adopted a proposal for a Council decision prolonging the JET project until 1996 to enable the installation to be used to test plasma control methods to be used in the Next Step device[3] and, secondly, Directives for negotiations on the continued participation of the Community[4] in the ITER pre-design activities together with Japan, the United States and the Soviet Union.[5] These Directives were adopted by the Council on 20 November.[6]

Human capital and mobility

296. Under the programme to stimulate the international cooperation and interchange needed by European research scientists (Science) (1988-92),[7] 601 proposals were submitted for evaluation; 135 of these were selected for Commission funding totalling ECU

---

[1]   Point 295 of this Report.
[2]   OJ C 261, 16.10.1990; Bull. EC 9-1990, point 1.2.67.
[3]   Bull. EC 9-1990, point 1.2.68.
[4]   Bull. EC 9-1990, point 1.2.82.
[5]   OJ L 102, 21.4.1988; Twenty-second General Report, point 381.
[6]   Bull. EC 11-1190, point 1.3.83.
[7]   OJ L 206, 30.7.1988; Twenty-second General Report, point 195.

45 million. During the same period, 227 applications were received for research bursaries and 181 for research grants, of which 113 and 75 respectively were approved. In addition, 29 applications for subsidies for high-level training courses were received, of which 12 were approved.

297.   The Community stimulation plan for economic science (SPES) was put into operation.[1]

298.   Work began on the 12 projects selected under the Community plan of support to facilitate access to large-scale scientific facilities (1988-92).[2] Seven new facilities were shortlisted, of which four were finally chosen. Study reports were also drawn up by expert groups on the following seven topics: neutron sources, high-power lasers, intense magnetic fields, hydraulics, seismics, oceanography and combustion technology. A round-table meeting on the subject of synchrotron radiation facilities was organized, bringing together the heads of four of the selected projects and representatives of user groups.

299.   On 30 May the Commission adopted a proposal for a new programme in the field of human capital and mobility (1990-94).[3] The aim of this programme is to develop a high-level decentralized research and training scheme in the Community. Host institutions, networks of centres of excellence and large-scale facilities capable of supervising high-level post-doctoral research will be selected and will then themselves select research scientists. The programme covers all the exact and natural sciences, and the areas of social and human sciences liable to have a major impact on European competitiveness. The proposed budget is ECU 518 million, of which ECU 25 million are for activities undertaken by the JRC. This proposal was examined by the Economic and Social Committee in September.[4]

Support for Community R&TD and other activities

300.   Work continued under the Community programme on strategic analysis, forecasting and assessment in research and technology (1989-92) (Monitor).[5] A first two-yearly report was prepared dealing with the social and economic implications of technological change and identifying the main problems confronting political decision-makers. Under the FAST programme the initial results of forecasting studies on economic and social

---

[1]   Point 55 of this Report.
[2]   OJ L 98, 11.4.1989; Twenty-third General Report, point 350.
[3]   OJ C 174, 16.7.1990; Bull. EC 5-1990, point 1.2.105.
[4]   Bull. EC 9-1990, point 1.2.75.
[5]   OJ L 200, 13.7.1989; Twenty-third General Report, point 351.

cohesion, the internationalization of the economy and anthropocentric production systems were published. Under the SAST programme,[1] a number of strategic analysis studies were initiated concerning the potential for scientific collaboration with the industrialized countries, problems of technological standards and the interaction between transport and the environment. Under the Spear programme[2] two studies were completed, dealing, respectively, with the impact of research programmes on economic and social cohesion, and training schemes. Three expert networks were set up to work on the economic impact of research, training in assessment and research impact indicators.

301. A number of programmes were also submitted for evaluation by panels of independent experts as part of the Community action plans in these fields:[3] Science, Brite/Euram (aerospace sector), medical research, training and mobility, and fusion. A start was also made on evaluating the work of three other programmes: large-scale facilities, science and technology for development, and COST cooperation.

302. Activities in the space sector continued.[4] Five working groups comprising representatives of the Community and the European Space Agency were set up, with remits to look at research and technology, earth observation, telecommunications, industrial competitiveness and trade policy and external relations. A study on the scope for the use of space data in the implementation of major Community policies was published. Further studies were initiated on soil infrastructure, methods of interpreting satellite data and analysis of socio-economic conditions for the development of earth observation services. In the field of microgravity research the Commission announced opportunities created within the Science, Brite/Euram, Esprit and Bridge programmes. A study was also launched to identify those areas of microgravity research liable to generate the greatest interest within industry. The Commission also published a communication proposing a common Community approach to satellite telecommunications.[5]

303. The JRC's Institute for Technology forecasting published two studies on science and the greenhouse effect and on technological responses to the problems of CO_2. It undertook a number of studies on future trends in air transport, and a study on the interaction between horizontal and vertical technologies. The Institute also contributed to the preparation of discussions on JRC strategy for the year 2000 and beyond, publishing three studies on science and technology forecasting.

---

[1] Strategic analysis in the field of science and technology.
[2] Support programme for a European assessment of research.
[3] OJ C 14, 20.1.1987; Twentieth General Report, point 363.
[4] Twenty-third General Report, point 312.
[5] Point 312 of this Report.

304.   On 26 September the Commission adopted medium-term guidelines for technical steel research (1991-95).[1] These guidelines identify the priority areas of the steel research programmes for the years ahead. They fall within the Commission's general steel objectives,[2] and are designed to help proposers prepare their research project submissions and the Commission departments to assess their admissibility. Under the 1990 programme the Commission selected 101 technical steal research projects totalling ECU 28 million and 14 pilot and demonstration projects in the steel industry totalling ECU 13 million. In addition, 16 projects were placed on a reserve list with a budget of nearly ECU 7 million.

305.   Acting under Article 55 of the ECSC Treaty and in accordance with the medium-term guidelines adopted in 1989,[3] the Commission decided to grant financial aid amounting to ECU 36 355 600 to 98 technical research projects on coal. It also decided, under the same provision, to grant financial aid of ECU 13 million to 68 projects on health, medicine and safety in ECSC industries, on mines safety and health, and on the technical control of nuisances at work and in the environment of coal and steel installations (ECSC social research).

306.   On 30 July and 21 August the Commission approved, in first reading, two draft memoranda on, respectively, a sixth programme of research on industrial hygiene in mines[4] and a sixth programme of ergonomic research for ECSC industries.[5] These two drafts were endorsed by the ECSC Consultative Committee in September[6] and by the Council in October.[7] Subject to available budgetary funds, the amounts allocated to these two programmes are, respectively, ECU 9 million for a period of four years as from 1990 and ECU 15 million for a period of five years as from the same date.

---

[1]   OJ C 252, 6.10.1990; Bull. EC 9-1990, point 1.2.78.
[2]   Point 215 of this Report.
[3]   OJ C 52, 1.3.1989; Twenty-third General Report, point 327.
[4]   Bull. EC 7/8-1990, point 1.3.126.
[5]   Bull. EC 7/8-1990, point 1.3.127.
[6]   Bull. EC 9-1990, points 1.2.80 and 1.2.81.
[7]   OJ C 269, 25.10.1990; OJ C 290, 20.11.1990; Bull. EC 10-1990, points 1.3.70 and 1.3.71.

Section 7

Telecommunications, information industries and innovation

Priority activities and objectives

307. The electronics, information technology (IT) and telecommunications industries have become strategic industries having a decisive influence on the competitiveness of the Community and world productive fabric. In 1990 world production in the sector was ECU 750 billion, or some 5% of world GDP. It will probably exceed 10% of GDP by the end of the decade, thus making information industries the world's top industrial sector.

An examination of the evolution of world production since 1980 reveals a fairly stable, though relatively low, level of production of European industry which accounted for 25% of the total in 1990 as against 26% in 1980. Comparing the evolution of trade balances, however, shows a continuing worsening of the trade balance in Europe which amounted to USD 34.2 billion in 1989, the recent but rapidly growing deficit of the United States, amounting to USD 7.7 billion, and a Japanese trade surplus exceeding USD 60 billion.

A quick analysis by product shows that European industry is under-represented in certain key areas such as consumer electronics; it has a precarious position in IT but is strong in software and IT services, telecommunications and advanced manufacturing equipment. The European information industry basically has great potential, and has made significant progress in certain areas over the past five years. The Community is the largest market in the industrialized world and is developed to a level which ensures a high potential demand for information industries. The university and research fabric has a high and varied cultural and intellectual level. The main European companies employ over 800 000 highly skilled staff in the Community and some 1 100 000 throughout the world. There are also some 13 000 IT service and engineering companies in the Community. For the first time in 1989, three European groups were classed among the world top 10 IT groups.

In this context, studies and measures undertaken to consolidate the position of the Community have been organized around three principal axes. The programmes of pre-competitive R&TD, Esprit and RACE continued to mobilize human, financial and technological resources, thereby bolstering the technological foundations of businesses. Each of them produced significant results, the first in the marked increase in results leading directly to the marketing of specific products and services, and the second in the number of detailed contributions made to standardization bodies. The AIM and Delta programmes, which drew to completion this year, made for both new collaboration networks and a high-quality technological base for the application of generic technology to health and remote learning. Following adoption by the Council of the third Community research and technological development framework programme (1990-94), [1] *proposals for specific programmes on information technologies, communications and the development of 'telematic' systems of general interest were approved by the Commission. Within the framework of the Community telecommunications policy, the opening of sectoral markets to competition and harmonization projects moved at a tremendous pace, especially where the development of networks and services is concerned. The Council adopted the framework directive on the provision of an open telecommunications network as well as a recommendation for the introduction of a pan-European public radio paging system. For its part the Commission adopted the directive on competition in the market for telecommunications services.*

The dissemination and utilization of Community R&DT results plus the promotion of innovation and technology transfer made great strides thanks to the implementation of the Value and Esprit programmes. The initial period of the Impact programme (1989-90) laid the foundations for the future European market in information services.

Information technology — Esprit

308. Esprit again achieved significant results in 1990. [2] Cooperation within this programme helped to further cooperation between companies themselves and between companies and universities. The latter were thus able to work on subjects of vital importance to industry. Esprit's own structure evolved, with the participation of a growing number of SMEs in projects and greater user involvement. In all, some 6 000 engineers, scientists and research workers, belonging to more than 1 500 organizations, work full time on Esprit projects. Furthermore, the basic research projects, begun in 1989, have set up an impressive network of respected academics and scientists.

309. The seventh annual Esprit conference was held from 12 to 15 November in Brussels, [3] on the theme 'New prospects for information technology and its impact on society'. Over 3 000 participants were able to see demonstrations of some 100 projects. The opening of the conference to the public, a new feature this year, proved a success.

---

[1]   Point 247 of this Report.
[2]   OJ L 118, 6.5.1988; Twenty-second General Report, point 405.
[3]   Bull. EC 11-1990, point 1.3.78.

310. Following calls for proposals in May and September 1989,[1] the Commission selected[2] 130 new projects costing an estimated total of ECU 690 million, half of which will be funded by the Community. All the projects selected relate to computer-integrated manufacturing, office and business systems or microelectronics.

311. Under the new research and technological development framework programme,[3] on 30 May the Commission adopted a proposal for a decision adopting a specific programme in the field of information technology for 1990-94.[4] This programme will cover five areas: microelectronics, software data-processing systems, advanced office and home automation systems, computer-integrated manufacturing and engineering, and basic research. The planned total financial envelope is ECU 1 352 million. The Economic and Social Committee endorsed the proposal in November[5] and Parliament endorsed it (first reading) in December.[6]

Telecommunications

312. The opening-up of telecommunications markets to competition and harmonization work are still the main lines of the development of Community telecommunications policy. In particular, in November the Commission adopted[7] a Green Paper on satellite telecommunications, which applies to this area the guidelines of the 1987 Green Paper on the development of the common market for telecommunications services and equipment.[8] This communication was favourably received by the Council in December.[9] Looking outside the Community, in June the Commission adopted[10] a communication on the role of telecommunications in the development of relations with Central and Eastern European countries, the Council stating its position on this subject in December.[9] New initiatives were taken within the framework of the lines of action agreed in 1986:[11]

(i) Framing of a common strategy for the development of telecommunications networks and services: in June the Commission adopted a Directive on competition in the

---

[1]   OJ C 134, 31.5.1989; OJ C 240, 20.9.1989; Twenty-third General Report, point 357.
[2]   Bull. EC 1/2-1990, point 1.1.115; Bull. EC 5-1990, point 1.2.109.
[3]   Point 247 of this Report.
[4]   OJ C 174, 16.7.1990; Bull. EC 5-1990, point 1.2.93.
[5]   Bull. EC 11-1990, point 1.3.68.
[6]   OJ C 19, 28.1.1991; Bull. EC 12-1990.
[7]   Bull. EC 11-1990, point 1.3.64.
[8]   Twenty-first General Report, point 353.
[9]   Bull. EC 12-1990.
[10]   Bull. EC 6-1990, point 1.3.94.
[11]   Twentieth General Report, point 401.

telecommunications services market.[1] The framework Directive on ONP[2] for telecommunications was adopted[3] by the Council, also in June, while the preparation of directives applicable to various specific sectors continued. Furthermore, the Commission prepared a second progress report[4] on the introduction of the integrated services digital network in the European Community (ISDN). In the conclusions[5] adopted in June on the basis of that report, the Council welcomed the substantial progress made in 1989. The proposal for a decision on the introduction of a single telephone number[6] for emergency calls was amended[7] following Parliament's first opinion[8] and was approved in principle by the Council in December.[9] Moreover, in October the Council adopted[10] a recommendation on the coordinated introduction of a pan-European public land-based paging system in the Community (Ermes)[11] and a Directive on the frequency bands to be reserved for the coordinated introduction of such a system. In June a resolution was also adopted on the strengthening of European cooperation in radio frequencies,[12] notably for pan-European services. The Commission also sent[13] the Council proposals for a recommendation and a Directive on DECT.[14] The Economic and Social Committee delivered a favourable opinion on these proposals in September,[15] as did Parliament in December,[16] the Council likewise adopting its common position and approving the recommendation in December.[17]

Having received a communication from the Commission[18] taking stock of the application of the Directive and recommendation of 1987,[19] the Council adopted a resolution on 14 December on the final stage of implementation of the coordinated introduction of

---

[1]   Point 209 of this Report
[2]   Open network provision.
[3]   OJ L 192, 24.7.1990; Bull. EC 6-1990, point 1.3.94; Commission proposal: OJ C 39, 16.2.1989; Twenty-second General Report, point 403; OJ C 236, 14.9.1989; Twenty-third General Report, point 360; Bull. EC 6-1990, point 1.3.96.
[4]   Bull. EC 3-1990, point 1.1.75.
[5]   Bull. EC 6-1990, point 1.3.103.
[6]   OJ C 269, 21.10.1989; Twenty-second General Report, point 360.
[7]   OJ C 275, 1.11.1990; Bull. EC 10-1990, point 1.3.69.
[8]   OJ C 231, 17.9.1990; Bull. EC 7/8-1990, point 1.3.121.
[9]   Bull. EC 11-1990, point 1.3.76.
[10]   OJ L 310, 9.11.1990; Bull. EC 10-1990, point 1.3.67; Commission proposal: OJ C 193, 31.7.1989; Twenty-second General Report, point 360; OJ C 43, 23.2.1990; Bull. EC 1/2-1990, point 1.1.114; Bull. EC 7/8-1990, point 1.3.120.
[11]   European radio messaging system.
[12]   OJ C 166, 7.7.1990; Bull. EC 6-1990, point 1.3.105; Commission proposal: Bull. EC 5-1990, point 1.2.86.
[13]   OJ C 187, 27.7.1990; Bull. EC 5-1990, point 1.2.85.
[14]   Digital European cordless telecommunications.
[15]   Bull. EC 9-1990, point 1.2.76.
[16]   OJ C 19, 28.1.1991; Bull. EC 12-1990.
[17]   Bull. EC 12-1990.
[18]   Bull. EC 11-1990, point 1.3.77.
[19]   OJ L 196, 25.6.1987; Twenty-first General Report, point 353.

public pan-European cellular digital land-based mobile communications in the Community.[1]

(ii) Creation of a Community-wide market for telecommunications equipment: in July the Council adopted[2] a common position on the Directive on the approximation of the laws of the Member States concerning telecommunications terminal equipment, including the mutual recognition of their conformity.[3] This proposal was amended[4] in June following an opinion delivered on first reading by Parliament,[5] the second reading being in December.[6] With a view to extending the single market to procurement for all public authorities, in September the Council adopted a Directive on public procurement procedures in the water, energy, transport and telecommunications sections.[7]

In the field of high-definition television (HDTV), in application of the Council decision establishing a strategic framework for the rapid introduction of HDTV services on a European scale,[8] a European economic interest grouping, Vision 1250, was set up in March.[9] In May the Commission adopted, for transmission to the Council, a report on the latest developments in the field.[10] At its plenary session in Düsseldorf from 21 May to 1 June, the International Radio Consultative Committee (IRCC) adopted[11] various recommendations which leave open the possibility of the later adoption of a single standard conforming to European proposals:[12]

(iii) Implementation of a Community programme to promote the development of certain less-favoured areas in the Community (STAR):[13] the current phase of the STAR programme comes to an end in 1991 and a second phase could not be launched until 1993, so the Commission decided to implement the Telematics programme, lasting two years, in order to ensure continuity between the two phases and to allow current work to continue. Two other Community initiatives, Prisma[14] and Leader,[15] should help to strengthen interconnections between regional centres and improve access to new telecommunications services in rural areas.

---

[1]   Bull. EC 12-1990.
[2]   Bull. EC 7/8-1990, point 1.3.122.
[3]   OJ C 211, 17.8.1989; Twenty-third General Report, point 360.
[4]   OJ C 187, 27.7.1990; Bull. EC 6-1990, point 1.3.102.
[5]   OJ C 113, 7.5.1990; Bull. EC 4-1990, point 1.1.70.
[6]   OJ C 19, 28.1.1991; Bull. EC 12-1990.
[7]   Point 121 of this Report.
[8]   OJ L 142, 25.5.1989; Twenty-third General Report, point 360.
[9]   Bull. EC 3-1990, point 1.1.74.
[10]   Bull. EC 5-1990, point 1.2.108.
[11]   Bull. EC 6-1990, point 1.3.109.
[12]   OJ L 363, 13.12.1989; Twenty-third General Report, point 360.
[13]   OJ L 305, 30.10.1986; Twentieth General Report, point 519.
[14]   Point 407 of this Report.
[15]   Point 434 of this Report.

(iv) Achievement of a social consensus on the measures taken to establish a 'European telecommunications area'; consultations about the changes taking place in and introduced by the new telecommunications technology have continued and the first meeting of the joint committee on telecommunications set up in 1989[1] took place in October.

(v) Setting-up of Community-level coordination in the postal sector; in June the Council adopted conclusions on cooperation on postal matters.[2] With the assistance of the senior officials group set up in 1989,[1] the Commission continued to study the situation of the sector and to prepare a Green Paper.

RACE

313. The research programme on advanced telecommunications technologies (RACE)[3] provides a unique environment in which telecommunications network operators and computerized telecommunications manufacturers can work together with leading-edge users of communication systems and services. The work will allow a new generation of technologies to be introduced and the quality and cost-effectiveness of traditional telecommunications services to be improved. It will also help to bring new types of services onto the market by 1995. All the current projects were subjected to a third technical audit which, as previously, stressed their high quality and showed technological developments to be on schedule for the introduction of an initial range of integrated broadband services in 1995. Over 200 detailed contributions were sent to the standards institutions concerning multimedia services, quality of services, user requirements, network architectures and network management. Four new patents on communications were registered, and over 400 scientific papers were published.

On 30 May the Commission adopted a proposal for a decision adopting a specific programme in the field of communications technologies (1990-94).[4] This programme is part of the new R&TD framework programme[5] and mainly covers intelligence in broadband networks, flexible communications management, mobile and personal communications, image and data communications, integrated services technologies, data security technologies, experiments in advanced communications, and testing installations. The planned Community contribution is ECU 489 million. The Economic and Social Committee delivered an opinion on this proposal in November[6] and Parliament (first reading) in December.[7]

---

[1]   Twenty-third General Report, point 360.
[2]   Bull. EC 6-1990; point 1.3.104.
[3]   OJ L 16, 21.1.1988; Twenty-first General Report, point 354.
[4]   OJ C 174, 16.7.1990; Bull. EC 5-1990, point 1.2.94.
[5]   Point 247 of this Report.
[6]   Bull. EC 11-1990, point 1.3.69.
[7]   OJ C 19, 28.1.1991; Bull. EC 12-1990.

Telematic services of general interest

Tedis

314. An activity report on the first phase of the Tedis programme (1988-89)[1] was adopted by the Commission in July.[2] Work in progress in 1988-89 was continued in 1990. It related essentially to the coordination of projects launched at the initiative of the various European industrial sectors, with the aim of implementing electronic data interchange (EDI), standardization of EDI messages, and activities relating to message security and the legal aspects of EDI. The 12 pilot projects involving small businesses, selected as a result of an invitation to tender[3] published in 1988, are now complete and their results due to be published; the same applies to the case studies which were carried out as a result of the invitation to tender published in September 1989.[4]

In November the Commission adopted[5] a communication on electronic data interchange using computer service networks and a proposal for a decision on a second phase of the Tedis programme.

Insis

315. The strategic study on the revision of the Insis programme[6] began this year. The essential aims of the study are to analyse the results and assess the benefits of the activities of the Insis programme and its standardization policy, and to make suggestions with a view to setting and adapting the objectives and activities of the programme on the basis of the consequences for the European institutions and national public administrations of the creation of a European economic and social area by 1993. Moreover, the activities of the programme concerning electronic communication with the Member States have grown considerably, preliminary projects or studies or operational implementations now being in progress with most of them.

---

1 OJ L 285, 8.10.1987; Twenty-first General Report, point 358.
2 Bull. EC 7/8-1990, point 1.3.123.
3 Twenty-second General Report, point 409.
4 Twenty-third General Report, point 362.
5 OJ C 311, 12.12.1990; Bull. EC 11-1990, point 1.3.79.
6 OJ L 368, 28.12.1982; Twentieth General Report, point 406.

Caddia

316. The Caddia programme[1] continued to work towards its objectives. In addition to the continuing study of the strategic aspects of the programme which began in 1989,[2] the year was marked by the launch of studies in several Member States aimed at defining and implementing, at national level, computer systems for data interchange between the Commission and the Member States, and by the active participation of several Member States in the project to introduce these national gateways.

Drive, AIM, Delta

317. In order to build on the experience gained under the three programmes on learning (Delta),[3] road transport (Drive)[3] and health (AIM),[4] to ensure continuity in research and to benefit from the communities of interest created, the Commission proposed[5] that these three areas of work should be included in a new specific programme on telematic systems of general interest under the new framework programme for 1990-94.[6] This programme should also cover three other areas: administrations most concerned by the implementation of the internal market, libraries, and linguistic research and engineering. After Parliament (first reading)[7] and the Economic and Social Committee[8] had delivered their opinions in November the Council adopted a common position on this proposal in December.[9]

318. Work continued on the 71 projects adopted under the Drive programme, three of them drawing to completion. All underwent an independent technical audit. A close working relationship has developed with similar projects in the Eureka framework, allowing a valuable synergy to be established between initiatives of public traffic control organizations and those of motor vehicle manufacturers. In addition, standardization initiatives for the identification of goods vehicles were taken with the European Committee for Standardization (CEN), and support was given to the European Conference of Postal and Telecommunications Administrations (CEPT) on the allocation of radio frequencies for road transport IT. A strategic consultative committee was set up to ensure cooperation between the motor industry and traffic management administrations.

---

1   OJ L 145, 5.6.1987; Twenty-first General Report, point 357.
2   Twenty-third General Report, point 363.
3   OJ L 206, 30.7.1988; Twenty-second General Report, point 406.
4   OJ L 314, 22.11.1988; Twenty-second General Report, point 406.
5   OJ C 174, 16.7.1990; Bull. EC 5-1990, point 1.2.95.
6   Point 247 of this Report.
7   OJ C 324, 24.12.1990; Bull. EC 11-1990, point 1.3.70.
8   Bull. EC 11-1990, point 1.3.70.
9   Bull. EC 12-1990.

319. The 42 projects adopted under the AIM programme, which brought together more than 250 organizations, underwent a final technical audit. This programme has stimulated a better mutual awareness of needs and technical capabilities between industry, including SMEs, research workers and users, especially regarding data protection and confidentiality in medical computing, the theme of a conference held in Brussels in March.[1] AIM was also instrumental in the creation within CEN of a technical committee on medical computing.

320. The 30 projects accepted under the Delta programme, which brought together more than 190 organizations, were completed in 1990, each one undergoing a technical audit. In addition to developing exchanges of information and experience, the programme focused on new forms of cooperation for the production of training materials, the development of common approaches and protocols for distance learning, and the search for new uses of satellite systems.

Libraries

321. As part of its proposal for a specific programme in the field of telematic systems of general interest,[2] the Commission intends to set up a programme to facilitate access to the wealth of knowledge contained in libraries in the European Community. The main objective will be to carry out pre-standardization and development work with a view to promoting the penetration of new technologies in this area. The work will concentrate on developing computerized catalogues, interconnecting library systems, stimulating new electronic services in libraries, and developing new types of computerized telecommunications products or services relevant to libraries. Exploratory studies and preliminary projects were launched in 1990 to prepare the ground.

Eurotra, linguistic research and engineering

322. The Eurotra research programme[3] was evaluated in its final phase by a panel of independent experts.[4] The report was adopted by the Commission on 31 July for transmission to the Council and Parliament.[5] In November the Council adopted a decision on a specific programme concerning the preparation of the development of an

---

[1] Bull. EC 3-1990, point 1.1.68.
[2] Point 317 of this Report.
[3] OJ L 317, 31.12.1982; Sixteenth General Report, point 598.
[4] OJ L 222, 12.8.1988; Twenty-second General Report, point 417.
[5] Bull. EC 7/8-1990, point 1.3.117.

operational Eurotra system.[1] The specific programme in the field of telematic systems of general interest, proposed by the Commission in May, includes linguistic research and engineering with the aim of developing a basic linguistic technology which could be built into a large number of computer applications where natural language is an essential element.

323.   As part of its fourth action plan for the improvement of information transfer between languages (1986-90),[2] the Commission continued to develop and implement the Systran machine translation system. Nine of the 16 language pairs under development are now accessible to all departments from Brussels and Luxembourg, with a resulting throughput of 25 000 pages over the year.

Standardization in IT and telecommunications

324.   The rapid evolution of information technology and telecommunications and the technical prerequisites to achieve the objectives linked to the completion of the internal market in these fields have led to a considerable increase in the standardization work given to the European standards institutions. A significant proportion of this work has related to the implementation of standards in specific areas such as the exchange of medical data, electronic identification in transport, exchange of messages between libraries, and identification and payment cards. In particular the European Telecommunications Standards Institute (ETSI) has made good progress on work in the telecommunications field. This covers the Integrated Services Digital Network, mobile communications, terminals, high-definition television and satellite communications. The growing role of standardization in the implementation of information systems has also led to the launching of projects for the practical implementation, in the public sector, of the Council Decision of December 1986 on standardization in the field of information technology and telecommunications.[3] Moreover, progress made in the fields of conformity testing and certification has paved the way in particular for the integration of the IT and telecommunications certification structure into the global approach to certification, for the launching of the first projects in the third phase of the verification of conformity programme and for a proposal to the Council for the setting-up, in the telecommunications sector, of a system of mutual recognition of approval certificates for telecommunications terminal equipment, and the appropriate measures for marketing them.[4] In addition, as in previous years, special attention was given to the problem

---

[1]   OJ L 358, 21.12.1990; Bull. EC 11-1990, point 1.3.66; Commission proposal: OJ C 7, 12.1.1990; Twenty-third General Report, point 374; OJ C 209, 22.8.1990; Bull. EC 7/8-1990, point 1.3.116.
[2]   Nineteenth General Report, point 701.
[3]   OJ L 36, 7.2.1987; Twentieth General Report, point 408.
[4]   Point 312 of this Report.

of the relations to be established between the various fields with a view to ensuring that the European standardization system remains consistent.

Dissemination and utilization of results of Community and national research and technological development programmes

325. Following the adoption of the specific programme Value in June 1989,[1] work on the dissemination and utilization of knowledge derived from the specific research and technological development programmes moved into gear in 1990. Traditional methods of disseminating results, in publications (some 600 a year) and conferences, have continued. At the same time, an electronic information service (Cordis)[2] has been developed and tested with the aim of making an experimental version available to the public by the end of the year. The initial phase of the service comprises three databases concerning, respectively, research and technological development programmes, research projects carried out under these programmes, and the results published in the form of books or reports. Management of the JRC patents portfolio and the associated exploitation activities have continued in order to facilitate industrial exploitation of the results. Exploitation activities, so far concentrated on a limited number of scientific and technical fields, are gradually spreading to all Community research activities, notably in biotechnology and information technology. Following the publication of the announcement of facilities for promoting Community research and technological development results,[3] 55 proposals were selected for analysis and evaluation. Initiatives are also in progress for developing joint activities or cooperation arrangements with related programmes or activities. The expansion of operational activities has also gone hand in hand with consideration of strategic aspects; and several studies were completed during 1990 aimed at better defining Member States' expectations concerning dissemination and exploitation, and at improving knowledge of exploitation methods and practices in the major industrialized countries.

326. The Commission adopted,[4] in December, a proposal for a decision on the dissemination and utilization of knowledge from specific Community research and technological development programmes, which, in application of the new framework programme for research,[5] is designed to define and implement centralized action and lay down general provisions regarding dissemination and utilization.

---

[1]   OJ L 200, 13.7.1989; Twenty-third General Report, point 369.
[2]   OJ C 202, 3.8.1988; Twenty-second General Report, point 412.
[3]   OJ C 134, 1.6.1990; Bull. EC 6-1990, point 1.3.101.
[4]   Bull. EC 12-1990.
[5]   Point 247 of this Report.

Promotion of innovation and technology transfer

327. The implementation of the main phase[1] of the strategic programme for innovation and technology transfer (Sprint)[2] has involved three categories of activities:

(i) the strengthening of the European infrastructure for innovation support services by the formation of networks of agents for technology transfer and innovation support, and by the launching of support measures to facilitate the formation of such networks and to improve their operational efficiency;

(ii) the launching of specific projects, concerned with transferring new technologies already applied in one sector or region to another sector or region in the Community where those technologies are not yet used; following the 1989 call for proposals,[3] a second one on the definition phase of such projects was published in July.[4] Some 30 projects were selected as a result of this call for proposals;

(iii) the launching, in July, of a first call for tenders[5] concerning work related to the development of a European innovation monitoring system.

In addition, a science park consultancy scheme was launched to improve the market-orientated definition, planning and chances of success of future science, research or technology park projects and business innovation centres.[5]

Development of an information services market

328. The Commission's work in the context of the plan of action for the establishment of an information services market (Impact)[6] has aimed to reduce legal and economic uncertainty in the market and to promote the use of electronic information services and to encourage European cooperation between market operators on pilot and demonstration projects. In the extension of the work undertaken on the legal problems of the information market,[7] a series of proposals relating to the protection of personal data and security of information systems were approved by the Commission in July.[8] The European information market observatory,[7] in cooperation with the Statistical Office, launched a series of activities aimed at gathering and improving the quality of economic

---

[1] OJ L 112, 25.4.1989; Twenty-third General Report, point 370.
[2] Strategic programme for innovation and technology transfer.
[3] Twenty-third General Report, point 370.
[4] OJ C 186, 27.7.1990; Bull. EC 7/8-1990, point 1.3.124.
[5] OJ C 186, 27.7.1990.
[6] OJ L 288, 21.10.1988; Twenty-second General Report, point 415.
[7] Twenty-third General Report, point 372.
[8] Point 186 of this Report.

data available on the information market. Its report on the most important events and developments in the information services market was approved by the Commission in September for communication to Parliament and the Council.[1] The Commission has also upgraded the help and guidance services offered by its ECHO[2] server so as to facilitate users' access to electronic information services.

Fourteen pilot and demonstration projects have been launched in the fields of intelligent interfaces, image banks, and information on patents, standards, road transport, tourism and libraries.

In accordance with the Council Decision of July 1988,[3] the Commission had an independent assessment carried out of the initial results of the Impact programme, the conclusions of which were communicated to Parliament and the Council.[4]

---

[1] Bull. EC 9-1990, point 1.2.77.
[2] European Commission host organization.
[3] OJ L 208, 21.10.1988; Twenty-second General Report, point 415.
[4] Bull. EC 9-1990, point 1.2.77.

Section 8

Coordination of structural policies

Priority activities and objectives

329.   Coordination of the structural policies, the objective and mainspring of the reform of the structural Funds,[1] continued under the impetus given by the Commission,[2] with the aim of increasing the effectiveness of assistance from the available instruments and achieving greater coherence between their activities and other Community policies.

The Commission, in partnership with the national and regional authorities, drew up the Community support frameworks (CSFs) for assistance under Objective 5(b) and launched 12 Community initiatives. It adopted implementing decisions, created the budgetary framework and took the necessary measures to improve and simplify management procedures. Coordinated initiatives were launched to realize technical assistance, and continued effort was put into information and training measures with a view to ensuring correct application of the reform.

The Commission adopted the first annual report on the implementation of the reform of the structural Funds on 24 October.[3]

The EIB, required to collaborate on the part-financing of the envisaged investments, cooperated in the implementation of the reform of the structural Funds by participating in the preparation and monitoring of the CSFs. In addition, it continued to provide assistance for projects not included in the CSFs by contributing to the development of the regions concerned.

Implementation of the reform of the structural Funds

330.   The Spanish CSFs for Objective 2 were adopted on 14 March[4] and those for Objectives 3 and 4 were adopted on 4 May.[5]

---

[1]   OJ L 185, 15.7.1988; OJ L 374, 31.12.1988; Twenty-second General Report, points 533 and 534.
[2]   Twenty-third General Report, points 481 to 486.
[3]   Bull. EC 10-1990, point 1.3.54.
[4]   Point 406 of this Report.
[5]   Point 341 of this Report.

As regards Objective 5(a), the Council extended the new rules governing the EAGGF Guidance Section under the reform[1] to include improvement of the conditions in which agricultural and forestry products are processed and marketed. At the same time, the Commission adopted rules on the part-financing rates, the eligibility criteria and the operational programmes for investments relating to such improvements.[2] As regards Objective 5(b), on 6 June[2] the Commission adopted 44 CSFs and allocated ECU 2 607 million among the rural areas of the Member States which are not eligible under Objective 1 (Belgium, Denmark, the Federal Republic of Germany, Spain, France, Italy, The Netherlands and the United Kingdom, not including Objective 1 regions).

331. The Commission adopted a number of operational programmes under the differents CSFs for Objectives 1,[3] 2,[3] 3 and 4.[4]

332. As a result of the Commission's agreement in principle of 2 May[5] regarding a second set of initiatives,[6] ECU 3 800 million were finally allocated to 12 Community initiatives, of which eight (Rechar, Envireg, Stride, Regis, Interreg, Regen, Prisma and Télématique) are regional in scope,[7] three (Euroform, NOW, Horizon) concern human resources[4] and one (Leader) concerns rural development.[2] Table 1 shows how this amount was allocated.

To this amount can be added ECU 1 700 million for Community programmes in hand (STAR,[8] Valoren,[8] Resider[9] and Renaval[10]), bringing the sum dedicated to Community initiatives for 1989-93 to ECU 5 500 million.

333. On 2 July, the Commission adopted the rules concerning interest in the event of late repayment of assistance from the structural Funds[11] and the use of the ecu for the budgetary management of the structural Funds.[11]

With a view to providing the Member States with coherent and coordinated information on the new opportunities offered by the reform of the structural Funds, a guide to technical assistance was drawn up. The guide deals with different aspects of technical assistance, which can be given within the framework of the partnership or on the Commission's initiative.

---

[1] OJ L 374, 31.12.1988; Twenty-second General Report, point 534.
[2] Point 432 of this Report.
[3] Point 408 of this Report.
[4] Point 341 of this Report.
[5] Bull. EC 5-1990, point 1.2.84.
[6] Twenty-third General Report, points 468 and 469.
[7] Points 407 and 419 of this Report.
[8] OJ L 305, 31.10.1986; Twentieth General Report, point 519.
[9] OJ L 33, 5.2.1988; Twenty-second General Report, point 519.
[10] OJ L 225, 15.8.1988; Twenty-second General Report, point 519.
[11] OJ L 170, 3.7.1990; Bull. EC 7/8-1990, point 1.3.40; Commission draft: Twenty-third General Report, point 485.

TABLE 1

Community initiatives — Indicative budgets

million ECU

Rechar	300
Envireg	500
Stride	400
Interreg	800
Regis	200
Regen	300
Télématique	200
Prisma	100
Euroform	300
NOW	120
Horizon	180
Leader	400
Total	3 800

Section 9

Employment and social policy

Priority activities and objectives

334.   Implementation of the Single Act[1] and the progress made on the programme set out in the White Paper on completing the internal market[2] have helped to create a context favourable to dynamic development which is expected to lead to more competitiveness, stable and managed growth and, in the final analysis, more scope for job creation. Adoption by 11 Member States of the Community Charter of Fundamental Social Rights of Workers at the European Council in Strasbourg and of the Commission's action programme on implementation of the Charter have given fresh impetus to this development.[3]

The programme was the subject of two European Parliament resolutions[4] and an own-initiative opinion from the Economic and Social Committee[5] and was largely put into effect in 1990. It was supported by the European Council, which expressed the wish at the Rome meeting in December that the programme would be actively implemented.[6]

The first proposals to be adopted concern what are regarded as the most urgent of the aspects covered by the Charter: organization of working time and non-standard forms of work; consultation, information and participation of workers; greater clarity in terms of the rights and duties of employers and employees within the context of enhanced worker mobility; continuation of the work initiated in 1988[7] under Article 118a of the Treaty in the field of health and safety at work; intensified effort to develop the social dialogue bringing together the two sides of industry on a permanent basis.

---

[1]   OJ L 169, 29.6.1987; Twenty-first General Report, point 1; Supplement 2/86 — Bull. EC.
[2]   Nineteenth General Report, points 162 to 166.
[3]   Twenty-third General Report, point 394.
[4]   OJ C 68, 19.3.1990; Bull. EC 1/2-1990, point 1.1.190; OJ C 260, 15.10.1990; Bull. EC 9-1990, point 1.2.54.
[5]   OJ C 225, 10.9.1990; Bull. EC 7/8-1990, point 1.3.81.
[6]   Bull. EC 12-1990.
[7]   Twenty-second General Report, point 499; Twenty-third General Report, point 427.

Employment

Dialogue with management and labour

335. The political-level steering group set up in 1989[1] under the social dialogue initiated on the basis of the conclusions reached at the Val Duchesse meeting on 12 November 1985[2] met on a number of occasions in 1990. In January it took note[3] of the adoption by the working party on training and education set up in March 1989[1] of a joint opinion in which the two sides of industry stressed the importance of a high level of initial occupational training accessible to all young persons, and with the emphasis on measures designed to facilitate the transition from school to work by way of apprenticeship and work experience/training schemes. The steering group and the Commission also agreed on a joint consultation procedure with the two sides of industry on the proposals designed to implement the Commission's action programme. In July the steering group formally adopted a joint opinion on creating a European occupational and geographical mobility area and improving the operation of the labour market in Europe, the main points of which concern the internal adaptability of firms by giving priority to continuing training, geographical mobility — including the various forms of transfrontier work — and the operation of the labour market.[4] In November it considered[5] the Commission's second annual report on employment in Europe.[6]

Employment and the labour market

336. On 4 July the Commission approved[7] its second annual report on employment in Europe (1990),[8] in which it analyses employment prospects, problems and policies. One of the main points is that the period 1985-88 was characterized by significant growth of the order of 4% and the creation of jobs essentially in the service sector, but with unemployment remaining a worrying factor, affecting some 12.5 million people, or 8.5% of the labour force.

337. With a view to ensuring a minimum of consistency between the highly varied forms of employment contract other than those of an open-ended type (in particular fixed-term contracts, part-time working, temporary work and seasonal work) which have developed

---

[1]   Twenty-third General Report, point 395.
[2]   Nineteenth General Report, point 74.
[3]   Bull. EC 1/2-1990, point 1.1.91.
[4]   Bull. EC 7/8-1990, point 1.3.85.
[5]   Bull. EC 11-1990, point 1.3.47.
[6]   Point 336 of this Report.
[7]   Bull. EC 7/8-1990, pointed 1.3.79.
[8]   First report: Twenty-third General Report, point 397.

in the Community over the years, the Commission adopted, on 13 June, a communication featuring three proposals for directives on atypical work, concerning, respectively, the approximation of the laws of the Member States relating to certain employment relationships with regard to working conditions (based on Article 100 of the Treaty), distortions of competition (based on Article 100a) and the introduction of measures to encourage improvements in the safety and health of temporary workers (based on Article 100a).[1] The Commission does not wish to question these specific forms of employment relationship, which are regarded as indispensable in terms of a coherent strategy for growth and employment, but wishes to combat abuses and prevent any spread in the increasing prevalence of insecurity and segmentation on the labour market. These proposals received favourable opinions from the Economic and Social Committee on 20 September.[2] On 24 October Parliament endorsed at first reading the two proposals concerning distortions of competition and improvements in the safety and health of temporary workers,[3] while rejecting, in November, the proposal concerning working conditions.[4] After the Commission had amended the first two proposals to take account of Parliament's views,[5] in December the Council agreed on a common position concerning the proposal to improve the safety and health of temporary workers.[6] On 10 July Parliament adopted a resolution on an initiative aimed at a proposal for a Directive on atypical employment contracts and terms of employment in which, for the first time, it calls on the Commission to adopt a proposal that Parliament had itself drafted.[7]

338.   The Standing Committee on Employment met on two occasions: in May it considered long-term unemployment and came out in favour of stepping up measures of identification and analysis, and the exchange of experiences;[8] in October it encouraged the Commission to explore ways of reducing the large pockets of unemployment persisting in disadvantaged urban and rural areas.[9]

Freedom of movement for workers and migration policy

339.   The Council and the Representatives of the Governments of the Member States adopted a resolution, on 29 May, on the fight against racism and xenophobia,[10] even

---

[1]   OJ C 224, 8.9.1990; Bull. EC 6-1990, points 1.3.70 to 1.3.73.
[2]   Bull. EC 9-1990, point 1.3.56.
[3]   OJ C 295, 26.11.1990; Bull. EC 10-1990, points 1.3.48 and 1.3.49.
[4]   OJ C 324, 24.12.1990; Bull. EC 11-1990, point 1.3.53.
[5]   OJ C 305, 5.12.1990; Bull. EC 10-1990, points 1.3.48 and 1.3.49.
[6]   Bull. EC 12-1990.
[7]   OJ C 231, 17.9.1990; Bull. EC 9-1990, point 1.3.87.
[8]   Bull. EC 5-1990, point 1.2.65.
[9]   Bull. EC 10-1990, point 1.3.50.
[10]   OJ C 157, 27.6.1990; Bull. EC 5-1990, point 1.2.247.

though the Commission had withdrawn its proposal of June 1988,[1] considering that the text had been stripped of some of its substance. Parliament stated its views on the resolution on 14 June[2] and addressed the subject again when it adopted a further resolution in October.[3]

The Commission decided, on 26 September, to send the Council an expert report on immigration policies and the social integration of immigrants.[4] This report, designed to supplement an examination of aspects relating to conditions of access to the Member States' territories, came in response to the request made by the Strasbourg European Council in December 1989 for an inventory of national positions on immigration. The situation of migrant workers from non-member countries was also the subject of a resolution adopted by Parliament on 14 June.[5]

European Social Fund and structural operations

Special measures for certain Member States

340. Under Regulation (EEC) No 815/84 on exceptional financial support in favour of Greece in the social field,[6] which was extended to 31 December 1991,[7] the Commission decided, on 26 January, to grant aid to the total sum of ECU 11 910 261 for 15 projects for 1989.[8]

European Social Fund

341. Further to the measures introduced in 1989,[9] the Commission approved, on 4 May, the Community support framework for assistance from the European Social Fund for Objectives 3 (long-term unemployment) and 4 (occupational integration of young people) in Spain[10] as defined under the reform of the structural Funds.[11]

---

[1]   OJ C 214, 16.8.1988; Twenty-second General Report, point 453.
[2]   OJ C 175, 16.7.1990; Bull. EC 6-1990, point 1.3.226.
[3]   Point 903 of this Report.
[4]   Bull. EC 9-1990, point 1.2.190.
[5]   OJ C 175, 16.7.1990; Bull. EC 6-1990, point 1.3.76.
[6]   OJ L 88, 31.3.1984; Eighteenth General Report, point 283.
[7]   OJ L 362, 30.12.1988; Twenty-second General Report, point 454.
[8]   OJ L 35, 7.2.1990; Bull. EC 1/2-1990, point 1.1.94.
[9]   OJ L 64, 13.3.1990; Twenty-third General Report, point 401.
[10] OJ L 146, 9.6.1990; Bull. EC 5-1990, point 1.2.63.
[11] OJ L 185, 15.7.1988; OJ L 374, 31.12.1988; Twenty-second General Report, points 533 and 534.

342. On 18 December the Commission adopted general guidelines on three Community initiatives for strengthening, at Community level, the bases for vocational training and improving employment prospects, with special reference to the most disadvantaged sections of the population.[1] With an overall budget of ECU 600 million and classed among the programmes eligible under the structural Funds, these initiatives are concerned with the development of new qualifications, new skills and new employment opportunities (Euroform), the promotion of equal opportunities for women in the field of employment and vocational training (NOW) and easier access to the employment market for handicapped persons and certain other disadvantaged groups (Horizon).

On 29 May the Council adopted a resolution on action to be undertaken under a Community initiative to assist the long-term unemployed.[2]

343. In 1990, available commitment appropriations totalled ECU 4 075 million.[3] These were committed gradually in line with the adoption of operational programmes and overall subsidies by the Commission. The amounts committed were distributed as set out in Table 2.

344. The sums granted to each Member State were approximately 20.5% to Spain, 16% to the United Kingdom, 14% to Italy, 11.4% to France, 10% Greece, 8.8% to Ireland, 7.9% to Portugal, 6.1% to the Federal Republic of Germany, 2.4% to The Netherlands, 1.8% to Belgium, 1% to Denmark, and 0.1% to Luxembourg.

TABLE 2

Appropriations committed

million ECU

Objective 1	
Regions whose development is lagging behind	1 787
Objective 2	
Regions affected by industrial decline	357
Objectives 3 and 4	
Long-term unemployment and occupational integration of young people	1 391
Objective 5(b)	
Development of rural areas	8
Transitional measures	—
Total	3 543

---

[1]   OJ C 327, 29.12.1990; Bull. EC 12-1990.
[2]   OJ C 157, 27.6.1990; Bull. EC 5-1990, point 1.2.64.
[3]   Full details on the Social Fund will be given in the 1990 annual report.

345.   Payment appropriations available for 1990 amounted to ECU 3 321.9 million, the amount entered in the budget the same year, since there were no appropriations remaining or transfers from 1989.

346.   In 1990 the Commission adopted many operational programmes associated with the implementation of the Community support frameworks.

The sums granted in respect of programmes under Objectives 3 and 4 are as follows: ECU 50.3 million for Belgium, ECU 35.8 million for Denmark, ECU 172.9 million for the Federal Republic of Germany, ECU 217.4 million for Spain, ECU 302.8 million for France, ECU 184.6 million for Italy, ECU 72.6 million for The Netherlands, and 356.9 million for the United Kingdom.

347.   On 12 July Parliament adopted a resolution on the European Social Fund and the utilization rate of commitment and payment appropriations at 15 June 1990, in which it called on the Commission to take measures to ensure speedier disbursement of appropriations granted for projects qualifying for assistance under the Fund and called on the Governments of the Member States to facilitate the utilization of the Fund by local authorities and voluntary organizations.[1]

Measures for ECSC workers

348.   In 1990, ECU 184 million was granted in respect of readaptation aid under Article 56(2)(b) and (1)(c) of the ECSC Treaty for workers, in the form of income support allowances in the event of unemployment or early retirement or to facilitate reintegration in new jobs. In 1990, the conventional aid programmes were supplemented by the grant of additional sums under the Community Rechar initiative (ECU 40 million) and under the accompanying social measures for steelworkers (ECU 50 million). The ECSC readaptation aid granted under the Rechar programme[2] was used to finance innovative measures which could not be supported previously, especially initial training for the less skilled categories of miners, and aid for transition to new jobs for persons engaged in a re-employment scheme.

Table 3 gives a breakdown by country and by industry of the total granted in the form of conventional aid and accompanying social measures.

349.   Under the 1990 instalment of aid granted under the 11th ECSC subsidized housing scheme, contracts were concluded with financial intermediaries in all the Member States

---

[1]   OJ C 231, 17.9.1990; Bull. EC 7/8-1990, point 1.3.83.
[2]   Point 407 of this Report.

TABLE 3

Readaptation aid — Appropriations committed in 1990

	Steel industry and iron ore mining				Coal industry			
	Conventional aid		Social measures		Conventional aid		Rechar	
	Workers	Amount (ECU)	Workers	Amount (ECU)	Workers	Amount (ECU)	Workers	Amount (ECU)
Belgium	297	795 366	279	44 445	3 125	9 242 322	3 392	10 348 429
Denmark								
Germany (FR)	5 411	14 583 524	7 357	18 200 000	4 856	13 031 357	4 667	15 344 874
Greece								
Spain	1 662	4 369 277	1 662	4 986 000	1 099	2 697 500	253	809 777
France	12 482	32 014 715	2 891	8 249 000	3 433	14 521 029	2 306	7 949 074
Ireland								
Italy	11 455	22 996 658	3 500	9 400 000				
Luxembourg	3 217	8 197 107	513	1 331 625				
Netherlands	1 338	3 045 788	252	756 000				
Portugal	4 477	7 125 819	200	600 000	135	234 769	15	29 800
United Kingdom	1 606	5 253 232	614	1 649 000	24 703	45 891 537	9 634	5 518 046
Total	41 945	98 381 486	17 268	45 216 070	37 351	85 618 514	20 267	40 000 000

totalling ECU 48 million.[1] On 4 October, in Longwy, France, the Commission celebrated the completion of 200 000 dwellings financed by ECSC loans since the foundation of the Community.

Aid for disaster victims

350.   In the course of the year the Commission granted emergency assistance in 19 cases totalling ECU 7.1 million to the families of disaster victims.[2] Parliament expressed its views in a number of resolutions, calling for action for people affected by a variety of natural disasters in the Community.[3]

---

[1]   Twenty-second General Report, point 490.
[2]   Bull. EC 1/2-1990, point 1.1.275.
[3]   OJ C 38, 19.2.1990; Bull. EC 1/2-1990, point 1.1.274; OJ C 96, 17.4.1990; Bull. EC 3-1990, point 1.1.196; OJ C 149, 18.6.1990; Bull. EC 4-1990, points 1.2.242 to 1.2.246; OJ C 260, 15.10.1990; Bull. EC 9-1990, points 1.2.191 to 1.2.196.

Social security and living and working conditions

Social security and other schemes

351.   On 26 November the Council adopted a decision on measures to help the elderly involving a series of initiatives to be carried out at Community level in the period 1 January 1991 to 31 December 1993 to meet the social and economic challenge of population ageing, to identify innovatory approaches to inter-generation solidarity and the integration of the elderly, and to develop and enhance the potential of the elderly in the Community.[1]

352.   The medium-term Community action programme concerning the economic and social integration of the less privileged groups in society[2] was launched on 29 and 30 March at a meeting held in Brussels attended by the persons responsible for the 39 selected projects, 27 of which were classed as 'model actions' and 12 as 'innovatory initiatives'.[3]

353.   During the 1989/90 academic year the Executive Committee of the Paul Finet Foundation examined 675 applications and awarded 596 scholarships representing a total amount of BFR 12 569 116.

Social security for migrant workers

354.   On 24 July the Commission adopted a new proposal[4] to amend Regulations (EEC) Nos 1408/71[5] and 574/72[6] on social security for migrant workers (employed and self-employed) and members of their families moving within the Community, to reflect changes made by the Member States in their national law and to effect certain changes of a technical nature. The Economic and Social Committee and Parliament delivered opinions on this proposal in November[7] and December,[8] respectively.

---

[1]   Bull. EC 11-1990, point 1.3.200. Commission proposal: OJ C 120, 16.5.1990; Bull. EC 3-1990, point 1.1.191.
[2]   OJ L 224, 2.8.1989; Twenty-third General Report, point 411; Supplement 4/89 — Bull. EC.
[3]   Bull. EC 3-1990, point 1.1.195.
[4]   OJ C 221, 5.9.1990; Bull. EC 7/8-1990, point 1.3.88.
[5]   OJ L 149, 5.7.1971.
[6]   OJ L 74, 27.3.1972.
[7]   Bull. EC 11-1990, point 1.3.51.
[8]   OJ C 19, 28.1.1991; Bull. EC 12-1990.

355.   The Court of Justice delivered 16 judgments on cases referred by national courts, [1] while 27 cases are still before the Court. [2]

Equal opportunities for men and women

356.   On 17 October the Commission adopted the third Community medium-term action programme on equal opportunities for men and women (1991-95). [3] Based on three priority lines of attack — application and development of the legal framework; promotion of occupational integration of women; improvement of women's status in society — the programme sets out to consolidate what has already been achieved and put to use the experience gained to date, to develop new initiatives in the fields of vocational training and employment, and to strengthen the partnership and complementarity elements of activities undertaken by the various groups and organizations.

357.   The proposal for a Directive adopted on 12 September seeks to protect the health and safety at work of pregnant women or women who have recently given birth, while maintaining the principle of equal opportunities. [4]

Bearing in mind the specific structural problems encountered by women on the labour market, the NOW initiative is intended to encourage the implementation of transnational activities on vocational training and the promotion of jobs for women. [5]

358.   On 29 May the Council adopted a resolution on the protection of the dignity of women and men at work. [6]

359.   In a resolution adopted on 15 May Parliament expressed its opinion on various aspects of the situation of women in the field of health care. [7]

---

[1]   Cases 168/88, 199/88, 228/88, 236/88, 293/88, 324/88, 342/88, 2/89, 12/89, 85/89, 99/89, 105/89, 108/89, 109/89, 117/89 and 163/89.
[2]   Cases 79/85, 197/85, 93/86, 159/87, 356/87, 369/87, 114/88, 140/88, 245/88, 178/89, 216/89, 227/89, 251/89, 317/89, 356/89, 10/90, 15/90, 18/90, 74/90, 93/90, 186/90, 188/90, 196/90, 198/90, 215/90, 297/90 and 302/90.
[3]   Bull. EC 10-1990, point 1.3.46. First programme: OJ C 22, 29.1.1982; Fifteenth General Report, point 295; Supplement 1/82 — Bull. EC. Second programme: OJ C 356, 31.12.1985; Nineteenth General Report, point 437; Supplement 3/86 — Bull. EC.
[4]   Point 371 of this Report.
[5]   Point 342 of this Report.
[6]   OJ C 157, 27.6.1990; Bull. EC 5-1990, point 1.2.67.
[7]   OJ C 149, 18.6.1990; Bull. EC 5-1990, point 1.2.237.

Social integration of the disabled

360. The Horizon initiative aims to facilitate the integration of handicapped persons and certain other disadvantaged groups by means of training adapted to market conditions and to develop conditions to facilitate the integration process.[5]

361. On 31 May the Council and the Ministers for Education meeting within the Council adopted a resolution on the integration of young handicapped persons in ordinary education.[1]

Labour law, industrial relations and living and working conditions

362. On 28 November the Commission adopted a proposal for a Directive on the establishment of a written statement concerning employment relationships.[2] Its main aims are to increase the transparency and comparability of employment situations while improving the means of inspection available to the labour inspectorate.

363. On 5 December the Commission adopted a proposal for a Directive on the establishment of a European works council for firms or groups of firms operating throughout the Community with a view to providing information for and consulting workers.[3]

364. On 27 November the Commission adopted a communication on the living and working conditions of Community citizens living in frontier areas, in particular frontier workers.[4] This communication supplements and updates the communication of 1985 on people working in frontier areas.[5]

European Foundation for the Improvement of Living and Working Conditions

365. The end of 1990 marked the mid-term of the Foundation's current four-year programme 1989-92.[6] The main topics covered in 1990 were: the development of the social dialogue, restructuring the work environment, promotion of health and safety, protection of the environment, the worker and the public, and raising living standards for all. The Foundation's findings have appeared in various publications.

---

[1]   Point 376 of this Report.
[2]   Bull. EC 11-1990, point 1.3.42.
[3]   Bull. EC 12-1990.
[4]   Bull. EC 11-1990, point 1.3.52.
[5]   Nineteenth General Report, point 289.
[6]   Twenty-second General Report, point 491.

Health and safety

Public health

366.   On 17 May the Council and the Ministers for Health meeting within the Council adopted conclusions on the medical and psychosocial care of AIDS patients.[1] In conclusions adopted on 3 December, they broached the subject of the role played by service and reception centres for drug addicts, and requested the Commission to develop exchanges of information, experiences and experts.[2] Parliament gave its opinion, in a resolution adopted on 18 January,[3] on the Sixth International Conference on AIDS held in San Francisco in June.

367.   At the meetings in May and December the Council and the Ministers for Health meeting within the Council also adopted conclusions on health and young people in Europe in the 1990s,[4] a resolution on Community action in the field of nutrition and health,[2] conclusions on the wholesomeness of food, beverages and water for human consumption,[2] conclusions on cardiovascular disease in the Community,[2] a resolution on Community action against drug abuse and the misuse of medication in sports,[2] and a resolution on better prevention and treatment of acute poisoning in man.[2] With respect to the campaign against drug abuse which they had previously considered in May,[5] they adopted conclusions[2] on 6 December on reduction of the demand for narcotics and psychotropic drugs, in which they identified the most pressing of the social and health measures listed by the European Committee to Combat Drugs (ECCD).[6] The Commission, responding to a request by the Dublin European Council,[7] had sent them a report in November on national programmes to reduce demand for drugs in the Community.[8]

368.   Two important steps were taken in the fight against cancer with the adoption of the new 1990-94 action programme and the adoption of the Directive on the maximum tar content of cigarettes.[9]

---

[1]   Bull. EC 5-1990, point 1.2.252.
[2]   OJ C 329, 31.12.1990; Bull. EC 12-1990.
[3]   OJ C 38, 19.2.1990; Bull. EC 1/2-1990, point 1.1.276.
[4]   Bull. EC 5-1990, point 1.2.253.
[5]   Bull. EC 5-1990, point 1.2.249.
[6]   Point 165 of this Report.
[7]   Bull. EC 6-1990, point I.16.
[8]   Bull. EC 11-1990, point 1.3.206.
[9]   Point 174 of this Report.

Health and safety at work

369.   On 22 May the Council adopted the Directives on the minimum health and safety requirements for the manual handling of loads where there is a risk particularly of back injury to workers,[1] and on the minimum safety and health requirements for work with display screen equipment,[2] i.e. the fourth and fifth individual Directives within the meaning of the framework Directive on the introduction of measures to encourage improvements in the health and safety of workers at work.[3] The sixth and seventh individual Directives — on the protection of workers from the risks related to exposure at work to carcinogens and to biological agents, respectively — were adopted on 28 June[4] and 26 November.[5]

370.   On 30 May the Commission adopted a proposal[6] for a Directive to amend Council Directive 83/477/EEC on the protection of workers from the risks related to exposure to asbestos at work.[7] As amended by the Commission[8] in line with the opinions of the Economic and Social Committee[9] and Parliament (first reading),[10] the proposal was the subject of a common position of the Council in December.[11]

371.   The Commission adopted a number of proposals for Directives on the minimum health and safety requirements for improved medical treatment on board vessels,[12] at temporary and mobile work sites,[13] on certain aspects of the organization of working time, particularly the protection of workers' health and safety in the event of changes in working patterns,[14] and protection at work of pregnant women or women who have

---

[1]   OJ L 156, 21.6.1990; Bull. EC 5-1990, point 1.2.69. Commission proposal: OJ C 117, 4.5.1988; Twenty-second General Report, point 499. OJ C 129, 25.5.1989; Twenty-third General Report, point 427; OJ C 118, 12.5.1990; Bull. EC 4-1990, point 1.1.46.
[2]   OJ L 156, 21.6.1990; Bull. EC 5-1990, point 1.2.70. Commission proposal: OJ C 113, 29.4.1988; Twenty-second General Report, point 499. OJ C 130, 26.5.1989; Twenty-third General Report, point 427; Bull. EC 5-1990, point 1.2.70.
[3]   OJ L 183, 29.6.1989; Twenty-third General Report, point 427.
[4]   OJ L 196, 26.7.1990; Bull. EC 6-1990, point 1.3.77. Commission proposal: OJ C 34, 8.2.1988; Twenty-second General Report, point 445; OJ C 229, 6.9.1989. Bull. EC 5-1990, point 1.2.68.
[5]   OJ L 374, 31.12.1990; Bull. EC 11-1990, point 1.3.50. Commission proposal: OJ C 150, 8.6.1988; Twenty-second General Report, point 502. OJ C 210, 24.8.1989.
[6]   OJ C 161, 30.6.1990; Bull. EC 5-1990, point 1.2.72.
[7]   OJ L 263, 24.9.1983; Seventeenth General Report, point 340.
[8]   OJ C 300, 29.11.1990; Bull. EC 11-1990, point 1.3.49.
[9]   Bull. EC 9-1990, point 1.2.58.
[10]   OJ C 284, 12.11.1990; Bull. EC 10-1990, point 1.3.51.
[11]   Bull. EC 12-1990.
[12]   OJ C 183, 29.7.1990; Bull. EC 6-1990, point 1.3.74.
[13]   OJ C 213, 28.8.1990; Bull. EC 7/8-1990, point 1.3.80.
[14]   OJ C 254, 9.10.1990; Bull. EC 7/8-1990, point 1.3.74.

recently given birth.[1] Some of these proposals have been examined by Parliament[2] and the Economic and Social Committee.[3]

372.   The Commission proposal on an action programme for the European Year of Safety, Hygiene and Health Protection at Work (1992)[4] was welcomed by the Council, which was in general agreement regarding the organization of such a year.

373.   On 22 May the Commission adopted a recommendation to the Member States concerning the adoption of a European schedule of occupational diseases,[5] designed to update the 1962[6] and 1966[7] recommendations.

Health and safety (ECSC)

374.   The Mines Safety and Health Commission held two plenary meetings at which it examined a draft proposal for a Directive on the minimum provisions ensuring the health and safety of workers in mines, and a report on the procedures and conditions for testing low-combustion liquids used in mines for hydrostatic and hydrokinetic mechanical transmission systems.

---

[1]   OJ C 281, 9.11.1990; Bull. EC 9-1990, point 1.2.57.
[2]   OJ C 19, 28.1.1991; Bull. EC 12-1990.
[3]   Bull. EC 9-1990, point 1.2.57; Bull. EC 11-1990, point 1.3.54; Bull. EC 12-1990.
[4]   OJ C 293, 23.11.1990; Bull. EC 11-1990, point 1.3.48.
[5]   OJ L 160, 26.6.1990; Bull. EC 5-1990, point 1.2.61.
[6]   OJ L 80, 31.8.1962.
[7]   OJ L 147, 9.8.1966.

Section 10

Human resources, education, training and youth

Priority activities and objectives

375.   The year 1990 was marked by the development of Community action in the fields of initial and continuing vocational training and by the provision of assistance to the countries of Central and Eastern Europe.

The importance accorded to vocational training was reinforced by the work of the two sides of industry in the social dialogue. Their joint opinion,[1] like the Council conclusions of 14 December 1989[2] and Parliament's resolution of 16 February,[3] highlighted the need for a comprehensive strategy based on existing actions and programmes. At the same time, the Commission laid down the guidelines for better coordination and rationalization of the programmes in this field.

Moreover, under Operation Phare[4] the adoption of the trans-European mobility scheme for university studies (Tempus) and the establishment of the European Training Foundation gave the Commission two important instruments of cooperation with the countries of Central and Eastern Europe.

Cooperation in education

*376.   On 31 May the Council and Ministers for Education meeting within the Council adopted conclusions on meetings of senior officials in the education sector,[5] reaffirming the usefulness of such meetings for improving mutual understanding of the various educational systems, comparing education policies and discussing problems of common concern. On the same date the Council and the Ministers also adopted a resolution on the integration of young people with disabilities into ordinary systems of education[6] and

---

[1]   Point 335 of this Report.
[2]   OJ C 27, 6.2.1990; Twenty-third General Report, point 435.
[3]   OJ C 68, 19.3.1990; Bull. EC 1/2-1990, point 1.1.273.
[4]   Point 669 of this Report.
[5]   OJ C 162, 3.7.1990; Bull. EC 5-1990, point 1.2.239.
[6]   OJ C 162, 3.7.1990; Bull. EC 5-1990, point 1.2.240.

conclusions on the equality of educational opportunity in the training of teachers.[1] And in a resolution adopted on 6 December they declared themselves in favour of strengthening the Eurydice education information network in the Community.[2]

Vocational training

377. On 21 August the Commission adopted a memorandum on the rationalization and coordination of Community vocational training programmes.[3] The aim of the memorandum is to establish an overall frame of reference to be used in locating and managing all Community initiatives and actions in the context of the development of a common vocational training policy based on Article 128 of the EEC Treaty. The rationalization measures proposed classify training activities in three principal sectors (initial vocational training and training of young people, higher education and advanced training, continuing education and training) and two horizontal actions (teaching of foreign languages and provision of assistance to the countries of Central and Eastern Europe).

378. On 1 June the Commission adopted an interim report[4] on the implementation of Council Decision 85/368/EEC on the comparability of vocational training qualifications between the Member States.[5] The report reviews the work accomplished and lists the measures adopted for completing it before the end of 1992. In a resolution adopted on 18 December the Council, taking note of this report, mentioned the possibility of extending the work to other occupations at all levels of training, in particular to qualifications connected with technological innovation.[6] The Council also underlined the need to ensure more effective implementation of Decision 85/368/EEC and invited the Member States and the Commission to draft proposals to this end.

In accordance with Decision 85/368/EEC the Commission published, on 2 April, a communication on the comparability of vocational training qualifications in the agricultural sector.[7] And on 24 October, acting under Directive 86/457/EEC on specific training in general medical practice,[8] it published the designations adopted by each Member State for the diplomas, certificates and other evidence of formal qualifications that they are required to recognize on a mutual basis.[9]

---

[1]   OJ C 162, 3.7.1990; Bull. EC 5-1990, point 1.2.241.
[2]   OJ C 329, 31.12.1990; Bull. EC 12-1990.
[3]   Bull. EC 7/8-1990, point 1.3.91.
[4]   Bull. EC 6-1990, point 1.3.78.
[5]   OJ L 199, 31.7.1985; Nineteenth General Report, point 427.
[6]   OJ C 19, 18.1.1991; Bull. EC 12-1990.
[7]   OJ C 83, 2.4.1990; Bull. EC 4-1990, point 1.1.44.
[8]   OJ L 267, 19.9.1986: Twentieth General Report, point 295.
[9]   OJ C 268, 24.10.1990.

Initial training

379. On 29 May the Council amended[1] Decision 84/636/EEC establishing a third joint programme to encourage the exchange of young workers,[2] extending its validity to 31 December 1991. The implementation of this programme in 1988 and 1989 was the subject of a report adopted by the Commission on 1 August.[3]

380. The Council having decided to extend the third programme pending the submission of a comprehensive proposal in the fields of technical and vocational education and initial training, the Commission adopted, on 10 October, a proposal for a decision[4] to amend Decision 87/569/EEC,[5] setting out an action programme for the vocational training of young people and their preparation for adult and working life. This proposal is designed to consolidate and extend the Petra programme, the progress of which over the period 1987-89 is reviewed in an interim report adopted by the Commission in March,[6] and to integrate into it the exchange programme for young workers.

Training for technological change

381. The Eurotecnet II programme[7] having become operational on 1 January, the Commission published, on 14 February, a notice of invitation to tender concerning the technical assistance to be provided for its implementation.[8]

Higher education

382. On 29 March and 27 July, respectively, the Council adopted decisions concerning the conclusion of agreements between the European Economic Community and the EFTA countries (Austria, Finland, Iceland, Norway, Sweden and Switzerland)[9] and Liechtenstein,[10] establishing cooperation in the field of training in the context of the

---

[1] OJ L 156, 21.6.1990; Bull. EC 5-1990, point 1.2.73. Commission proposal: OJ C 89, 7.4.1990; Bull. EC 3-1990, point 1.1.55.
[2] OJ L 331, 19.12.1984; Eighteenth General Report, point 297.
[3] Bull. EC 7/8-1990, point 1.3.92.
[4] OJ C 322, 21.12.1990: Bull. EC 10-1990, point 1.3.52.
[5] OJ L 346, 10.12.1987; Twenty-first General Report, point 395.
[6] Bull. EC 3-1990, point 1.1.57.
[7] OJ L 393, 30.12.1989; Twenty-third General Report, point 440.
[8] OJ C 34, 14.2.1990; Bull. EC 1/2-1990, point 1.1.99.
[9] OJ L 156, 21.6.1990; Bull. EC 3-1990, point 1.1.53. Commission proposals: OJ C 53, 5.3.1990.
[10] Bull. EC 7/8-1990, point 1.3.93. Commission proposal: OJ C 109, 3.5.1990; Bull. EC 3-1990, point 1.1.54.

implementation of Comett II (1990-94).[1] These agreements were concluded pursuant to the Council Decision of 29 May 1985.[2]

The 1989 activity report on the first phase[3] and second phase[1] of Comett was adopted by the Commission in April.[4] In July the Commission published a notice of invitation to tender concerning the evaluation of the Comett programme.[5]

383. On 22 May the Commission adopted a report[6] on the implementation of the Erasmus programme[7] and the Lingua programme (Action II: measures to promote the learning of foreign languages in universities and in particular to develop the initial training of foreign language teachers)[8] for the academic year 1990/91. From a total of 2 754 projects submitted (24% more than the previous year), the Commission accepted 1 748 proposed inter-university cooperation programmes (ICPs), of which 1 592 concerned student mobility, 277 teaching-staff mobility, 99 joint curriculum development and 114 intensive programmes. The total budget for the academic year was ECU 58.8 million.

384. The Commission also adopted, on 11 June, a communication to the Council[9] concerning negotiating directives for the extension of the Erasmus programme[7] to the EFTA countries.

385. There were also specific initiatives concerning vocational training in the audiovisual sector[10] and the cultural field.[11]

Continuing training

386. On 29 May the Council adopted Decision 90/267/EEC establishing an action programme for the development of continuing vocational training in the European Community (the Force programme).[12] The aim of this four-year programme (1 January 1991 to 31 December 1994) is to support and complement the policies and activities

---

[1]   OJ L 13, 17.1.1989; Twenty-second General Report, point 464.
[2]   Twenty-third General Report, point 442.
[3]   OJ L 222, 8.8.1986; Twentieth General Report, point 473.
[4]   Bull. EC 4-1990, point 1.1.51.
[5]   OJ C 191, 31.7.1990; Bull. EC 7/8-1990, point 1.3.94.
[6]   Bull. EC 5-1990, point 1.1.238.
[7]   OJ L 395, 30.12.1989; Twenty-third General Report, point 437.
[8]   OJ L 239, 16.8.1989; Twenty-third General Report, point 434.
[9]   Bull. EC 6-1990, point 1.3.265.
[10] Point 179 of this Report.
[11] Point 181 of this Report.
[12] OJ L 156, 21.6.1990; Bull. EC 5-1990, point 1.2.62. Commission proposal: OJ C 12, 18.1.1990; Twenty-third General Report, point 441. OJ C 130, 29.5.1990; Bull. EC 4-1990, point 1.1.49.

developed by and in the Member States in the area of continuing vocational training. The estimated amount needed to finance the programme during the first two years was ECU 24 million. A notice of invitation to tender concerning the implementation of the programme was published on 14 July.[1] On 17 December the Commission proposed amendments[2] to this Decision and to Decision 89/657/EEC establishing the Eurotecnet II programme,[3] with a view to setting up a joint advisory committee for education and continuing training.

European Centre for the Development of Vocational Training

387.   In 1990 the European Centre for the Development of Vocational Training continued the task of rationalizing activities in the fields of research, documentation and implementation of Community decisions. Considerable resources were devoted to furthering the comparability of qualifications and defining occupational profiles. The Centre also conducted surveys on imbalances between Community regions in relation to certain declining industries and disadvantaged groups. Special attention was also given to the training of trainers and to developing the training of managers of small and medium-sized businesses. Work on exchanges of experience and of experts at Community level was carried out in close cooperation with the Commission. The dialogue on the priorities with regard to vocational training was continued at the forum of research directors, which was also attended by representatives of the countries of Central Europe. The Centre also contributed to the development of cooperation between the two sides of industry from the point of view of the creation of a European area of social dialogue.

Youth

Community initiatives to assist young people

388.   On 10 October the Commission adopted a memorandum on young people in the European Community, which provides a basis for discussion concerning future Community activities in relation to young people in the following areas: creativity and initiative, exchanges and mobility, training of youth workers, young persons' associations and information.[4] On the same date the Commission also adopted a proposal for a decision establishing the second phase of the 'Youth for Europe' programme, in which the

---

[1]   OJ C 173, 14.7.1990; Bull. EC 7/8-1990, point 1.3.95.
[2]   Bull. EC 12-1990.
[3]   Point 381 of this Report.
[4]   Bull. EC 10-1990, point 1.3.220.

Commission proposes support for youth exchange and mobility projects, particularly those involving disadvantaged young persons, and for an experimental action to promote the performance of voluntary service in the cultural, social and educational fields in another Member State.[1] This proposal, with a scheduled budget of ECU 10 million for 1992, is based on the experience gained during the first phase of the programme,[2] the 1988/89 annual report of which was adopted on 1 August.[3]

Youth Forum of the European Communities

389.   The Commission continued to support the activities of the Youth Forum, which focused in particular on youth policy and the social dimension of the internal market.

Training assistance for the countries of Central and Eastern Europe

Higher education

390.   On 7 May the Council adopted Decision 90/233/EEC establishing a trans-European mobility scheme for university studies (Tempus), the aim of which is to contribute towards providing training assistance for the eligible countries of Central and Eastern Europe.[4]

European Training Foundation

391.   Regulation (EEC) No 1360/90, adopted by the Council on 7 May, established a European Training Foundation, the main purpose of which is to contribute towards adapting training systems to the new market conditions.[5] The Regulation will enter into force once the Council has decided where the Foundation is to be located.

---

[1]   OJ C 308, 8.12.1990; Bull. EC 10-1990, point 1.3.220.
[2]   OJ L 158, 25.6.1988; Twenty-second General Report, point 468.
[3]   Bull. EC 7/8-1990, point 1.3.316.
[4]   OJ L 131, 23.5.1990; Bull. EC 5-1990, point 1.3.2. Commission proposal: OJ C 85, 3.4.1990; Bull. EC 1/2-1990, point 1.2.6. OJ C 116, 11.5.1990; Bull. EC 4-1990, point 1.2.5.
[5]   OJ L 131, 23.5.1990; Bull. EC 5-1990, point 1.3.2. Commission proposal: OJ C 86, 4.4.1990; Bull. EC 1/2-1990, point 1.2.6. OJ C 119, 15.5.1990; Bull. EC 4-1990, point 1.2.5.

European University Institute

392.   The Commission contributed ECU 2 650 000 to the academic and research activities of the European University Institute in Florence (research projects, research unit on European policy, research unit on European culture, library, publications, summer school, Jean Monnet scholarships for senior researchers, Jean Monnet chair, Community chairs and Jean Monnet lecture, training courses for researchers preparing theses, Centre for Documentation and Research on European Integration). [1]

393.   On 23 November, Mr G. Spadolini, President of the Italian Senate and former President of the Council, gave the annual Jean Monnet lecture on the crisis of the societies in the East and the return to a common Europe.

394.   The Institute participated in five Erasmus programmes during the 1989/90 academic year and will participate, from the start of 1990/91, in two Tempus programmes covering agreements with the main universities in Poland and Hungary. The Commission was associated with various research projects, colloquia and seminars organized by the Institute.

---

[1]   The activities of the European University Institute are described in a brochure which can be obtained from the Institute at Badia Fiesolana, 5 via dei Roccettini, San Domenico di Fiesole, I-50016 Florence.

Section 11

Regional policies

Priority activities and objectives

395.   Following the adoption in 1989 of the Community support frameworks (CSFs) for the regions whose development is lagging behind[1] and declining industrial areas[2] (Objectives 1 and 2 of the reform of the structural Funds), 1990 saw the adoption of a large number of operational programmes drawn up under the CSFs, and a series of Community initiatives and pilot projects.

Formulation and launching of regional policies

Formulation of regional policies

396.   The conference on regional policy in the context of the single market, organized by the Commission and the Council Presidency and held in Dublin on 10 and 11 June,[3] brought together the ministers responsible for regional policy in the Member States, and European, American and Japanese business representatives. Particular attention was paid to the factors likely to influence decisions on where to invest, and to the role of regional policy in this respect.

397.   In November the Commission adopted communication 'Europe 2000' on the outlook for the development of the Community's territory.[4] The aim of this preliminary document is to promote discussion of the factors determining the development of the territory so that a global study can be implemented which will serve as a reference framework for public authorities and businesses, facilitating their long-term planning and decision-making processes.

398.   The Consultative Council of Local and Regional Authorities set up by the Commission in 1988[5] held full meetings on 21 and 22 June[6] and in November.[7] During

---

[1]   OJ L 370, 19.12.1989; Twenty-third General Report, point 465.
[2]   OJ L 153, 19.6.1990; OJ L 154, 20.6.1990; OJ L 155, 21.6.1990; OJ L 157, 22.6.1990; OJ L 158, 23.6.1990; Twenty-third General Report, point 466.
[3]   Bull. EC 6-1990, point 1.3.79.
[4]   Bull. EC 11-1990, point 1.3.55.
[5]   OJ L 247, 6.9.1988; Twenty-second General Report, point 516.
[6]   Bull. EC 6-1990, point 1.3.90.
[7]   Bull. EC 11-1990, point 1.3.62.

these meetings it gave opinions on the Community initiatives Stride,[1] Interreg[1] and Leader;[2] it also adopted resolutions on partnership in the framework of implementing the reform of the structural Funds and on the role of local and regional authorities in the context of the reform of the Treaties.[3]

399.   The Committee on the development and conversion of the regions held five meetings in 1990, during which it gave opinions on the Community initiatives and on the fourth periodic report on the social and economic situation and development of the regions.[4]

Guidelines

400.   On 28 March, the Economic and Social Committee adopted an opinion on the declining industrial areas[5] in which it made a number of recommendations for improving Community action in those areas.

401.   On 17 May, Parliament adopted a resolution on the need to give preference to undertakings located in the less-favoured areas and the regions in decline when public works contracts are awarded.[6]

Social and economic situation and development
of the regions (periodic report)

402.   In December,[7] after consulting the Committee on the development and conversion of the regions, the Commission adopted the fourth periodic report on the social and economic situation and development of the regions of the Community.[8] This is the first report since the reform of the structural Funds. It gives a detailed analysis of the regional disparities at the beginning of the implementation of the reform, particularly as regards the regions with problems, and evaluates the regional effects of economic integration and of the Community's other policies. It also includes an initial assessment of the social and economic situation of the regions of the former German Democratic Republic and the countries of Central and Eastern Europe.

---

[1]   Point 407 of this Report.
[2]   Point 434 of this Report.
[3]   Point 1 et seq. of this Report.
[4]   Point 402 of this Report.
[5]   OJ C 124, 21.5.1990; Bull. EC 3-1990, point 1.1.61.
[6]   OJ C 149, 18.6.1990; Bull. EC 3-1990, point 1.2.133.
[7]   Bull. EC 12-1990.
[8]   Third report: Twenty-first General Report, point 461.

Regional impact assessment

403.   The Commission has launched a number of studies with a view to assessing the impact of completion of the internal market on the regions; these concern appraisal of regional competitiveness factors in regions with problems and the socio-economic consequences of opening the single market on regions with an industrial tradition.

Regional development at Community level

404.   The Commission continued its activities[1] in the context of the opportunities offered under Regulation (EEC) No 4254/88.[2] In the context of the Community initiative Interreg,[3] it launched a pilot project called 'Observatory for transfrontier cooperation' which aims to help border regions to exploit the opportunities provided by the completion of the internal market and overcome the specific problems arising from their relative isolation in the national economies and in the Community as a whole. The Commission also continued to study solutions to major urban problems at Community level. The pilot projects for London and Marseilles were begun,[4] and new pilot projects were launched for Berlin, Rotterdam,[5] Athens, Dublin, Neunkirchen, Brussels and Gibraltar.[6] As part of its campaign to encourage inter-regional cooperation it launched a number of pilot projects intended to encourage the sharing of experience and regional and local cooperation on development.

Implementation of the reform of the Funds as regards regional objectives

Eligibility of regions and areas

405.   On 18 April,[7] the Commission adopted the list of regions eligible under the Rechar programme for the economic conversion of coal-mining areas,[3] totalling 29 areas in six Member States. As a result, an amendment had to be made[8] to the list of declining industrial areas eligible under Objective 2[9] to include certain parts of the coal-mining areas concerned in the Federal Republic of Germany, France and the United Kingdom.

---

1   Twenty-third General Report, point 460.
2   OJ L 374, 31.12.1988; Twenty-second General Report, point 534.
3   Point 407 of this Report.
4   Bull. EC 1/2-1990, point 1.1.100.
5   Bull. EC 9-1990, point 1.2.61.
6   Bull. EC 12-1990.
7   Bull. EC 4-1990, point 1.1.53.
8   OJ L 206, 4.8.1990.
9   OJ L 112, 25.4.1989; Twenty-third General Report, point 462.

The Commission also decided that a number of areas were eligible under Community programmes for the conversion of steel areas (Resider)[1] and shipbuilding areas (Renaval).[2] The areas concerned were six Italian areas[3] and two Spanish areas[4] for Resider; and three French areas,[5] three Italian areas,[6] one Portuguese area and seven British areas[7] for Renaval. These areas were added to those selected in 1989.[8]

Regional plans and Community support frameworks

406.   In addition to the decisions adopted in 1989,[9] the Commission adopted the Objective 2 CSF for Spain on 14 March[10] and the Objective 1 CSF for Greece on 30 March.[11]

In June, after examining and discussing the development plans for Objective 5(b) rural areas in partnership with the competent national and regional authorities, the Commission adopted the 44 Objective 5(b) CSFs, most of which were drawn up at regional level.[12]

Community initiatives

407.   In the framework of the financial provisions adopted in November 1989[13] and supplemented in May,[14] the Commission formally adopted, on 25 July, the guidelines for operational programmes under the three Community initiatives Interreg, Stride and Regis, concerning the development of internal and external border areas of the Community,[15] the strengthening of regional capacities for research, technology and innovation[16]

---

[1]   OJ L 33, 5.2.1988; Twenty-second General Report, point 519.
[2]   OJ L 225, 15.8.1988; Twenty-second General Report, point 519.
[3]   OJ L 43, 17.2.1990; Bull. EC 1/2-1990, point 1.1.105; OJ L 223, 18.8.1990; Bull. EC 7/8-1990, point 1.3.110.
[4]   OJ L 209, 8.8.1990; Bull. EC 7/8-1990, point 1.3.110.
[5]   OJ L 106, 26.4.1990; Bull. EC 4-1990, point 1.1.52; OJ L 231, 25.8.1990; Bull. EC 7/8-1990, point 1.3.112.
[6]   OJ L 231, 25.8.1990; Bull. EC 7/8-1990, point 1.3.112.
[7]   OJ L 162, 18.6.1990; Bull. EC 6-1990, point 1.3.88; OJ L 231, 25.8.1990; Bull. EC 7/8-1990, point 1.3.112; OJ L 315, 15.11.1990; Bull. EC 10-1990, point 1.3.58.
[8]   Twenty-third General Report, point 471.
[9]   OJ L 370, 19.12.1989; Twenty-third General Report, point 466; OJ L 153, 19.6.1990; OJ L 154, 20.6.1990; OJ L 155, 21.6.1990; OJ L 157, 22.6.1990; OJ L 158, 23.6.1990; Twenty-third General Report, point 466.
[10]   OJ L 141, 2.6.1990; Bull. EC 3-1990, point 1.1.62.
[11]   OJ L 106, 26.4.1990; Bull. EC 3-1990, point 1.1.59.
[12]   Point 432 of this Report.
[13]   Twenty-third General Report, point 468.
[14]   Point 332 of this Report.
[15]   OJ C 215, 30.8.1990; Bull. EC 7/8-1990, point 1.3.106.
[16]   OJ C 196, 4.8.1990; Bull. EC 7/8-1990, point 1.3.108.

and the most remote regions,[1] respectively. On 27 January and 2 May, it adopted guidelines for initiatives concerning the economic conversion of coalmining areas (Rechar)[2] and protection of the environment in coastal areas (Envireg),[3] which had been agreed on in principle at the end of the previous year.[4] In addition, the criteria for granting the redeployment aids available under Article 56 of the ECSC Treaty and provided for in the Rechar programme were fixed in July.[5]

On 2 May and 25 July, the Commission also approved on first reading four new draft initiatives concerning energy network (Regen),[6] the preparation of industries for the single market (Prisma),[7] telecommunications networks and services for regional development (Télématique),[8] and rural development (Leader) in both Objective 1 and Objective 5(b) rural areas.[9] The Economic and Social Committee gave favourable opinions on the first three initiatives in September[10] and Parliament did so in October[11] and December.[12]

Operational programmes in the regions
(including integrated approaches and IMPs)

408. During the course of 1990 the Commission adopted a large number of operational programmes arising from the implementation of the Community support frameworks. The Objective 1 programmes concerned Greece (ECU 2 647.5 million), Spain (ECU 2 140.6 million), France (ECU 312.8 million), Ireland (ECU 866 million), Italy (ECU 1 844.7 million), Portugal (ECU 2 152.5 million), and the United Kingdom (Northern Ireland) (ECU 202.4 million).

The Objective 2 programmes concerned Belgium (ECU 696 million), Denmark (ECU 17.4 million), the Federal Republic of Germany (ECU 260 million), Spain (ECU 367.57 million), France (ECU 277.7 million), Italy (ECU 149 million), The Netherlands (ECU 28.46 million) and the United Kingdom (ECU 178 million).

---

[1]   Point 419 of this Report.
[2]   OJ C 20, 27.1.1990; Bull. EC 1/2-1990, point 1.1.106; Twenty-third General Report, point 469.
[3]   OJ C 115, 9.5.1990; Bull. EC 5-1990, point 1.2.77.
[4]   Twenty-third General Report, point 469.
[5]   OJ C 185, 26.7.1990; Bull. EC 7/8-1990, point 1.3.109.
[6]   Bull. EC 5-1990, point 1.2.74.
[7]   Bull. EC 7/8-1990, point 1.3.101.
[8]   Bull. EC 7/8-1990, point 1.3.102.
[9]   Point 432 of this Report.
[10] Bull. EC 9-1990, point 1.2.65.
[11] OJ C 295, 26.11.1990; Bull. EC 10-1990, point 1.3.61.
[12] OJ C 19, 28.1.1991; Bull. EC 12-1990.

409.   The Commission also adopted Community programmes to assist the conversion of steel areas (Resider)[1] and shipbuilding areas (Renaval).[2] The former related to one programme in Belgium,[3] two in the Federal Republic of Germany,[4] two in France[5] and one in Portugal;[6] the latter related to two programmes in Denmark,[7] three in the Federal Republic of Germany,[8] two in France,[9] two in The Netherlands[10] and four in the United Kingdom. In addition, one operational programme, in France, was adopted under the Community initiative to assist the conversion of coal-mining areas (Rechar).[11]

410.   In accordance with Regulation (EEC) No 2088/85 on the integrated Mediterranean programmes (IMPs),[12] the Commission adopted, on 19 July[13] and 14 December respectively, the content of and the detailed schedule for the second phase (1989-92) of the IMPs for Attica[14] and information technology concerning which negotiations with the Greek authorities were begun in 1989.[15]

In December, Parliament adopted a resolution[16] on the second activities report on implementation of the IMPs covering the 1988 financial year.[15]

Global grants

411.   Relatively little use was made of the global grant facility[17] in the context of the first Community support frameworks. However, 15 global grants are already being negotiated under the regional policies, or are under preparation, mainly in Objective 1 regions and mostly for purposes of assistance to local development.

---

[1]   OJ L 33, 5.2.1988; Twenty-second General Report, point 519.
[2]   OJ L 225, 15.8.1988; Twenty-second General Report, point 519.
[3]   Bull. EC 11-1990, point 1.3.61.
[4]   Bull. EC 3-1990, point 1.1.65.
[5]   Bull. EC 5-1990, point 1.2.78.
[6]   Bull. EC 10-1990, point 1.3.60.
[7]   Bull. EC 7/8-1990, point 1.3.111; Bull. EC 9-1990, point 1.2.66.
[8]   Bull. EC 3-1990, point 1.1.66; Bull. EC 7/8-1990, point 1.3.113; Bull. EC 10-1990, point 1.3.59.
[9]   Bull. EC 11-1990, point 1.3.59; Bull. EC 12-1990.
[10] Bull. EC 6-1990, point 1.3.89.
[11] Bull. EC 12-1990.
[12] OJ L 197, 27.7.1985; Nineteenth General Report, points 465 to 467.
[13] Bull. EC 7/8-1990, point 1.3.114.
[14] OJ L 140, 7.6.1988; Twenty-first General Report, point 475.
[15] Twenty-third General Report, point 470.
[16] OJ C 19, 28.1.1991; Bull. EC 12-1990.
[17] Twenty-third General Report, point 474.

Transitional measures

412. To ensure the continuity of financial flows to the less-favoured regions, the Commission decided to grant aid for a certain number of projects. The amount and the allocation of the aid and information on all ERDF assistance for 1990 can be found in Tables 4 and 5.

Technical assistance and studies

413. The Commission prepared a guide to help the Member States and the regions to make full use of the opportunities for technical assistance offered by the structural Fund regulations. [1] In accordance with the guidelines laid out in this document, the financial envelope in the CSFs for Objectives 1 and 2 earmarked for the financing of technical assistance was used to develop a system for monitoring the CSFs, with computer support, and to prepare the envisaged operational programmes. The Commission supplemented these measures with actions undertaken on its own initiative, particularly as regards the implementation and assessment of the CSFs. In addition, it continued its programme of information meetings on the CSFs for employers and workers in the regions.

TABLE 4

ERDF commitments in 1990 — Broken down by Objective

million ECU

Member States	Objective 1	Objective 2	Objective 5(b)	Transitional measures	Innovative measures (Art. 10)	Technical assistance (Art. 7)	Total
Belgium	—	59.608	—	7.159	—	0.036	66.803
Denmark	—	9.614	1.866	6.910	—	—	18.390
Germany (FR)	—	40.869	28.762	38.910	5.400	—	113.941
Greece	561.675	—	—	—	—	0.018	561.693
Spain	1 470.164	224.439	6.184	100.919	0.520	—	1 802.226
France	72.496	245.480	53.908	66.038	4.817	—	442.739
Ireland	289.673	—	—	—	—	2.324	291.997
Italy	776.030	61.083	—	—	—	—	837.113
Luxembourg	—	2.975	—	—	—	—	2.975
Netherlands	—	24.359	4.586	14.102	2.630	—	45.677
Portugal	533.675	—	—	—	—	0.047	533.722
United Kingdom	34.197	371.341	57.783	1.127	5.100	—	469.548
Commission	—	—	—	—	38.854	1.893	40.747
Total	3 737.910	1 039.768	153.089	235.165	57.321	4.318	5 227.571

---

[1]   Point 330 of this Report.

TABLE 5

ERDF commitments in 1990 — Broken down by type of assistance

million ECU

Member States	Community programmes and initiatives; non-quota measures	National programmes of Community interest (NPCI) and operational programmes	Innovative measures (Articles 7 and 10)	Total
Belgium	5.634	61.133	0.036	66.803
Denmark	12.468	5.922		18.390
Germany (FR)	36.377	72.164	5.400	113.941
Greece	26.156	535.519	0.018	561.693
Spain	123.381	1 678.325	0.520	1 802.226
France	52.843	385.079	4.817	442.739
Ireland	64.387	225.286	2.324	291.997
Italy	179.600	657.513		837.113
Luxembourg	—	2.975		2.975
Netherlands	14.102	28.945	2.630	45.677
Portugal	26.149	507.526	0.047	533.722
United Kingdom	41.254	423.194	5.100	469.548
Commission			40.747	40.747
Total	582.351	4 583.581	61.639	5 227.571

Other operations

Conversion loans

414.   New ECSC conversion loans[1] granted by the Commission in 1990 totalled ECU 1 143.1 million and were to help create 76 504 jobs. Of the ECU 69 million committed to finance interest rate subsidies under the 1990 ECSC budget, 65.7% was used to increase the amounts allocated for previous loans.

Business and innovation centres

415.   The Commission continued to support the development of European business and innovation centres (EBICs) and their network. It also provided financial assistance for the creation of seven new centres in addition to the 50 existing ones which have been

---

[1]   OJ C 273, 1.7.1987; Twentieth General Report, point 535.

TABLE 6

ECSC conversion loans

Member States	1975-89		1990		1975-90	
	1	2	1	2	1	2
Belgium	237.7	14 487	16.6	1 242	254.3	15 729
Denmark	11.7	854	—	—	11.7	854
Germany (FR)	1 413.5	97 392	315.8	23 679	1 729.3	121 071
France	477.0	34 015	285.2	21 388	762.2	55 403
Ireland	4.4	420	—	—	4.4	420
Italy	648.0	42 162	135.2	10 141	783.2	52 303
Luxembourg	25.8	2 100	—	—	25.8	2 100
Netherlands	33.5	2 372	—	—	33.5	2 372
United Kingdom	1 825.6	104 262	390.3	19 617	2 215.9	123 875
Greece	5.0	375	—	—	5.0	375
Spain	123.0	9 223	—	—	123.0	9 223
Portugal	20.0	1 500	—	—	20.0	1 500
Saar/Lorraine Luxembourg transfrontier operation	100.0	5 000	—	—	100.0	5 000
Community	4 925.2	314 162	1 143.1	76 504	6 068.3	390 666

[1] Amount of loans granted (million ECU).
[2] Number of jobs created/to be created.

functioning since the programme was launched in 1984.[1] It continued its efforts to increase the effectiveness of the centres in the EBN network (European Business and Innovation Centre Network),[1] in particular by encouraging the exchange of information and experience and the development of common methods.

Also with a view to creating new activities in regions covered by the objectives of the reform of the structural Funds, the Commission launched a research measure concerning trials for a European support centre for activities for the rural economy (Cesar).

Seed capital

416. The Commission continued the implementation of the Community pilot scheme to stimulate the creation of seed capital funds for investment in new businesses launched in 1989 for a period of five years.[2]

---

[1] Eighteenth General Report, point 335.
[2] Point 240 of this Report.

Section 12

Measures to assist the Community's remoter regions

417.   The Commission continued its work on implementing a Community approach to its remoter regions, the first practical result of which was adoption of the Poseidom programme[1] in December 1989,[2] and on certain products peculiar to those regions. The Community approach to its remoter regions involves adoption of multisectoral and multiannual measures for each region in the form, where necessary, of variations in the application of Community policies so as to offset as far as possible the problems arising from their considerable isolation, their insular nature, their specific products and the small scale of their economies. These activities are coordinated by the interdepartmental group for the French overseas departments and territories, the Canary Islands, Ceuta and Melilla, the Azores and Madeira under the authority of the President of the Commission.

418.   This year saw the preparation of Commission proposals on three matters of particular concern to the remoter regions: the beginning of implementation of the Poseidom programme in the French overseas departments, the preparation of an appropriate framework, similar to Poseidom, for application of the common policies in the Azores and Madeira, and changes in the status of the Canary Islands within the Community to integrate them more fully into the common policies and permitting application in those islands of a suitable framework similar in design to those for the other remoter regions. The Commission also continued work on the preparation of common measures for the Community market in bananas, a product of great economic importance for most of the remoter regions.

419.   Efforts to help the economies of those regions, all of which come under Objective 1 of the reform of the structural Funds,[3] to catch up led to adoption of the first operational programmes under the Community support frameworks and of a specific Community initiative for the most remote regions, Regis.[4] Regis has an allocation of

---

[1]   Programme of options specific to the remote and insular nature of the French overseas departments.
[2]   OJ L 399, 30.12.1989; Twenty-third General Report, point 490.
[3]   OJ L 185, 15.7.1988; Twenty-second General Report, point 533.
[4]   OJ C 196, 4.8.1990; Bull. EC 7/8-1990, point 1.3.107.

ECU 200 million and is intended to help diversify the economies of those regions, consolidate their links with the rest of the Community and promote cooperation between them and with neighbouring countries.

The French overseas departments

420. Poseidom entered its implementation phase; this was marked by frequent consultations between the Commission and the French authorities under the partnership arrangements.

421. The Commission prepared a proposal, to be presented in early 1991, for a framework regulation on specific agricultural measures. The proposal includes a range of measures covering both the special conditions governing the provision of certain supplies to the overseas departments and the development of production in those areas.

422. On the taxation front, 1990 saw the first application of Council Decision 89/688/EEC on dock dues in the overseas departments,[1] the Commission raising no objection following notification of a proposal to increase the tax.

423. The Commission ensures that account is taken of the Poseidom guidelines in its proposals under the various common policies, on air transport for example. It likewise assured consistency on regional cooperation between overseas departments, overseas territories and African and Caribbean States in the Caribbean and the Indian Ocean, which is now governed by uniform, expanded provisions set out in the various relevant texts.[2]

The Canary Islands (Spain), the Azores and Madeira (Portugal)

424. On 17 January the Commission adopted a report to the Spanish authorities on the Canary Islands[3] and subsequently sent it for information to the Council and Parliament. The report, which closely followed the resolution of the Islands' Parliament on accession to the Community,[4] concentrated on the capacity of Community law to respond to the problems raised by the arrangements for the Canary Islands instituted

---

[1]   OJ L 399, 30.12.1989; Twenty-third General Report, point 490.
[2]   Point 786 of this Report.
[3]   Bull. EC 1/2-1990, point 1.1.101.
[4]   Twenty-third General Report, point 494.

by the Act of Accession of Spain.[1] On 19 December, following the report, the Commission adopted, at the request of Spain and in accordance with the Act of Accession, two proposals drawn up in cooperation with the Spanish national and regional authorities concerned.[2] The first deals with changes to status with a view to strengthening the integration of the Canary Islands into Community policies, while the second, which implements the first, is in the form of a decision of the Poseidom type and introduces a programme (called Poseican) laying down the principles for a varied application of Community policies in the sectors where this approach is required.

425.   In its report on the Azores and Madeira, adopted on 17 January and sent to the Portuguese authorities before being transmitted for information to the Council and Parliament,[3] the Commission looked at the specific problems of the two Portuguese autonomous regions and set out possible measures which could facilitate application of the common policies. Portugal welcomed this approach in April. On 19 December the Commission adopted a proposal for a Council decision introducing a programme of measures specific to the remote and insular nature of the Azores and Madeira, similar to Poseidom and prepared in partnership with the Portuguese national and regional authorities concerned.[2] The programme, called Poseima, includes a number of measures for appropriate application of Community policies, particularly in the fields of agriculture, energy and the craft industry.

Common measures for bananas

426.   In view of the completion of the internal market the Commission has stepped up its work on the preparation of measures to achieve common measures for the banana market with a view to adopting initial guidelines on the matter in the near future, after which the Commission will draw up appropriate proposals.

---

[1]   OJ L 302, 15.11.1985; Nineteenth General Report, points 720 to 743.
[2]   Bull. EC 12-1990.
[3]   Bull. EC 1/2-1990, point 1.1.101.

Section 13

Agriculture[1]

Priority activities and objectives

427.   As a result of decisions taken in previous years, and particularly the progress made in 1989 with regard to the completion of the necessary adjustments to the market regulations and the introduction of a new structural policy, 1990 was the first year in which the common agricultural policy (CAP) was fully applied as adapted and reformed in accordance with the guidelines laid down by the European Council at its meeting in February 1988 in Brussels.[2]

In accordance with those guidelines, where market management is concerned, the prudent price policy followed during previous years has been continued, as has the strict application of the stabilizers, which have now been introduced in all the sensitive sectors.

With regard to structures and rural development, the decisions taken during the previous year have been supplemented this year with all the necessary implementing provisions, allowing, inter alia, *the regional programmes presented by the Member States to be adopted.*

This year also saw the continuing agricultural negotiations of the Uruguay Round,[3] increased Community assistance to the countries of Central and Eastern Europe,[4] German unification and extension of the CAP to cover the territory of the former German Democratic Republic,[5] as well as the beginning of the second transitional stage in the accession of Spain and Portugal.

In addition, during the course of the year the Commission presented a series of proposals to amend certain market organizations.

---

[1]   For further details see *The Agricultural Situation in the Community — 1990 Report*, published in conjunction with this Report (available from the Office for Official Publications).
[2]   Twenty-second General Report, point 2.
[3]   Point 817 of this Report.
[4]   Point 668 of this Report.
[5]   Point 24 of this Report.

Content of the common agricultural policy

Agricultural prices for 1990/91

428. On 27 April,[1] the Council reached an agreement (formally adopted on 7 and 14 May)[2] on agricultural prices for the 1990/91 marketing year. As in previous years, the concern was to control production and restore the balance between supply and demand. This decision does not differ substantially from the previous year's decisions,[3] being based on the strict use of stabilizers and improved intervention mechanisms. Thus the CAP continues to be consistent with the approach presented in the Uruguay Round negotiations by the Community to its partners in GATT.[4] The decisions resulted in an average reduction of 1.1% in prices, expressed in ecus, in relation to the previous marketing year. However, the agrimonetary adjustments which had taken place since the last price decisions led to an average increase of 1.6% in prices expressed in national currencies, which is nevertheless significantly lower than the average rate of inflation in the Community as a whole.

Adjustment of the agricultural market organizations

429. Following the substantial adjustments decided on in recent years, the adjustments made to the market organizations in 1990 were relatively minor. They mainly concern the special aid schemes, such as those in favour of small-scale producers. The Council decided to grant a premium per hectare for certain cereals of lesser importance[5] and to introduce a new scheme of aid per hectare for small field crop producers,[5] allowing the Member States to choose between applying the new scheme or continuing to apply the previous provisions. The decisions fixing the agricultural prices for 1990/91[5] also included the possibility of granting the suckler cow premium to small milk producers with mixed herds and gave the Member States the opportunity to buy back milk quotas with a view to reallocating them to small producers in mountain, hill and less-favoured areas.[6] Special aid for producers growing cotton on less than 2.5 hectares was also

---

[1]   Bull. EC 4-1990, point 1.1.92.
[2]   OJ L 119, 11.5.1990; OJ L 132, 23.5.1990; OJ L 134, 28.5.1990; Bull. EC 5-1990, point 1.2.142; Commission proposals: OJ C 49, 28.2.1990; Twenty-third General Report, point 567; Bull. EC 1/2-1990, point 1.1.144.
[3]   Twenty-third General Report, point 558.
[4]   Point 821 of this Report.
[5]   OJ L 134, 28.5.1990; Bull. EC 5-1990, point 1.2.142; Commission proposal: OJ C 49, 28.2.1990; Bull. EC 1/2-1990, point 1.1.144.
[6]   OJ L 119, 11.5.1990; Bull. EC 5-1990, point 1.2.142; Commission proposal: OJ C 49, 28.2.1990; Bull. EC 1/2-1990, point 1.1.144.

introduced.[1] In addition, the common organization of the market in products processed from fruit and vegetables[2] was amended to renew the production aid scheme for dried grapes.[3]

430.   The Commission, whilst continuing to adjust its markets policy, and given certain set dates, sent the Council proposals to extend the sugar market organization for two years with some adjustments.[4] It also presented a proposal for the olive oil market organization[5] as a result of the end, on 31 December, of the transitional period provided for in the Act of Accession of Spain and Portugal.[6]

431.   Pursuant to the Act of Accession,[6] in December[7] the Council adopted a series of proposals for Regulations on agricultural products subject in Portugal to the phased transitional arrangements for integration into the common organization of the markets. These proposals are based on the solutions put forward by the Commission in its report, adopted in June,[8] on the progress made towards the specific objectives and the implementation of structural measures in Portugal.

Rural development

432.   In the context of the implementation of the reform of the structural Funds,[9] on 6 and 27 June[10] the Commission formally adopted the 44 Community support frameworks (CSFs) for the regions eligible under Objective 5(b) (development of rural areas), on which it had agreed in principle in May.[11] These support frameworks concern rural areas in Belgium, Denmark, the Federal Republic of Germany, Spain, France, Italy, Luxembourg, The Netherlands and the United Kingdom. In order to make optimum use of existing resources and so as to have a maximum impact on rural development, the measures envisaged concentrate on five priorities: developing other sectors of the economy, particularly small and medium-sized businesses; tourism and recreation; environmental protection; human resources.

---

[1]   OJ L 116, 8.5.1990; Bull. EC 4-1990, point 1.1.115; Commission proposal: OJ C 2, 5.1.1990.
[2]   OJ L 49, 27.2.1986.
[3]   OJ L 201, 31.7.1990; Bull. EC 7/8-1990, point 1.3.171; Commission proposal: OJ C 49, 28.2.1990; Bull EC 1/2-1990, point 1.1.144.
[4]   OJ L 258, 13.10.1990; Bull. EC 7/8-1990, point 1.3.165.
[5]   OJ C 277, 5.11.1990; Bull. EC 7/8-1990, point 1.3.191 to 1.3.197.
[6]   OJ L 302, 15.11.1985; Nineteenth General Report, points 730 and 731.
[7]   OJ L 362, 27.12.1990; Bull. EC 12-1990; Commission proposal: OJ C 297, 27.11.1990; Bull. EC 9-1990, point 1.2.107.
[8]   Bull. EC 6-1990, point 1.3.147.
[9]   OJ L 185, 15.7.1988; OJ L 374, 31.12.1988; Twenty-second General Report, points 533 and 534.
[10] OJ L 322, 21.11.1990; Bull. EC 6-1990, point 1.3.145.
[11] Bull. EC 5-1990, point 1.2.137.

The overall financial guidelines for Objective 5(b) for 1989-93, approved in 1989,[1] and the indicative allocation of funds between the Member States[2] were revised on 2 May.[3] The indicative allocation of the sum of ECU 2 607 million to the CSFs was as follows: ECU 32.5 million for Belgium, ECU 23 million for Denmark, ECU 525 million for the Federal Republic of Germany, ECU 285 million for Spain, ECU 960 million for France, ECU 385 million for Italy, ECU 2.5 million for Luxembourg, ECU 44 million for The Netherlands and ECU 350 million for the United Kingdom.

In March the Council adopted a new Community aid scheme for investments in the marketing and processing of agricultural products.[4] This scheme replaced the arrangements introduced in 1977[5] and applies to both agricultural and forestry products. In June the Commission fixed the selection criteria to be adopted for investments under the new rules.[6]

433.   On 24 July the Council adopted Regulation (EEC) No 2176/90[7] amending Regulation (EEC) No 797/85 on improving the efficiency of agricultural structures.[8] The aim of this amendment is to adjust the current scheme of aid to encourage the set-aside of arable land with a view to promoting non-food uses of agricultural products. Regulation (EEC) No 797/85[8] was also amended in March[9] as regards the rates of reimbursement applicable to set-aside.

434.   On 25 July, the Commission approved on first reading a communication to the Member States laying down guidelines in the context of a Community initiative for rural development called 'Leader' (links between actions for the development of the rural economy)[10] The Economic and Social Committee gave its opinion on this initiative in October.[11] On 7 June,[12] the Commission adopted a proposal for a decision on the setting up of a network of rural development information centres dealing with rural development initiatives and agricultural markets, called Miriam. The Economic and Social Committee gave its opinion on this proposal in September,[13] and Parliament in Novem-

---

[1] Twenty-third General Report, point 482.
[2] Twenty-third General Report, point 561.
[3] Bull. EC 5-1990, point 1.2.137.
[4] OJ L 91, 6.4.1990; Bull. EC 3-1990, point 1.1.108; Commission proposals: OJ C 240, 20.9.1989; Twenty-third General Report, point 561.
[5] OJ L 51, 23.2.1977; Eleventh General Report, point 310.
[6] OJ L 163, 29.6.1990; Bull. EC 6-1990, point 1.3.148.
[7] OJ L 198, 28.7.1990; Bull. EC 7/8-1990, point 1.3.167; Commission proposal: OJ C 31, 9.2.1990; Twenty-third General Report, point 562; OJ C 203, 14.8.1990; Bull. EC 7/8-1990, point 1.3.167.
[8] OJ L 93, 30.3.1985; Nineteenth General Report, point 548.
[9] OJ L 83, 30.3.1990; Bull. EC 3-1990, point 1.1.105; Commission proposal: OJ C 268, 20.10.1989.
[10] Bull. EC 7/8-1990, point 1.3.164.
[11] Bull. EC 10-1990, point 1.3.114.
[12] OJ C 158, 28.6.1990; Bull. EC 6-1990, point 1.3.146.
[13] Bull. EC 9-1990, point 1.2.111.

ber.[1] The Commission also transmitted to the Council a communication on Community actions for rural tourism.[2]

435.   On 25 July, the Commission adopted a proposal for a Regulation on the introduction and the maintenance of agricultural production methods compatible with the requirements of the protection of the environment and the maintenance of the countryside.[3] The proposal is to introduce an effective instrument which will fully guarantee that agriculture meets environmental protection requirements and reflects market realities.

436.   The proposal for a Regulation on Community plant variety rights, adopted on 23 July, introduces a special form of industrial property right for the development of new plant varieties.[4] The Economic and Social Committee gave its opinion on the proposal in December.[5]

437.   On 17 October,[6] the Commission adopted a report on inter-branch cooperation in agriculture, in which it stresses the need to set up flexible structures for cooperation and collaboration between the various occupational categories involved in the production, processing and marketing of agricultural products.

438.   This was the first year of implementation of the forestry action programme adopted by the Council on 29 May 1989.[7] Forestry operational programmes or sections on forestry in more general operational programmes were approved in the context of regional development measures. In addition, aid for the afforestation of agricultural land was strengthened. With regard to the protection of forests against atmospheric pollution and fires,[8] the Commission decided in 1990 to grant ECU 16 million of financial aid to 86 projects. At international level, the Commission participated, in particular, in the preparation and running of the Pan-European Conference on forest protection,[9] and extended its participation in the international programme for the surveillance and assessment of the effects of atmospheric pollution on forests.

439.   These aspects of the CAP were the subject of resolutions by Parliament on, for example, the crisis in the agricultural sector[10] and damage caused by drought.[11]

---

[1]   OJ C 324, 24.12.1990; Bull. EC 11-1990, point 1.3.116.
[2]   Point 246 of this Report.
[3]   OJ C 267, 23.10.1990; Bull. EC 7/8-1990, point 1.3.163.
[4]   OJ C 244, 28.9.1990; Bull. EC 7/8-1990, point 1.3.166.
[5]   Bull. EC 12-1990.
[6]   Bull. EC 10-1990, point 1.3.110.
[7]   OJ L 165, 15.6.1989; Twenty-third General Report, point 565.
[8]   OJ L 326, 17.11.1986; Twentieth General Report, point 618.
[9]   Point 509 of this Report.
[10]   OJ C 260, 15.10.1990; Bull. EC 9-1990, point 1.2.108.
[11]   OJ C 260, 15.10.1990; Bull. EC 9-1990, point 1.2.113.

Management of the common agricultural policy

Market organization

Crop products

440.   As the 1988/89 harvest[1] exceeded the maximum guaranteed quantity (MGQ), pursuant to the stabilizers decided on by the European Council in February 1988,[2] cereals prices were reduced for 1989/90; 1989/90 production was fixed by the Commission in October 1989 at 160.5 million tonnes (t), slightly in excess of the MGQ. Since this overrun was felt to be negligible, and in view of the situation as regards the income of cereals producers affected by the drought that struck a large part of the Community, it was decided not to collect the additional co-responsibility levy. Benefiting from the continuing shortfall of production in relation to consumption on the world market in 1989 for breadmaking cereals and fodder grain, the Community was able to export 32 million t of cereals and cereal products, with common wheat accounting for about 18.8 million t, barley for 10 million t, durum wheat for 1.7 million t and maize for 1.6 million t. Despite these sales, intervention stocks increased from 9.2 to 11.8 million t by the end of the 1989/90 marketing year, because of the large harvest.

The Commission took a number of measures to ensure implementation of the agreement between the Community and the United States,[3] opening an annual import quota into Spain of maize and sorghum until 1990.

In the context of its policy in favour of rural society, the Community introduced a system of aid for the production of canary grass, millet and buckwheat. In addition, a new aid scheme for small producers was introduced to soften the impact of the stabilizers.[4] In view of the structural difficulties on the market in cereals, namely excess supply and the existence of large stocks in the Community, and the possibilities for putting cereals to non-food uses, which are sufficiently advanced in both technical and economic terms, the Council decided to adjust the aid scheme to encourage the set-aside of arable land by providing for specific aid for the use of arable land for non-food purposes.[5]

To ensure the integration of the cereal production of the former German Democratic Republic, the Commission authorized the German authorities to derogate from several provisions in the cereals regulations.[6]

---

[1]   Twenty-third General Report, point 568.
[2]   OJ L 110, 29.4.1988; OJ L 132, 28.5.1988; Twenty-second General Report, point 625.
[3]   OJ L 98, 10.4.1987; Twenty-first General Report, point 558.
[4]   Point 428 of this Report.
[5]   Point 433 of this Report.
[6]   OJ L 267, 29.9.1990; Bull. EC 9-1990, point 1.1.3.

441.   Rice production in 1989/90 fell slightly, particularly as a result of the drought in Spain, to 2.01 million t of paddy. The loss of certain export markets and the size of the Italian harvest forced producers to sell 95 000 t of rice into intervention for the first time since 1972. Spanish prices for 1990/91 were aligned on Community prices. [1]

442.   In the sugar sector, the 1989/90 world harvest of 109 million t of raw sugar brought an end to the growing production shortfall of the four previous years, which had caused a considerable contraction in world stocks. The low levels of stocks, particularly in the main exporting countries, were clearly reflected in the free market sugar prices, which increased considerably and also affected the marketing year in question. As a result prices reached their highest level since August 1961, at 16.25 cents per pound. Since then, prices have been falling slowly but steadily.

In 1989, although the area under sugarbeet remained relatively stable (1 855 000 ha or an increase of 1.5% in relation to 1988), favourable weather conditions meant that sugar production increased considerably, to 14 334 million t. However, this area represents only about 1.4% of the utilizable agricultural area (UAA) in the Community. The number of holdings producing sugarbeet, which has been falling continually since 1970, seems now to have stabilized at around 367 000 units. The average Community yield of sugar per hectare is now at 7.59 t (an all-time record), thereby exceeding last year's yield (7.41 t) which was already considered satisfactory, and considerably outstripping the average yield for the five previous years (6.96 t/ha). Total sugar consumption in the Community, estimated at 10 950 million t, increased, in particular human consumption. The degree of self-sufficiency in sugar in the Community was at 131.8% in 1989/90, as compared to 127.8% in 1988/89. In 1989/90, ecu prises for sugar in the Community fell by 2% after having been kept at the same level for a long period. Total exports of unprocessed sugar were estimated at about 4.9 million t of which 2.3 t were non-quota, or 'C' sugar. Sugar exports guaranteed by the Community were carried out exclusively under tendering procedures.

Proposals were made concerning the possible continuation, from 1991/92, of the sugar market organization, where each sugar undertaking is allocated a production quota, with different guarantees for A or B sugar. [2]

443.   Community production of olive oil, at about 1 450 000 t, accounts for approximately 80% of world production, which is estimated at around 1 800 000 t. The 1989/90 harvest was estimated at 1 551 500 t, compared with an actual production of 1 143 000 t in 1988/89. There was little change in the area under olive trees, which available data put at 4.4 million ha and a total of 422 million trees. About two million families are

---

[1]   OJ L 198, 28.7.1990; Bull. EC 7/8-1990, point 1.3.174; Commission proposal: OJ C 187, 27.7.1990; Bull. EC 6-1990, point 1.3.156.
[2]   Point 430 of this Report.

engaged in olive cultivation. Community consumption in 1988/89 amounted to 1 420 000 t, or 75% of world consumption. Consumption of oil in small containers, at 650 000 t, accounts for most of the consumption in the Community of Ten. Farm consumption is still considerable. At the beginning of 1989/90, intervention stocks were 84 000 t; at the end of the marketing year they were 65 000 t. Greece and Spain are the main suppliers and Italy remains the chief purchaser, although it also produces and exports. Except for exceptional cases, the only imports are under the Tunisian quota of 46 000 t. Exports, which have been increasing since 1981, reached 150 000 t in 1989/90, as compared to 120 000 t in 1988/89. A stabilizer was introduced in 1987/88, with an MGQ of 1 350 000 t.[1] Although in that year the co-responsibility mechanism came into play, leading to a reduction of 31% in the aid, the MGQ was not reached in 1988/89 and is unlikely to be reached in 1989/90. In view of the end of the transitional period in Spain and Portugal on 31 December, and the consequences thereof, the Commission presented proposals to the Council to extend the rules to cover the whole of the Community territory.[2]

444.   In the wine sector, the most recent data put the 1989 harvest at 167 million hectolitres (hl), an increase of 10.8 million hl in relation to the previous year, although these levels are relatively low compared to production levels attained over the last 10 years as a result of weather conditions, particularly in Spain. The 1990 harvest is expected to be slightly larger, at 175 million hl, i.e. an increase of 4.8%. Total domestic use, taking account of the distillation operations decided on, should amount to 157.5 million hl. Prices for table wine rose slowly but steadily during 1990. The initial results of the strengthening of the grubbing arrangements in 1988[3] were encouraging in France, Italy and Greece, where Community premiums were paid for the abandonment of production on about 27 000 ha, 15 000 ha and 1 000 ha, respectively. In Spain, grubbing operations related to 1 000 ha and did not lead to a large reduction in production capacity because of the low yields per hectare. In 1989[4] the Commission implemented a programme for the disposal of stocks of vinous alcohol from compulsory distillation. The programme provides for these stocks to be sold by tendering procedure both outside the Community and on the internal market, as well as for uses which would not disrupt the markets in alcohol and spirit drinks. The Commission made its first report on the progress of the programme in a communication adopted on 4 July.[5]

445.   In the fresh fruit and vegetables sector, intervention thresholds were exceeded during 1989/90 for cauliflower, peaches, nectarines, lemons, satsumas and oranges. The basic and intervention prices for 1990/91 for each of these products were therefore

---

[1]   OJ L 89, 6.4.1988; Twenty-second General Report, point 650.
[2]   Point 431 of this Report.
[3]   OJ L 132, 28.5.1988; Twenty-second General Report, point 625.
[4]   Twenty-third General Report, point 571.
[5]   Bull. EC 7/8-1890, point 1.3.182.

reduced by 4%, 6%, 20%, 3%, 20% and 10%, respectively. From 1990/91 Portugal is included in the system of intervention thresholds. The aid scheme for processing lemons was aligned on the system in force for other citrus fruit. The minimum price which processors must pay producers is not directly linked to the withdrawal price, which is now the same regardless of size and packaging. The quantities of lemons delivered for processing under the aid scheme are added to the quantities offered for intervention for the purposes of determining whether the intervention threshold has been exceeded. The threshold has been raised accordingly.

446.   Community policy for tobacco encouraged conversion to the more sought-after varieties and applied the system of stabilizers. The MGQs for the popular varieties were therefore increased for the 1990/91 harvests and those for the problem varieties were reduced. The intervention price policy remained the same.

447.   Aid for hops was fixed at ECU 340, ECU 390 and ECU 400 per hectare for the aromatic, bitter and other varieties, respectively.[1] In addition, the Council permitted the extension of the aid to cover experimental varieties under certain conditions.[2] It also granted Spain an additional period of two years in which to implement the varietal conversion programme.[3]

448.   Although not widely grown in the Community, cotton plays an important role in those regions where cultivation is concentrated. In 1990 the area under cotton in the Community was 350 000 ha, of which 268 000 ha are in Greece, 84 000 in Spain, and a few dozen in Italy, with an estimated production of 1 035 000 t of unginned cotton, of which Greece accounted for 750 000 t and Spain for 285 000. Cotton is a deficit crop in the Community, as its production of cotton fibre covers only 30% of the 1 300 000 t or so which it consumes. Because of the large increase in production, the MGQ has been exceeded each year since 1986/87, which has led to a reduction in the target price and the level of aid. As a result of these measures, the steady increase in the area under cotton has ceased. Special aid for small producers was introduced in April.[4]

449.   The cultivation of flax in the Community has been increasing, with 79 300 ha under flax in 1990. Flax straw is processed into fibre by about 180 retting and scutching undertakings. The Community harvest provides about 110 000 t of fibre. The area under hemp reached 4 000 ha in 1989. The market for fibre is expected to be difficult in

---

[1]   OJ L 190, 21.7.1990; Bull. EC 7/8-1990, point 1.3.205; Commission proposal: OJ C 127, 23.5.1990; Bull. EC 4-1990, point 1.1.113.
[2]   OJ L 265, 28.9.1990; Bull. EC 9-1990, point 1.2.133; Commission proposal: OJ C 153, 22.6.1990; Bull. EC 5-1990, point 1.2.171.
[3]   OJ L 367, 29.12.1990; Bull. EC 12-1990; Commission proposal: OJ C 279, 7.11.1990; Bull. EC 10-1990, point 1.3.136.
[4]   Point 429 of this Report.

1990/91: although there is unlikely to be a major reduction in stocks of short flax fibre and hemp fibre, stocks of long flax fibre are expected to fall from this year.

450. In the seed sector, the Commission fixed the new reference prices for hybrid maize and hybrid sorghum for sowing for 1990/91[1] and the new countervailing charges for hybrid maize and hybrid sorghum.[2] It also adopted a new list of the different varieties of *Lolium perenne L.*[3]

Livestock products

451. When the Council fixed the agricultural prices,[4] it adjusted the target price for milk, which was reduced by 3.5% for 1990/91, and the intervention price for Italian cheeses in line with the reductions which had already been made to the intervention prices. The threshold prices were reduced accordingly. At the same time, the Council decided to amend the quota arrangements by approving Community financing, to the tune of 500 000 t, for a programme of buying back quotas for reallocation to small producers. In addition, on the basis of the conclusions of a Commission report,[5] the Council laid down general rules on the use of casein and caseinates in the manufacture of cheese, seen as most vulnerable to speculative use.[6]

The drop in world demand, particularly that of Central and Eastern Europe and the Middle East, and the fall in consumption in almost all the OECD countries, led to a deterioration in the situation on the world market. The fall in prices on the Community market, which reflects the trend on international markets, triggered off intervention buying again. The accumulation of stocks of butter (250 000 t) and skimmed milk (350 000 t) reflects the worsening of the sector's situation in 1990.

452. The market for beef, at both production and consumption level, was hit by a series of unfavourable circumstances to do with weather, health problems and politics. As a consequence, prices, which were already falling as result of a cyclical upswing in production, dropped sharply, in relation to 1989, by about 9% for beef from large male animals and by as much as 18% for beef from cows. In the 1990/91 price decisions,[4] the Council decided to pay a premium for the maintenance of no more than 10 eligible suckler cows per small milk producer. With such a depressed market, price support could be guaranteed only through direct intervention buying, either under a tendering proce-

---

1   OJ L 168, 30.6.1990; Bull. EC 6-1990, point 1.3.192.
2   OJ L 168, 30.6.1990.
3   OJ L 173, 6.7.1990.
4   Point 428 of this Report.
5   Bull. EC 3-1990, point 1.1.129.
6   OJ L 201, 31.7.1990; Bull. EC 7/8-1990, point 1.3.184; Commission proposal: OJ C 135, 2.6.1990; Bull. EC 5-1990, point 1.2.160.

dure or, in Spain, at a fixed price.[1] To alleviate the market situation, refunds were increased for exports to certain countries in the Near and Middle East and Africa, meat in intervention storage was sold at reduced prices to Brazil and meat of cull dairy cows sold to certain non-member countries in Central and Eastern Europe in the context of agreements concluded by the former German Democratic Republic with those countries.

453.   The market for sheepmeat and goatmeat also experienced difficulties for a variety of reasons all occurring together: an increase in production and sales, particularly in northern Europe, drought, monetary fluctuations, low prices for wool and hides and uncertainty regarding imports from Central and Eastern Europe, particularly the former German Democratic Republic. Production forecasts show an increase of 3.6%, or 1 132 000 t, in 1990, with a particularly large increase in Ireland, Spain and the United Kingdom, while consumption is expected to increase by only 2.4%, or 1 358 000 t. The Community's level of self-sufficiency is therefore still rising, and is set to reach 83%. The Community market price could fall by 10% in 1990. In view of the disturbance on the market, the Commission fixed the first advance for the ewe premium in July and the second in September. Tendering procedures for private storage aid were introduced at the beginning of the year.

454.   The outbreak of swine fever in Belgium had repercussions on the market in pigmeat, and supply was significantly down during the first six months of the year. On top of the fall in pig numbers in 1989, this reduction resulted in exceptionally high prices until the end of July. Thereafter, the raising of the animal health restrictions on pigs originating in Belgium at the end of August and the increase in imports from the former German Democratic Republic led to a marked drop in prices from September. Nevertheless, market conditions did not warrant private storage aid, except in Belgium, where it was needed to keep up prices during the outbreak of the disease.[2] The levy and refund were adjusted in line with price trends.

455.   Production of poultrymeat increased by 1.5% in 1990. Balance was restored in the chicken sector, while the situation in the turkey and duck sectors was difficult in the spring and summer, particularly because of an excessive increase in Community supply at the end of 1989 and the beginning of 1990. No support is applied on the internal market for poultrymeat. The measures governing trade with non-member countries have been adapted to the situation on the world market. In June the Council adopted a regulation on marketing standards for poultrymeat.[3]

---

[1]   OJ L 121, 12.5.1990.
[2]   OJ L 67, 15.3.1990; Bull. EC 3-1990, point 1.1.116; OJ L 93, 10.4.1990; Bull. EC 4-1990, point 1.1.97;
       OJ L 120, 11.5.1990; Bull. EC 5-1990, point 1.2.146; OJ L 131, 23.5.1990; Bull. EC 5-1990, point 1.2.147;
       OJ L 141, 2.6.1990, OJ L 152, 16.6.1990; Bull. EC 6-1990, point 1.3.157.
[3]   OJ L 173, 6.7.1990; Bull. EC 6-1990, point 1.3.159.

In the egg sector, after a 4% drop in production in 1989, laying hen numbers are growing again in 1990. In view of the shrinking opportunities on the world market, Community supply has exceeded demand slightly since the spring. Given the continual fall in the price of feedingstuffs, the situation gives no cause for concern and production is expected to increase somewhat in 1991. As regards trade, export refunds have been kept at the same level to reflect the situation on the internal and world markets. Finally, the Council adopted a new Regulation on marketing standards for eggs.[1]

Other work

Approximation of laws

456.   For the approximation of laws on public and animal health, feedingstuffs, plant health products and seeds and propagating material, see 'Harmonization of veterinary and plant health rules' in Chapter III, Section 2 ('Completing the internal market') of this Report.[2]

Agrimonetary measures

457.   By adjusting the green rates applied in the context of the CAP when it made the price decisions for the 1990/91 marketing year, the Council dismantled the remaining monetary gaps between the Member States, thereby respecting the principal disciplines of the European Monetary System (EMS), with the exception of the cereals sector in the Federal Republic of Germany and The Netherlands. In addition, the entry of the lira in the group of currencies held within the 2.25% margin of fluctuation[3] gave rise to the implementation of automatic dismantling; and the readjustment of the green lira rate made it possible to abolish all the Italian monetary compensatory amounts (MCAs). The entry of the pound sterling into the exchange-rate mechanism of the EMS in October[2] entailed a 0.56% revaluation of the ecu, which triggered the automatic dismantling of the green rates. The agrimonetary situation has therefore improved considerably in 1990 and the only gaps remaining are those for certain currencies not held within the narrow margin of the EMS.

---

[1]   OJ L 173, 6.7.1990; Bull. EC 6-1990, point 1.3.160.
[2]   Points 38 to 40.
[3]   Point 38 of this Report.

Food aid for the needy

458.   The Community continued[1] its programme of food aid for the needy.[2] This year about ECU 150 million was shared among the 12 Member States to assist the distribution of foodstuffs through social and charitable associations. However, during the course of the year the German authorities ceased to participate in the operation and the amount allocated to that country was divided among the other Member States involved.

Income aid

459.   In May[3] the Commission amended the detailed implementing rules[4] allowing Member States to introduce systems of direct aid to agricultural incomes in accordance with Council Regulation (EEC) No 768/89.[5] The Netherlands and France have already set up such schemes under conditions which should make it possible to grant income aid to about 60 000 farmers; the Community's contribution could amount to ECU 70 million. The German and Italian authorities have submitted five-year programmes to the Commission.

Competition[6]

460.   The Commission has paid special attention to the aids granted by Member States to their farmers and farming industries. When implementing this policy, it has generally given favourable decisions with respect to aid relating to environmental protection, plant health measures, research and compensation for disasters. The Article 93(2) procedure was initiated against a Belgian measure,[7] two German measures,[8] three Spanish measures,[9] two French measures,[10] and four Italian measures.[11] The procedure was terminated in respect of two Spanish measures.[12] one Italian measure[13] and one

---

[1]   Twenty-third General Report, point 591.
[2]   OJ L 352, 15.12.1987; Twenty-first General Report, point 588.
[3]   OJ L 126, 16.5.1990; Bull. EC 5-1990, point 1.2.141.
[4]   OJ L 371, 20.12.1989; Twenty-third General Report, point 562.
[5]   OJ L 84, 29.3.1989; Twenty-third General Report, point 562.
[6]   For more detailed information, see the *Twentieth Report on Competition Policy (1990)* issued in association with this Report and scheduled to appear in 1991. (Available from the Office for Official Publications.)
[7]   Bull. EC 6-1990, point 1.3.217.
[8]   Bull. EC 5-1990, point 1.2.200; Bull. EC 12-1990.
[9]   Bull. EC 5-1990, point 1.2.209; Bull. EC 6-1990, point 1.2.172; Bull. EC 12-1990.
[10] Bull EC 5-1990, point 1.2.202; Bull. EC 6-1990, point 1.3.218.
[11] Bull. EC 1/2-1990, point 1.1.241; Bull. EC 5-1990, point 1.2.203; Bull. EC 6-1990, point 1.3.219; Bull. EC 10-1990, point 1.3.172.
[12] Bull. EC 6-1990, point 1.3.220; Bull. EC 11-1990, point 1.3.170.
[13] Bull. EC 6-1990, point 1.3.221.

Luxembourgish measure.[1] The Commission sent a negative recommendation to France[2] and also to the United Kingdom.[3]

Farm accountancy data network (FADN)

461.   The FADN handles individual and confidential data on the accounts of agricultural holdings. These are selected by the 12 Member States to represent commercial agriculture in the Community. The sample now includes over 57 000 holdings. The management committee responsible for the general coordination and management of the network held two meetings in 1990, at which it examined the standard results for the 1986/87 to 1988/89 accounting years prior to their publication, as well as the outlook for 1990 on the basis of the available data. A large number of economic analyses were based on FADN data and were generally descriptions of the situation of agricultural holdings, providing a reference base for the CAP and for a knowledge of the sector. The most significant studies were on set-aside, direct income aids and structural aspects of agricultural production. In addition, studies on the definition of economic indicators for agricultural holdings, the economics of oilseed production, the gross margin of businesses and the profitability of various products were carried out by outside consultancies following a call for tenders.

Advisory committees and relations with professional organizations

462.   The advisory committees made up of representatives of the professional farming and consumer organizations, created at Community level, have been kept regularly informed of the application of the CAP. Sixty-five meetings were held, at which the committee members gave their opinions. The Advisory Committee for Cotton, which was set up last year, held its first meetings in 1990 and a new advisory committee was set up for cork.

---

[1]   Bull. EC 6-1990, point 1.3.222.
[2]   Bull. EC 12-1990.
[3]   Bull. EC 10-1990, point 1.3.173.

TABLE 7

The agricultural management and regulatory committees

Committees	From 1 January to 31 December 1990			
	Meetings[1]	Favourable opinion	No opinion	Unfavourable opinion
Management Committee for Cereals	47	633	29	0
Management Committee for Pigmeat	22	41	4	0
Management Committee for Poultrymeat and Eggs	15	61	2	0
Management Committee for Fruit and Vegetables	22	117	7	0
Management Committee for Wine	36	83	1	0
Management Committee for Milk and Milk Products	27	153	37	0
Management Committee for Beef and Veal	32	126	5	0
Management Committee for Sheep and Goats	17	44	17	0
Management Committee for Oils and Fats	25	110	5	0
Management Committee for Sugar	51	133	4	0
Management Committee for Live Plants	6	6	0	0
Management Committee for Products Processed from Fruit and Vegetables	13	48	4	0
Management Committee for Tobacco	10	32	1	0
Management Committee for Hops	3	6	0	0
Management Committee for Flax and Hemp	6	7	0	0
Management Committee for Seeds	6	9	0	0
Management Committee for Dried Fodder	5	8	0	0
Management Committee for Agricultural Income Aids	5	4	1	0
Implementation Committee for Spirit Drinks	8	5	0	0
Joint meetings of management committees[1]	6	3	3	0
EAGGF Committee	18	19	1	0
Standing Committee on Feedingstuffs	6	9	0	0
Standing Veterinary Committee	26	83	1	0
Standing Committee on Seeds and Propagating Material for Agriculture, Horticulture and Forestry	7	11	0	0
Committee on Agricultural Structures and Rural Development	14	116	3	0
Community Committee on the Farm Accountancy Data Network	2	1	0	0
Standing Committee on Agricultural Research	3	1	0	0
Standing Committee on Plant Health	9	20	0	0
Standing Committee on Zootechnics	1	5	0	0
Standing Forestry Committee	8	0	0	0
Ad hoc Committee on the Supplementary Trade Mechanism	0	0	0	0

[1] Except those on trade mechanisms (11 meetings) and agrimonetary questions (13 meetings).

Financing the common agricultural policy: the EAGGF

Guarantee Section

463.   The 1990 budget, adopted on 13 December 1989,[1] provided EAGGF guarantee appropriations amounting to ECU 28 024 million, broken down as follows:

EAGGF Guarantee Section (Titles 1 and 2)	ECU	26 452 million
Set-aside of farmland (part financed by the Guarantee Section)	ECU	70 million
Market organization for fishery products	ECU	32 million
Reimbursement of Member States' expenditure on depreciation of stocks and disposal of butter	ECU	1 470 million
Total	ECU	28 024 million

The figure of ECU 26 452 million includes a provisional appropriation of ECU 21 million to finance anti-fraud measures in the EAGGF Guarantee Section. In addition to the ECU 26 452 million, the monetary reserve in a specific chapter of the budget set aside a further ECU 1 000 million to cover any additional expenditure arising from major and unforeseeable fluctuations in the exchange rate between the US dollar and the ecu compared with the rate used for the budget. This reserve does not count against the agricultural guideline.

In relation to this guideline for maximum agricultural expenditure,[2] covering only Titles 1 and 2 and the share (50%) of the set-aside measure financed by the Guarantee Section, which is fixed at ECU 30 630 million for 1990, the unused margin amounts to ECU 4 108 million.

464.   The preliminary draft budget for 1991, adopted by the Commission on 13 June,[3] was sent to the budgetary authority in the following month.

The breakdown of the appropriations for the Guarantee Section is as follows:

EAGGF Guarantee Section (Subsection B.1)	ECU 31 356 million
Including:	
the part (50%) of the set-aside payments financed by the Guarantee Section (former Article 390)	

[1]   OJ L 24, 29.1.1990; Twenty-third General Report, point 88.
[2]   Twenty-second General Report, point 671.
[3]   Point 988 *et seq.* of this Report

appropriations from the monetary reserve
(ECU 1 000 million) only available under
certain conditions

Other appropriations to which the detailed
rules for Guarantee Section financing apply:

Market organization for fishery products
(Chapter B 2-90)   ECU   29 million

Reimbursement of Member States' expenditure
on depreciation of stocks and disposal of
butter (Chapter B0-10)   ECU   810 million

Total   ECU   32 195 million

At ECU 30 356 million (excluding the monetary reserve), agricultural expenditure is therefore ECU 2 155 million lower than the agricultural guideline of ECU 32 511 million fixed for 1991. The increase in appropriations in relation to 1990 and hence, also, of foreseeable expenditure, can be attributed to three main factors: the amendments to the cereals co-responsibility levy and the detailed rules for the payment of production aid for olive oil; the impact of the decisions on agricultural prices and related measures for 1990/91; the ecu/US dollar rate used for the 1991 budget, which is lower than the rate used for 1990. [1]

465. With respect to the Community's own resources, agricultural levies and sugar sector levies will, according to the preliminary draft budget, yield an estimated ECU 1 218 million and ECU 1 212.7 million, respectively, in 1991.

The proceeds of the co-responsibility levies in the cereals and dairy sectors do not count as own resources but are treated as agricultural market intervention; these are estimated, for 1991, at ECU 934 million for cereals and ECU 313 million for milk and milk products.

Extension of the CAP following German unification

466. Acceleration of the unification of Germany led the Commission to propose a series of transitional measures to ensure the rapid integration of the former East Germany into the Community. In principle the measures are applicable until the end of 1992. [2] As far as agriculture is concerned, the financial consequences of German unification for the EAGGF Guarantee Section can be considered to be negligible in 1990. However, the additional expenditure to be incurred in 1991 as a result of integration could be anywhere between ECU 850 million and ECU 1 350 million.

---

[1]   Bull. EC 10-1990, point 1.3.153.
[2]   Point 24 of this Report.

TABLE 8

EAGGF guarantee appropriations, by sector

million ECU

	1988 expenditure	1989 expenditure	1990 appropriations[1]	Proposed 1990 appropriations[2]
Milk and milk products[3]	5 983.5	5 040.7	4 489	5 063
Cereals and rice[3]	4 511.5	3 340.3	4 611	5 261
Fruit and vegetables, wine, tobacco	3 219.9	3 305.2	3 740	4 370
Beef, sheepmeat, goatmeat and pigmeat	3 985.1	4 142.3	3 730	4 127
Olive oil, oilseeds and protein crops[3]	4 606.1	4 781.0	5 717	6 737
Sugar[3]	2 081.8	1 979.8	2 127	1 885
Other products	708.1	918.6	954	1 046
Refunds on processed products	602.4	552.1	693	715
Monetary compensatory amounts	569.5	364.3	171	245
Impact of account clearance decisions	29.2[4]	− 202.7	token entry	token entry
Other				
Interest payable to Member States following financial reform	37.5	48.5	49	60
Distribution of agricultural products to the needy	65.8	132.9	150	150
Fraud control	—	—	21[5]	21
Rural development activities related to the operation of markets	—	—	—	576
Subtotal for Titles 1 and 2 of budget	26 400.4	24 403.0	26 452	30 256
Set-aside of arable land (50% to be borne by EAGGF Guarantee Section)	—	3.0	70	100
Total financed within guideline	26 400.4	24 406.0	26 522	30 356
Initial appropriations	27 500.0	26 761.0	26 522	30 356
Guideline	27 500.0	28 624.0	30 630	32 511
Fisheries	46.9	24.0	32	29
Depreciation of stocks and disposal of butter	1 240.0	1 442.9	1 470	810
Total	27 678.3	25 872.9	28 024[6]	31 195[6]

[1] Budget.
[2] Preliminary draft budget.
[3] Including refunds for Community food-aid operations.
[4] Balance from the clearance of the accounts for 1985 and previous years.
[5] Provided for in Chapter 100.
[6] Not including the additional ECU 1 000 million set aside in the monetary reserve.

Intensification of fraud control

467. In 1990 the Commission continued and stepped up its efforts to control fraud. Political sensitivity to this problem meant that a number of the measures in the Commission's work programme were able to be implemented, in particular in the field of agriculture.[1]

Guidance Section

468. Since 1 January 1989 funding from the EAGGF Guidance Section has been provided as part of the general scheme of the structural Funds.[2] This is illustrated in Table 9, which shows the breakdown of 1989 appropriations by objective for expenditure qualifying for contributions from this Section, i.e. the adjustment of regions whose development is lagging behind (Objective 1), the adjustment of agricultural structures (Objective 5(a)), and the development of rural areas (Objective 5(b)). The appropriations entered in the 1990 budget[3] totalled ECU 1 700 million for commitments (15.2% of the total for the structural Funds) and ECU 1 651.5 million for payments. However, in the context of a transfer of appropriations within the total amount allocated to the structural Funds, the budget of the EAGGF Guidance Section was increased to ECU 1 821 million. As a result of the definitive adoption of the Community support frameworks for the regions covered by Objectives 1[4] and 5(b),[5] the 1991 draft budget[6] was increased to ECU 2 424 million for commitments and ECU 2 022 million for payments. The commitment appropriations account for 18% of the total for the structural Funds.

The budget for the set-aside scheme,[7] financed equally by both Sections of the EAGGF, will be increased from ECU 140 million in 1990 to ECU 220 million in 1991. As yet there has been no actual expenditure on agricultural income aids,[8] for which the 1990 budget provided ECU 155 million.

Where the Guidance Section of the EAGGF is concerned, the reform of the structural Funds required amendments to the legal basis as regards checks and verifications which, since 1 January 1989, are governed by Regulation (EEC) No 4253/88.[9] Since the new

---

[1] Point 1010 of this Report.
[2] OJ L 185, 15.7.1988; OJ L 374, 31.12.1988; Twenty-second General Report, point 641.
[3] OJ L 24, 29.1.1990; Twenty-third General Report, point 88.
[4] OJ L 370, 19.12.1989; Twenty-third General Report; point 406 of this Report.
[5] Point 432 of this Report.
[6] Point 988 et seq. of this Report.
[7] OJ L 106, 21.4.1988; Twenty-second General Report, point 642.
[8] Point 459 of this Report.
[9] OJ L 374, 31.12.1988; Twenty-second General Report, point 534.

TABLE 9

EAGGF Guidance Section: Summary of 1989 budget implementation
(Commitment appropriations)

million ECU

Type of financing	Total	Objec-tive 1	Objec-tive 5(a)	Objec-tive 5(b)	Transi-tional
Direct	398.937	210.738	161.625	9.619	16.955
Regional	37.322	4.748	6.000	9.619	16.955
General	361.615	205.990	155.625	—	—
Indirect	1 047.616	638.366	354.579	17.237	37.434
Regional	364.362	309.691	—	17.237	37.434
General	683.254	328.675	354.579	—	—
Operational programmes	12.857	12.857	—	—	—
Regional	12.857	12.857	—	—	—
Marketing/processing	—	—	—	—	—
Community initiatives	—	—	—	—	—
Pilot projects, etc. (Article 22, Reg. 797; Article 8, Reg. 4256)	2.581	0.168	—	—	2.413
Global grant					
Total	1 461.991	862.129	516.204	26.856	56.802

provisions are, in the main, identical to those previously in force, particularly Regulation (EEC) No 729/70,[1] the transition from one system to the other posed no difficulties. In particular, Regulation (EEC) No 4253/88[2] provides an adequate basis for carrying out on-the-spot checks, either to ensure that national administrative measures are suitable and effective or to verify doubtful or problem cases.

International provisions

469.   As a result of the political and economic developments in Central and Eastern Europe and, in particular, the events in Romania at the end of 1989 and the beginning of this year, the Community decided to supply, free of charge, certain available agricultural products, namely cereals, beef, butter and olive oil. In January,[3] the Council authorized the supply of the first instalment of products to Romania, the full cost of which was borne by the EAGGF. The supply of a second instalment of equal quantities

---

[1]   OJ L 94, 28.4.1970.
[2]   OJ L 374, 31.12.1988; Twenty-second General Report, point 534.
[3]   OJ L 31, 2.2.1990; Bull. EC 1/2-1990, point 1.2.19.

at the same cost was decided on a month later.[1] In February[2] a new emergency operation[3] in favour of Poland was also decided. These operations were carried out during 1990 and the products thus supplied were sold on the local markets, thereby creating counterpart funds in local currency. These funds are to be used for projects to restructure local agriculture; the operation is under way in Poland and is currently being negotiated with Romania. In line with the decisions taken at the Rome European Council,[4] food-aid operations in favour of the countries of Central and Eastern Europe will be intensified in 1991 and proposals aimed at facilitating their implementation were adopted by the Commission in December.[5]

Common provisions

470.   On 5 September the Commission adopted, for transmission to the Council and Parliament, the 19th financial report (1990) on the activities of the EAGGF.[5]

---

[1]   OJ L 48, 24.2.1990; Bull. EC 1/2-1990, point 1.2.20.
[2]   OJ L 48, 24.2.1990; Bull. EC 1/2-1990, point 1.2.18.
[3]   OJ L 216, 27.7.1990; Twenty-third General Report, point 592.
[4]   Bull. EC 12-1990.
[5]   Bull. EC 9-1990, point 1.2.160.

Section 14

Fisheries

Priority activities and objectives

471.   In view of the importance of the fisheries sector and related activities for the Mediterranean coastal regions, the Commission drew up a discussion paper on the outline of a common fisheries system in the Mediterranean[1] with a view to implementing a common policy of conservation and management of fish stocks taking into account the specific conditions in that area. The approach involves two main stages: the introduction in the waters of the Member States concerned of a common management model based on control of fishing effort via the establishment of a system controlling access to stocks and on the use of gear, and the formulation of an overall policy of cooperation between all the Mediterranean coastal and high-sea fishery countries.

On 28 November, the Commission also adopted a communication on the common fisheries policy in which it presented an overall analysis of the fisheries and aquaculture sectors indicating the current major problems and the general guidelines for future policy.[2] The Commission, confronted with a marked imbalance between available stocks and existing fishing capacity, the high degree of dependence of third countries on access to Community waters and the structural shortcomings of the Community market in fishery products, advocates better management of and more efficient controls on fishing activities, in particular a closer synergy between the various aspects of the common fisheries policy and possible recourse to other structural instruments. In November the Parliament also expressed an opinion on conservation measures in the fisheries sector.[3]

As regards the fisheries structures, the improvement of which is vital to development of the common fisheries policy, the Commission proposed an amendment to Regulation (EEC) No 4028/86 on Community measures in this field, thereby giving priority to exploratory fishing, the adjustment of capacity, temporary joint ventures and the promotion of fishery products. In addition, the Community support frameworks for the Member States have been adapted for the purposes of applying the new Regulation on the processing and marketing of fishery and aquaculture products.

---

[1]   Bull. EC 7/8-1990, point 1.3.259.
[2]   Bull. EC 11-1990, point 1.3.171.
[3]   OJ C 324, 24.12.1990; Bull. EC 11-1990, point 1.3.173.

A number of regulations were adopted in December fixing the fishing opportunities for 1991 for vessels of the Member States in the Community fishing zone and in Norwegian, Swedish, Faeroese and Greenland waters and the waters covered by the Northwest Atlantic Fisheries Organization (NAFO).

In addition, the Commission continued and developed its policy of informing and consulting the European Parliament, for which it organized two seminars, and the professional organizations, particularly at the meetings of the Advisory Committee on Fisheries.

Internal resources and policy on conservation and monitoring

Internal measures

Community measures

472.   On 22 March[1] and 27[2] and 29[3] June the Council amended Regulation (EEC) No 4047/89[4] fixing, for certain fish stocks and groups of fish stocks, the total allowable catches (TACs) for 1990, the share of these available to the Community, the allocation of that share among the Member States and certain conditions under which the quotas may be fished. In December it fixed the TACs and quotas for 1991.[5] As required by the Act of Accession, in December the Council also adopted regulations determining certain fishing opportunities in 1991 for vessels of the Member States fishing in Spanish and Portuguese waters and for Spanish and Portuguese vessels fishing in the waters of the other Member States.[5]

473.   On 11 June[6] the Council amended Regulation (EEC) No 2245/85 laying down certain technical measures for the conservation of fishery resources in the Antarctic.[7] In February it laid down similar measures for the Regulatory Area of the Northwest Atlantic Fisheries Organization (NAFO).[8] In addition, the Commission presented to the Council a proposal[9] for the tenth amendment to Regulation (EEC) No 3094/86 laying down certain technical measures for the conservation of fishery resources.[10]

---

[1]   OJ L 82, 29.3.1990; Bull. EC 3-1990, point 1.1.164; Commission proposal: Bull. EC 1/2-1990, point 1.1.243.
[2]   OJ L 171, 4.7.1990; Bull. EC 6-1990, point 1.3.223; Commission proposal: Bull. EC 6-1990, point 1.3.223.
[3]   OJ L 172, 5.7.1990; Bull. EC 6-1990, point 1.3.224.
[4]   OJ L 389, 30.12.1990; Twenty-third General Report, point 599.
[5]   Bull. EC 12-1990.
[6]   OJ L 151, 15.6.1990; Bull. EC 6-1990, point 1.3.225; Commission proposal: Bull. EC 5-1990, point 1.2.207.
[7]   OJ L 210, 7.8.1985; Nineteenth General Report, point 592.
[8]   OJ L 36, 8.2.1990; Bull. EC 1/2-1990, point 1.1.246.
[9]   Bull. EC 7/8-1990, point 1.3.261.
[10]   OJ L 288, 11.10.1986; Twentieth General Report, point 662.

474. The Scientific and Technical Committee for Fisheries held meetings in Brussels in May and September and drew up its 16th and 17th reports.

National measures

475. The Commission enquired into 90 national conservation measures, of which 85 were notified by the Member States, while the others were examined on the Commission's initiative; 73 measures were the subject of comments or were approved by the Commission, and 17 are still under examination.

Monitoring

476. Monitoring compliance with the TACs and quotas in Community, non-member country and international waters led to the closing of 75 fisheries during the year following exhaustion of a TAC or quota. In December, the Commission adopted two regulations remedying the prejudice caused by the halting of fishing for certain species by vessels flying the flag of a Member State in 1989.[1] A number of preliminary infringement procedures relating to overfishing were initiated. Procedures relating to overfishing in previous years (from 1985 to 1988) were continued in 1990.[2] The Commission also monitored observance of conservation measures, fisheries agreements with non-member countries and international agreements. At the Commission's request, irregularities discovered in certain Member States were the subject of administrative inquiries, with the participation of Commission departments. Steps were taken to remedy the shortcomings which were ascertained. The Community continued its surveillance in the Regulatory Area of the Northwest Atlantic Fisheries Organization (NAFO). With a view to coordinating surveillance in that Area, certain principles for collaboration were established with the Canadian authorities. Within the framework of Council Decision 89/631/EEC,[3] the Commission adopted, on 18 December, its first decision on the eligibility of programmes presented by the Member States for the acquisition and improvement of means of surveillance and inspection.[4] In May, it also adopted a proposal for a regulation on the checks and penalties applicable under the common agricultural and fisheries policies.[5]

---

[1] OJ L 350, 14.12.1990; Bull. EC 12-1990.
[2] For further information, see the Eighth Annual Report to Parliament on Commission monitoring of the application of Community law (1990).
[3] OJ L 364, 14.12.1989; Twenty-third General Report, point 598.
[4] Bull. EC 12-1990.
[5] Point 467 of this Report.

External resources

477.   On 25 April[1] and 24 July,[2] the Council adopted regulations on the conclusion of fisheries agreements with Sierra Leone and Cape Verde.

In addition, the Commission transmitted to the Council proposals concerning the conclusion of such agreements with Tanzania[3] and Côte d'Ivoire[4] in December. In October, the Council also authorized the Commission to open negotiations with a view to concluding agreements with Argentina, Chile, Colombia, Mexico, Peru and Uruguay.[5]

New protocols to the fisheries agreements with Guinea-Bissau,[6] Equatorial Guinea,[7] Mozambique,[8] Guinea,[9] Greenland,[10] the Seychelles,[11] the Gambia[12] and Angola were also concluded. In addition, the Council decided on the provisional application of similar protocols with Senegal,[13] Morocco[14] and Mauritania.[15]

478.   The Joint Committees responsible for the management of the fisheries agreements with Mozambique, Madagascar and Guinea met in October and November. The Joint Committee responsible for the management of the agreement with Morocco met twice, in Brussels in January and in Rabat in March.

479.   Bilateral consultations on fishing rights and conditions for 1991 were followed by the conclusion of agreements with Sweden on 28 November, with the Faeroes on 3 December and with Norway on 7 December.

---

1   OJ L 125, 15.5.1990; Bull. EC 4-1990, point 1.1.145; Commission proposal: OJ C 55, 7.3.1990.
2   OJ L 212, 9.8.1990; Bull. EC 7/8-1990, point 1.3.263; Commission proposal: OJ C 115, 9.5.1990.
3   OJ L 379, 31.12.1990; Bull. EC 12-1990; Commission proposal: OJ C 187, 27.7.1990; Bull. EC 6-1990, point 1.3.228.
4   OJ L 379, 31.12.1990; Bull. EC 12-1990; Commission proposal: OJ C 220, 4.9.1990; Bull. EC 7/8-1990, point 1.3.271.
5   Bull. EC 10-1990, point 1.3.180; Commission proposal: Bull. EC 7/8-1990, point 1.3.270.
6   OJ L 125, 15.5.1990; Bull. EC 4-1990, point 1.1.143; basic agreement: OJ L 226, 29.8.1980; Fourteenth General Report, point 394.
7   OJ L 125, 15.5.1990; Bull. EC 4-1990, point 1.1.144; basic agreement: OJ L 188, 16.10.1984; Eighteenth General Report, point 466.
8   OJ L 140, 1.6.1990; Bull. EC 5-1990, point 1.2.209; basic agreement: OJ L 98, 10.4.1987; Twentieth General Report, point 671.
9   OJ L 212, 9.8.1990; Bull. EC 7/8-1990, point 1.3.264; basic agreement: OJ L 111, 27.4.1983; Seventeenth General Report, point 474.
10   OJ L 252, 15.9.1990; Bull. EC 7/8-1990, point 1.3.262; basic agreement: OJ L 29, 1.2.1985; Nineteenth General Report, point 596.
11   OJ L 306, 6.11.1990; Bull. EC 10-1990, point 1.3.179.
12   Bull. EC 12-1990.
13   OJ L 208, 7.8.1990; Bull. EC 7/8-1990, point 1.3.266.
14   OJ L 208, 7.8.1990; Bull. EC 7/8-1990, point 1.3.268.
15   OJ L 334, 30.11.1990; Bull. EC 11-1990, point 1.3.174.

480.   In December, the Council agreed on how the 1991 fishing quotas in Norwegian, Faeroese and Swedish waters should be shared out among the Member States and adopted regulations laying down for 1991 the conservation measures applicable to vessels flying the flag of Norway, the Faeroes or Sweden fishing in the Community zone.[1] In May[2] and June[3] it had amended certain provisions adopted in December 1989 with regard to conservation measures and the management of stocks applicable to vessels registered in the Faeroes, and the allocation of additional catch quotas between the Member States for vessels fishing in Swedish waters.[4]

481.   Also in December,[1] the Council decided how the quotas agreed with Greenland in the Protocol on conditions relating to fishing should be shared out among the Member States.[5] On the same day it agreed on the 1991 fishing levels for Community vessels operating in the Regulatory Area of the Northwest Atlantic Fisheries Organization (NAFO).[1] The quotas for 1990[6] were amended in May[2] and June[7] for the Greenland waters and in October for the area covered by the NAFO convention.[8]

482.   On 11 September the European Parliament adopted a resolution dealing with matters relating to fisheries agreements and external aspects of the management of stocks.[9]

483.   The Community participated, either as a member or as an observer, in the work of a number of international fisheries organizations: the sixth technical consultation on the Balearic Islands and the Golfe du Lion of the General Fisheries Council for the Mediterranean (OGPM), held from 28 May to 2 June; the seventh session of the North Atlantic Salmon Conservation Organization, held from 12 to 15 June; the 47th meeting of the Inter-American Tropical Tuna Commission, held on 25 and 26 June; the 42nd meeting of the International Whaling Commission, held from 2 to 6 July; the 11th meeting of the Committee for the Management of Indian Ocean Tuna, held from 9 to 12 July;[10] the 12th annual session of the Northwest Atlantic Fisheries Organization, held from 10 to 14 September,[11] and the meetings of the scientific council of NAFO held in June and September; the 16th annual session of the International Baltic Sea

---

[1]   Bull. EC 12-1990.
[2]   OJ L 133, 24.5.1990; Bull. EC 5-1990, point 1.2.205; Commission proposal: Bull. EC 4-1990, point 1.1.142.
[3]   OJ L 155, 21.6.1990; Bull. EC 6-1990, point 1.3.229; Commission proposal: Bull. EC 5-1990, point 1.2.206.
[4]   OJ L 389, 30.12.1989; Twenty-third General Report, point 608.
[5]   Point 477 of this Report.
[6]   OJ L 389, 30.12.1989; Twenty-third General Report, point 609.
[7]   OJ L 171, 4.7.1990; Bull. EC 6-1990, point 1.3.230; Commission proposal: Bull. EC 6-1990, point 1.3.230.
[8]   OJ L 281, 12.10.1990; Bull. EC 10-1990, point 1.3.175; Commission proposal: Bull. EC 7/8-1990, point 1.3.272.
[9]   OJ C 260, 15.10.1990; Bull. EC 9-1990, point 1.2.173.
[10]   Bull. EC 7/8-1990, point 1.3.274.
[11]   Bull. EC 9-1990, point 1.2.176.

Fishery Commission, held from 17 to 21 September;[1] the statutory session of the International Council for the Exploration of the Sea, held from 3 to 9 October;[2] the ninth meeting of the Commission for the Conservation of Antarctic Marine Living Resources, held from 22 October to 2 November;[3] the 12th ordinary session of the Commission for the International Convention on the Conservation of Atlantic Tunas, held in Madrid from 5 to 9 November,[4] and the seventh special session of that Commission, held from 12 to 16 November; and the ninth annual session of the Northeast Atlantic Fisheries Commission, held from 21 to 23 November.[5] The cooperation agreement between the latter organization and the Community[6] was extended by a new exchange of letters.[7] In December, the Commission also adopted a proposal[8] for a regulation on the application of the monitoring and inspection arrangements in accordance with the Convention on the Conservation of Antarctic Marine Living Resources.[9]

Market organization

484.   To improve and simplify the arrangements for communication of information for the purposes of the common organization of the market in fisheries, the Commission adopted, on 18 April, a regulation mainly intended to bring together various provisions in force.[10]

485.   In the context of market management, the Commission adopted a number of regulations on the grant of compensation to producers' organizations in respect of tuna delivered to the canning industry during certain periods of 1988 and 1989.[11]

486.   In view of the crisis on the Community market for squid, the Commission adopted two regulations granting private storage aid to producers for two species (*Loligo patagonica* and *Illex argentinus*).[12] In addition, to prevent serious market disturbances,

---

[1]   Bull. EC 9-1990, point 1.2.177.
[2]   Bull. EC 10-1990, point 1.3.182.
[3]   Bull. EC 11-1990, point 1.3.175.
[4]   Bull. EC 11-1990, point 1.3.176.
[5]   Bull. EC 11-1990, point 1.3.177.
[6]   OJ L 149, 10.6.1987; Twenty-first General Report, point 609.
[7]   Bull. EC 7/8-1990, point 1.3.273.
[8]   Bull. EC 12-1990; Commission proposal; Bull. EC 10-1990, point 1.3.181.
[9]   OJ L 252, 5.9.1981; Fifteenth General Report, point 456.
[10] OJ L 111, 1.5.1990; Bull. EC 4-1990, point 1.1.148.
[11] OJ L 76, 22.3.1990; Bull. EC 3-1990, points 1.1.169 and 1.1.170; OJ L 112, 3.5.1990; Bull. EC 5-1990, point 1.2.212; OJ L 188, 20.7.1990; Bull. EC 7/8-1990, point 1.3.277.
[12] OJ L 173, 6.7.1990; Bull. EC 7/8-1990, point 1.3.275.

the Commission adopted, on 5 July, a regulation making imports of certain frozen squid subject to observance of the reference price.[1]

487. In December, in the context of the Community's market supply policy, the Council opened autonomous tariff quotas for certain fishery products so that the processing industries could obtain supplies at competitive prices without harming the interests of Community fishermen.[2]

488. On 20 November, the Council set the guide prices for fishery products for 1991.[3] On 19 December, the Commission adopted implementing provisions for these prices.[4] In March,[5] it had amended the provisions adopted in December 1989 with regard to products subject to the supplementary trade mechanism.[6]

Structural policy

489. Observing the alarming situation as regards certain stocks, and that the conditions of access to third-country waters are becoming increasingly difficult, the Commission adopted, on 25 July,[7] a proposal for an amendment to Regulation (EEC) No 4026/86 on Community measures to improve and adapt structures in the fisheries and aquaculture sector.[8] The Commission proposes to intensify support measures with a view to facilitating the adaptation of structural policy to the requirements of the common policy, particularly as regards the conservation of stocks and the reorientation of the activities of those undertakings most affected by the reduction of the fishing effort. In addition, the proposal provides in particular for small-scale fisheries and the extension of the measures concerning the search for new markets to cover certain aquaculture products and the application of the amended Regulation to fishing vessels in the Canary Islands and Ceuta and Melilla. The proposal, on which the Parliament[9] and the Economic and Social Committee[10] gave their opinions in November and in December, was agreed in principle by the Council in December.[11]

---

[1] OJ L 173, 6.7.1990; Bull. EC 7/8-1990, point 1.3.276.
[2] OJ L 376, 31.12.1990; Bull. EC 12-1990.
[3] OJ L 346, 11.12.1990; Bull. EC 11-1990, point 1.3.172.
[4] OJ L 371, 31.12.1990; Bull. EC 12-1990.
[5] OJ L 59, 8.3.1990; Bull. EC 3-1990, point 1.1.168.
[6] OJ L 385, 30.12.1989; Twenty-third General Report, point 615.
[7] OJ C 243, 28.9.1990; Bull. EC 7/8-1990, point 1.3.260.
[8] OJ L 376, 31.12.1986; Twentieth General Report, point 684.
[9] OJ C 19, 28.1.1991; Bull. EC 12-1990.
[10] Bull. EC 11-1990, point 1.3.179.
[11] Bull. EC 12-1990.

490.   In the context of Regulation (EEC) No 4028/86,[1] the Commission granted, for the 1990 budget year, total aid of about ECU 117.3 million to 797 projects for the construction and modernization of fishing vessels and 265 projects for aquaculture facilities and artificial reefs.[2] In addition, it granted total aid of about ECU 4.824 million to 22 projects concerning facilities for fishing ports in 1990. In the context of the exploratory fishing scheme provided for by the same Regulation, the Commission granted incentive premiums in respect of 16 projects submitted by Spain, The Netherlands, France, Ireland, Portugal and Italy for a total amount of approximately ECU 3.9 million and, with regard to joint ventures, it approved aid of ECU 1.1 million to three projects. In June, the Commission also approved the specific programmes concerning the provision of facilities at fishing ports submitted by the United Kingdom, Ireland, Greece and Portugal (Azores and Madeira).[3]

On 14 May the Commission laid down the maximum total amount of eligible expenditure by the Member States on measures to adjust capacity. This was updated by a decision of 29 November to stand at ECU 99.8 million.

By way of specific measures under Regulation (EEC) No 4028/86,[4] the Commission decided, on 13 June, to grant aid of ECU 0.74 million for the establishment of data media for the compilation of fishing vessel registers in Ireland and Greece.[5] It also granted financial assistance totalling ECU 0.5 million to promotion campaigns for fishery products in The Netherlands and Ireland.

491.   As new Regulation (EEC) No 4042/89[6] provides for the possibility, until 31 December 1990, of submitting projects under Regulation (EEC) No 355/77 on common measures to improve the conditions under which agricultural and fishery products are processed and marketed,[7] the Commission granted aid totalling ECU 52.117 million to 170 projects relating to the processing and marketing of fishery products.[8]

492.   Within the framework of Regulation (EEC) No 4042/89,[6] the Commission adopted, on 17 December, the draft Community support frameworks for each Member State, providing for Community assistance totalling ECU 157 million for 1991-93.[9]

---

[1]   OJ L 376, 31.12.1986; Twentieth General Report, point 684.
[2]   OJ C 123, 19.5.1990; Bull. EC 5-1990, point 1.2.213; Bull. EC 6-1990, point 1.3.233; Bull. EC 10-1990, point 1.3.187.
[3]   OJ L 180, 13.7.1990; Bull. EC 6-1990, point 1.3.232.
[4]   OJ L 376, 31.12.1986; Twentieth General Report, point 684.
[5]   OJ L 162, 28.6.1990; Bull. EC 6-1990, point 1.3.231.
[6]   OJ L 388, 30.12.1989; Twenty-third General Report, point 618.
[7]   OJ L 51, 23.2.1977; Eleventh General Report, point 354.
[8]   Bull. EC 6-1990, point 1.3.234.
[9]   Bull. EC 12-1990.

The European Parliament gave its opinion on the fisheries and aquaculture structures when it adopted two resolutions in January[1] and December.[2]

493.   Under Council Regulation (EEC) No 3252/87 on the coordination and promotion of research in the fisheries sector,[3] the Commission, following up the call for proposals published in December 1989,[4] selected 38 projects to qualify for financial assistance totalling ECU 8.2 million (shared-cost research contracts). With regard to coordination measures, to encourage the exchange of research workers, the Commission awarded a sectoral grant and a research allocation and organized a visit to a Danish research centre by a group of young European research workers. It decided to approve the part-financing of seven conferences and five workshops as well as the publication of the results of two research projects, at a total cost of ECU 0.235 million. Several meetings of the four sectoral working parties set up in 1989[5] were held, chiefly with a view to drawing up an overall report on the state of research in the fisheries and aquaculture sector in the Member States.

494.   As required by Articles 92 and 93 of the Treaty, the Member States notified the Commission of 12 draft national aid schemes in the fisheries and aquaculture sector. The Commission also examined seven schemes which had not been notified. It took 17 final decisions, 12 of which were in respect of schemes notified in 1989 or 1988. The Commission raised no objection to 11 schemes. However, it decided to initiate the Article 93(2) scrutiny procedure in respect of three schemes. It issued a decision finding against schemes notified by Spain. Lastly, it decided to terminate the procedure in respect of three notified schemes.

---

[1]   OJ C 38, 19.2.1990; Bull. EC 1/2-1990, point 1.1.242.
[2]   OJ C 19, 28.1.1991; Bull. EC 12-1990.
[3]   OJ L 314, 4.11.1987; Twenty-first General Report, point 620.
[4]   OJ C 313, 13.12.1989; Twenty-third General Report, point 619.
[5]   Twenty-third General Report, point 619.

Section 15

Environment

Priority activities and objectives

495.   At its June meeting in Dublin the European Council agreed on the need for a more determined and systematic approach to environmental management in the Community. [1] In its statement it called for action by the Community and its Member States to be developed on a coordinated basis in keeping with the principles of sustainable development and giving precedence to preventive measures. The European Council also defined the areas of activity to which priority should be given, thereby determining the direction of Community environment policy for the years ahead.

Against this background, and with the objective of establishing a fifth environmental action programme in 1991, the Commission and the Council paid particular attention to the opportunities offered by greater use of economic and fiscal instruments in the environment sector.

Appreciable progress was also made in the legislative field, including the adoption of a Regulation establishing the European Environment Agency and the Directive on the freedom of access to information. The Commission also expressed its desire for more effective implementation of existing Community legislation.

At the international level, the Community and its Member States played an important role in the efforts to find solutions to global problems such as world climate change and the destruction of tropical forests.

---

[1]   Bull. EC 6-1990, point I.36.

Horizontal measures

Implementation of Community law[1]

496. The Commission continued to monitor the proper application of Community environment legislation. In an effort to improve communications with the national administrations it held numerous meetings to discuss the various aspects of proceedings in progress and cases which were not yet the subject of a Commission decision. It also proposed to the Council that national reporting on the implementation of existing Community Directives should be standardized and rationalized.[2] Parliament[3] and the Economic and Social Committee[4] delivered their opinions on the proposal in December. Parliament also expressed its concern on this matter in a resolution adopted in February.[5]

Taking the environment into account in other policies

497. Taking environmental protection requirements into account in the other policies is an obligation that arises out of Article 130e of the EEC Treaty. The Commission is discharging this obligation in the context of its structural activities by insisting that applications for part-financing submitted under the reform of the Funds comply with the Community's environmental policy and contain the information needed to verify such compliance. The Community's Envireg[6] initiative is also designed to help solve certain environmental problems in eligible regions (chiefly coastal areas). In addition, the aid arrangements for farmers who undertake to introduce or retain agricultural production practices that are compatible with the need to protect the environment[7] continued to be applied; since the introduction of these arrangements in June 1987, 33 programmes have been deemed eligible for assistance by a Community decision. As at 31 December 1989, 2.3 million ha had been designated as areas which are sensitive as regards protection of the environment and approximately 18% of that area had been used for farming practices compatible with environmental requirements. Some 34 000 farmers had received a premium amounting on average to ECU 111 per hectare per year.

---

[1] For further details, see the eighth annual report from the Commission to Parliament on monitoring the application of Community law (1990).
[2] OJ C 214, 29.8.1990; Bull. EC 7/8-1990, point 1.3.147.
[3] OJ C 19, 28.1.1991; Bull. EC 12-1990.
[4] Bull. EC 12-1990.
[5] OJ C 68, 19.3.1990; Bull. EC 1/2-1990, point 1.1.133.
[6] Point 407 of this Report.
[7] OJ L 93, 30.3.1985; Nineteenth General Report, point 548; OJ L 167, 26.6.1987; Twenty-first General Report, point 553.

In February,[1] Parliament invited the Commission to report to it on the action taken in response to its 1986 resolution on agriculture and the environment.[2]

498.   In July, the Commission, for its part, adopted a proposal for a Regulation on the introduction and maintenance of agricultural production methods compatible with the requirements of the protection of the environment and the maintenance of the country-side.[3]

499.   On 19 September the Economic and Social Committee adopted an own-initiative opinion on environmental policy and the single European market,[4] following up its 1989 opinion on environmental policy,[5] a fundamental aspect of economic and social development.

500.   In July Parliament adopted a resolution on the measures needed to protect the environment from potential damage caused by mass tourism,[6] as part of European Tourism Year.[7]

Economic aspects and employment

501.   A group of national experts, set up at the request of the Council and chaired by a Commission representative, examined the scope for greater use of economic and fiscal instruments in the context of environment policy. Three conclusions emerge from its report, namely that the use of economic incentives and market mechanisms to attain environment policy objectives is consistent with the philosophy underlying the internal market; there is a need at European level to develop economic and fiscal instruments which can contribute to environmental protection; and it is particularly important to take environmental considerations into account in the harmonization of indirect taxation. This report also showed that, in the long run, the introduction of environment levies and taxes could generate considerable resources at national level.

In conclusions adopted in October,[8] the Council also expressed the wish that such instruments should be introduced in support of the current rules. It was agreed that it would be appropriate to examine the possibility of Community action in this field, specifying the areas where particular attention was warranted. In December the Com-

---

[1]   OJ C 68, 19.3.1990; Bull. EC 1/2-1990, point 1.1.131.
[2]   OJ C 68, 24.3.1986.
[3]   Point 435 of this Report.
[4]   Bull. EC 9-1990, point 1.2.98.
[5]   OJ C 56, 7.3.1990; Twenty-third General Report, point 500.
[6]   OJ C 233, 17.9.1990; Bull. EC 7/8-1990, point 1.3.145.
[7]   Point 245 of this Report.
[8]   Bull. EC 10-1990, point 1.3.78.

mission submitted to the Council a working paper[1] on policy options for a Community objective for the stabilization of CO_2 in which it sets out economic and fiscal measures to limit the energy consumption which causes this type of pollution.

Public awareness, information and training

502.   On 7 May the Council adopted Regulation (EEC) No 1210/90 on the establishment of the European Environment Agency and the European environment monitoring and information network.[2] However, in the absence of a decision on its seat, the Agency has been unable to start work. In June, Parliament called for the seat of the Agency to be decided without delay.[3]

503.   On 22 March the Council extended until the end of 1990[4] the Corine programme on an experimental project for gathering, coordinating and ensuring the consistency of information on the state of the environment and natural resources in the Community.[5]

504.   On 7 June the Council adopted Directive 90/313/EEC on the freedom of access to information on the environment.[6] The purpose of this Directive is to guarantee freedom of access to, and the dissemination of, information on the environment held by public authorities and to lay down the terms and conditions on which such information is to be made accessible.

505.   On 28 November, the Commission adopted a proposal for a Regulation on the award of a Community environmental label for identifying products which are least harmful to and have the lowest overall impact on the environment.[7]

506.   The Commission sent the Council a proposal for a decision adopting a four-year programme (1990-93) for the regular compilation of official statistics on the environment.[8]

---

[1]   Bull. EC 12-1990.
[2]   OJ L 120, 11.5.1990; Bull. EC 5-1990, point 1.2.115; Commission proposal: OJ C 217, 23.8.1989; Twenty-third General Report, point 502; Bull. EC 3-1990, point 1.1.77.
[3]   OJ C 175, 16.7.1990; Bull. EC 6-1990, point 1.3.115.
[4]   OJ L 81, 28.3.1990; Bull. EC 3-1990, point 1.1.88; Commission proposal: OJ C 269, 21.10.1989; Twenty-third General Report, point 503; OJ C 101, 21.4.1990; Bull. EC 3-1990, point 1.1.88.
[5]   OJ L 176, 6.7.1985; Nineteenth General Report, point 515.
[6]   OJ L 158, 23.6.1990; Bull. EC 6-1990, point 1.3.125; Commission proposal: OJ C 335, 30.12.1988; Twenty-second General Report, point 555; OJ C 102, 24.4.1990; Bull. EC 3-1990, point 1.1.89.
[7]   Bull. EC 11-1990, point 1.3.88.
[8]   Point 976 of this Report.

507.   The prize-giving for the 1990 'Enterprise and environment' competition was held in Paris on 24 April.[1]

International cooperation

508.   The Community continued to take part in the work of the United Nations Environment Programme (UNEP), whose governing council held a special session in August.[2] From 14 to 16 May the Commission took part in the Bergen Conference on the Environment,[3] which culminated in the adoption of a declaration on sustainable development, and in the first meeting of the working party preparing the United Nations Conference on Environment and Development. In addition, the Council authorized the Commission to take part in the negotiations within the Economic Commission for Europe on the outline agreement on transfrontier environmental impact assessment.[4]

509.   Cooperation with the countries of Central and Eastern Europe was stepped up during the year. The first conference of environment ministers from these countries and from the Member States was held in Dublin on 16 June, and was attended by the Commission.[5] This conference lent fresh momentum to the cooperation between both sides. Substantial financial support was granted to Poland, Hungary, Czechoslovakia and the former German Democratic Republic under the Phare programme.[6] In agreement with the governments concerned, the Commission took steps to ensure that the purpose of the projects funded was not only to bring about a direct improvement in the environmental situation but also to pave the way for a coherent policy in this area. The Commission matched the funding contributed by the United States for the establishment of the Regional Centre for the Environment, inaugurated in Budapest in September. Furthermore, with the Council's authorization,[7] the Commission negotiated and signed the Convention on the International Commission for the Protection of the Elbe[8] with the Federal Republic of Germany and Czechoslovakia. The Commission was also instructed by the Council[7] to take part in the pan-European Conference on the Protection of Forests in Europe,[9] one of the aims of which was to increase awareness in the countries of Central and Eastern Europe of the need to protect forestry resources.

510.   Contacts with the EFTA countries were stepped up in the framework of the negotiations on the creation of a European economic area, which include environmental

---

[1]   Bull. EC 4-1990, point 1.1.82.
[2]   Point 858 of this Report.
[3]   Bull. EC 5-1990, point 1.2.123.
[4]   Bull. EC 9-1990, point 1.2.99; Commission proposal; Twenty-third General Report, point 511.
[5]   Bull. EC 6-1990, point 1.3.114.
[6]   Point 669 of this Report.
[7]   Bull. EC 9-1990, point 1.2.95; Commission proposal; Bull. EC 7/8-1990, point 1.3.142.
[8]   Bull. EC 10-1990, point 1.3.89.
[9]   Bull. EC 12-1990.

issues.[1] The second EEC-EFTA Ministerial Conference on the Environment,[2] which was held in November in Geneva, enabled participants, including the Commission, jointly to prepare their negotiating position concerning the reduction and stabilization of CO_2 emissions prior to the World Climate Conference.[3] In the annual high-level talks with the United States[4] a consensus was reached on most of the issues that are currently the subject of international negotiations and on the desirability of practical cooperation between the two parties on chemicals and biotechnology.

511.   The Community, represented by the Presidency of the Council and by the Commission, took part in the Third International Conference on the Protection of the North Sea held in The Hague on 7 and 8 March;[5] the Commission undertook to translate the main decisions of this conference into proposals for legally binding measures. Parliament adopted a resolution on the Commission's statement in April.[6] The Conference on environmental management and protection in the Mediterranean, which brought together 17 Mediterranean countries at the Commission's invitation in April,[7] ended in the adoption of the Nicosia Charter setting out a priority programme and a precise timetable. Also in April the Commission took part in the forum on international environment law in Sienna.[8] In September it signed the declaration adopted at the end of the Conference on the Baltic Sea held in Ronneby, Sweden,[9] which proposes a series of measures to reduce pollution in the Baltic. The Commission also took part in the conference on the Mediterranean[10] held in Palma de Mallorca as part of the Conference on Security and Cooperation in Europe, the sixth ministerial conference of the environment ministers of the member countries of the Council of Europe in October in Brussels,[11] and, in November, the eighth session of the executive body of the Geneva Convention on Transboundary Air Pollution.

512.   In March the Council decided to conclude an agreement on cooperation on management of water resources in the Danube basin.[12]

---

1   Point 688 of this Report.
2   Bull. EC 11-1990, point 1.3.90.
3   Point 537 of this Report.
4   Bull. EC 9-1990, point 1.2.93.
5   Bull. EC 3-1990, point 1.1.79.
6   OJ C 113, 7.5.1990; Bull. EC 4-1990, point 1.1.75.
7   Bull. EC 4-1990, point 1.1.76.
8   Bull. EC 4-1990, point 1.1.83.
9   Bull. EC 9-1990, point 1.2.87.
10   Point 870 of this Report.
11   Bull. EC 10-1990, point 1.3.93.
12   OJ L 90, 5.4.1990; Bull. EC 3-1990, point 1.1.80; Commission proposal: OJ C 98, 19.4.1989; Twenty-third General Report, point 511.

513.   On 17 October the Commission signed the cooperation agreement for the protection of the North-east Atlantic against accidental pollution,[1] which the Council had
authorized it to negotiate.[2] In November and December, the Council adopted Directives
for the negotiation of an international convention on oil pollution preparedness and
response[3] and of an agreement on the conservation of the white stork.[4]

Prevention and reduction of pollution and nuisances

Protection of the aquatic environment

514.   On 27 July the Council amended Annex II[5] to Directive 86/280/EEC on limit
values and quality objectives for discharges of certain dangerous substances.[6]

515.   In response to Parliament's opinion,[7] on 24 October the Commission amended[8]
its proposal for a Directive concerning municipal waste water treatment,[9] on which the
Economic and Social Committee had delivered an opinion in April.[10]

516.   On 19 June the Council adopted a resolution on the prevention of accidents
causing marine pollution.[11] Parliament also expressed its concern on several occasions
about marine pollution due to accidental or other causes.[12] The Commission was also
called upon to give technical advice in two cases of accidental pollution.

517.   On 2 February the Commission adopted a proposal[13] amending Council Directive
76/464/EEC on pollution caused by certain dangerous substances discharged into the
aquatic environment,[14] with a view to setting limit values and quality objectives.
Opinions on this proposal were delivered by the Economic and Social Committee in

---

[1]   Bull. EC 10-1990, point 1.3.79.
[2]   Bull. EC 10-1990, point 1.3.79; Commission proposal: Bull. EC 9-1990, point 1.2.28.
[3]   Bull. EC 11-1990, point 1.3.89; Commission proposal: Bull. EC 6-1990, point 1.3.118.
[4]   Bull. EC 12-1990, Commission proposal: Bull. EC 7/8-1990, point 1.3.140.
[5]   OJ L 219, 14.8.1990; Bull. EC 7/8-1990, point 1.3.134; Commission proposal: OJ C 253, 29.9.1988;
      Twenty-second General Report, point 569.
[6]   OJ L 181, 4.7.1986; Twentieth General Report, point 551.
[7]   OJ C 260, 15.10.1990; Bull. EC 9-1990, point 1.2.86.
[8]   OJ C 287, 15.11.1990; Bull. EC 10-1990, point 1.3.81.
[9]   OJ C 300, 29.11.1989; OJ C 1, 4.1.1990; Twenty-third General Report, point 515.
[10] OJ C 160, 10.7.1990; Bull. EC 4-1990, point 1.1.74.
[11] OJ C 206, 18.8.1990; Bull. EC 6-1990, point 1.3.117.
[12] OJ C 38, 19.2.1990; Bull. EC 1/2-1990, points 1.1.124 and 1.1.125; OJ C 149, 18.6.1990; Bull. EC 5-1990,
      point 1.2.116.
[13] OJ C 55, 7.3.1990; Bull. EC 1/2-1990, point 1.1.122.
[14] OJ L 129, 18.5.1976; Tenth General Report, point 277.

July[1] and by Parliament in October.[2] Also on 2 February the Commission amended[3] its proposal for a Directive concerning the protection of fresh, coastal and marine waters against pollution caused by nitrates from diffuse sources.[4]

518.   In July the Commission published its seventh report on the quality of bathing water[5] drawn up pursuant to Council Directive 76/160/EEC.[6] Particular attention is also to be devoted to reducing the damage caused by tourism to the environment in coastal areas and improving planning in these areas.

Air pollution

519.   On 20 December the Council reached agreement in principle on a common position[7] on the proposed amendment[8] of Directive 70/220/EEC on measures to be taken against air pollution by emissions from motor vehicles.[9] The proposal for a consolidated Directive had been amended in October[10] in response to the opinions of the Economic and Social Committee[11] and Parliament (first reading).[12]

520.   On 2 May the Commission adopted a proposal[13] amending Council Directive 88/77/EEC on the measures to be taken against the emission of gaseous pollutants from diesel engines for use in vehicles.[14] The purpose of this proposal, on which the Economic and Social Committee delivered an opinion in November,[15] is to reduce gaseous emissions still further and establish limit values for particulate emissions.

521.   On 21 May the Council adopted conclusions on energy and the environment which outlined various possible approaches in the energy sector to help combat air pollution.[16]

[1]   OJ C 225, 10.9.1990; Bull. EC 7/8-1990, point 1.3.137.
[2]   OJ C 284, 12.11.1990; Bull. EC 10-1990, point 1.3.80.
[3]   OJ C 51, 2.3.1990; Bull. EC 1/2-1990, point 1.1.123.
[4]   OJ C 54, 3.3.1989; Twenty-second General Report, point 572.
[5]   Bull. EC 7/8-1990, point 1.3.133.
[6]   OJ L 31, 5.2.1976; Nineteenth General Report, point 237.
[7]   Bull. EC 12-1990.
[8]   OJ C 81, 30.3.1990; Twenty-third General Report, point 518.
[9]   OJ L 76, 6.4.1970; OJ L 81, 14.4.1970; Fourteenth General Report, points 28 and 64.
[10] OJ C 281, 9.11.1990; Bull. EC 10-1990, point 1.3.82.
[11] OJ C 225, 10.9.1990; Bull. EC 7/8-1990, point 1.3.136.
[12] OJ C 260, 15.10.1990; Bull. EC 9-1990, point 1.2.89.
[13] OJ C 187, 27.7.1990; Bull. EC 5-1990, point 1.2.113.
[14] OJ L 36, 9.2.1988; Twenty-first General Report, point 504.
[15] Bull. EC 11-1990, point 1.3.93.
[16] Point 600 of this Report.

522.   Pursuant to the 1984 Directive on the combating of air pollution from industrial plants, [1] and in order to ensure the harmonized and effective implementation at Community level of the provisions on the use of the best available technology, the Commission organized an exchange of information in the form of the establishment and publication of technical memoranda concerning a number of industrial activities and defining the best available technologies, the conditions for their use, emission levels and other aspects which were relevant to the implementation of the Directive.

Control of chemicals, industrial hazards and biotechnology

523.   On 23 April the Council adopted two Directives dealing, respectively, with the contained use and the deliberate release into the environment of genetically modified organisms. [2]

524.   On 9 October the Council again adapted to technical progress[3] Directive 67/548/EEC on the classification, packaging and labelling of dangerous substances. [4] The proposal amending the Directive for the seventh time[5] was the subject of an opinion by the Economic and Social Committee in September[6] and by Parliament in October, [7] before being amended by the Commission in November. [8]

525.   On 4 July the Commission adopted a proposal for a Regulation on the evaluation and the control of the environmental risks of existing substances; [9] its purpose is to establish a procedure for drawing up priority lists of chemicals requiring immediate attention, determining methods of data gathering, imposing testing requirements and evaluating the risks to human beings and the environment.

---

[1]   OJ L 188, 16.4.1984; Eighteenth General Report, point 365.
[2]   OJ L 117, 8.5.1990; Bull. EC 4-1990, points 1.1.78 and 1.1.79; Commission proposal: OJ C 198, 28.7.1988; Twenty-second General Report, point 590; OJ C 246, 27.9.1989; Twenty-third General Report, point 528.
[3]   OJ L 287, 19.10.1990; Bull. EC 10-1990, point 1.3.84; Commission proposal: Bull. EC 7/8-1990, point 1.3.137.
[4]   OJ 196, 16.8.1967.
[5]   Twenty-third General Report, point 527; OJ C 33, 13.2.1990; Bull. EC 1/2-1990, point 1.1.126.
[6]   Bull. EC 9-1990, point 1.2.92.
[7]   OJ C 284, 12.11.1990; Bull. EC 10-1990, point 1.3.83.
[8]   OJ C 318, 18.12.1990; Bull. EC 11-1990, point 1.3.94.
[9]   OJ C 276, 5.11.1990; Bull. EC 7/8-1990, point 1.3.132.

Management of environmental resources

Conservation of the natural heritage

526.   In December the Council reached agreement[1] on the proposal for a Regulation on action by the Community for the protection of the environment in the Mediterranean region (Medspa).[2]

527.   On 7 March the Commission adopted annexes[3] supplementing the proposal for a Directive on the protection of natural and semi-natural habitats and of wild fauna and flora.[4] The proposal, together with the annexes, was examined in October by the Economic and Social Committee[5] and by Parliament.[6]

In order to cover the Community's entire marine and coastal environment, and in particular the especially sensitive and endangered areas of the North Sea and the Baltic Sea, on 17 December the Commission adopted a proposal for a Regulation supplementing the latter to protect the environment of the Irish Sea, North Sea, Baltic Sea and North-east Atlantic Ocean (Norspa).[1]

528.   On 17 January the Commission amended[7] the 1982 Council Regulation on the implementation in the Community of the Convention on international trade in endangered species of wild fauna and flora (Cites),[8] in order to incorporate the provisions on a prohibition on importing raw or worked ivory derived from the African elephant into the Community contained in the relevant Commission Regulation of August 1989,[9] which was thereby repealed.

529.   On the basis of Regulation (EEC) No 2242/87 covering the financing of action by the Community relating to the environment (ACE),[10] the Commission during the year approved the granting of financial aid amounting to ECU 3 052 000 to six projects to promote the conservation of biotopes of particular importance for the Community. It also proposed an increase of ECU 500 000 in funding for a project approved in 1989.

On 2 May the Commission approved a proposal for a Regulation on Community measures for nature conservation (Acnat),[11] thereby making the biotopes section of

---

1   Bull. EC 12-1990.
2   OJ C 80, 30.3.1990; Twenty-third General Report, point 533.
3   OJ C 195, 3.8.1990; Bull. EC 3-1990, point 1.1.87.
4   OJ C 247, 21.9.1988; Twenty-second General Report, point 592.
5   Bull. EC 10-1990, point 1.3.87.
6   OJ C 324, 24.12.1990; Bull. EC 11-1990, point 1.3.96.
7   OJ L 29, 31.1.1990; Bull. EC 1/2-1990, point 1.1.129.
8   OJ L 384, 31.12.1982; Sixteenth General Report, point 374.
9   OJ L 240, 17.8.1989; Twenty-third General Report, point 531.
10   OJ L 207, 29.7.1987; Twenty-first General Report, point 486.
11   OJ C 137, 6.6.1990; Bull. EC 5-1990, point 1.2.114.

Regulation (EEC) No 2242/87[1] into a new independent instrument. This proposal was examined by the Economic and Social Committee in October[2] and by Parliament in December.[3]

530. On 17 May Parliament adopted a resolution on the moratorium on commercial whaling adopted in 1982.[4]

531. In January the Commission set up an advisory committee on the protection of animals used for experimental and other scientific purposes.[5]

Waste management

532. On 7 May the Council adopted a resolution on waste policy[6] in which it endorsed the Community strategy on waste management outlined by the Commission in its communication of September 1989.[7] In December it reached agreement in principle[8] on the proposal for a Directive on dangerous wastes.[9]

533. On 2 April the Council accepted, on behalf of the Community, the OECD decision-recommendation on the control of the transfrontier movements of hazardous wastes[10] to which it had agreed in principle in March 1989.[11] On 26 July the Commission adopted a proposal for a decision on the conclusion, on behalf of the Community, of the Basle Convention[12] signed in March 1989.[13] The proposal was endorsed by the Economic and Social Committee in October.[14] On 19 September the Commission also adopted a proposal for a Regulation on the supervision and control of shipments of waste within, into and out of the European Community,[15] the aim of this proposal being to replace the Directive of 6 December 1984[16] to take account in particular of the provisions of the Basle and Lomé IV Conventions.[11, 17]

---

[1]   OJ L 207, 29.7.1987; Twenty-first General Report, point 486.
[2]   Bull. EC 10-1990, point 1.3.86.
[3]   OJ C 19, 28.1.1991; Bull. EC 12-1990.
[4]   OJ C 260, 15.10.1990; Bull. EC 9-1990, point 1.2.94.
[5]   OJ L 44, 20.2.1990; Bull. EC 1/2-1990, point 1.1.130.
[6]   OJ C 122, 18.5.1990; Bull. EC 5-1990, point 1.2.119.
[7]   Twenty-third General Report, point 537.
[8]   Bull. EC 12-1990.
[9]   OJ C 295, 19.11.1988; Twenty-second General Report, point 597.
[10] OJ L 92, 7.4.1990; Bull. EC 4-1990, point 1.1.80; Commission proposal: Twenty-third General Report, point 539.
[11] Twenty-third General Report, point 539.
[12] Bull. EC 7/8-1990, point 1.3.139.
[13] Twenty-third General Report, point 506.
[14] Bull. EC 10-1990, point 1.3.85.
[15] OJ C 289, 17.11.1990; Bull. EC 9-1990, point 1.2.84.
[16] OJ L 326, 13.12.1984; Eighteenth General Report, point 378.
[17] Twenty-third General Report, point 846.

534. On 17 September and 29 October, respectively, the Council adopted common positions[1,2] on the proposal for a Directive on batteries and accumulators containing dangerous substances[3] and the proposal for a Directive[4] amending Directive 75/442/EEC.[5] In December Parliament delivered its opinion on both proposals.[6] On 21 March the Commission amended[7] its proposal for a Directive on sewage sludge in agriculture.[8] The proposal for a Directive on civil liability for damage caused by waste[9] was examined by the Economic and Social Committee in March[8] and by Parliament (first reading) in November.[10] In December Parliament also gave its opinion[6] on the proposal for a Directive on the disposal of polychlorinated biphenyls (PCBs) and polychlorinated terphenyls (PCTs).[11]

535. Pursuant to Regulation (EEC) No 2242/87 on action by the Community relating to the environment (ACE),[12] the Commission approved the granting of financial aid to 21 demonstration projects in the field of soil decontamination (13 projects) and environment quality measuring techniques (eight projects), amounting to a total of ECU 5.4 million.

Urban environment

536. On 6 June, following on from work begun in 1989,[13] the Commission adopted a Green Paper on the urban environment;[14] this is a policy document outlining what the Community intends to do in order to tackle the environmental problems of Europe's major towns and cities. In December the Council adopted a resolution[15] embodying some of the conclusions and short-term measures proposed in the Green Paper. This effort to improve the urban environment was also backed up by a set of planned or already adopted measures on combating air pollution[16] and noise abatement.

---

[1]   Bull. EC 9-1990, point 1.2.91.
[2]   Bull. EC 10-1990, point 1.3.78.
[3]   OJ C 6, 7.1.1989; Twenty-second General Report, point 600; OJ C 11, 17.1.1990; Twenty-third General Report, point 540.
[4]   OJ C 295, 19.11.1988; Twenty-second General Report, point 597; OJ C 326, 30.12.1989; Twenty-third General Report, point 540.
[5]   OJ L 194, 25.7.1975; Nineteenth General Report, point 237.
[6]   OJ C 19, 28.1.1991; Bull. EC 12-1990.
[7]   OJ C 114, 8.5.1990; Bull. EC 3-1990, point 1.1.85.
[8]   OJ C 112, 7.5.1990; Bull. EC 3-1990, point 1.1.84.
[9]   OJ C 251, 4.10.1989; Twenty-third General Report, point 538.
[10] OJ C 324, 24.12.1990; Bull. EC 11-1990, point 1.3.95.
[11] OJ C 319, 12.12.1988; Twenty-second General Report, point 598.
[12] OJ L 207, 29.7.1987; Twenty-first General Report, point 486.
[13] Twenty-third General Report, point 541.
[14] Bull. EC 6-1990, point 1.3.113.
[15] Bull. EC 12-1990.
[16] Points 519 to 522 of this Report.

Global environment

537. With regard to energy and the environment, and more particularly to the aspects associated with the greenhouse effect and climatic change, the Commission, in March, adopted a communication on the Community's policy objectives in this field.[1] Following the conclusions of the Council on 29 October[2] which had decided that emissions should be stabilized, throughout the Community, by the year 2000 at their 1990 levels, the Commission examined a set of guidelines designed to restrict CO_2 emissions in the Community and improve the security of energy supply. At international level, the Commission took an active part in the work of the conference on global warming in April in Washington[3] and of the second World Conference on Climatic Change which was held at ministerial level in November in Geneva.[4]

538. At its meeting in June in Dublin, the European Council asked the Commission to continue and speed up its work on preserving the tropical forests,[5] in accordance with the guidelines laid down in the Commission's 1989 communication.[6] The Council and Parliament gave their opinion on this communication in May[7] and October,[8] respectively. In accordance with the requests from the European Council in Dublin and the summit of the industrialized countries held in July in Houston,[9] the Commission made initial contact with the Brazilian authorities and the World Bank to draw up a pilot scheme for dealing with the threat to the tropical rainforests in Brazil.

539. With regard to the protection of the ozone layer, the Commission adopted a proposal,[10] in January, which seeks to amend Regulation (EEC) No 3322/88[11] by providing for the elimination, as from 1997, of the substances destroying the ozone layer, with the exception of halons, which it is proposed to eliminate by the year 2000. In September the proposal was examined by the Economic and Social Committee,[12] and was the subject of a substantive agreement by the Council in December.[13] In May the Commission adopted a communication on participation by the developing countries in the Montreal Protocol,[14] and in June two recommendations on the reduction of the use

---

[1]   Bull. EC 3-1990, point 1.1.81.
[2]   Bull. EC 10-1990, point 1.3.77.
[3]   Bull. EC 4-1990, point 1.1.77.
[4]   Bull. EC 11-1990, point 1.3.90.
[5]   Bull. EC 6-1990, point I.14.
[6]   OJ C 264, 16.10.1989; Twenty-third General Report, point 529.
[7]   Bull. EC 5-1990, point 1.3.41.
[8]   OJ C 295, 26.11.1990; Bull. EC 10-1990, point 1.3.90.
[9]   Point 691 of this Report.
[10] OJ C 86, 4.4.1990; Bull. EC 1/2-1990, point 1.1.120.
[11] OJ L 298, 31.10.1988; Twenty-second General Report, point 546.
[12] Bull. EC 9-1990, point 1.2.90.
[13] Bull. EC 12-1990.
[14] Bull. EC 5-1990, point 1.2.118.

of chlorofluorocarbons by the plastic foam and refrigeration industries,[1] which complement the one addressed in 1989 to the aerosol industry.[2] At international level, the
Commission took part, in June in London, in the second conference[3] of the parties to
the Montreal Protocol.[4] This work led to a strengthening of the protective measures in
the protocol, and in December, the Commission transmitted to the Council a proposal
for a Directive on the conclusion by the Community of this amendment to the protocol.[5]

540.   Lastly, in November the Commission took part in the international work initiated
by the United Nations Environment Programme on the protection of biodiversity and
in the conference of the parties to the Wellington Treaty on Antarctica.

---

[1]   OJ L 227, 21.8.1990; Bull. EC 6-1990, point 1.3.123.
[2]   OJ L 144, 27.5.1989; Twenty-third General Report, point 524.
[3]   Bull. EC 6-1990, point 1.3.121; Negotiation Directives: Bull. EC 6-1990, point 1.3.120.
[4]   Twenty-first General Report, point 484.
[5]   Bull. EC 12-1990.

Section 16

Consumers

Priority activities and objectives

541.   The Commission continued and stepped up its activities to protect and promote consumer interests. On 28 March, acting on the Council resolution of 9 November 1989 setting out future priorities for relaunching policy in this area, [1] *the Commission adopted a three-year action plan* [2] *the purpose of which is to allow the 340 million consumers within the Community to derive maximum benefit from the internal market and to participate actively in it. Based on the principle of subsidiarity, the action plan comprises 22 measures in four main areas: consumer representation, health and safety of consumers, commercial transactions involving consumers, and consumer information and education.*

Consumer representation

542.   The Consumers Consultative Council set up following the revision of the rules governing the Consumers Consultative Committee, [3] held its inaugural meeting on 23 April. [4] This body, which will deliver opinions on Commission proposals relating to consumers, consists of representatives of the main European consumer organizations, the national organizations, the disabled and the elderly.

In addition, the Commission provided greater financial support for the national consumer organizations, in particular in southern Europe and Ireland.

---

[1]   OJ C 294, 22.11.1989; Twenty-third General Report, point 542.
[2]   Bull. EC 3-1990, point 1.1.93.
[3]   OJ L 38, 10.2.1990; Twenty-third General Report, point 543.
[4]   Bull. EC 4-1990, point 1.1.86.

Consumer information and education

543. Two consumer information centres were set up in Luxembourg and in Lille (France) as part of pilot projects to provide better information for consumers who make frequent cross-border purchases.

At the Commission's request, further price surveys were carried out in the border areas of the Community and within the Member States in order to provide better information for consumers about price differences for certain consumer goods and services.

544. As part of the child safety information and awareness campaign (1988-90),[1] the Commission drew conclusions from the trial use in various schools in the Member States of the teaching material known as the 'Safety Pack' for children aged between 11 and 14 aimed at preventing accidents in the home.[2]

Health, physical safety and quality

545. On 11 June, in the light of the opinions of the Economic and Social Committee[3] and of the European Parliament (first reading),[4] given on 31 January and 15 March, respectively, concerning the proposal for a directive on general product safety,[5] the Commission adopted an amended proposal[6] which nevertheless maintains the basic principles of the initial proposal, namely harmonization of Member States' approaches in this area and authorization for the Commission to intervene in the event of a grave and immediate risk.

546. On 29 June the Council adopted Decision 90/352/EEC[7] amending Decision 89/45/EEC concerning the Community system for the rapid exchange of information on the dangers arising from the use of consumer products,[8] in order to extend its validity until the date by which Member States have to comply with the general directive on product safety.

---

[1]   Twenty-first General Report, point 531.
[2]   Twenty-third General Report, point 554.
[3]   OJ C 75, 26.3.1990; Bull. EC 1/2-1990, point 1.1.137.
[4]   OJ C 96, 17.4.1990; Bull. EC 3-1990, point 1.1.94.
[5]   OJ C 193, 31.7.1989; Twenty-third General Report, point 544
[6]   OJ C 156, 27.6.1990; Bull. EC 6-1990, point 1.3.130.
[7]   OJ L 173, 6.7.1990; Bull. EC 6-1990, point 1.3.129; Commission proposal: OJ C 135, 2.6.1990; Bull. EC 5-1990, point 1.2.126.
[8]   OJ L 17, 21.1.1989.

In June the Commission also laid down detailed procedures[1] for the operation of this system which had been the subject of an assessment report adopted on 4 May.[2]

547. On 22 October the Council adopted a decision[3] amending Decision 86/138/EEC concerning a demonstration project with a view to introducing a Community system of information on accidents involving consumer products (Ehlass — the European home and leisure accident surveillance system).[4] The purpose of this amendment is mainly to establish a budget for the last two years of the demonstration project (1990 and 1991), lay down the breakdown of funds, and make for greater decentralization.

548. In December, in connection with the implementation of the toy safety Directive,[5] which entered into force on 1 January, the Commission adopted a report to the Council on the risk of damage to hearing resulting from noise emitted by toys.[6] In addition, European standards on mechanical and physical properties, flammability and the migration of certain elements were published in the Member States.

549. On 29 October the Commission adopted a proposal for a directive[7] consolidating all the successive amendments to Directive 76/768 concerning cosmetic products. On 20 February it once again adapted the Directive to technical progress.[8] On 4 April it amended[9] Directive 82/434/EEC relating to methods of analysis.[10]

550. In accordance with the Council resolution of November 1989[11] — which assigns priority to providing consumers with better information about product quality — on 28 November[12] the Commission adopted a proposal for a regulation on the award of a Community environmental label; and on 5 December it adopted two proposals for regulations on the protection of geographical descriptions and designations of origin for agricultural products and foodstuffs,[6] and on certificates of specific character for foodstuffs.[6]

551. Turning to services, the Commission took the view that priority should be given at Community level to action to protect the victims of faulty services. On 24 October

---

[1]   Bull. EC 6-1990, point 1.3.128.
[2]   Bull. EC 5-1990, point 1.2.125.
[3]   OJ L 296, 27.10.1990; Bull. EC 10-1990, point 1.3.100; Commission proposal: OJ C 300, 29.11.1989; Twenty-third General Report, point 546.
[4]   OJ L 109, 26.4.1986; Twentieth General Report, point 587.
[5]   OJ L 187, 16.7.1988; Twenty-second General Report, point 602.
[6]   Bull. EC 12-1990.
[7]   Bull. EC 10-1990, point 1.3.99.
[8]   OJ L 71, 17.3.1990; Bull. EC 1/2-1990, point 1.1.138.
[9]   OJ L 108, 28.4.1990; Bull. EC 4-1990, point 1.1.85
[10] OJ L 185, 30.6.1982; Sixteenth General Report, point 387.
[11] Point 541 of this Report.
[12] Point 505 of this Report.

it therefore adopted a proposal for a directive on the liability of suppliers of services,[1] which provides for the reversal of the burden of proof if the supplier of the service is at fault, and compensation in that event for physical damage suffered by the victim and damage to property.

Transactions involving consumers

552.   On 22 February the Council adopted Directive 90/88/EEC[2] amending Directive 87/102/EEC on consumer credit.[3] The Directive provides for the harmonization, from 1 January 1993, of the method of calculating the cost of consumer credit for amounts between ECU 200 and 20 000.

553.   On 13 June the Council adopted Directive 90/314/EEC on package travel, including package holidays and package tours.[4] Under the terms of the Directive, there will be a greater onus on operators to ensure that consumers are properly informed and on operators and retailers to honour their contractual obligations, whether they themselves or third parties are responsible for their performance.

554.   On 18 July the Commission adopted a proposal for a directive on unfair terms in consumer contracts,[5] which seeks to eliminate such terms and remedy omissions which might make a contract unfair. To this end the proposal defines the concept of unfairness and lists unfair terms which should not be included in consumer contracts.

555.   A recommendation adopted by the Commission in February concerning cross-border financial transactions[6] relates, among other things, to the information to be supplied to consumers by banks.

---

[1]   OJ C 12, 18.1.1991; Bull. EC 10-1990, point 1.3.98.
[2]   OJ L 61, 10.3.1990; Bull. EC 1/2-1990, point 1.1.140; Commission proposal: OJ C 155, 14.6.1988; Twenty-second General Report, point 612; OJ C 155, 23.6.1989; Twenty-third General Report, point 550; OJ C 30, 8.2.1990.
[3]   OJ L 42, 12.2.1987; Twentieth General Report, point 589.
[4]   OJ L 158, 23.6.1990; Bull. EC 6-1990, point 1.3.127; Commission proposal: OJ C 96, 12.4.1988; Twenty-second General Report, point 611; OJ C 190, 27.7.1989; Twenty-third General Report, point 551; OJ C 158, 28.6.1990; Bull. EC 5-1990, point 1.2.124.
[5]   OJ C 243, 28.9.1990; Bull. EC 7/8-1990, point 1.3.150.
[6]   Point 129 of this Report.

Section 17

Transport

Priority activities and objectives

556. Since transport is, by definition, an international activity, external relations in the transport field are becoming increasingly important as the Community is called upon to adopt a position vis-à-vis third countries. This year, therefore, the Commission has focused on the external aspects of the common transport policy. In February it sent the Council a proposal for a consultation and authorization procedure for agreements concerning commercial aviation relations between Member States and third countries. In June the Council decided to give the Commission a mandate for opening negotiations with Norway and Sweden on scheduled air services. The Commission had originally requested authorization to open negotiations with all the EFTA countries.

Considerable progress was also made towards liberalization of air transport services. In June the Council adopted a package of regulations on the second stage of Community policy. The measures adopted, with a view to setting up a Community organization for air transport in Europe, relate to fares, access to the market and the sharing of passenger capacity. The Commission, for its part, tabled proposals on overbooking, on consultation between airports and their users, on the operation of air cargo services and on slots allocation.

In view of the importance of developing the infrastructure to enable goods and persons to move freely within the single market, the Council decided to give its support to projects of interest to the Community within the framework of a three-year programme (1990-92). It also welcomed a communication from the Commission on the European high-speed rail network and called on it to pursue its efforts on the basis of the master plan put forward. Lastly, the decisions adopted by the Council in December completed the implementation of the legislative measures relating to the liberalization of services in the field of intra-Community international carriage by road.

Infrastructure

557. The interim report on Europe-wide networks, adopted by the Commission in July, reviews the progress made in the four areas selected in 1989, including transport infrastructure.[1]

558. On 19 September, the Economic and Social Committee adopted an own-initiative opinion on the Channel Tunnel and its impact on transport policy.[2]

Financial support for projects of Community interest

559. On 20 November the Council adopted a three-year programme (1990-92) granting financial support for projects of Community interest falling within the scope of the seven priorities selected:[3] high-speed rail network, Alpine transit route, combined transport network of Community interest, trans-Pyrenean road links, road links in and with Ireland, the Scanlink, and the strengthening of land communication in Greece. ECU 328 million, of which ECU 60 million in 1990, ECU 118 million in 1991 and ECU 160 million in 1992, has been earmarked for these projects.

560. In December the Commission adopted a proposal for a decision concerning the permanent introduction of a system for observing the markets in the inland carriage of goods.[4] The proposal, which is accompanied by a report on the existing system, has a double purpose: (i) to inform all the parties concerned about the present situation, and (ii) to enable the competent authorities to take the necessary steps by detecting market disturbances as and when they occur.

Inland transport

Railways

561. In July[5] and December,[6] respectively, the Economic and Social Committee and Parliament delivered their opinions on all the proposals for a common railway policy,

---

[1]   Point 60 of this Report.
[2]   Bull. EC 9-1990, point 1.2.180.
[3]   OJ L 326, 24.11.1990; Bull. EC 11-1990, point 1.3.181; Commission proposal: OJ C 270, 19.10.1988; Twenty-second General Report, point 714; OJ C 170, 5.7.1989; Twenty-third General Report, point 623.
[4]   Bull. EC 12-1990.
[5]   OJ C 225, 10.9.1990; Bull. EC 7/8-1990, point 1.3.285.
[6]   OJ C 19, 28.1.1991; Bull. EC 12-1990.

adopted by the Commission in November 1989.[1]

562. In accordance with the Council resolution of December 1989,[2] the Commission drafted a communication including a master plan for the European high-speed rail network,[3] identifying priority projects and proposing courses of action to ensure technical compatibility between the different parts of the network. The communication was welcomed by the Council, which called on the Commission to examine certain aspects in greater depth together with the Member States and representatives of railway undertakings and the railway industry.[3]

563. On 7 December,[3] in accordance with Regulation (EEC) No 2830/77, the Commission adopted its eleventh report (1987) on the annual accounts of railway undertakings.[4]

Road transport

Access to the market

564. On 25 April the Council adopted a regulation increasing by 40% the 1990 Community quota for the carriage of goods by road between Member States.[5] In December it decided on a 40%-a-year increase of the Community quota for 1991 and 1992 to be shared among the Member States.[6] On the same occasion the Council adapted the Community quota to take German unification into account.[7]

565. On 24 July[8] the Council amended Directive 84/647/EEC on the use of vehicles hired without drivers for the carriage of goods by road.[9]

566. On 21 December the Council adopted a regulation on the introduction of the final regime for the organization of the market for the carriage of goods by road, aimed at introducing a safeguard mechanism to deal with any market disturbances and to specify what measures to apply in the event of a crisis in the sector.[10]

---

[1]   OJ C 34, 14.2.1990; Twenty-third General Report, point 624.
[2]   Twenty-third General Report, point 625.
[3]   Bull. EC 12-1990.
[4]   OJ L 334, 24.12.1977; Eleventh General Report, point 376.
[5]   OJ L 108, 28.4.1990; Bull. EC 4-1990, point 1.1.149; Commission proposal: OJ C 316, 16.12.1989; Twenty-third General Report, point 627.
[6]   OJ L 375, 31.12.1990; Bull. EC 12-1990; Commission proposal: OJ C 316, 16.12.1989; Twenty-third General Report, point 627.
[7]   Bull. EC 12-1990; Commission proposal: OJ C 323, 22.12.1990; Bull. EC 11-1990, point 1.2.4.
[8]   OJ L 202, 31.7.1990; Bull. EC 7/8-1990, point 1.3.284; Commission proposal: OJ C 296, 24.11.1989; Twenty-third General Report, point 628; OJ C 150, 19.6.1990; Bull. EC 5-1990, point 1.2.218.
[9]   OJ L 335, 22.12.1984; Eighteenth General Report, point 488.
[10] OJ L 375, 31.12.1990; Bull. EC 12-1990; Commission proposal: OJ C 87, 5.4.1990; Bull. EC 1/2-1990, point 1.1.254; OJ C 294, 24.11.1990; Bull. EC 10-1990, point 1.3.191.

567.   The entry into force on 1 July of Regulation (EEC) No 4059/89 laying down the conditions under which non-resident carriers may operate national road haulage services within a Member State introduced a limited right of cabotage, so putting an end to the compartmentalization of the national transport markets.[1]

568.   On 6 April Parliament adopted a resolution on the taxation of commercial vehicles.[2] The issue of tax harmonization in the transport sector was also addressed by the Council of Ministers and the European Council.[3]

569.   On 12 July, in response to the Commission's application for the adoption of interim measures, the Court of Justice ordered the Federal Republic of Germany, pending its substantive judgment, to suspend collection of the road tax introduced by the law of 30 April.[4] This law, concerning taxes to be levied on the use by heavy goods vehicles of roads and motorways in the Federal Republic, lays down that, from 1 July, all vehicles weighing more than 18 tonnes — regardless of their place of registration — were liable to a tax on the use of such infrastructure, the amount of the tax depending upon the vehicles' characteristics. With the support of five Member States, the Commission, in the main action, asked the Court to declare this law incompatible with the Treaty and secondary legislation. To reduce distortion of competition among Community carriers resulting from tax legislation while ensuring that the fixed costs of the infrastructure are shared out more equitably, on 22 November the Commission amended its proposal for a directive on the allocation of transport infrastructure costs to certain commercial vehicles, to ensure that national road tax procedures are brought into line and that uniform minimum rates are applied which take account of the road tolls paid.[5]

Technical aspects

570.   In December[6] the Council gave its approval to the amendment of Directive 85/3/EEC on the weights and dimensions of commercial road vehicles in respect of the maximum authorized dimensions for road trains.[7] The maximum total length of road trains will be 18.35 m, the maximum length of load will be 15.65 m, and the total maximum length of load including the distance between the tractor unit and the trailer will be 16 m.

---

[1]   OJ L 390, 30.12.1989; Twenty-third General Report, point 629.
[2]   OJ C 113, 7.5.1990; Bull. EC 4-1990, point 1.1.150.
[3]   Bull. EC 6-1990, point I.6; Bull. EC 12-1990.
[4]   Order of 12 July 1990, Case C-195/90R *Commission* v *Federal Republic of Germany* (OJ C 199, 8.8.1990).
[5]   Bull. EC 11-1990, point 1.3.182.
[6]   Bull. EC 12-1990; Commission proposal: OJ C 316, 16.12.1989; Twenty-third General Report, point 632; OJ C 268, 24.10.1990; Bull. EC 10-1990, point 1.3.188.
[7]   OJ L 2, 3.1.1985; Eighteenth General Report, point 493.

On 17 October the Commission adopted a new proposal for an amendment to that Directive with a view to defining a parametric equivalent to air suspension and extend its use to the drive axle of all vehicles used for international transport and falling within the scope of the Directive.[1]

571. On 11 May the Commission adopted a communication on a consistent approach as regards the dimensions of commercial vehicles, in which it examines the policy objectives, both general (e.g. safety and the environment) and specific.[2]

572. On 16 November[3] the Commission adopted a regulation adapting to technical progress Council Regulation (EEC) No 3821/85[4] on recording equipment in road transport. The purpose of this Regulation is to adapt the technical provisions so that the automatic recording of driving time starts as soon as the vehicle begins to move, and to ensure that any interruption in the operation of the electronic tachographs is shown clearly on the record sheets of the apparatus.

Inland waterways

573. The structural improvements in inland waterway transport pursuant to Council Regulation (EEC) No 1101/89,[5] and to the Commission's implementing measures, began on 1 January.[5] Applications for the scrapping of some 1 600 vessels, totalling more than 1 million dead-weight tonnes, were submitted within the time-limit. This reduction in the fleet capacity of the Member States concerned should lead in the short term to an improvement in the economic situation of their inland waterway operators. The Council also adopted a number of measures extending this scheme to the fleet of the former German Democratic Republic.[6]

---

[1]   OJ C 292, 22.11.1990; Bull. EC 10-1990, point 1.3.190.
[2]   Bull. EC 5-1990, point 1.2.216.
[3]   OJ L 318, 17.11.1990; Bull. EC 11-1990, point 1.3.184.
[4]   OJ L 370, 31.12.1985.
[5]   OJ L 116, 27.4.1989; Twenty-third General Report, point 634.
[6]   Point 24 of this Report.

Sea transport

Application of the 1986 Regulations

574. On 1 August[1] the Commission adopted a report on the implementation of the four Regulations of December 1986 on maritime transport.[2] The report deals, in particular, with the steps taken by the Member States to amend their legislation on unilateral restrictions and the procedures for progressively abolishing or adapting the cargo-sharing arrangements in existing bilateral agreements. The Commission considers that, as a whole, implementation of the Regulations is advancing in a satisfactory manner though the pace is uneven and, in certain respects, slower than anticipated. In the Commission's view, however, their cumulative impact is real and significant.

575. The Commission has undertaken examination of 20 individual complaints or requests for exemption submitted under Regulation (EEC) No 4056/86.[1] It has also persevered in its action to safeguard free access to cargoes in trade with West and Central African countries. It has discussed a number of specific problems with third countries, in particular Kenya, the Republic of Korea (which has taken significant steps towards liberalization), Indonesia (which has abolished a tax on port services supplied to vessels in ports of call), Japan and Brazil. Furthermore, in the light of consultations between the Commission and Community trade circles, a protocol relating to exemption for Community by shipowners from the freight tax imposed by Taiwan was signed on 1 August by representatives of commercial ports in Taiwan and in the Community.

Increased competitiveness for the Community fleet

576. On 1 June[3] the Commission adopted a proposal for a regulation on the transfer of ships from one register to another within the Community. This proposal is the practical follow-up to one of the initiatives proposed in July 1989[4] to improve, by means of positive measures, the operating conditions and competitiveness of the Community merchant fleet on which Parliament had delivered a favourable opinion in October.[5] In December the new proposal was examined by the Economic and Social Committee[6] and by Parliament[7] and was also the subject of a Council joint position.[6]

---

[1]   Bull. EC 7/8-1990, point 1.3.287.
[2]   OJ L 378, 31.12.1986; Twenty-third General Report, point 711.
[3]   OJ C 153, 22.6.1990; Bull. EC 6-1990, point 1.3.243.
[4]   OJ C 263, 10.10.1989; Twenty-third General Report, point 637.
[5]   OJ C 295, 26.11.1990; Bull. EC 10-1990, point 1.3.193.
[6]   Bull. EC 12-1990.
[7]   OJ C 19, 28.1.1991; Bull. EC 12-1990.

577.   On 30 October the Council adopted a decision extending until 31 December 1991 the collection of information concerning the activities of carriers in certain areas of operation. [1]

Air transport

Implementation of the common policy

578.   In December the Council approved in principle a regulation on the operation of air cargo services liberalizing the rules on market access, operational flexibility and cargo rates. [2]

579.   Also in December the Council approved in principle a regulation on common rules for a denied-boarding compensation system, to protect passengers against the abuses of overbooking. Its purpose is to harmonize the disparate policies applied by airlines and to provide greater protection of passengers' interests. [3]

580.   On 28 March the Commission adopted a proposal for a regulation to organize regular exchanges of information between airports and their users with regard both to infrastructure projects and charges, and to traffic and fleet forecasts. [4] The Economic and Social Committee and Parliament delivered their opinions on this proposal in October [5] and December, [6] respectively.

581.   On 26 March, [7] the Council adopted conclusions on air traffic system capacity problems, confirming its resolution of July 1989. [8]

582.   The Commission published an explanatory note on the interpretation of the code of conduct for the use of computerized reservation systems. [9]

---

[1]   OJ L 311; 10.11.1990; Bull. EC 10-1990, point 1.3.194; Commission proposal: Bull. EC 7/8-1990, point 1.3.286.
[2]   Bull. EC 12-1990, Commission proposal: OJ C 88, 6.4.1990; Bull. EC 1/2-1990, point 1.1.255.
[3]   Bull. EC 12-1990, Commission proposal: OJ C 129, 24.5.1990; Bull. EC 4-1990, point 1.1.151.
[4]   OJ C 147, 16.6.1990; Bull. EC 3-1990, point 1.1.177.
[5]   Bull. EC 10-1990, point 1.3.197.
[6]   OJ C 19, 28.1.1991; Bull. EC 12-1990.
[7]   Bull. EC 3-1990, point 1.1.183.
[8]   OJ C 189, 26.7.1989; Twenty-third General Report, point 640.
[9]   OJ C 184, 25.7.1990; Bull. EC 7/8-1990, point 1.3.289.

583.   In December the Commission adopted a draft regulation on the allocation of slots for civil aircraft, establishing the rules for sharing out among the airlines the allotted take-off and landing slots in Community airports. [1]

Second stage of the common policy

584.   Development of the common air transport policy continued with the adoption by the Council, on 24 July, [2] of regulations on fares, access to the market, the sharing of passenger capacity in addition to the Regulation on the application of Article 85(3) of the Treaty to certain categories of agreements and concerted practices in the air transport sector. [3] This package of measures, which entered into force on 1 November, substantially transforms the organization of air transport in Europe. The purpose of the Regulation on fares is to make the system of fares on intra-Community routes more flexible and introduce three 'zones' of flexibility: a normal fare zone, a discount zone and a deep-discount zone. The system of 'double disapproval' of fares is to be fully introduced by 1 January 1993, but is nevertheless immediately applicable in certain cases. The Regulation on market access and on the sharing of passenger capacity establishes third-, fourth- and fifth-freedom traffic rights between all airports in the Member States. (These freedoms mean, respectively: the right of a carrier to put down, in a particular State, passengers taken up in the State in which it is registered; the right of a carrier to take on, in a particular State, passengers for disembarkation in the State in which it is registered; and the right of a carrier to pick up passengers in a State other than that in which it is registered and set them down in a third State.) The Regulation introduces more liberal provisions with regard to multiple designation and aims at the gradual removal of bilateral restrictions on passenger capacity until such restrictions are completely abolished with the completion of the internal air transport market. There are special capacity provisions for markets dominated by non-scheduled services.

The Economic and Social Committee and Parliament have delivered opinions on the proposed regulations annexed to the memorandum on the application of the competition rules to air transport. [3]

---

[1]   Bull. EC 12-1990.
[2]   OJ L 217, 11.8.1990; Bull. EC 7/8-1990, point 1.3.288; Commission proposal: OJ C 258, 11.10.1989; Twenty-third General Report, point 641; OJ C 164, 5.7.1990; Bull. EC 6-1990, points 1.3.240 to 1.3.243.
[3]   Point 190 of this Report.

Technical aspects

585.   On 27 September the Commission adopted a proposal for a directive on the harmonization of technical requirements and procedures applicable to civil aircraft.[1] This proposal concerns the harmonization of provisions relating to the certification, operation and maintenance of aircraft and their equipment, within the framework of the Joint Aviation Requirements (JAR).

Multimodal transport

Development of combined transport

586.   On 30 October the Council adopted a resolution on the establishment of a European combined transport network calling on the Commission to convene a high-level working party with the task of defining the future network and the conditions under which such a network can operate effectively.[2]

587.   In December[3] the Council approved a proposal for a Directive[4] amending Directive 75/130/EEC on the establishment of common rules for certain types of combined carriage of goods between Member States.[5] The Directive lays down in particular that all hauliers, established in a Member State, licensed to carry out international transport operations will be authorized to carry out initial or terminal road haulage operations forming an integral part of intra-Community combined transport, regardless of their nationality or place of establishment. Initial or terminal road haulage forming part of a combined transport operation will also be exempted from compulsory tariff regulations.

---

[1]   OJ C 270, 26.10.1990; Bull. EC 9-1990, point 1.2.179.
[2]   Bull. EC 10-1990, point 1.3.199.
[3]   Bull. EC 12-1990.
[4]   OJ C 34, 14.2.1990; Twenty-third General Report, point 643.
[5]   OJ L 48, 22.2.1975; Ninth General Report, point 367.

International cooperation

Transit through non-Community countries

588.   The Commission pursued its transit traffic negotiations with Austria, Switzerland and Yugoslavia[1] on the basis of the directives adopted by the Council in December 1988[2] relating to the second stage of the negotiations.[3]

Air traffic rights

589.   On 23 February the Commission adopted a proposal for a decision on a consultation and authorization procedure for agreements concerning commercial aviation relations between Member States and third countries.[4] The purpose of this proposal is to confer upon the Community responsibility for defending the Member States' interests in this field: it would have sole competence over the provision of services, under Article 113 of the Treaty, and a greater or lesser degree of competence — depending on the situation — over technical, social and safety matters. Parliament[5] and the Economic and Social Committee[6] delivered their opinions on this proposal in September.

590.   On 18 June the Council gave the Commission a mandate to conduct negotiations with Norway and Sweden on scheduled air services.[7]

591.   The Commission took part for the second time[8] in the joint meeting of the European Conference of Ministers of Transport (ECMT) and the Council for Mutual Economic Assistance (CMEA), held in Stockholm on 1 October.[9]

---

[1]   Bull. EC 1/2-1990, point 1.1.250; Bull. EC 5-1990, point 1.2.222; Bull. EC 7/8-1990, point 1.3.283.
[2]   Twenty-second General Report, point 751.
[3]   First stage: Twenty-first General Report, point 649; Twenty-second General Report, point 751.
[4]   Bull. EC 1/2-1990, point 1.1.256.
[5]   OJ C 260, 15.10.1990; Bull. EC 9-1990, point 1.2.183.
[6]   Bull. EC 9-1990, point 1.2.183.
[7]   Bull. EC 6-1990, point 1.3.245; Commission recommendation: Bull. EC 1/2-1990, point 1.1.257.
[8]   Twenty-third General Report, point 656.
[9]   Bull. EC 10-1990, point 1.3.200.

Transport safety

Road safety

592. On 14 November[1] the Commission adopted an amendment to its proposal for a directive on the compulsory use of safety belts in vehicles of less than 3.5 tonnes, so as to include child restraint systems.[2]

593. On 14 September[3] Parliament adopted a favourable opinion on the proposal for a directive on speed limits for commercial vehicles.[4]

Safety at sea

594. The safety of ferry boats was the subject of resolutions adopted by Parliament on 17 May[5] and by the Council and Representatives of the Member States' Governments meeting within the Council on 19 June.[6] On that occasion the Council also adopted a resolution on the prevention of accidents causing marine pollution.[7] Furthermore, Parliament asked for an immediate ban of the transport of nuclear waste by ferry.[8]

595. In the light of the opinion of Parliament,[9] on 31 October[10] the Commission amended its proposal for a directive concerning minimum requirements for vessels entering or leaving Community ports carrying packages of dangerous goods.[11]

Social conditions

596. On 30 October the Council authorized the Commission to conduct negotiations, on behalf of the Community, with a view to revising the European Agreement concerning the Work of Crews of Vehicles engaged in International Road Transport (AETR),

---

[1]   OJ C 308, 8.12.1990; Bull. EC 11-1990, point 1.3.183.
[2]   OJ C 298, 23.11.1988; Twenty-second General Report, point 735.
[3]   OJ C 260, 15.10.1990; Bull. EC 9-1990, point 1.2.182.
[4]   OJ C 33, 9.2.1989; Twenty-third General Report, point 651.
[5]   OJ C 149, 18.6.1990; Bull. EC 5-1990, point 1.2.219.
[6]   OJ C 206, 18.8.1990; Bull. EC 6-1990, point 1.3.249.
[7]   Point 516 of this Report.
[8]   Point 654 of this Report.
[9]   OJ C 175, 16.7.1990; Bull. EC 6-1990, point 1.3.248.
[10] OJ C 294, 24.11.1990; Bull. EC 10-1990, point 1.3.192.
[11] OJ C 147, 14.6.1989; Twenty-third General Report, point 648.

in consultation with the Member States and on the basis of current Community legislation.[1]

597.   On 9 October, the Commission adopted a proposal for a directive to codify all the legislation on the right to take up the occupations of road haulage operator and road passenger transport operator in national and international transport.[2]

598.   The proposal[3] for a directive on the mutual recognition of licences and qualifications of persons exercising an occupation in civil aviation was the subject of opinions delivered by the Economic and Social Committee[4] and Parliament.[5] A Joint Committee on Civil Aviation was also set up.[6]

Research and technological development

599.   On 21 December the Council adopted a specific research and technological development programme in the field of transport (Euret) 1990-93.[7] With a budget of ECU 25 million, the programme deals with issues covering competitiveness, safety and environmental protection. Three aims are singled out: optimum network exploitation; logistics and reduction of harmful externalities.

---

[1]   Bull. EC 10-1990, point 1.3.201; Commission proposal: Bull. EC 7/8-1990, point 1.3.291.
[2]   OJ C 286, 14.11.1990; Bull. EC 10-1990, point 1.3.189.
[3]   OJ C 10, 16.1.1990; Twenty-third General Report, point 645.
[4]   OJ C 124, 21.5.1990; Bull. EC 3-1990, point 1.1.181.
[5]   OJ C 284, 12.11.1990; Bull. EC 10-1990, point 1.3.195.
[6]   OJ L 230, 24.8.1990; Bull. EC 7/8-1990, point 1.3.86.
[7]   OJ C 295, 26.11.1990; Bull. EC 10-1990, point 1.3.64.

Section 18

Energy

Priority activities and objectives

600. The Commission submitted to the Council in 1989 a set of proposals for directives or regulations which represented a first stage towards the gradual completion of the internal energy market. Two of these pieces of legislation relating to the transparency of gas and electricity prices charged to industrial end-users and the transit of electricity through the major systems were adopted this year. The Commission also adopted a working document which reviews a series of measures designed to maintain the security of the Community's energy supply, given the completion of the internal market.

A significant step in the promotion of efficient energy technologies was the adoption by the Council of the Thermie programme.

Efforts to take greater account of environmental considerations in energy policies continued along the lines set out in the communication of November 1989 from the Commission.[1] Using this as a basis, at their joint meeting of 29 October,[2] the Ministers for Energy and for the Environment reached conclusions reflecting the Community's position on the policy to be pursued on the issue of climate change, in preparation for the second World Climate Conference,[3] especially as regards the restriction of carbon dioxide emissions.

The Gulf crisis once again underlined the risks inherent in high oil dependency.[4] It prompted the Commission to put forward a series of proposals designed to ensure greater security of supply and better coordination of measures to be taken in the event of crisis.

At its meeting in Rome in December, the European Council, acting largely on proposals put forward by the Netherlands Government, felt the need to establish long-term cooperation on energy with the countries of Central and Eastern Europe.[5] It hoped an international conference could be organized in 1991 in order to draft a pan-European charter

---

[1] Twenty-third General Report, point 657.
[2] Bull. EC 10-1990, point 1.3.77.
[3] Point 510 of this Report.
[4] Point 734 of this Report.
[5] Bull. EC 12-1990.

for energy, a project backed by Mr Delors, the President of the Commission, at the summit of Heads of State or Government of the CSCE. [1]

Internal energy market

601.   On 29 June the Council adopted Directive 90/377/EEC concerning a Community procedure on the transparency of gas and electricity prices charged to industrial end-users. [2]

602.   On 29 October the Council also adopted Directive 90/547/EEC on the transit of electricity through the major European networks. [3]

603.   On 31 January and 5 April opinions were delivered by the Economic and Social Committee [4] and Parliament, [5] respectively, concerning the proposal for a Regulation [6] amending Council Regulation (EEC) No 1056/72 on investment projects of interest to the Community. [7] On 21 May the Council agreed [8] on the need to concentrate first on more effective implementation of the existing Regulation and to return to the Commission proposal in due course. This proposal was amended [9] on 12 June to incorporate certain amendments adopted by Parliament.

604.   In December the Council adopted [10] its common position on the proposal for a Directive on the transit of natural gas through the major systems, [11] which had been amended [12] by the Commission in September in the light of the opinions delivered by the Economic and Social Committee [13] and by Parliament (first reading). [14]

---

[1]   Point 871 of this Report.
[2]   OJ L 185, 17.7.1990; Bull. EC 6-1990, point 1.3.253; Commission proposal: OJ C 257, 10.10.1989; Twenty-third General Report, point 658; OJ C 164, 5.7.1990; Bull. EC 6-1990, point 1.3.253.
[3]   OJ L 313, 13.11.1990; Bull. EC 10-1990, point 1.3.213; Commission proposal: OJ C 8, 13.1.1990; Twenty-third General Report, point 676; OJ C 144, 16.6.1990; Bull. EC 5-1990, point 1.2.229; OJ C 284, 12.11.1990; Bull. EC 10-1990, point 1.3.213.
[4]   OJ C 75, 26.3.1990; Bull. EC 1/2-1990, point 1.1.260.
[5]   OJ C 113, 7.5.1990; Bull. EC 4-1990, point 1.1.154.
[6]   OJ C 250, 3.10.1989; Twenty-third General Report, point 659.
[7]   OJ L 120, 25.5.1972; Sixth General Report, point 335.
[8]   Bull. EC 5-1990, point 1.2.225.
[9]   OJ C 187, 27.7.1990; Bull. EC 6-1990, point 1.3.254.
[10] Bull. EC 12-1990.
[11] OJ C 247, 28.9.1989; Twenty-third General Report, point 673.
[12] OJ C 268, 24.10.1990; Bull. EC 9-1990, point 1.2.185.
[13] OJ C 75, 26.3.1990; Bull. EC 1/2-1990, point 1.1.264.
[14] OJ C 231, 17.9.1990; Bull. EC 7/8-1990, point 1.3.298.

605. In its working document on security of supply, the internal energy market and energy policy, adopted on 4 July,[1] the Commission proposes an approach which seeks to strike a balance between the benefits resulting from such security for the Member States and the adverse effects of the fiscal and administrative measures having equivalent effect to national aid which they adopt.

606. In May the Commission published an initial report on work already accomplished and the work remaining to be done to complete the internal energy market.[2] In addition, in its progress report on trans-European networks,[3] the Commission reviewed the progress of its work in the four sectors chosen, which include the transport of electricity and gas.

607. Under the heading of accompanying measures and in the context of regional policy the Commission adopted a new Community initiative on energy networks (Regen).[4] As part of its action in connection with regional energy planning it granted financial support of ECU 2.6 million towards 33 projects selected following an invitation to submit proposals published in March.[5]

Promotion of energy technologies

608. The Thermie programme was adopted by the Council on 29 June.[6] The purpose of this five-year programme (1990-94), which has an initial budget of ECU 350 million for the period 1990-92, is to create the conditions for the granting of Community financial support to projects that promote energy technology in the fields of rational use of energy, renewable energies, solid fuels and hydrocarbons. Under this programme the Commission approved[5] an initial tranche of ECU 45 million for 1990 and, on 30 August, issued a second invitation to tender for 1991.[7] A first technology dissemination programme with a budget of ECU 6.2 million was established.

---

1   Bull. EC 7/8-1990, point 1.3.292.
2   Bull. EC 5-1990, point 1.2.224.
3   Point 60 of this Report.
4   Point 407 of this Report.
5   OJ C 77, 27.3.1990.
6   OJ L 185, 17.7.1990; Bull. EC 6-1990, point 1.3.256; Commission proposal: OJ C 101, 22.4.1989;
    Twenty-third General Report, point 661; OJ C 111, 5.5.1990; Bull. EC 5-1990, point 1.2.223.
7   OJ C 215, 30.8.1990; Bull. EC 7/8-1990, point 1.3.301.

Community energy strategy and objectives for 1995

609.   The Commission continued[1] its exploratory investigations with a view to identifying the priority themes which will provide a basis for new energy objectives beyond 1995. These objectives were also the subject of a resolution adopted by the European Parliament in April.[2]

Relations with third countries producing or importing energy

610.   In its contacts with the oil-exporting countries, the Commission continued its technical cooperation with the Organization of Petroleum Exporting Countries. From 4 to 6 June a joint seminar was held in Fez, Morocco, with the Organization of Arab Petroleum Exporting Countries to discuss the integration of the Community's energy market and that of the Arab world.[3]

611.   On 24 October the Commission adopted a communication to the Council proposing guidelines for negotiations for the accession of the Community to the International Energy Agency (IEA).[4]

612.   At the 33rd annual session of the general conference of the International Atomic Energy Agency, held in Vienna from 17 to 21 September,[5] the Commission reported on developments in the Community nuclear industry and confirmed the Commission's support for the Agency's activities. As in 1989 the Council Presidency made a statement on behalf of the Community and its Member States concerning the growth of nuclear electricity production in the Community, nuclear safety, the environment and non-proliferation.[6]

613.   In the nuclear energy field the Commission was authorized by the Council[7] to negotiate an amendment to the 1959 Cooperation Agreement between Euratom and Canada,[8] with a view to extending the scope of the Agreement to include tritium, tritium separation equipment and tritium separated using such equipment. This Agreement was initialled on 22 October. Under the trade and commercial and economic agreement with

---

[1]   Twenty-third General Report, point 664.
[2]   OJ C 113, 7.5.1990; Bull. EC 4-1990, point 1.1.153.
[3]   Bull. EC 6-1990, point 1.3.258.
[4]   Bull. EC 10-1990, point 1.3.215.
[5]   Bull. EC 9-1990, point 1.2.186.
[6]   Twenty-third General Report, point 668.
[7]   Bull. EC 4-1990, point 1.1.156; Commission proposal: Bull. EC 1/2-1990, point 1.1.267.
[8]   OJ 60, 24.11.1959.

the Soviet Union,[1] the Commission[2] submitted to the Council, on 1 August, draft negotiating directives in respect of three cooperation agreements between Euratom and the Soviet Union in the fields of controlled nuclear fusion, nuclear safety[3] and matters relating to trade in nuclear materials. In addition, the Commission began to implement intra-European cooperation arrangements for the operation of nuclear power stations. The first countries to benefit from the programme, which seeks to improve nuclear plant safety through twinning arrangements between operators, were Poland and Czechoslovakia.

614. Following the first meeting[4] in July 1989, a further high-level meeting with United States energy officials was held in Brussels in May.[5]

615. International energy cooperation programmes advanced appreciably in 1990, primarily with the countries of Central and Eastern Europe under the Phare programme,[6] but also with the countries of Asia, Latin America[7] and the Mediterranean basin. A budget of ECU 6.7 million will allow more than 60 cooperation programmes to be financed.

Sectoral aspects

Oil and petroleum products

616. The outbreak of the Gulf crisis pushed prices sharply upwards on world markets.[8] Prices continued to rise even when it became apparent that additional production from other oil-exporting countries would offset the embargo on Iraqi and Kuwaiti exports.

In the light of the situation, on 24 October the Commission adopted a communication on the steps to be taken in the event of oil supply difficulties and on stocks of petroleum products, together with two proposals for Directives.[9] The purpose of these proposals, which are based on an analysis of the short-term market prospects, is to amend the 1968

---

[1]   Twenty-third General Report, point 797; Point 685 of this Report.
[2]   Bull. EC 7/8-1990, point 1.3.302.
[3]   Point 656 of this Report.
[4]   Twenty-third General Report, point 665.
[5]   Bull. EC 5-1990, point 1.2.230.
[6]   Point 669 of this Report.
[7]   Points 763 and 764 of this Report.
[8]   Point 734 of this Report.
[9]   Bull. EC 10-1990, points 1.3.204 to 1.3.206.

Directive on reserve oil stocks[1] and the 1973 Directive on measures to mitigate the effects of difficulties in the supply of crude oil and petroleum products.[2]

On 29 October the Council adopted conclusions[3] in which it stressed that there was no real supply crisis, but confirmed its endorsement of the positions adopted by the IEA and its intention to coordinate the Community's response in the event of such a crisis.

The European Parliament also expressed its view on the rise in oil prices, adopting three resolutions at its first October part-session.[4]

617.   Prior to the events in the Gulf the Council had adopted,[5] in May, a Regulation adapting the reporting requirements introduced in 1979 as regards crude oil imports in the Community[6] to the trading conditions prevailing on international markets.

Natural gas

618.   The Directive concerning a Community procedure on the transparency of gas and electricity prices charged to industrial end-users was adopted by the Council on 29 June;[7] in December the Council also adopted a common position on the proposal for a Directive on the transit of natural gas through the major networks.[7]

619.   On 29 October the Council reached agreement[8] on a position in favour of the proposal for a Directive[9] repealing Directive 75/404/EEC on the restriction of the use of natural gas in power stations,[10] in the light of technological advances. The Economic and Social Committee had delivered a favourable opinion on this proposal on 18 October.[8]

Solid fuels

620.   Acting under Decision No 2064/86/ECSC establishing Community rules for State aid to the coal industry,[11] the Commission authorized the granting of aid to the industry

---

[1]   OJ L 308, 23.12.1968.
[2]   OJ L 228, 16.8.1973; Seventh General Report, point 382.
[3]   Bull. EC 10-1990, point 1.3.207.
[4]   OJ C 284, 12.11.1990; Bull. EC 10-1990, points 1.3.208 to 1.3.210.
[5]   OJ L 133, 24.5.1990; Bull. EC 5-1990, point 1.2.228; Commission proposal: Bull. EC 1/2-1990, point 1.1.263.
[6]   OJ L 220, 30.8.1979; OJ L 297, 24.11.1979; Thirteenth General Report, point 398.
[7]   Point 601 of this Report.
[8]   Bull. EC 10-1990, point 1.3.211.
[9]   OJ C 203, 14.8.1990; Bull. EC 7/8-1990, point 1.3.297.
[10]   OJ L 178, 9.7.1975; Ninth General Report, point 355.
[11]   OJ L 177, 1.7.1986; Twentieth General Report, point 737.

in the Federal Republic of Germany[1] and Portugal[2] in 1989, and in Belgium,[3] France,[3] Spain[4] and Germany[5] in 1990. Furthermore, the Commission authorized supplementary aid for 1989-90 in the United Kingdom,[6] for 1988 and 1989 in the Federal Republic of Germany and for 1987, 1988 and 1989 in Spain.[7] As in the case of Germany in 1989,[8] the Commission accompanied the latter authorization with a request to the Spanish authorities to submit a plan for reducing compensatory payments to electricity producers and a plan for restructuring, rationalizing and modernizing the coal industry.

621.   On 18 July the Commission repealed[9] the 1959[10] and 1962[11] recommendations on commercial policy measures concerning imports of coal from third countries into the Federal Republic of Germany. On the same date it authorized[12] Spain to exclude from Community treatment, up to 31 December, coal of third country origin imported after having been put into free circulation in another Member State.

622.   On 23 March the Commission approved on first reading the report on the solid fuels market in the Community in 1989 and the outlook for 1990.[13] The ECSC Consultative Committee was consulted twice on this report, in March[14] and September,[15] the purpose of the latter meeting being to revise the forecasts for 1990. The Commission formally adopted the report on 10 September, and on 14 December it approved the draft report on the outlook for 1991.[16]

Electricity

623.   In May and October, respectively, the Council adopted Directives concerning a Community procedure on the transparency of gas and electricity prices charged to the industrial end-user[17] and, secondly, the transit of electricity through the major European networks.[17]

---

[1]   OJ L 105, 25.4.1990.
[2]   OJ L 5, 8.1.1991.
[3]   OJ L 133, 24.5.1990; Bull. EC 3-1990, point 1.1.188.
[4]   OJ L 5, 8.1.1991; Bull. EC 7/8-1990, point 1.3.296.
[5]   OJ L 346, 11.12.1990.
[6]   OJ L 346, 11.12.1990; Bull. EC 3-1990, point 1.1.188.
[7]   OJ L 105, 25.4.1990.
[8]   Twenty-third General Report, point 674.
[9]   OJ L 228, 22.8.1990; Bull. EC 7/8-1990, point 1.3.294.
[10]   OJ 8, 11.2.1959.
[11]   OJ 116, 12.11.1962.
[12]   OJ L 228, 22.8.1990; Bull. EC 7/8-1990, point 1.3.295.
[13]   Bull. EC 3-1990, point 1.1.185.
[14]   Bull. EC 3-1990, point 1.1.186.
[15]   Bull. EC 9-1990, point 1.2.184.
[16]   Bull. EC 12-1990.
[17]   Point 601 of this Report.

624. The Commission pressed ahead with its work to improve the efficiency of electricity use, in line with the Council Decision of June 1989 instituting a Community action programme on this subject.[1] In particular it collected information on specific current and future initiatives in the Member States and drew up a document listing a series of action projects to be undertaken at Community level. A number of activities were continued, dealing, in particular, with the problems and possibilities involved in introducing Community energy labelling and standards for the efficiency of electrical appliances.

The Commission also embarked, in collaboration with the national administrations, electricity distributors and consumers, on a study of the scope for third-party access to electricity grids in the Community. It also continued its policy debate on a number of topics liable to be the subject of proposals in future: electricity supply structures in the Community, network optimization, costs and electricity prices.

Nuclear energy

625. The update[2] of the Community's illustrative nuclear programme (PINC)[3] was published on 7 February,[4] and work began on implementing the recommendations in this document: second phase of the European Fast Reactor project; bilateral agreements between electricity producers with a view to a subsequent multilateral agreement on light-water reactors; debate on the standardization of nuclear power plant components, in particular the interface with safety.

626. On 22 January the Council adopted[5] a negotiating brief for a safeguards agreement between Euratom, the United Kingdom and the IAEA in accordance with the Tlatelolco Treaty establishing a nuclear-free zone in Latin America.

New and renewable energy sources

627. As part of its efforts to promote renewable energy sources the Commission, in collaboration with the Spanish authorities, organized a conference on wind energy in Madrid in May, which culminated in proposals for a Community strategy in this field. It published[6] an invitation to submit proposals for a study on the economic and technical

---

[1]   OJ L 157, 9.6.1989; Twenty-third General Report, point 681.
[2]   Twenty-third General Report, point 679.
[3]   Eighteenth General Report, point 528.
[4]   Bull. EC 1/2-1990, point 1.1.265.
[5]   Bull. EC 1/2-1990, point 1.1.269; Commission proposal: Twenty-third General Report, point 679.
[6]   OJ C 239, 25.9.1990.

outlook for renewable energies to the year 2010 and funded a project for the systematic compilation of statistics on renewable energy sources. It endorsed the creation in May of the European Association for Biomass and published an invitation for proposals for studies of the biomass market. The Commission confirmed its endorsement of the activities of the European Small Hydro Association, funding the publication of the proceedings of the Hydro-Energy '89 Conference and supporting studies on mini-hydro-power stations.

Energy savings and rational use

628.   On 3 October the Commission adopted[1] a proposal for a Regulation on the promotion of energy efficiency in the Community (SAVE programme).[2] This programme, which will take five years to complete, begins on 1 January 1991 and complements project carried out elsewhere by the Community and the Member States: the programme will take the form of medium- and long-term projects covering technical, financial and fiscal aspects, and the setting-up of a system of information exchange and the adoption of legislation. The first such piece of legislation, a Directive on the efficiency requirement for new hot-water boilers using liquid or gaseous fuels, was proposed by the Commission on the same date.[3]

Euratom Supply Agency

629.   As in 1989,[4] the supply of natural uranium and enrichment services to Community users and the provision of services for the whole fuel cycle continued smoothly in 1990, with the exception of the reprocessing of highly enriched uranium. The Community depended on imports for more than 70% of its supplies of natural uranium. Of the eight external supplier countries, none accounted for more than 25% of total supplies.

Given the termination or suspension of nuclear programmes in a number of Western countries, both the supply of natural uranium and enrichment services, as well as the provision of services for the whole fuel cycle, seem reasonably secure in the short to medium term. The probable shortfall of uranium production in relation to demand is likely to continue to be covered by the running down of stocks and by increased supplies from the countries of Central and Eastern Europe. In the longer term, too, supply seems secure as long as economic trends are not distorted by political factors or the number

---

1   OJ C 301, 30.11.1990; Bull. EC 10-1990, point 1.3.202.
2   Specific actions for vigorous energy efficiency.
3   OJ C 292, 22.11.1990; Bull. EC 10-1990, point 1.3.203.
4   Twenty-third General Report, point 683.

of producers is not reduced by an excessive fall in prices. The Agency takes the view that security of supply can best be guaranteed by the conclusion of long-term purchasing contracts, while specific contracts could be considered for unforeseen needs, thereby ensuring market stability and the diversification of sources of supply.

630.   The primary market, both in natural uranium, uranium and in enrichment services again remained quiet this year. In spite of a slight upturn during the second half of the year, 44 long-term contracts for uranium procurement and 4 long-term contracts for enrichment services were concluded out of a total of some 243 contracts signed by the Agency in 1990 (101 for natural uranium and 142 for the supply of enrichment services and special fissile materials).

631.   On the market for natural uranium, most transactions by the Agency were for spot purchases or swap transactions, generally involving intermediaries. On the market for special fissile materials and enrichment services, the focus was also on spot purchases. Since the market was oversupplied, the downward price trend persisted:[1] the average price paid by the electricity producers for natural uranium under long-term contracts (accounting for some 90% of supplies) is likely to be about ECU 69/kg of U_3O_8. World spot market prices fell from ECU 8.2/lb of U_3O_8 in December 1989 to ECU 8.6 in September 1990 (from ECU 24.5 to ECU 29.6/kg U). As regards enriched uranium there was an excess of production capacity in all enrichment plants; high availability in the Soviet Union together with surplus stocks of enriched uranium kept spot prices relatively low.

---

[1]   Twenty-third General Report, point 685.

Section 19

Euratom safeguards

632.   In 1990 the Euratom Safeguards Directorate conducted physical and accounting checks on average stocks of some 180 tonnes of plutonium, 12 tonnes of highly enriched uranium and 194 000 tonnes of low-enrichment uranium, natural uranium, depleted uranium, thorium and heavy water. These materials were held in over 800 nuclear installations in the Community and gave rise to nearly 500 000 operator entries concerning physical movements and stocks. As in the past, the checks also covered equipment subject to external commitments under cooperation agreements with non-member countries. The anomalies and irregularities detected by the Directorate were followed up rigorously by additional inspections; some of these are still being looked into.

633.   On 26 January the Commission adopted Regulation (Euratom) No 220/90[1] amending Regulation (Euratom) No 3227/76[2] in order to establish an inventory change for the recording of nuclear material obtained from substances not subject to safeguards, as a result of attaining the minimum concentration requirements. In addition, the 'particular safeguard provisions' referred to in Articles 7 and 8 of Regulation (Euratom) No 3227/76 entered into force for 18 nuclear reactors in Belgium, the Federal Republic of Germany and Spain.

634.   It had emerged from discussions between the various European authorities on the subject of nuclear energy that it was both desirable and necessary to prepare a report on the operational aspects of safeguards. The latter, adopted by the Commission on 19 March,[3] seeks to provide an overview of safeguard activities in the nuclear fuel cycle for civil use, including research and other related activities. It was favourably received by the Council in December.[4] The Council reiterated the importance it attaches to safeguards and emphasized the need to maintain high safety standards.

635.   For the first time the Commission applied a sanction under Article 83 of the Euratom Treaty, deciding on 1 August to place the undertaking Advanced Nuclear Fuels

---

[1]   OJ L 22, 27.1.1990; Bull. EC 1/2-1990, point 1.1.266.
[2]   OJ L 363, 31.12.1976; Tenth General Report, point 432.
[3]   Bull. EC 3-1990, point 1.1.187.
[4]   Bull. EC 12-1990.

GmbH under administration following infringement of Article 79 of the Euratom Treaty. [1] The sanction will last for a period of four months and will concern only the safeguards aspects.

In consultation with the French authorities, the Commission established the practical arrangements for the safeguards for the new UP$_3$ reprocessing plant at La Hague.

636.   On 4 October, after on-the-spot visits and a seminar in Berlin for operators of nuclear installations, safeguards inspectors began the first inspection activities in the nuclear installations situated on the territory of the former German Democratic Republic. [2]

637.   Special attention was paid to the laboratories on the spot which should be able to analyse the large number of samples of nuclear materials taken, in particular in the reprocessing plants, and to produce the results very quickly, thus avoiding the high costs and risks involved in transporting the samples to distant laboratories, generally at the Joint Research Centre.

---

[1]   OJ L 209, 8.8.1990; Bull. EC 7/8-1990, point 1.3.299.
[2]   Bull. EC 10-1990, point 1.3.95.

Section 20

Nuclear safety

Priority activities and objectives

*638.   The Community continued its activities in accordance with the guidelines adopted
following the Chernobyl accident in 1986.[1] At international level it expanded its activities
with regard to the Central and Eastern European countries, in particular under the Phare
programme[2] which, at the request of Poland and Czechoslovakia, has been extended to
include cooperation projects in the field of nuclear safety. The Commission also requested
the Council for authorization to negotiate a cooperation agreement in the field of nuclear
safety with the Soviet Union. The Commission stepped up its cooperation with other
international organizations, in particular the International Atomic Energy Agency: Commission representatives took part, for example, in nuclear safety missions organized by
the Agency in various European countries.*

Radiation protection

639.   On 22 March the Council extended,[3] until 31 March 1995, Regulation (EEC)
No 3955/87[4] on the conditions governing imports of agricultural products originating in
third countries following the Chernobyl accident. In 1989 the Regulation had been
extended until 31 March 1990.[5] The Regulation as extended also provides for measures
designed to bring about a gradual return to normal.

640.   On 4 December the Council adopted a Directive on the operational protection
of outside workers exposed to ionizing radiation during their activities in installations
in which such radiation is used.[6] The Directive supplements, as regards this particular

---

[1]   Twentieth General Report, point 759.
[2]   Point 668 of this Report.
[3]   OJ L 82, 29.3.1990; Bull. EC 3-1990, point 1.1.90; Commission proposal: Bull. EC 1/2-1990, point 1.1.135.
[4]   OJ L 371, 30.12.1987; Twenty-first General Report, point 695.
[5]   OJ L 382, 30.12.1989; Twenty-third General Report, point 692.
[6]   OJ L 349, 13.12.1990; Bull. EC 12-1990; Commission proposal: Twenty-third General Report, point 694;
      Bull. EC 1/2-1990, point 1.1.134; Bull. EC 11-1990, point 1.3.99.

category of workers, Directive 80/836/Euratom,[1] which lays down basic standards for the health protection of the general public and workers against the dangers of ionizing radiation. The Commission also began preparatory work on a partial revision of the Directive to adapt it to the latest scientific developments in this area.

641.   On 29 March the Commission adopted Regulation (Euratom) No 770/90 laying down maximum permitted levels of radioactive contamination of feedingstuffs following a nuclear accident or any other case of radiological emergency.[2] With the adoption of this Regulation, all the maximum levels provided for by Council Regulation (Euratom) No 3954/87,[3] as amended in 1989,[4] have been laid down.

642.   On 21 February the Commission adopted a recommendation on the protection of the public against indoor exposure to radon in which it proposes the establishment, in the Member States, of a system for limiting exposure to indoor radon concentrations.[5]

643.   In accordance with its decision to resume the inspections provided for in Article 35 of the Euratom Treaty,[6] the Commission verified the operation and efficiency of the relevant facilities at the Philippsburg nuclear power station (Federal Republic of Germany).

644.   Acting under Article 33 of the Euratom Treaty, the Commission delivered seven opinions on draft radiation protection provisions submitted by Denmark, Italy, Portugal and the United Kingdom.

645.   On 7 December the Commission adopted a recommendation on the application of Article 37 of the Euratom Treaty.[7] This recommendation replaces that of 3 February 1982[8] in the light of the judgment of the Court of Justice of 22 September 1988.[9] Under Article 37 the Commission delivered four opinions concerning plans for the discharge of radioactive effluent from various types of nuclear installations.

646.   Some 100 multinational research projects were selected for funding under the radiation protection research and training programme 1990-91.[10]

---

[1]   OJ L 246, 17.9.1980; Fourteenth General Report, point 265.
[2]   OJ L 83, 30.3.1990; Bull. EC 3-1990, point 1.1.91.
[3]   OJ L 371, 30.12.1987; Twenty-first General Report, point 694.
[4]   OJ L 211, 22.7.1989; Twenty-third General Report, point 691.
[5]   OJ L 80, 27.3.1990; Bull. EC 1/2-1990, point 1.1.121.
[6]   Twenty-third General Report, point 697.
[7]   OJ L 6, 9.1.1991; Bull. EC 12-1990.
[8]   OJ L 83, 29.3.1982; Sixteenth General Report, point 542.
[9]   Judgment of 22.9.1988, Case 187/87 *Saarland* v *Minister for Industry, P and T and Tourism* (OJ C 271, 20.10.1988); Twenty-second General Report, point 1098.
[10]   Point 286 of this Report.

A proposal for a specific programme in the field of nuclear fission safety as part of the framework programme of research and technological development 1990-94 was adopted by the Commission on 1 August.[1] It contains a radiation protection section for 1992-93.

647.　On 15 March the European Parliament adopted a resolution on safety at the Sellafield nuclear plant in which it expressed concern about the results of epidemiological studies carried out in the United Kingdom concerning the statistical relationship between leukaemia in children and the occupational exposure of their parents.[2]

Plant safety

648.　On 26 March the Council adopted conclusions[3] on the Commission report[4] on the technological problems of nuclear safety which takes stock of the work carried out concerning the harmonization of safety requirements in the light of the Council resolution of 22 July 1975.[5] The Council reaffirmed its commitment to the goal of levelling up safety requirements in the Community and at international level.

649.　The research and training programme in the field of remote handling in hazardous and disordered nuclear environments (Teleman) got under way with the selection of 16 multinational research projects.[6]

650.　A proposal for a specific programme in the field of nuclear fission safety as part of the framework programme of research and technological development 1990-94 was adopted by the Commission on 1 August.[6] contains a section on reactor safety which will be implemented as an intensified concerted action project.

Radioactive waste

651.　On 17 July, in the light of the opinion delivered by the Economic and Social Committee[7] on the 1989 proposal,[8] the Commission adopted a proposal for a Directive[9] amending Directive 80/836/Euratom,[10] which lays down basic safety standards for the

---

[1]　Point 286 of this Report.
[2]　OJ C 96, 17.4.1990; Bull. EC 3-1990, point 1.1.52.
[3]　Bull. EC 3-1990, point 1.1.92.
[4]　Bull. EC 1/2-1990, point 1.1.36.
[5]　OJ C 185, 14.8.1975, Ninth General Report, point 302.
[6]　Point 289 of this Report.
[7]　OJ C 168, 10.7.1990; Bull. EC 4-1990, point 1.1.84.
[8]　OJ C 5, 10.1.1990; Twenty-third General Report, point 701.
[9]　OJ C 210, 23.8.1990; Bull. EC 7/8-1990, point 1.3.149.
[10]　OJ L 246, 17.9.1980; Fourteenth General Report, point 265.

health protection of the general public and workers against the dangers of ionizing radiation, as regards prior authorization for shipments of radioactive waste.

652.   In December the Council adopted conclusions[1] on the Commission communication on objectives, standards and criteria for radioactive waste disposal.[2] In its conclusions the Council emphasized in particular the importance of formulating a common approach at Community level to radioactive waste management strategies and practices, and recommended the Commission to submit proposals in this connection.

653.   The fourth programme of research and technological development in the field of the management and storage of radioactive waste, which was approved by the Council in December 1989, gets under way this year.[3]

654.   In October the European Parliament adopted a resolution on the transport of nuclear waste by ferry and the storage and processing of nuclear waste.[4]

Decommissioning of nuclear installations

655.   The third programme on the decommissioning of nuclear installations (1989-93) got under way with the selection of 51 multinational research projects and the start of work on four pilot dismantling projects.[5]

International action

656.   In August the Commission submitted to the Council a draft decision setting out guidelines for the Commission for the negotiation of a cooperative agreement with the Soviet Union in the field of nuclear safety,[6] covering reactor safety, radiation protection, management of nuclear waste, decommissioning, decontamination and dismantling of nuclear installations, and research and development concerning the monitoring of nuclear materials.

657.   The Commission took part in the assessment carried out in the IAEA framework of the exposure and consequences in the Soviet Union of the Chernobyl accident.

---

[1]   Bull. EC 12-1990.
[2]   Bull. EC 11-1990, point 1.3.80.
[3]   Point 288 of this Report.
[4]   OJ C 295, 26.11.1990; Bull. EC 10-1990, point 1.3.96.
[5]   Point 290 of this Report.
[6]   Point 613 of this Report.

Chapter IV

External relations

Section 1

Priority activities and objectives

658.   *Owing to the political and economic reforms in the countries of Central and Eastern Europe, there was a considerable upgrading of relations and cooperation between the Community and those countries in 1990. The programme of aid for the economic reconstruction of Poland and Hungary (Phare) set up by the Commission at the beginning of the year was extended to Czechoslovakia, Bulgaria, Yugoslavia and the German Democratic Republic until unification, with a final total of ECU 500 million being earmarked for assistance to the countries concerned. In view of the additional difficulties confronting them as a result of the Gulf crisis, as well as the adoption of convertible currencies as a means of payment in commercial transactions and the establishment of world market prices in trade within the Council for Mutual Economic Assistance, the European Council meeting in Rome in December agreed that steps should be taken,* inter alia *in the framework of the Group of 24, to help the countries involved cope with their financing requirements. As well as economic aid of this type, the* rapprochement *between the Central and Eastern European countries and the Community should, as the countries concerned carry out the requisite political and economic reforms, take the form of a move towards a new type of relations. This is the object of the 'European agreements' on which negotiations with Poland, Hungary and Czechoslovakia opened in December. These agreements, one of the main objects of which is the progressive setting up of a free-trade zone and increased economic, scientific and technical cooperation, should also supply the proper institutional framework for the conduct of genuine political dialogue. In relation to the Soviet Union, the European Council, on the basis of the outcome of the work done by the Commission at its behest, decided to make food aid worth up to ECU 750 million*

available in the short term and, in the longer term, to supply technical assistance of the kind which would help put the Soviet economy back on its feet.

659.   Following the ministerial meeting in December 1989 at which it was decided to embark on formal negotiations between the Community and the EFTA countries, these opened on 20 June. Their purpose is ultimately the establishment of a European economic area in which freedom of movement for goods, services, individuals and capital is guaranteed as well as greater cooperation in the field of flanking policies and a reduction in economic and social disparities. Considerable progress was made in the course of the year, mainly in respect of joint action to identify the existing Community provisions suitable for inclusion in a future agreement and of institutional and judicial matters. The ministerial meeting of 19 December was an opportunity to take stock of progress and pinpoint the difficulties still to be resolved. The two sides expressed the wish to step up their discussions so that they would be in a position to sign an agreement by the summer of 1991.

660.   The Community and the United States of America established closer and broader relations in line with the joint ministerial-level decision of December 1989. As a result, contacts between the Commission and the US Administration were stepped up at every level. The two sides sought to further cooperation between them, not just by giving greater depth to their existing dialogue but also by seeking out new areas of common interest. This desire culminated in the adoption by the United States and the Community and its Member States of a joint declaration in November, a sign of the importance of transatlantic relations for political stability and economic progress in Europe and throughout the world. A similar declaration, inspired by the same considerations, was signed with Canada. Trade questions continued to crop up in relations between the Community and the United States, but the problems discussed in the Uruguay Round were put in abeyance until the negotiations in question were completed.

661.   This year saw the resumption of ministerial-level meetings between the Commission and Japan after a break of nearly three years. Emphasis was placed on the need to strengthen and deepen cooperation between the two sides in a large number of areas of common interest, particularly science and technology, and in the social, cultural, environmental and development aid fields. Progress still has to be made, however, on opening up the Japanese market to European products and investment, given the large and continuing deficit in the Community's trade balance with Japan.

662.   In the area of the Community's relations with the Mediterranean countries, the Commission took three major initiatives on overhauling its Mediterranean policy as a whole and on relations with Yugoslavia and Turkey. Substantial progress was made on the first two points, with the Council in December adopting a comprehensive decision on Mediterranean policy, including a considerable sum in funding, and adopting guide-

lines for the negotiation of the third financial protocol with Yugoslavia. Applications for membership from Cyprus and Malta were confirmation of the Community's continuing and undoubted drawing power.

663.   The Gulf crisis was an opportunity for the Community and its Member States to display their cohesion, firmness and solidarity. They categorically condemned the Iraqi invasion of Kuwait and responded both by launching a huge emergency aid operation and taking immediate steps to impose an embargo in line with UN Security Council resolutions and by their decision to give financial assistance to the neighbouring countries most immediately affected by the consequences of events in the Gulf.

664.   In December the Council approved the guidelines for cooperation with the developing countries of Asia and Latin America in the coming decade. The Community stepped up its relations with the countries belonging to the Association of South-East Asian Nations and with the Association itself. It strengthened its bilateral ties with the major Southern Asian countries and re-established diplomatic relations with Vietnam. At the same time it consolidated its presence in Latin America by drafting and concluding several cooperation agreements, setting up a regional payments system in Central America and responding favourably to the cooperation requirements of the countries involved in combating drugs.

665.   In the area of relations between the Community and the African, Carribbean and Pacific States, 1990 was spent drawing up the new convention signed in Lomé on 15 December 1989. The Convention has to be ratified by the Member States and at least two thirds of the ACP States before it enters into force. By the end of the year two Member States and 33 ACP States had completed the process. As the financial protocol cannot be put into effect until the Convention is ratified, the Commission has made an urgent appeal to the States concerned to ensure that the procedures now under way are completed as soon as possible. However, the adoption of transitional measures as far back as 1 March enabled certain major provisions of the Convention to be put into force straight away, particularly the trading arrangements which it lays down. The process of planning the Community's aid to the ACP States, a vital stage in the implementation of the Convention, was carried through actively and successfully in a spirit of openness and dialogue. Namibia, independent since 21 March, acceded to the Convention and thus became the 69th ACP State. The Lomé Convention therefore now covers the whole of sub-Saharan Africa apart from South Africa. In view of developments in that country, and in line with the conclusions of the Dublin European Council of 25 and 26 June, the Community decided to increase the funds earmarked under its programme of positive measures to aid the victims of apartheid, especially in terms of meeting the requirements created by the return of exiles.[1] In conclusion, the Community took a step with

---

[1]   Bull. EC 6-1990, point 1.4.48.

far-reaching political implications in proposing the cancellation of the debts contracted to the Community by the ACP States under previous Conventions. The proposed measures are an encouraging signal to what are some of the poorest countries in the world to persevere with their attempts at reform and revival in relation to economic and social development.

666.   On a multilateral level the Community worked to make sure that the Uruguay Round trade talks would be a success by playing an active part in all the work on the various areas under discussion, through putting forward constructive proposals. Despite significant progress on certain issues, the ministerial conference held in Brussels from 3 to 7 December failed to bring the negotiations to a successful conclusion, largely because of disagreements over reforming agricultural policy. The Community will give its full backing to the efforts which are to be made shortly to iron out these differences and find realistic solutions to the problems still outstanding.

667.   In 1990 the number of diplomatic missions from non-Community countries accredited to the European Communities rose to 142. The Commission opened delegations in Warsaw, Budapest, Nicosia and Manila and made preparations for opening others in Malta, Moscow, Lima, Windhoek, Santo Domingo and Port-au-Prince, thereby increasing the number of its external delegations to 93.

Section 2

Relations with the countries of Central and Eastern Europe

Operation Phare

Coordination of the Group of 24

668.   The Commission continued to coordinate economic assistance from the 24 Western countries (G-24) associated with Operation Phare; this task was entrusted to the Commission by the Paris Western Economic Summit.[1] Operation Phare initially concerned only Poland and Hungary, but during the year it was extended to other Central and Eastern European countries.

G-24 assistance to Poland and Hungary included measures facilitating access for Polish and Hungarian products to G-24 markets,[2] the establishment of a USD 1 billion fund comprising contributions from many G-24 countries to help Poland stabilize its currency, the granting by the Community of the first and second tranches (ECU 350 million and ECU 260 million respectively) of a USD 1 billion medium-term loan to help Hungary overcome its balance of payments difficulties,[3] and the financing of economic restructuring projects and programmes and of initiatives to promote export (credit insurance) and investments, costing a total of more than ECU 11 billion. The Community set aside ECU 300 million for economic aid in the form of grants, plus up to ECU 1 billion in loans from the European Investment Bank over three years[4] and ECSC loans to finance investment in the coal and steel industries in Hungary and Poland.[5] The food aid to Poland approved in 1989 was also continued.[6]

The second ministerial meeting of the Group of 24 was held in Brussels on 4 July;[7] work continued throughout the year at senior official level.[8] At the July meeting Ministers

---

[1]   Twenty-third General Report, point 786.
[2]   Points 669 and 848 of this Report.
[3]   Point 50 of this Report.
[4]   Point 49 of this Report.
[5]   Point 51 of this Report.
[6]   Point 469 of this Report.
[7]   Bull. EC 7/8-1990, point 1.4.1.
[8]   Bull. EC 1/2-1990, point 1.2.8; Bull. EC 3-1990, point 1.2.3; Bull. EC 5-1990, point 1.3.4; Bull. EC 10-1990, point 1.4.6.

decided to extend assistance to the German Democratic Republic, Czechoslovakia, Bulgaria and Yugoslavia in order to support the reform process under way in those countries. Romania was granted only humanitarian aid. The new action plan for coordinated assistance proposed by the Commission[1] was adopted by the G-24 Ministers, who agreed to develop joint programmes and projects in priority areas. This led to measures by G-24 countries and by the Community aimed at improving market access for products originating in the new recipient countries[2] and to the necessary funds being made available.[3]

The Community adopted a budget of ECU 200 million for the financing of economic restructuring projects.[4] The Community proposed to extend the guarantee given by the Community to the EIB at the beginning of the year on loans to projects in Poland and Hungary to cover projects in Czechoslovakia, Bulgaria and Romania, and to extend to Czechoslovakia, Bulgaria and Yugoslavia the entitlement to ESCS loans that had been granted in March to Poland and Hungary.[5] It further proposed stepping up export credit insurance and the protection and promotion of investment in the countries of Central and Eastern Europe.[6] The European Council meeting in Rome in December[7] announced that the Community, under the G-24 umbrella, would support Czechoslovakia's programme to stabilize and modernize its economy and to achieve full convertibility for its currency. It also decided to grant emergency food aid worth ECU 100 milion to Bulgaria and Romania.

These measures were supplemented by more general initiatives: establishment of the European Bank for Reconstruction and Development,[8] setting-up of the European Training Foundation and the Tempus programme,[9] and inauguration of the Budapest regional environment centre, in which Hungary is joined by certain G-24 countries, including various Community Member States.[10]

---

[1]   Bull. EC 5-1990, point 1.3.3.
[2]   Points 670 and 795 of this Report.
[3]   Points 669 and 1025 of this Report.
[4]   Point 669 of this Report.
[5]   Point 51 of this Report.
[6]   Point 837 of this Report.
[7]   Bull. EC 12-1990.
[8]   Point 54 of this Report.
[9]   Point 390 of this Report.
[10]   Point 509 of this Report.

Community contribution

669.   On 17 September, following the decision of the Group of 24,[1] the Council amended[2] Regulation (EEC) No 3906/89 on economic aid to Hungary and Poland[3] in order to extend assistance to other Central and Eastern European countries.

The Commission, which attaches the highest priority to this latest operation, swiftly set up the necessary machinery for implementing the aid programme. From the beginning of the year it cooperated closely on a permanent basis with the Polish and Hungarian authorities, and the first financial programmes were launched as early as March. Following the extension of the programme in September, financing decisions concerning the new countries were adopted the same month.

The financial programmes take the form of direct aid; rather than subsidizing individual projects, the emphasis is on providing sectoral support for the process of economic restructuring and encouraging the changes necessary to build an economy based on market forces and private enterprise. It includes financial and technical assistance to help establish an environment favourable to the emergence of a modern market economy, assistance in the preparation and implementation of sectoral development plans, support for pump-priming projects which can act as catalysts for subsequent complementary assistance from other G-24 countries and, where appropriate, the provision of vital supplies to maintain the production of goods and services which are essential for the economy of the countries concerned. Financing decisions taken in this framework gave priority to modernizing agriculture, restructuring the financial sector, privatization (especially of small and medium-sized firms), promoting investment, protecting the environment, and education and training.[4] A number of emergency food aid and humanitarian aid operations were also financed, many of them in Romania, which is not yet receiving economic aid. Table 10 gives the breakdown of the financial aid granted.

Trade arrangements

670.   Imports from Eastern European countries of products not liberalized at Community level continued to be subject to arrangements which differ considerably from one

---

[1]   Point 668 of this Report.
[2]   OJ L 257, 21.9.1990; Bull. EC 9-1990, point 1.3.3; Commission proposal: OJ C 191, 31.7.1990; Bull. EC 7/8-1990, point 1.4.2.
[3]   OJ L 375, 23.12.1989; Twenty-third General Report, point 786.
[4]   Bull. EC 3-1990, point 1.2.5; Bull. EC 5-1990, point 1.3.5; Bull. EC 7/8-1990, point 1.4.10; Bull. EC 9-1990, point 1.1.8; Bull. EC 10-1990, point 1.4.5; Bull. EC 11-1990, point I.44; Bull. EC 12-1990.

Member State to another; it has not so far been possible to establish entirely uniform arrangements for these products.

TABLE 10

Operation Phare: Financial aid granted

million ECU

Beneficiaries	Sectors							Total
	Agri-culture	Industry/finance	Environ-ment	Education, training	Health, social development	Humani-tarian aid	Other	
Poland	100	56	22	16.6				194.6
Hungary	20	35.3	27	12	3			97.3
Bulgaria	16		3.5	4	5			28.5
Czechoslovakia			30	1				31
GDR (before unification)			20				14[1]	34
Romania					4.4	11.1		15.5
Yugoslavia		35						35
Other						51[2]	12.9	63.9
Total	136	126.3	102.5	33.6	12.4	62.1	26.9	500

[1] Regional restructuring (various items).
[2] Food aid.

The import quotas to be opened by the Member States in 1990 were agreed by the Council on 27 July.[1] At the same time, quantitative restrictions applied at Community level were gradually liberalized. Extension to other Central and Eastern European countries of Operation Phare[2] resulted in the adoption by the Council of Regulation (EEC) No 2727/90,[3] replacing the Regulations which previously applied to Poland and Hungary[4] and providing for the elimination or suspension of quantitative restrictions on imports from the countries of Central and Eastern Europe from 1 October, subject in the case of Romania to the entry into force of the trade and cooperation Agreement.[5] As a temporary measure connected with German unification,[6] the Council suspended,

[1]   OJ L 259, 24.9.1990; Bull. EC 7/8-1990, point 1.4.73; Commission proposal: Bull. EC 5-1990, point 1.3.58.
[2]   Point 668 of this Report.
[3]   OJ L 262, 26.9.1990; Bull. EC 9-1990, point 1.3.4; Commission proposal: Bull. EC 7/8-1990, point 1.4.3.
[4]   OJ L 326, 11.11.1989; OJ L 362, 12.12.1989; Twenty-third General Report, point 787.
[5]   Point 680 of this Report.
[6]   Point 22 of this Report.

from 3 October 1990 to 31 December 1991, the Common Customs Tariff duties on products entered for free circulation in the territory of the former German Democratic Republic and originating in countries of Central and Eastern Europe which have agreements with the former GDR. On 2 October the Commission approved a request regarding a suspension until 31 December 1991 of the remaining quantitative restrictions on imports into the Federal Republic of Germany of the products in question originating in the USSR, to enable the preferential arrangement to be applied in full.[1] The Council also eliminated a significant number of Community and regional quantitative restrictions and suspended a number of other regional quantitative restrictions[2] before the deadline laid down in the Agreement with the Soviet Union.[3]

Bilateral relations

General aspects

671.   As the European Council recorded on several occasions, the Community made a significant contribution to the process of political and economic reform in the countries of Central and Eastern Europe.[4]

672.   The impact of developments in Central and Eastern Europe on the Community's relations with the countries concerned was the subject of a communication from the Commission dated 17 January in which it proposed new Community initiatives to support the changes under way and supplement the network of Agreements with the countries concerned.[5] Further guidelines were adopted following the informal meeting of Foreign Ministers in Dublin on 20 January,[6] the Commission referring to possible new association agreements and giving an indication of the assistance these countries needed from the Community and from the Group of 24. With the Council's backing[7] and while G-24 assistance was being extended,[8] the Commission moved quickly to ensure that trade and cooperation Agreements were concluded with those countries not yet covered by such agreements and specified the objectives and content of the future association agreements. The thinking behind these 'European agreements', the first of

---

[1]   OJ C 254, 9.10.1990.
[2]   OJ L 138, 31.5.1990; Bull. EC 5-1990, point 1.3.16; Commission proposal: Bull. EC 4-1990, point 1.2.13.
[3]   Point 685 of this Report.
[4]   Bull. EC 4-1990, point I.8; Bull. EC 6-1990, point I.20; Bull. EC 10-1990, points I.7 to I.9; Bull. EC 12-1990.
[5]   Bull. EC 1/2-1990, point 1.2.1.
[6]   Bull. EC 1/2-1990, point 1.2.3.
[7]   Bull. EC 1/2-1990, point 1.2.5.
[8]   Point 668 of this Report.

which were to be negotiated with Poland, Hungary and Czechoslovakia, was presented in a communication dated 27 August.[1] Their implementation was to be linked to compliance with the principles of democracy and economic liberalization in the future associated countries. The agreements were to contain sections on political dialogue, free trade and freedom of movement, economic, financial and cultural cooperation, and institutional provisions. The Council adopted the appropriate directives on 18 December,[2] and the negotiations got under way before the end of the year, the Rome European Council[3] declaring that the Community wished to conclude the agreements as quickly as possible, thus marking a new stage in the development of ever-closer relations with the countries concerned.

673.   The Commission identified the prospects for cooperation with the countries of Central and Eastern Europe in the fields of industry,[4] research[5] and technological development.[5]

674.   The various aspects of relations with the countries of Central and Eastern Europe were the subject of numerous resolutions in Parliament[6] and an own-initiative opinion of the Economic and Social Committee.[7]

Specific aspects

Bulgaria

675.   Signed on 8 May[8] and concluded by the Council on 24 September,[9] the trade and commercial and economic cooperation Agreement entered into force on 1 November. Mr Andrei Lukanov, Prime Minister, visited the Commission in April,[10] and again in May[11] to sign the Agreement; Mr Christophersen paid an official visit to Bulgaria in September.[12] The first meeting of the Joint Committee was held in Sofia in November.

---

[1]   Bull. EC 7/8-1990, point 1.4.5.
[2]   Bull. EC 12-1990; Commission proposal: Bull. EC 11-1990.
[3]   Bull. EC 12-1990.
[4]   Point 212 of this Report.
[5]   Point 251 of this Report.
[6]   OJ C 38, 19.2.1990; Bull. EC 1/2-1990, point 1.2.2; OJ C 113, 7.5.1990; Bull. EC 5-1990, point 1.2.4; OJ C 231, 17.9.1990; Bull. EC 7/8-1990, point 1.4.9; OJ C 284, 12.11.1990; Bull. EC 10-1990, points 1.4.3 and 1.4.4; OJ C 324, 24.12.1990; Bull. EC 11-1990, point 1.4.2.
[7]   OJ C 124, 21.5.1990; Bull. EC 3-1990, point 1.2.1.
[8]   Bull. EC 5-1990, point 1.3.7.
[9]   OJ L 291, 23.10.1990; Bull. EC 9-1990, point 1.3.5; Commission proposal: Bull. EC 4-1990, point 1.2.6.
[10]   Bull. EC 4-1990, point 1.2.7.
[11]   Bull. EC 5-1990, point 1.3.8.
[12]   Bull. EC 9-1990, point 1.3.6.

Hungary

676. Following an appeal from the Hungarian Government regarding its serious economic difficulties, the European Council indicated at its extraordinary meeting in Rome in October[1] that the Community and its Member States would help Hungary to overcome its problems, particularly as regards energy supplies.

The third meeting of the EEC-Hungary Joint Committee set up under the trade and commercial and economic cooperation Agreement signed in 1988[2] was held in Budapest on 26 and 27 November.

Mr Geza Jeszenszky, Foreign Minister, and Mr Jozsef Antall, Prime Minister, visited the Commission in June[3] and July[4] respectively; Mr Christophersen visited Budapest in June.[5]

677. On 13 September Parliament adopted a resolution on political aspects of the situation in Hungary and its relations with the Community.[6]

Poland

678. The Polish Prime Minister, Mr Tadeusz Mazowiecki, visited the Commission on 1 February and had talks with Mr Delors and Mr Andriessen.[7] Relations were intensified through a whole series of meetings, in Brussels and Poland, between members of the Polish Government and the Commission.[8]

The second meeting of the EEC-Poland Joint Committee provided for in the 1989 trade and commercial and economic cooperation Agreement[9] was held in Warsaw in September.

679. In February Parliament adopted resolutions on the political aspects of the situation in Poland and economic and trade relations between the Community and Poland.[10]

---

1   Bull. EC 10-1990, point I.9.
2   OJ L 327, 30.11.1988; Twenty-third General Report, point 906.
3   Bull. EC 6-1990, point 1.4.1.
4   Bull. EC 7/8-1990, point 1.4.8.
5   Bull. EC 6-1990, point 1.4.2.
6   OJ C 260, 15.10.1990; Bull. EC 9-1990, point 1.3.7.
7   Bull. EC 1/2-1990, point 1.2.14.
8   Bull. EC 1/2-1990, point 1.2.13; Bull. EC 6-1990, points 1.4.3 and 1.4.4; Bull. EC 9-1990, point 1.3.2; Bull. EC 10-1990, point 1.4.8.
9   OJ L 339, 22.11.1989; Twenty-third General Report, point 790.
10   OJ C 68, 19.3.1990; Bull. EC 1/2-1990, points 1.2.15 and 1.2.16.

Romania

680. Initialled in June[1] following negotiations on the basis of directives issued by the Council in May,[2] the signing of the Agreement between the EEC, the EAEC and Romania on trade and commercial and economic cooperation was suspended on account of the events in Romania in June;[1] the decision to suspend the signing of the Agreement was approved by Parliament.[3] The Agreement was eventually signed in October[4] after the Council had given its approval in September.[5]

681. The EEC-Romania Joint Committee set up under the 1980 Trade Agreement,[6] meetings of which had been suspended, met again on 19 March in Brussels.[7] Mr Mihai Draganescu, Deputy Prime Minister, also had private talks with Mr Andriessen.[8]

682. In 1990 Romania received food products,[9] emergency food and medical aid and humanitarian aid costing ECU 53 million. The humanitarian aid was used mainly to carry out projects to help orphanages.[10]

Czechoslovakia

683. Negotiated on the basis of directives issued by the Council in March,[11] a trade and commercial and economic cooperation Agreement was signed on 8 May[12] and concluded by the Council on behalf of the EEC on 24 September[13] and by the Commission on behalf of the EAEC on 27 September.[13] It entered into force on 1 November.

Mr Delors had talks with Mr Marián Calfa, Prime Minister, in Brussels in Ma[14] and paid an official visit to Czechoslovakia in September.[15] The various aspects of cooperation between the two parties were also discussed during the visits of Mr Jirí Dienstbier,

---

[1]   Bull. EC 6-1990, point 1.4.5.
[2]   Bull. EC 5-1990, point 1.3.12; Commission proposal: Bull. EC 4-1990, point 1.2.11.
[3]   OJ C 233, 17.9.1990; Bull. EC 7/8-1990, point 1.4.13.
[4]   Bull. EC 10-1990, point 1.4.9.
[5]   Bull. EC 9-1990, point 1.3.8.
[6]   OJ L 352, 29.12.1980; Fourteenth General Report, point 705.
[7]   Bull. EC 3-1990, point 1.2.12.
[8]   Bull. EC 3-1990, point 1.2.13.
[9]   Point 469 of this Report.
[10]   Bull. EC 7/8-1990, point 1.4.12; Bull. EC 10-1990, point 1.4.10.
[11]   Bull. EC 3-1990, point 1.2.15; Commission proposal: Bull. EC 1/2-1990, point 1.2.22.
[12]   Bull. EC 5-1990, point 1.3.13.
[13]   OJ L 291, 23.10.1990; Bull. EC 9-1990, points 1.3.9 and 1.3.10; Commission proposal: Bull. EC 4-1990, point 1.2.12.
[14]   Bull. EC 5-1990, point 1.3.14.
[15]   Bull. EC 9-1990, point 1.3.1.

Foreign Minister, to Brussels in March,[1] Mr Christophersen to Prague in July,[2] and Mr Vaclav Vales, Deputy Prime Minister, to Brussels in November.[3]

Soviet Union

684.   Anxious to mark its support for the efforts of the Soviet Union to make progress towards a democratic system and a market-oriented economy, the European Council, at its meeting in Dublin in June,[4] asked the Commission, in cooperation with the IMF, the World Bank, the EIB, the OECD and the President designate of the EBRD, to consult the government of the Soviet Union with a view to preparing proposals covering short-term credits and longer-term support for structural reform. On the basis of the guidelines put forward in a Commission report, the European Council decided in December to grant food aid of up to ECU 750 million, including ECU 250 million in grants from the 1990 budget, and technical assistance worth ECU 400 million in 1991 to support the restructuring of the Soviet economy.[5] Priority would be given to training in public administration and business management, financial services, energy, transport and the distribution of foodstuffs. On 17 December the Council adopted the financial arrangements for the food aid not included in the first tranche of ECU 250 million; it approved the granting of medium-term credit guarantees to exporters for a period of three years from the Community budget.[5] The Council reiterated the conditions laid down by the European Council for the guarantees to ensure that the aid actually reaches the intended recipients and does not compromise the transition to normal supplies on market terms.

685.   The trade and commercial and economic cooperation Agreement signed in December 1989[6] was concluded in February by the Council and the Commission on behalf of the EEC and the EAEC respectively.[7] The first meeting of the Joint Committee set up by the Agreement was held in Moscow in May and attended by Mr Andriessen and Mr Eduard Shevardnadze, Soviet Foreign Minister.[8] The Joint Committee agreed to establish subcommittees on environmental and nuclear issues, scientific and technological cooperation, and customs matters. It also paved the way for faster elimination of quantitative restrictions on Soviet imports.[9]

---

[1]   Bull. EC 3-1990, point 1.2.14.
[2]   Bull. EC 7/8-1990, point 1.4.14.
[3]   Bull. EC 11-1990, point 1.4.6.
[4]   Bull. EC 6-1990, point I.19.
[5]   Bull. EC 12-1990.
[6]   Twenty-third General Report, point 797.
[7]   OJ L 68, 15.3.1990; Bull. EC 1/2-1990, points 1.2.23 and 1.2.24; Commission proposal: OJ C 58, 8.3.1990.
[8]   Bull. EC 5-1990, point 1.3.1.5.
[9]   Point 670 of this Report.

686. Following the entry into force of the framework cooperation Agreement, the Commission sent the Council draft negotiating directives for three agreements on nuclear energy.[1]

Relations with the Council for Mutual Economic Assistance

687. Meetings between experts from the Commission and the CMEA Secretariat continued on the basis of the Joint Declaration of June 1988 on the establishment of official relations between the Community and the CMEA.[2]

---

[1] Point 613 of this Report.
[2] OJ L 157, 24.6.1988; Twenty-second General Report, point 908.

Section 3

European Free Trade Association[1]

Relations with EFTA

688.   As a result of the ministerial meeting held in December 1989[2] the Commission resumed[3] in January the preliminary contacts with a view to examining in more depth the issues related to the establishment of a European economic area (EEA) to include the Community, the EFTA countries and Liechtenstein. These discussions were aimed at identifying the essential Community rules to be adopted by the EFTA countries which embody the four freedoms enshrined in the Treaty, examining the opportunities for increased cooperation in other fields and analysing legal and institutional aspects of the EEA. Senior officials concluded their work on 20 March and a report was presented to the Council at the beginning of April.

On 28 April[4] the European Council in Dublin reaffirmed the great interest attached by the Community to an early agreement on the establishment of a European economic area, and on 8 May[5] the Commission adopted a communication recommending negotiating directives to the Council, whch the latter adopted on 18 June.[6] Parliament adopted a first resolution on 5 April,[7] followed by two resolutions on 12 June,[8] confirming its interest in the establishment of the EEA, which was also the subject of an own-initiative opinion issued by the Economic and Social Committee on 30 May.[9]

At a meeting held in Gothenburg on 13 and 14 June,[10] for part of which Mr Delors and Mr Andriessen were present, the Heads of Government and the Ministers of the EFTA countries indicated their willingness to enter into negotiations. These were officially opened on 20 June, thus keeping the political undertaking given at the ministerial meeting of December 1989 to initiate the negotiations before the end of June 1990, and

---

[1]   Austria, Finland, Iceland, Norway, Sweden and Switzerland.
[2]   Twenty-third General Report, point 781.
[3]   Twenty-third General Report, point 780.
[4]   Bull. EC 4-1990, point I.7.
[5]   Bull. EC 5-1990, point 1.3.17.
[6]   Bull. EC 6-1990, point 1.4.6.
[7]   OJ C 113, 7.5.1990; Bull. EC 4-1990, point 1.2.15.
[8]   OJ C 175, 16.7.1990; Bull. EC 6-1990, point 1.4.9.
[9]   OJ C 182, 23.7.1990; Bull. EC 5-1990, point 1.3.18.
[10]   Bull. EC 6-1990, points 1.4.7. and 1.4.8.

this was welcomed by the European Council meeting on 25 and 26 June in Dublin.[1] A high-level working party made up of senior officials from both sides was entrusted with the task of conducting the negotiations and work was shared out among five groups dealing with goods, services and capital, persons, accompanying measures, and legal and institutional issues.

A joint ministerial meeting held in Brussels on 19 December[2] reviewed the state of negotiations. It was observed in a joint statement that definition of the substance of the agreement, 'the relevant Community rules', was virtually complete and that, in several important fields, a wide convergence of views had been reached. The ministers expressed their wish to see the negotiators actively seek solutions on matters still unresolved and for every effort to be made to enable the agreement establishing the European economic area to be signed before the summer of 1991.

Bilateral relations with the EFTA countries

689.   Closer cooperation and contacts were established with the EFTA countries at all levels. Over and above the meetings of the Joint Committees set up under the free trade Agreements, high-level consultations under the chairmanship of Mr Andriessen and his counterparts at ministerial level took place with Norway, Sweden, Finland and Austria on 28 June,[3] 10 September,[4] 5 October[5] and 27 November[6] respectively. Mr Delors, Mr Andriessen and other members of the Commission had talks in Brussels with Mr Ingvar Carlsson, Swedish Prime Minister, in January[7] and Mr Jean-Pascal Delamuraz, President of the Swiss Federal Council, in July[8] in their double capacity as current chairman of the EFTA Council and Head of Government. The Swedish Foreign Trade Minister, Mrs Anita Gradin, visited the Commission in March[9] as representative of the country holding the EFTA chairmanship.

Mr Syse, Prime Minister of Norway, Mr Hermansson, Prime Minister of Iceland, and Mr Holkeri, Prime Minister of Finland, met Mr Delors and other Members of the

---

[1]   Bull. EC 6-1990, point I.18.
[2]   Bull. EC 12-1990.
[3]   Bull. EC 6-1990, point 1.4.11.
[4]   Bull. EC 9-1990, point 1.3.12.
[5]   Bull. EC 10-1990, point 1.4.12.
[6]   Bull. EC 11-1990, point 1.4.7.
[7]   Bull. EC 1/2-1990, point 1.2.25.
[8]   Bull. EC 7/8-1990, point 1.4.15.
[9]   Bull. EC 3-1990, pont 1.2.16.

Commission in January,[1] April[2] and May[3] respectively. Moreover, relations between the Commission and the EFTA countries were fostered by a series of meetings held both in Brussels[4] and in the capitals of those countries[5] between Members of the Commission and members of their respective governments.

690.   Agreements on the Science programme[6] with all EFTA countries except Iceland were adopted by the Council on 12 February. In the field of education, on 29 March the Council adopted the agreements concerning the implementation of Comett II.[7] In June it authorized the Commission to begin negotiations with Norway and Sweden on scheduled air passenger services[8] and in September[9] it approved the agreement concluded with the EFTA countries concerning the exchange of information on draft technical rules.

---

[1]   Bull. EC 1/2-1990, point 1.2.27.
[2]   Bull. EC 4-1990, point 1.2.17.
[3]   Bull. EC 5-1990, point 1.3.20.
[4]   Bull. EC. 1/2-1990, point 1.2.26; Bull. EC 3-1990, points 1.2.18 to 1.2.20; Bull. EC 4-1990, point 1.2.14; Bull. EC 6-1990, point 1.4.10; Bull. EC 7/8-1990, point 1.4.16.
[5]   Bull. EC 3-1990, point 1.2.17; Bull. EC 4-1990, point 1.2.16; Bull. EC 5-1990, point 1.3.21; Bull. EC 6-1990, point 1.3.111; Bull. EC 7/8-1990, point 1.4.17; Bull. EC 11-1990, point 1.4.8.
[6]   Point 253 of this Report.
[7]   Point 382 of this Report.
[8]   Point 590 of this Report.
[9]   Point 108 of this Report.

Section 4

Relations with the United States of America, Japan and other industrialized countries

Western Economic Summit

691. The Western Economic Summit was held in Houston from 9 to 11 July.[1] At the close of the Summit, the participants adopted an economic declaration and political declarations concerning the advance of democracy in the world, terrorism and the non-proliferation of nuclear, chemical and biological weapons. The main economic talking points were the continuation of aid already granted for the process of reform in Central and Eastern Europe, the liberalization efforts currently under way in the Soviet Union and the possibility of aid to the Soviet Union. The Summit's participants agreed to ask the IMF, the World Bank, the OECD and the president-designate of the European Bank for Reconstruction and Development to undertake, in close consultation with the Commission, a detailed study of the Soviet economy, to make recommendations for its reform and to establish the criteria under which Western economic assistance could effectively support such reform. They also discussed the international trading system and still-unresolved Uruguay Round issues, the debt problem, the control of narcotics trafficking and environmental protection; the participants confirmed their commitment to seek a solution for global problems by means of enhanced international cooperation.

United States of America

692. The nature of EC-US relations changed substantially over the year in line with the joint statement adopted in December 1989, in which the two parties reaffirmed the importance they attached to closer cooperation and to a stronger relationship.[2] Both sides share the view that EC-US relations constitute an important element of political stability on the changing political scene. The US is now fully aware that the Community

---

[1]   Bull. EC 7/8-1990, point 1.4.18 and points 2.2.1 to 2.2.5.
[2]   Twenty-third General Report, point 753.

can serve as a model for the reforms which are to take place in Central and Eastern Europe. On the whole, the Community and the US also share a similar interest and responsibility in assuring an open, stable and growing international economy.

693. The changing nature of the relationship led to an intensification of the EC-US dialogue at all levels, with more frequent meetings between Members of the Commission and their US counterparts.[1] For the first time, two ministerial meetings between members of the US Government and Members of the Commission, jointly chaired by Mr Delors and US Secretary of State James Baker, were held during the year, one in Washington[2] and the other in Brussels.[3] The European Council, meeting in Dublin in June, welcomed the development of cooperation along the lines it had mapped out in April,[4] and referred to the possibility of a transatlantic declaration, which would include Canada.[5] This declaration was concluded between the United States and the Community and its Member States in November.[6] The two parties thus confirmed the importance of strengthening and expanding their partnership on an equal footing and, to achieve this goal, agreed to consult each other on important matters of common interest and to expand their dialogue within a formal framework of contacts.

The will to develop positive and constructive collaboration in areas of common interest resulted in the extension of sector-based cooperation to new areas, including research and technological development[7] higher education and continuing training.[8] In view of the volume of trade, commercial issues remained a major concern for both parties.

694. The US Omnibus Trade and Competitiveness Act continued to be a source of difficulties,[9] although the US implemented this legislation with relative restraint and reaffirmed that the successful conclusion of the Uruguay Round remained its top trade priority. The Community continued nevertheless to press for the elimination of all unilateral provisions of US legislation as part of the final Uruguay Round package. The action introduced by the US Shipbuilding Council against the Federal Republic of Germany and other, non-Community, countries under Section 301 of the Trade Act was suspended after negotiations began within the OECD on a multilateral agreement on fair and normal competition in the commercial shipbuilding industry.[10]

---

[1]   Bull. EC 1/2-1990, point 1.2.29; Bull. EC 3-1990, point 1.2.2.1; Bull. EC 4-1990, point 1.2.18; Bull. EC 6-1990, point 1.4.13; Bull. EC 9-1990, points 1.3.13 and 1.3.14; Bull. EC 12-1990.
[2]   Bull. EC 4-1990, point 1.2.18.
[3]   Bull. EC 11-1990, point 1.4.11.
[4]   Bull. EC 4-1990, point I.10.
[5]   Bull. EC 6-1990, point I.22.
[6]   Bull. EC 11-1990, point 1.5.3.
[7]   Point 255 of this Report.
[8]   Bull. EC 11-1990, point 1.3.199.
[9]   Twenty-second General Report, point 757.
[10]   Point 844 of this Report.

695. As indicated in the EC report on US trade barriers and unfair trade practices published in April,[1] a number of areas of US trade legislation can give rise to the imposition of unilaterial measures and deviations from multilateral obligations. The list of measures and practices identified in the report shows that the USA is not free from the types of trade barriers which it condemns elsewhere, and that the fragmentation of the US market in areas such as standards and financial and professional services creates serious handicaps for Community exporters.

696. The USA continued to apply retaliatory measures such as those imposed unilaterally in January 1989[2] in response to the Directive prohibiting the use in livestock farming of certain substances having a hormonal effect.[3] In July the Italian tomato canning industry submitted a formal complaint to the Commission under Regulation (EEC) No 2641/84 on the strengthening of the common commercial policy with regard in particular to protection against illicit commercial practices.[4] A decision on the supply of US meat to US military commissaries in Europe, which would normally buy European beef, was the subject of ministerial correspondence.

697. Three other bilateral trade issues attracting attention were: the discovery in samples of wine imported from the Community of traces of a fungicide (procymidone) which is accepted in the Community but for which the producer had not requested a level of tolerance on importation; a problem of tariff classification and possible fraud in relation to US exports of maize germ cake to the Community; the one-year extension to 31 December 1991[5] of the agreement reached in 1986[6] and concluded in 1987 following enlargement of the Community to ensure that Spain imported a minimum level of maize and sorghum every year.

698. On telecommunications, two further meetings were held in the series of contacts with the US administration started in 1989.[7] They provided an opportunity for an exchange of information on Community legislation in the context of the single market and on telecommunications issues in the United States, without prejudice to the trade issues under negotiation in the Uruguay Round.

699. Proposals presented by the Community[8] permitted the resumption in March of bilateral discussions on trade in civil aircraft.[9] In order to end the existing dispute the

---

[1]   Bull. EC 4-1990, point 1.2.19.
[2]   Twenty-third General Report, point 754.
[3]   OJ L 382, 31.12.1985; Nineteenth General Report, point 203; Twentieth General Report, point 195.
[4]   OJ L 252, 20.9.1984; Eighteenth General Report, point 620.
[5]   Bull. EC 12-1990.
[6]   Twentieth General Report, point 822.
[7]   Twenty-third General Report, point 758.
[8]   Bull. EC 10-1990, point 1.4.59.
[9]   Twenty-third General Report, point 759.

Commission adopted in October a communication on the opening of formal negotiations with the United States and, subsequently, with other GATT contracting parties with a view to the conclusion of new arrangements in this area.[1]

700.   The adoption by the Community in October 1989 of the Directive on television without frontiers[2] prompted the United States to request GATT consultations. In its view, the Directive's provisions requiring Member States to reserve a major proportion of their transmission time for European works is contrary to the GATT. The Community agreed to hold consultations even though it considered that the matter was not covered by GATT provisions.

701.   The dialogue on standards and certification issues was carried on through a series of meetings dealing with industrial products and also with foodstuffs, human biology, medicines and medical systems. Information was also exchanged on health and phytosanitary matters.

Japan

702.   EC-Japan relations were marked by growing cooperation in numerous fields, reflecting the increasingly important economic, financial and political role played by Japan, the ever-increasing role of the Community on the world stage and the approach of 1992.

703.   The Japanese Prime Minister, Mr Toshiki Kaifu, visited the Commission on 10 January and discussed major international and bilateral issues with Mr Delors and Mr Andriessen.[3] Bilateral relations were discussed again at the ministerial meeting in May, at which trade problems and the prospects for cooperation in various fields were reviewed.[4] The two sides agreed to set up a working party on trade issues to examine barriers to the Japanese market. They also signed an Agreement on nuclear safety.[5] Cooperation was further strengthened by various meetings between Members of the Commission and Japanese ministers.[6] Mr Andriessen also represented the Commission at the Emperor's coronation ceremony.[7]

---

[1]   Point 851 of this Report.
[2]   OJ C 298, 17.10.1989; Twenty-third General Report, point 227.
[3]   Bull. EC 1/2-1990, point 1.2.28.
[4]   Bull. EC 5-1990, point 1.3.23.
[5]   Point 656 of this Report.
[6]   Bull. EC 3-1990, point 1.2.22; Bull. EC 9-1990, point 1.3.15; Bull. EC 11-1990, points 1.4.12 and 1.4.13.
[7]   Bull. EC 11-1990, point 1.4.13.

704.   Japan's economic situation remained favourable in 1990 and its economy grew by an estimated 5%. During the first six months of the year Community exports to Japan increased by 13%, while imports from Japan fell by 2.5%. In spite of these more favourable results for the Community, the trade deficit with Japan in 1990 is likely to be broadly similar to that in 1989. Investment in the Community by Japanese firms increased substantially during the 1989 tax year, rising from 19.4% to 21.9% of total Japanese investment abroad. Japanese investment continues to be focused in the United Kingdom (USD 5.24 billion) and the Netherlands (USD 4.55 billion), but also increased substantially in Spain (from USD 161 million to USD 501 million) and Portugal (from USD 9 million to USD 48 million).

705.   Community exports and investment are still restrained by a number of problems of access to the Japanese market and structural barriers. The whole range of trade problems, concerning in particular processed agricultural products, fishery products, leather and footwear, was examined by the working party set up at the May ministerial meeting. [1] The working party met twice and drafted a report for the high-level consultations held in Tokyo in October. At the close of these consultations the two parties stated their intention to make every effort to resolve the difficulties of access to the Japanese market during the Uruguay Round and to continue their bilateral discussions on the matter if no multilateral solutions were found.

706.   On a number of occasions the Commission reminded the Japanese authorities of the importance of structural reforms, in particular to bring about a better balance in Japan's trade with the Community. Following Japan's discussions with the United States on structural barriers, the Commission urged that the concessions made to the United States be applied in a non-discriminatory fashion so that all Japan's trading partners could benefit.

707.   Consultations with a view to the abolition of the remining quantitative restrictions on imports from Japan, started in 1988, [2] resulted in a further round of liberalization. [3]

708.   In agreement with the Member States, the Commission held informal discussions with the Japanese authorities on the trade implications of its December 1989 communication on the single market for motor vehicles. [4]

709.   The Commission stepped up its efforts to promote exports to Japan. It launched a major campaign with the aim of increasing the scope for sales by specific branches of European industry over the next three years. It also started informal talks with the

---

[1]   Point 703 of this Report.
[2]   Twenty-second General Report, point 891.
[3]   Point 832 of this Report.
[4]   Twenty-third General Report, point 276.

Japanese authorities with a view to establishing a link between its own programme and the Japanese import promotion measures.

710.   As agreed during the high-level consultations in November 1989,[1] a first meeting of experts in Brussels in June was held to exchange information on standards and certification systems.[2] The two parties agreed to continue these contacts and bring in specialists from the various sectors involved.

Other industrialized countries

Canada

711.   Preceded by the eighth meeting of the Joint Cooperation Committee set up under the Framework Agreement of 1976, the annual ministerial meeting was held in Ottawa in May and provided an opportunity for the two parties to confirm the importance they attach to developing bilateral relations.[3]

712.   The dialogue between Canada and the Community was boosted by a number of visits by ministers. Mr Donald Mazankowski, Deputy Prime Minister and Minister for Agriculture, visited the Commission in April[4] and took part in a wide-ranging exchange of views on agriculture and the Uruguay Round. In May Mr Marín, Vice-President of the Commission, made an official visit to Canada and his talks on this occasion helped reduce differences in the fisheries sector.[5] Mr John Crosbie, the Minister for Trade, and Mr Bernard Valcourt, the Valcourt, the Minister for Fisheries, continued this discussion when they visited the Commission on 30 November. Mr Crosbie also discussed bilateral and multilateral trade problems with Mr Andriessen in Brussels on 3 December.[6]

The strengthening of relations between the two parties was officialized in November when Canada and the Community and its Member States adopted a declaration,[7] which is based on the preferential relations introduced by the Framework Cooperation Agreement signed in 1976[8] and reinforces the institutional framework for consultations in order to give them a long-term horizon.

---

[1]   Twenty-third General Report, point 774.
[2]   Bull. EC 6-1990, point 1.4.14.
[3]   Bull. EC 5-1990, point 1.3.22.
[4]   Bull. EC 4-1990, point 1.2.20.
[5]   Bull. EC 5-1990, point 1.2.211.
[6]   Bull. EC 12-1990.
[7]   Bull. EC 11-1990, point 1.5.4.
[8]   OJ L 260, 24.9.1976; Tenth General Report, point 541.

713.   The Community retained its position as Canada's second-largest trading partner, accounting for some 10% of Canada's external trade. Bilateral trade was estimated at ECU 17 billion in 1990, resulting in a trade surplus of ECU 2 billion for the Community.

714.   Negotiations continued on the elimination of discriminatory practices affecting beer but have so far not produced any results[1] and Canada took further measures towards eliminating discrimination affecting wine and spirits, as it agreed to do in December 1988.[2] However, Canada continued to refuse to apply the decision of the GATT panel condemning the imposition of countervailing duties on Community exports of beef and veal.[3] An independent arbitrator confirmed that certain Canadian rights concerning exports of wheat to the Community, dating back to 1962 and 1975, were legal.

715.   In April the Council adopted negotiating directives for an amendment to the 1959 Agreement between Euratom and Canada.[4] This amendment was initialled by the two parties in October.

Australia

716.   The eighth EC-Australia ministerial consultations, held in Brussels on 5 June,[5] enabled the two parties to review recent developments in Europe and the Pacific, the prospects for the Uruguay Round and the main aspects of bilateral trade and cooperation relations.[5] It became apparent that in spite of differences over agriculture, Australia wished to strengthen and diversify its relations with the Community, particularly in the fields of science and technology, the environment and cooperation between small and medium-sized businesses.

Agricultural issues were at the centre of discussions when the Minister for Trade Negotiations, Mr Michal Duffy, visited the Commission in February and his successor,[6] Mr Neal Blewett, visited the Commission in July.[7] On 1 December,[8] on the eve of the ministerial meeting of the Uruguay Round held in Brussels,[9] Mr Blewett met Mr Andriessen to discuss the obstacles to the prospects of a successful outcome to the conference.

---

[1]   Twenty-third General Report, point 765.
[2]   Twenty-second General Report, point 910.
[3]   Twenty-first General Report, point 891.
[4]   Point 613 of this Report.
[5]   Bull. EC 6-1990, point 1.4.12.
[6]   Bull. EC 1/2-1990, point 1.2.30.
[7]   Bull. EC 7/8-1990, point 1.4.19.
[8]   Bull. EC 12-1990.
[9]   Point 821 of this Report.

New Zealand

717.   Normal good relations continued between the Community and New Zealand. The situation of the world market for dairy products, which account for a large share of New Zealand's export earnings, and the prospects for the Uruguay Round, with particular reference to agriculture, were the main topics discussed when Mr Mike Moore, then Minister for External Relations and Trade, visited Brussels on 1 August. The possible impact of food aid to the Soviet Union,[1] particularly as regards butter, on this country's traditional imports from New Zealand was discussed in November during the first meetings which the new Minister for Trade and Industry, Mr Burdon, had with Mr Andriessen and Mr Mac Sharry.[2]

---

[1]   Point 684 of this Report.
[2]   Bull. EC 11-1990, point 1.4.14.

Section 5

Relations with Mediterranean, Gulf and Arabian Peninsula countries

Mediterranean countries

718.   On 22 May the Commission adopted a communication[1] containing the proposal to the Council requested by the latter in February[2] for an action programme to redirect the Communities' Mediterranean policy, the principles of which had been agreed by the European Council in Strasbourg in the light of a previous communication.[3] The Commission proposed improvements in the instruments for cooperation and a substantial increase in the financial resources deployed to meet the vast needs of the countries in the region and improve support for efforts undertaken to implement economic reforms. In the conclusions following the September meeting,[4] the Council confirmed the need — particularly in the present crisis situation in the Gulf — to step up work on the Commission proposals. In April[5] the Economic and Social Committee produced a supplement to the own-initiative opinion issued in July 1989.[6]

On 18 December the Council reached a comprehensive decision on the three aspects of this policy,[7] namely, the guidelines for negotiations on the four financial protocols with the Maghreb and Mashreq countries and Israel, covering the period from 1 November 1991 to 31 October 1996 and involving a financial package of ECU 2 375 million, including 1 075 million charged to the general budget and 1 300 million from the EIB's own funds; across-the-board financial cooperation involving all the Mediterranean countries, to which an indicative amount of ECU 230 million is to be allocated, intended *inter alia* to support regional cooperation; and specific trade concessions involving various improvements in terms of access to the Community market for certain products from the Mediterranean non-Community countries.

---

[1]   Bull. EC 5-1990, point 1.3.24.
[2]   Bull. EC 1/2-1990, point 1.2.31.
[3]   Twenty-third General Report, point 799.
[4]   Bull. EC 9-1990, point 1.3.23.
[5]   OJ C 168, 10.7.1990; Bull. EC 4-1990, point 1.2.21.
[6]   OJ C 221, 28.8.1989; Twenty-third General Report, point 799.
[7]   Bull. EC 12-1990.

Turkey

719. At its meeting on 3 February[1] the Council endorsed the conclusions contained in the opinion delivered by the Commission in December 1989[2] on Turkey's application to join the Community.[3] Nevertheless it was recognized that it was desirable to strengthen relations with Turkey and in June, in response to its request, the Commission adopted a communication[4] accompanied by a proposal for a decision on the conclusion of the fourth financial protocol, initialled in 1981.[5] In addition, the Commission proposed the completion of the EEC-Turkey customs union by 1995, the development of cooperation in industrial and technological sectors and the promotion of political and cultural cooperation.

720. The EC-Turkey Joint Parliamentary Committee met on three occasions: in Antalya in March,[6] Strasbourg in July[7] and Istanbul in November.[8] The state of relations between the Community and Turkey and prospects for the future were also the focus of discussion when Dr Ali Bozer, Turkish Foreign Minister, met several members of the Commission in March during a visit to Brussels.[9] Mr Matutes visited Turkey in December.[10]

721. As one of the countries most directly affected by the Gulf crisis, Turkey is to receive financial aid under the Regulation adopted by the Council in December.[11] Two new financing agreements were also signed in Ankara in February[12] under the special action agreed upon in 1980.[13]

Cyprus

722. On 4 July, during talks with Mr Gianni De Michelis, President of the Council, Mr George Iacovou, Foreign Minister of Cyprus, presented an application from the Republic of Cyprus for accession to the European Communities in accordance with

---

[1]   Bull. EC 1/2-1990, point 1.2.32.
[2]   Twenty-third General Report, point 801.
[3]   Twenty-first General Report, point 783.
[4]   Bull. EC 6-1990, point 1.4.15.
[5]   Fifteenth General Report, point 736.
[6]   Bull. EC 3-1990, point 1.2.26.
[7]   Bull. EC 7/8-1990, point 1.4.27.
[8]   Bull. EC 11-1990, point 1.4.21.
[9]   Bull. EC 3-1990, point 1.2.25.
[10]   Bull. EC 12-1990.
[11]   Point 814 of this Report.
[12]   Bull. EC 1/2-1990, point 1.2.33.
[13]   Fourteenth General Report, point 644.

Articles 237, 98 and 205 of the EEC, ECSC and Euratom Treaties respectively.[1] On 17 September the Council decided to initiate the procedures laid down in the Articles referred to above, which provide for the Commission to be consulted.[2]

723.   The third financial protocol, signed in 1989,[3] entered into force on 1 June.[4] The 13th meeting of the EEC-Cyprus Association Council was held in Brussels in May.[5] The development of relations between the two parties was also discussed during the visits paid by Mr Matutes to Cyprus in February,[6] and by Mr Iacovou, Foreign Minister, and Mr Vassiliou, President of Cyprus, to the Commission in March[7] and May[8] respectively. The failure of the intercommunal talks held on the initiative of the United Nations Secretary-General formed the subject of a Parliament resolution in March.[9]

Malta

724.   On 16 July Mr Guido de Marco, Deputy Prime Minister and Minister for Foreign Affairs and Justice, presented to Mr De Michelis, President of the Council, an application from the Republic of Malta for accession to the European Communities in accordance with Articles 237, 98 and 205 of the EEC, ECSC and Euratom Treaties respectively.[10] On 17 September the Council decided to initiate the procedures laid down in the Articles referred to above, which provide for the Commission to be consulted.[11] The possibility of an application had been discussed during an official visit to Malta by Mr Matutes in March.[12]

725.   The sixth meeting of the EEC-Malta Association Council was held in Brussels in July.[13] The first meeting of the Committee for economic and trade cooperation between the two parties took place in February. In December[14] the Council concluded the protocol prolonging the first phase of the Association Agreement until 31 December 1991[15] and consequently extended the term of validity of the arrangement governing

---

[1]   Bull. EC 7/8-1990, poin 1.4.24.
[2]   Bull. EC 9-1990, point 1.3.24.
[3]   Twenty-third General Report, point 803.
[4]   OJ L 82, 29.3.1990; Bull. EC 1/2-1990, point 1.2.35.
[5]   Bull. EC 5-1990, point 1.3.26.
[6]   Bull. EC 1/2-1990, point 1.2.34.
[7]   Bull. EC 3-1990, point 1.2.27.
[8]   Bull. EC 5-1990, point 1.3.27.
[9]   OJ C 96, 17.4.1990; Bull. EC 3-1990, point 1.2.28.
[10]   Bull. EC 7/8-1990, point 1.4.25.
[11]   Bull. EC 9-1990, point 1.3.25.
[12]   Bull. EC 3-1990, point 1.2.30.
[13]   Bull. EC 7/8-1990, point 1.4.28.
[14]   OJ L 358, 21.12.1990; Bull. EC 12-1990; Commission proposal: OJ C 311, 12.12.1990; Bull. EC 11-1990, point 1.4.19.
[15]   OJ L 61, 14.3.1971; Fifth General Report, point 410.

trade. Financing was also granted for several operations[1] under the third financial protocol, which entered into force in August 1989.[2]

Andorra

726.   A trade agreement in the form of an exchange of letters was signed in Luxembourg on 28 June[3] and concluded by the Council on 26 November.[4] Initialled in December 1989,[5] the agreement, which enters into force on 1 January 1991, establishes a customs union between the Community and Andorra for industrial products. Provisions concerning the duty-free allowance for travellers are included to reflect Andorra's special circumstances. In the agricultural sector the Community grants duty-free access to certain products originating in Andorra.

San Marino

727.   On 18 December the Council adopted draft negotiating directives with a view to the conclusion of an agreement in the form of an exchange of letters between the Community and the Republic of San Marino.[6] The draft directives provide for the establishment of a customs union between the Community and San Marino in respect of all products covered by the Treaty of Rome. There are also special provisions, particularly in the area of indirect taxation, the social field and transport.

Yugoslavia

728.   Relations with Yugoslavia were reviewed at the request of the Yugoslav Government which, in the light of current developments in the country and in Europe more generally, considered that they needed redefining. Yugoslavia's requests were discussed, among other topics, during the visit paid by Mr Ante Markovic, Prime Minister, to the Commission in March,[7] and Mr Matutes' visit to Yugoslavia in April.[8] In this context, the Commission transmitted to the Council a communication on relations between the two parties calling, in particular, for the opening of negotiations with a view to

---

[1]   Bull. EC 3-1990, point 1.2.29; Bull. EC 7/8-1990, point 1.4.29.
[2]   OJ L 180, 27.6.1989; Twenty-third General Report, point 804.
[3]   Bull. EC 6-1990, point 1.4.17.
[4]   OJ L 374, 31.12.1990; Bull. EC 11-1990, point 1.4.18; Commission proposal: Bull. EC 4-1990, point 1.2.22.
[5]   Twenty-third General Report, point 806.
[6]   Bull. EC 12-1990; Commission proposal: Bull. EC 11-1990, point 1.4.20.
[7]   Bull. EC 3-1990, point 1.2.23.
[8]   Bull. EC 4-1990, point 1.2.23.

concluding a third financial protocol. [1] The Council adopted guidelines for this purpose on 18 December. [2] In September the Council decided to extend to Yugoslavia the economic aid to the countries of Central and Eastern Europe agreed upon by the Group of 24 at its meeting of 4 July. [3]

In 1990 cooperation initiatives matched in number and scope those undertaken in 1989, with a specific bias, however, towards activities aimed at bringing Yugoslavia's rules closer to those of the Community, in particular as regards standards. The Cooperation Council met at ministerial level in December and adopted a decision concerning the pursuit of bilateral cooperation in 1991 and a statement on future relations between the two sides. [2]

Maghreb (Algeria, Morocco, Tunisia), Mashreq (Egypt, Jordan, Lebanon and Syria) and Israel

729.   Implementation of the third financial protocols [4] continued satisfactorily. As at 31 December a large share of the funds earmarked under the protocols, namely ECU 986 million, i.e. 61% of the total ECU 1 618 million, had already been allocated through financing decisions. Israel is entitled only to EIB loans under its financial protocol, but cooperation activities were also financed, as in previous years, from Community budget funds. However, the Commission suspended implementation of all new scientific cooperation programmes in view of the closure by the Israeli authorities of universities located in the Occupied Territories.

On 17 September the Council authorized the Commission to negotiate the third financial protocol with Syria, which had never been concluded owing to the state of relations between the Community and that country. [5] A financial package of ECU 146 million is being made available in the form of grants (ECU 36 million) and EIB loans with an interest-rate subsidy of two percentage points (ECU 110 million). In December, at the end of the negotiations, the Commission put before the Council a recommendtion for a decision on the conclusion of the protocol. [2]

730.   The Council decided to grant financial aid to Egypt and Jordan, which, together with Turkey, are among the countries most directly affected by the Gulf crisis. [6] The aid, amounting for the three countries to ECU 500 million, will be used in particular to

---

[1]   Bull. EC 5-1990, point 1.3.25.
[2]   Bull. EC 12-1990.
[3]   Point 668 of this Report.
[4]   Twenty-second General Report, point 928.
[5]   Bull. EC 9-1990, point 1.3.22.
[6]   Point 719 of this Report.

TABLE 11

Third financial protocols

Breakdown at 31 December 1990 of financing decisions in respect of the
Maghreb and Mashreq countries and Israel (Commission and EIB)

Sector	Amount (ECU million)	%
Agriculture	252	25.6
Energy	97	9.8
Industry	261	26.5
Distributive trades	19	1.9
Infrastructure	294	29.8
Education and training[1]	43	4.4
Health and environment	2	0.2
Scientific cooperation	18	1.8
Total	986	100.0

[1] Project-linked training operations are included in the relevant project sector.

finance imports, and will take the form of balance-of-payment support.[1] Emergency aid totalling ECU 58 million was granted for the repatriation of refugees living in Egypt and Jordan.

731.   The third meeting of the EEC-Algeria Cooperation Council,[2] the eighth meeting of the EEC-Israel Cooperation Council[3] and the sixth meeting of the EEC-Egypt Cooperation Council[4] were held in Brussels in September and December. Mr Matutes made official visits to Egypt in March[5] and Tunisia in April.[6] During the year the Commission played host to Mr Nouri Zorgati, Tunisian Minister for Agriculture,[7] Mr Habib Boulares, Tunisian Minister for Foreign Affairs, Mr Sid Ahmed Ghozali, Algerian Foreign Minister,[8] Mr Hadj Nasser, Governor of Algeria's Central Bank, Prince Hassan of Jordan[9] and Mr Ghazi Hidouci, Algerian Minister for the Economy.[10]

---

[1]   Point 734 of this Report.
[2]   Bull. EC 9-1990, point 1.3.26.
[3]   Bull. EC 9-1990, point 1.3.27.
[4]   Bull. EC 12-1990.
[5]   Bull. EC 3-1990, point 1.2.32.
[6]   Bull. EC 4-1990, point 1.2.24.
[7]   Bull. EC 1/2-1990, point 1.2.36.
[8]   Bull. EC 9-1990, point 1.3.26.
[9]   Bull. EC 10-1990, point 1.4.14.
[10]   Bull. EC 11-1990, point 1.4.17.

On 12 November the Foreign Ministers of the Community and the Arab Maghreb Union met informally for the first time in Brussels.[1] The ministers had an exchange of views, focusing on the situation in the Gulf and the prospects for cooperation between the two regions.

732.   Agricultural exports to the Community from the West Bank and the Gaza strip (the 'Occupied Territories') under preferential arrangements introduced in 1986 increased significantly. Development aid to the Palestinian people from the Community totalled ECU 6 million. Direct aid was in addition to the aid given through UNRWA, the United Nations Relief and Works Agency for Palestine Refugees in the Near East.

Countries of the Gulf and the Arabian Peninsula

733.   The Cooperation Agreement between the Community and the States of the Gulf Cooperation Council, the GCC,[2] entered into force on 1 January. The first practical demonstration of the Agreement was the holding of a conference on industrial cooperation in Grenada from 18 to 22 February;[3] a number of areas of the economy in which there were excellent prospects for cooperation were discussed. The Cooperation Council set up by the Agreement met for the first time in Muscat (Sultanate of Oman) on 17 March;[4] in addition to purely political matters and exchanges of information on developments in the two regions, the meeting was an opportunity to set up the instruments of cooperation whose task would be to select priority objectives for the Cooperation Agreement. At the instigation of the Commission[5] and the Council,[6] against the backcloth of events at the beginning of August, negotiations with a view to the conclusion of a free-trade agreement[7] opened on 18 October,[8] following the signing of a standstill agreement.[9] This meeting, the first of its kind, was an opportunity for identifying the many issues on which a consensus already exists between the Community and the GCC.

734.   The Iraqi invasion of Kuwait prompted a firm and rapid response from the Community and its Member States. As the many declarations by the Twelve show,[10]

---

[1]   Bull. EC 11-1990, point 1.4.23.
[2]   OJ L 54, 25.2.1989; Twenty-third General Report, point 814.
[3]   Bull. EC 1/2-1990, point 1.2.37.
[4]   Bull. EC 3-1990, point 1.2.24.
[5]   Bull. EC 4-1990, point 1.3.16.
[6]   Bull. EC 9-1990, point 1.3.19.
[7]   Twenty-third General Report, point 814.
[8]   Bull. EC 10-1990, point 1.4.17.
[9]   Bull. EC 6-1990, point 1.4.18.
[10]   Point 881 of this Report.

they unreservedly condemned this act of aggression and did everything in their power to help find a solution to the crisis in the framework of the UN Security Council resolutions. Shortly after the invasion took place, the Community provided substantial amounts of humanitarian aid as a contribution to the repatriation of refugees.[1]

The Community also took the decisions required for the imposition of a complete embargo on trade with the two countries. An initial Regulation, combined with an EGSC Decision, both adopted on 8 August, prohibited all trade with Iraq and Kuwait except for products intended for strictly humanitarian uses.[2] In October these measures were strengthened by a second Regulation extending the embargo to air transport and to the provision of non-financial services with the object or effect of boosting the economy of the two countries.[3] A system for the exchange of information and coordination was set up in close cooperation with the Member States, to ensure that the provisions were implemented consistently and effectively.

On 4 December the Council adopted a Regulation on financial assistance for the countries most directly affected by the Gulf crisis,[4] under which the Community, from the beginning of 1991 onwards, will grant aid to Egypt, Jordan and Turkey. The estimated ECU 500 million required, to be granted principally in the form of non-refundable aid and otherwise as loans, will have to be charged to the budget for the next financial year.[5]

735.   The Joint Cooperation Committee established under the Cooperation Agreement between the Yemen Arab Republic and the Community[6] held its third meeting in Sana'a in January.[7]

Euro-Arab Dialogue

736.   Following the Euro-Arab ministerial conference held in Paris on 22 December 1989,[8] the sixth meeting of the General Committee of the Euro-Arab Dialogue took place in Dublin on 7 and 8 June.[9] The meeting adopted an organizational and procedural code containing a code of financial procedure. The General Committee also approved

---

[1]   Bull. EC 7/8-1990, points 1.4.65 and 1.4.67; Bull. EC 9-1990, points 1.3.18, 1.3.42 and 1.3.43.
[2]   OJ L 213, 9.8.1990; Bull. EC 7/8-1990, points 1.4.21 and 1.4.22; Commission proposal: Bull. EC 7/8-1990, point 1.4.20.
[3]   OJ L 304, 1.11.1990; Bull. EC 10-1990, point 1.4.15; Commission proposal: Bull. EC 9-1990, point 1.3.17.
[4]   OJ L 347, 12.12.1990; Bull. EC 12-1990; Commission proposal: Bull. EC 9-1990, points 1.3.20 and 1.3.21.
[5]   Point 992 of this Report.
[6]   OJ L 26, 31.1.1985.
[7]   Bull. EC 1/2-1990, point 1.2.38.
[8]   Twenty-third General Report, point 816.
[9]   Bull. EC 6-1990, point 1.4.16.

the six priority projects selected by the Paris ministerial conference. It appointed the co-chairmen and co-vice-chairmen of each of the three working committees (on economic, technical and social and cultural affairs) and defined their tasks. A meeting of all the co-chairmen, co-vice-chairmen and co-rapporteurs and a meeting of the ministerial 'troika' were scheduled for the end of 1990, but were postponed because of events in the Gulf.

Section 6

Relations with the countries of Asia and Latin America

Asia

South Asia

737.   The EC-Pakistan,[1] EC-Bangladesh[2] and EC-India[3] Joint Committees met in the first half of the year. The parties expressed their satisfaction with the outcome of the meetings, during which they were able to broaden and deepen bilateral relations.

738.   The new economic prospects opened up by the single European market were stressed when Mr Inder Kumar Gujral, India's Minister for External Affairs, visited the Commission in March.[4] During his visit to the Commission in May, to coincide with the meeting of the Joint Committee,[3] Mr Arun Nehru, India's Minister for Commerce, confirmed his country's commitment to strengthening the multilateral trading system. Mr Matutes emphasized the prospects for greater cooperation in various areas of mutual interest, including fisheries and tourism.

739.   In response to the Gulf crisis the Community decided to allocate financial aid to facilitate the repatriation of Bangladeshi, Indian, Pakistani and Sri Lankan nationals from Iraq and Kuwait,[5] expected to total some ECU 36.4 million. The Commission favoured granting aid to Afghan refugees and continued its programme of humanitarian aid to displaced persons in the North and North-East of Sri Lanka.

740.   Mr Hussain Mohammad Ershad, President of the People's Republic of Bangladesh, visited the Commission on 18 October.[6] Talks focused on the results of, and outlook for, Community aid and on the effects of the Gulf crisis on the Bangladeshi economy and financial assistance for the worst-affected countries.

---

[1]   Bull. EC 3-1990, point 1.2.34.
[2]   Bull. EC 5-1990, point 1.3.29.
[3]   Bull. EC 5-1990, point 1.3.30.
[4]   Bull. EC 3-1990, point 1.3.30.
[5]   Point 814 of this Report.
[6]   Bull. EC 10-1990, point 1.4.21.

Association of South-East Asian Nations

741. The eighth annual meeting of Asean and Community Foreign Ministers was held in Kuching, Malaysia, on 16 and 17 February;[1] the Community was represented by Mr Matutes. The meeting enabled the two sides to take stock of bilateral relations and examine various regional and international political and economic issues, such as the Uruguay Round. The Ministers agreed on the need to intensify further their cooperation and to give priority to the private sector, trade development, investment and market access. The other subjects under discussion included aid for rural development in the Asean countries, industrial and scientific cooperation, drug abuse control, the role of women in development, and environmental issues, including protection of the tropical forests, the subject of a conference held in Brussels in October.[2] As regards political issues, the Ministers had a detailed exchange of views on the Cambodian question.

742. The 23rd Ministerial meeting of the Asean countries took place in Jakarta on 24 and 25 July. It was followed, from 27 to 29 July, by the post-ministerial conference, attended by Asean's main partners, the Commission being represented by Mr Matutes.[3] The Asean Ministers highlighted the difficulties currently being experienced by most developing countries, i.e. a deterioration in the terms of trade and weak economic growth, and their feat that recent events in Europe would result in the deflection of financial and trade flows to Central and Eastern Europe. Other issues, such as the Uruguay Round, the situation in Indo-China and, in particular, the Cambodian question, were also discussed. The Community pointed out that any assessment of developments in Europe should take account of 1992, since Asean was one of the geographical areas which would benefit most from the single market. Turning to the refugee problem, Mr Matutes outlined an initiative for the return of the boat people to Vietnam.[4]

743. Mr Matutes paid an official visit to Thailand and the Philippines in January,[5] and to Indonesia in February.[6] Mr Chatchai Chunhawan, Thailand's Prime Minister, visited the Commission in March,[7] and an Asean interparliamentary delegation visited the Commission in May.[8]

---

[1]   Bull. EC 1/2-1990, point 1.2.39.
[2]   Bull. EC 10-1990, point 1.4.22.
[3]   Bull. EC 7/8-1990, point 1.4.35.
[4]   Point 748 of this Report.
[5]   Bull. EC 1/2-1990, points 1.2.41 and 1.2.42.
[6]   Bull. EC 1/2-1990, point 1.2.43.
[7]   Bull. EC 3-1990, point 1.2.35.
[8]   Bull. EC 5-1990, point 1.3.31.

744. In October[1] the Council approved the Protocol renewing, subject to certain amendments, the 1982 Agreement with Thailand on manioc production, marketing and trade.[2] The Protocol was signed in Brussels on 15 November.[3]

China

745. The restrictive measures adopted at the Madrid European Council in June 1989[4] affected relations between the People's Republic of China and the Community until October 1990. During that period there were no high-level meetings between representatives of the Commission and representatives of the Chinese Government, and no new cooperation projects were concluded. However, scientific and technical cooperation projects approved before 4 June 1989 were continued, in so far as they remained meaningful under the new circumstances. On 22 October the Twelve decided to progressively normalize their relations with China.

Republic of Korea

746. On 24 July the Prime Minister of the Republic of Korea, Mr Kang Young Hoon, accompanied by members of his Government, had talks with Mr Delors and Mr Andriessen;[5] they discussed various bilateral issues and international matters of common interest, including developments in Central and Eastern Europe and their implications for the dialogue between North Korea and the Republic of Korea. During his official visit in March,[6] Mr Andriessen had talks with several Korean Ministers on various bilateral issues, the Uruguay Round and developments in Central and Eastern Europe.

Other Asian countries

747. During a visit to Hong Kong in March,[7] Mr Andriessen had meetings with the local authorities and a large number of businessmen, with whom he discussed the Community's relations with China and Hong Kong as the internal market nears com-

---

[1] OJ L 347, 12.12.1990; Bull. EC 10-1990, point 1.4.23; Commission proposal: OJ C 170, 12.7.1990; Bull. EC 6-1990, point 1.4.22.
[2] OJ L 219, 28.7.1982; Sixteenth General Report, point 699.
[3] Bull. EC 11-1990, point 1.4.29.
[4] Twenty-third General Report, point 828.
[5] Bull. EC 7/8-1990, point 1.4.36.
[6] Bull. EC 3-1990, point 1.2.36.
[7] Bull. EC 3-1990, point 1.2.37.

pletion. In October the Governor of Hong Kong, Sir David Wilson, had talks with Mr Andriessen and Sir Leon Brittan, focusing on the Uruguay Round.[1]

748.   Diplomatic relations with the Socialist Republic of Vietnam were established in November. Parliament had called for the re-establishment of diplomatic relations in a resolution adopted in May.[2] In December the Commission adopted an initiative for the repatriation and resettlement of Vietnamese exiles not having refugee status ('boat-people').[3]

749.   Following the establishment of diplomatic relations between the Community and Mongolia in 1989, the Commission sent a mission to Ulan Bator in October to identify possible areas for cooperation. Mongolia further expressed the wish to conclude a trade and economic cooperation agreement with the Community.

Latin America

Relations with regional bodies

750.   The Rome Ministerial Conference in December[3] marked the institutionalization of relations between the Community and the countries of Latin America, the document adopted constituting the basis for the future development of relations. The Community continued its dialogue with the Rio Group[4] on international political and economic matters of mutual interest. Two Ministerial meetings were held, one in Dublin in April,[5] the other in New York in September, at the time of the United Nations General Assembly. The Group of Latin America Heads of Mission to the Communities met the Permanent Representatives of the Member States in Brussels on 3 May and 16 November.

751.   The sixth Ministerial Conference between the Community and its Member States and the countries of Central America, Panama, Colombia, Mexico and Venezuela — all countries with which the Community has cooperation ties — took place in Dublin on 9 and 10 April.[4] At the close of this conference on political dialogue and economic cooperation — part of the dialogue started at San José, Costa Rica, in 1984[6] — a joint political declaration and a joint economic communiqué were adopted.[7]

---

[1]   Bull. EC 10-1990, point 1.4.24.
[2]   OJ C 149, 18.6.1990; Bull. EC 5-1990, point 1.3.32.
[3]   Bull. EC 12-1990.
[4]   Argentina, Bolivia, Brazil, Chile, Colombia, Ecuador, Mexico, Paraguay, Peru, Uruguay, Venezuela.
[5]   Bull. EC 4-1990, point 1.2.26.
[6]   Eighteenth General Report, point 707.
[7]   Bull. EC 4-1990, points 2.2.1 and 2.2.2.

752. The fourth meeting of the Joint Committee set up under the Cooperation Agreement between the Community and Central America[1] was held in Tegucigalpa, Honduras, on 17 and 18 July. The various areas of cooperation were receiwed and guidelines for future action drawn up. The Community increased and diversified its aid to Central America to well over ECU 100 million in 1990, thus contributing to economic and social consolidation in the region.[2]

753. The Commission took part in the first international follow-up meeting to the international conference on refugees in Central America,[3] held in New York in June. It announced its decision to fund 10 projects for the repatriation and settlement of refugees and displaced persons, costing some ECU 22 million.

754. At the request of the Latin American Economic System, the Commission decided in June to proceed with an exchange of letters under which the two institutions agreed to a number of provisions aimed at strengthening their cooperation.[4]

755. Cooperation with the Andean Pact continued satisfactorily. The second meeting of the Joint Committee, held in Lima on 10 and 11 December,[5] provided an opportunity to take stock of cooperation so far and to consider ways of improving it.

756. In January the Economic and Social Committee adopted an own-initiative opinion on economic and commercial cooperation with Latin America, in which it called for the establishment of a more structured framework for relations between the Community and its Member States on the one hand and Latin America and its regions on the other.[6]

Bilateral relations

757. The President of the United Mexican States, Mr Carlos Salinas de Gortari, accompanied by several members of his Government, paid an official visit to the Commission on 31 January.[7] The discussions concerned the strengthening of cooperation, President Salinas calling for the 1975 Cooperation Agreement[8] to be replaced by

---

[1]   OJ L 172, 30.6.1986; Twentieth General Report, point 889; OJ L 58, 28.2.1987; Twenty-first General Report, point 817.
[2]   Bull. EC 1/2-1990, point 1.2.47; Bull. EC 7/8-1990, points 1.4.46 and 1.4.48; Bull. EC 9-1990, point 1.3.31; Bull. EC 11-1990, point 1.4.32.
[3]   Twenty-third General Report, point 837.
[4]   Bull. EC 6-1990, point 1.4.31.
[5]   Bull. EC 12-1990.
[6]   OJ C 75, 26.3.1990; Bull. EC 1/2-1990, point 1.2.46.
[7]   Bull. EC 1/2-1990, point 1.2.44.
[8]   OJ L 247, 23.9.1975; Ninth General Report, point 498.

a new agreement. The Council approved negotiatinig directives for such an agreement in October.[1]

758.   In February the Council recorded the Community's solidarity with the Andean countries in the fight against drugs;[2] in October, in response to the special cooperation plan drawn up by Colombia to support the fight against drugs by means of economic cooperation measures, the Council adopted a Regulation[3] extending to Colombia, Bolivia, Peru and Ecuador generalized tariff preferences applied in 1990 to certain least developed countries.[4] A decision of the representatives of the Governments of the ECSC Member States meeting within the Council did the same for ECSC products.[3] In a resolution the Council stressed the importance of coordinating Community and bilateral aid.[3] In December the Commission adopted proposals to enable the new arrangements to be applied from 1991.[5] In June the Commission decided to grant increased financial support to Colombia, amounting to a total of ECU 60 million for the period 1990-93.[6] The Community's support for the fight against drugs in producer countries was one of the main themes discussed during visits to the Commission in April by Mr Virgilio Barco Vargas, President of the Republic of Colombia,[7] and Mr Jaime Paz Zamora Lamoro, President of the Republic of Bolivia,[8] and in November by Mr Ballivian, Bolivia's Foreign Minister.[9]

759.   Initialled in Brussels in February,[10] the Framework Agreement for Trade and Economic Cooperation between the Community and Argentina was signed in Luxembourg on 2 April.[11] Negotiations had started in 1989.[12] The Agreement contains a number of innovations, including a clause making respect for democratic principles and human rights the basis for all cooperation between the parties. The Council approved the conclusion of the Agreement in October.[13] Mr Matutes visited Argentina in July as part of his official tour of countries in the southern cone of South America, during which he opened the meetings of the EEC-Brazil and EEC-Uruguay Joint Committees.[14] Mr Matutes had already visited Brazil in March, for the inauguration of

---

[1]   Bull. EC 10-1990, point 1.4.27; Commission proposal: Bull. EC 7/8-1990, point 1.4.45.
[2]   Bull. EC 1/2-1990, point 1.2.48.
[3]   OJ L 308, 8.11.1990; Bull. EC 10-1990, point 1.4.25; Commission proposals: OJ C 173, 14.7.1990; Bull. EC 6-1990, points 1.4.23 to 1.4.26.
[4]   OJ L 383, 30.12.1989; Twenty-third General Report, point 873.
[5]   OJ L 370, 31.12.1990; Bull. EC 12-1990.
[6]   Bull. EC 6-1990, point 1.4.27.
[7]   Bull. EC 4-1990, point 1.2.27.
[8]   Bull. EC 4-1990, point 1.2.28.
[9]   Bull. EC 11-1990, point 1.4.33.
[10]   Bull. EC 1/2-1990, point 1.2.45.
[11]   Bull. EC 4-1990, point 1.2.29.
[12]   Twenty-third General Report, point 842.
[13]   OJ L 295, 26.10.1990; Bull. EC 10-1990, point 1.4.26; Commission proposal: OJ C 87, 5.4.1990; Bull. EC 3-1990, point 1.2.39.
[14]   Bull. EC 7/8-1990, points 1.4.39 to 1.4.42.

President Fernando Collor de Mello.[1] Relations with this country were characterized by a clear wish to step up industrial cooperation and by the development of new forms of cooperation in the protection of the environment.

760. Relations with Chile revived as the country returned to democracy. Mr Matutes represented the Commission at the ceremonies for the inauguration of the new President, Mr Patricio Aylwin Azocar, on 12 March.[1] In May Parliament adopted a resolution calling on the Community and its Member States to step up cooperation with Chile.[2] In July[3] the Council authorized the Commission to negotiate a framework cooperation agreement with Chile covering a number of new areas. The Agreement was signed in Rome in December.[4] On 17 December the Commission adopted two draft Council decisions authorizing it to negotiate cooperation agreements with Uruguay and Paraguay.[4]

761. In June Mr Matutes had talks in Brussels with Mr Ricardo Arias Calderón, First Vice-President of Panama; they discussed the political and economic situation in Central America and Panama's external aid requirements. The prospects opened up by the elections in Nicaragua were the subject of a parliamentary resolution in March.[5] Mr F. Da Silvio, Minister for the Economy, visited the Commission in November.[4]

762. On 16 July Mr Reinaldo Figueredo Planchart, Venezuela's Minister for Foreign Affairs, paid an official visit to the Commission.[6]

Cooperation with the countries of Asia and Latin America

763. On 12 June, in response to an invitation from the Council in November 1989,[7] the Commission adopted a communication on guidelines for cooperation with the developing countries of Latin America and Asia.[8] It proposed that the Community increase funding and adapt the cooperation instruments to the needs of the countries concerned, while maintaining a consistent approach in parallel with the policies towards the ACP countries, the countries of Central and Eastern Europe and the Mediterranean developing countries. The proposals focus on development aid targeted on the poorest

---

1   Bull. EC 3-1990, point 1.2.38.
2   OJ C 149, 18.6.1990; Bull. EC 5-1990, point 1.3.36.
3   Bull. EC 7/8-1990, point 1.4.44; Commission proposal: Bull. EC 3-1990, point 1.4.41.
4   Bull. EC 12-1990.
5   OJ C 96, 17.4.1990; Bull. EC 3-1990, point 1.2.40.
6   Bull. EC 7/8-1990, point 1.4.47.
7   Twenty-third General Report, point 826.
8   Bull. EC 6-1990, point 1.4.19.

countries and the poorest sections of the population of those countries, and economic cooperation with countries or regions which have major commercial potential. In November the Council expressed its satisfaction with these proposals;[1] it approved the guidelines in December,[2] setting an indicative aid package of ECU 2 750 million for the next five years, 10% of which is earmarked for the environment, mainly for the protection of the Amazonian forest. On 22 June the Commission adopted its 13th report on the use of financial and technical aid at 31 December 1989.[3] The Council adopted the general guidelines for 1990 on 29 June.[4]

764.   Financial and technical cooperation with the countries of Latin America absorbed ECU 110 million in commitment appropriations: the main operations focused on regional integration in Central America and in the Andean countries. The main economic cooperation projects concerned trade promotion (ECU 5.5 million) and training (ECU 4.5 million). Some ECU 8 million was devoted to industrial cooperation, ECU 3.8 million to energy cooperation and ECU 2 million to the promotion of regional integration. A major humanitarian aid operation was mounted for the repatriation of Nicaraguan nationals.

765.   On 28 November[5] the Commission adopted a communication proposing that the experimental phase of the EC International Investment Partners system continue for a further five years, with a regulation specifying the objectives and operating criteria. The proposal takes account of the positive evaluation of the role played by the system since 1988;[6] the Commission emphasized the contribution which it could make to closer economic cooperation with Latin America and Asia, and also with the Mediterranean countries.

---

[1]   Bull. EC 11-1990, point 1.4.25.
[2]   Bull. EC 12-1990.
[3]   Bull. EC 6-1990, point 1.4.21.
[4]   Bull. EC 6-1990, point 1.4.20.
[5]   Bull. EC 11-1990, point 1.4.24.
[6]   Twenty-second General Report, point 1000.

Section 7

Relations with the African, Caribbean and Pacific countries and the overseas countries and territories

Implementation of the new Lomé Convention

766. With the third Lomé Convention expiring on 28 February,[1] the transitional measures to apply pending the entry into force of the fourth Convention, signed in Lomé on 15 December 1989,[2] were adopted at the beginning of the year.[3] These measures entered into force on 1 March and have wide political and practical scope. They are designed to ensure continuity of cooperation by extending all the necessary provisions of the previous Convention not covered by anticipatory measures, and also to pave the way for implementing the greater part of the results obtained during the negotiations — with the exception of the financial provisions — without waiting for the end of the ratification process. In this way the rules concerning the general objectives and principles of cooperation, trade arrangements, institutions and the procedure for Namibia's accession to the Convention were all brought into force.

767. Following Parliament's assent on 16 May to the conclusion of the Convention,[4] the Commission presented to the Council in July a proposal for a Decision providing for a single concluding act, to be signed by the Council and also by the Commission under the powers conferred upon it by the ECSC Treaty.[5]

768. On 22 October the Council adopted the Community position in readiness for the negotiations on the accession to the Convention of Namibia,[6] which had applied for accession immediately it became independent.[7] The specific arrangements for its accession, in particular the establishment of annual quotas for beef and veal and the granting of the status of least-developed country, were agreed in November by the

---

[1] OJ L 86, 31.3.1986; Twentieth General Report, point 939.
[2] Twenty-third General Report, point 846.
[3] OJ L 84, 30.3.1990; Bull. EC 3-1990, points 1.2.45 to 1.2.48; Commission proposals: OJ C 44, 24.2.1990; Bull. EC 1/2-1990, point 1.2.49.
[4] OJ C 149, 18.6.1990; Bull. EC 5-1990, point 1.3.37.
[5] Bull. EC 7/8-1990, point 1.4.49.
[6] Bull. EC 10-1990, point 1.4.28; Commission proposal: Bull. EC 7/8-1990, point 1.4.51.
[7] Bull. EC 3-1990, point 1.2.44.

ACP-EEC Committee of Ambassadors, acting on the authorization of the ACP-EEC Council of Ministers,[1] and the accession papers were signed in Brussels on 18 December.[2]

769.   On 14 November the Commission adopted a communication on reducing the burden of debt contracted by the ACP countries with the Community.[3] In line with the logic of the new Convention, the planned operation is informed by the special relations existing between the Community and the ACP countries, based more on the concept of partnership for development rather than on a creditor-debtor relationship. The proposed measures concern debt incurred in connection with the operation of the financial instruments provided for under the various Lomé Convention — EDF special loans, including Sysmin; Stabex transfers; EDF risk capital — with the exception, accordingly, of loans from the EIB's own resources and bilateral debts, the reduction of which is the responsibility of the Member States.

770.   In October Parliament adopted a resolution on ACP debt, calling on the ACP-EEC Council of Ministers to examine measures to cancel the ACP countries' debt to the Community.[4]

771.   At the internal Community level, the Council approved the new Internal Agreement on the financing and administration of Community aid.[5] Its provisions are mainly of a technical nature but they also have a political dimension, namely the concern to speed up the cooperation process and make Community aid more effective. In June the Commission adopted a draft Financial Regulation, applicable to development financing cooperation under the Convention, laying down the rules governing operations under the seventh EDF in accordance with the Internal Agreement.[6] The draft, which was amended in September,[7] was the subject of an opinion by Parliament in December.[8]

In December the Council adopted a regulation on safeguard measures, with the aim of replacing national procedures by a Community procedure.[9]

772.   On the operational front, once the breakdown of programmable resources was settled, the Commission embarked on the process of programming for the next five years. In this the Commission had three aims to keep in view: to consolidate the Lomé III approach of supporting sector-based policies through dialogue and the focus-

---

[1]   Bull. EC 11-1990, point 1.4.40.
[2]   Bull. EC 12-1990.
[3]   Bull. EC 11-1990, point 1.4.36.
[4]   OJ C 295, 26.11.1990; Bull. EC 10-1990, point 1.4.29.
[5]   Bull. EC 6-1990, point 1.4.32.
[6]   OJ C 165, 6.7.1990; Bull. EC 6-1990, point 1.4.33.
[7]   OJ C 267, 23.10.1990; Bull. EC 9-1990, point 1.3.34.
[8]   OJ C 19, 28.1.1991; Bull. EC 12-1990.
[9]   OJ L 358, 21.12.1990; Bull. EC 12-1990; Commission proposal: Bull. EC 7/8-1990, point 1.4.50.

ing of aid on a limited number of sectors; to incorporate in the programming exercise the new ideas brought in under Lomé IV, so that they could be given practical effect; and to give due consideration to structural adjustment policies, in consultation with the Member States and the international finance bodies. In addition, some flexibility was built in to the national programmes to allow for changing political and economic situations. By the end of the year the process had been completed for virtually all the ACP countries, and nine indicative programmes were already signed. The Commission also made a start on regional programming, by giving details of the amount to be allocated to each region and maintaining active contact with national authorizing officers and the various regional bodies concerned.

773. On 22 November the Commission adopted a proposal on the establishment of the joint committee to be set up under the new Convention with a view to seeking appropriate solutions to the problems encountered in the commodities sector.[1]

Trade cooperation

774. The importance of developing trade and services is highlighted in the new ACP-EEC Convention and the scope for assistance in this area has been broadened appreciably. The new guidelines were presented at a symposium organized in Brussels in July. On the practical side, efforts to develop trade and services in 1990 were concerned mainly with establishing and carrying out a number of action programmes, including one worth ECU 4 628 000 to support trade organizations dealing with tropical fruit and out-of-season vegetables. A regional programme was allocated ECU 4 932 000 to meet the cost of attendance — 296 persons in all — at trade and tourist events, the organization of seminars at the Brussels, Lisbon and Bari fairs, and technical assistance to 24 ACP countries to help them participate in trade events.

Stabex

775. Stabex operations in 1990 concerned the ACP countries' export earnings in 1989, the last trading year for the earnings stabilization system under the third Lomé Convention.[2] The Commission received a total of 70 requests for transfers in respect of 1989, from 32 countries. Upon examination, 36 of the requests were rejected while 34 others,

---

[1]   Bull. EC 11-1990, point 1.4.37.
[2]   OJ L 86, 31.3.1986; Twentieth General Report, point 939.

affecting 20 countries, were found to be admissible and gave rise to transfer bases totalling over ECU 495 million. The size of this amount, which though appreciably down on the transfer bases for the 1987 and 1988 trading years was for the third year running well in excess of the financial resources ordinarily available under Stabex for the year (ECU 141 million), [1] is explained by the continuing slump on the agricultural commodity markets, in particular for coffee — accounting for two-thirds of the total — but also for cocoa and oleaginous products. Application of the Lomé Convention provisions for

TABLE 12

Beneficiary countries	Product	Amount of transfer (ECU)
Benin	Palm oil	145 900
Burundi	Coffee	19 255 556
Cameroon	Cocoa products	33 563 345
	Coffee	30 104 618
Central African Republic	Coffee	2 898 962
	Cotton	347 888
	Sawn wood	707 074
Comoros	Vanilla	807 570
	Cloves	655 356
Côte d'Ivoire	Coffee	59 955 369
	Wood	11 138 057
Dominica	Bananas	1 208 418
Equatorial Guinea	Cocoa	3 004 810
	Coffee	229 932
Ethiopia	Beans	418 130
Gambia	Groundnuts	447 739
	Groundnut oil	695 055
Grenada	Cocoa	719 293
Kenya	Coffee	11 082 250
Malawi	Groundnuts	1 183 487
	Coffee	1 167 337
Papua New Guinea	Cocoa	4 224 193
	Coffee	1 337 001
	Palm products	510 383
Rwanda	Coffee	18 855 083
Samoa	Cocoa	157 790
	Copra oil	1 194 923
	Oil cake	26 298
Somalia	Hides and skins	543 312
Togo	Cocoa	1 713 208
	Coffee	2 729 873
Tonga	Copra oil	270 905
	Bananas	296 070
Vanuatu	Copra	783 826
	Total	212 369 011

---

[1]   Twentieth General Report, point 1006; Twenty-third General Report, point 848.

dealing with a shortfall in resources under the system brought the transfer bases total down to around ECU 413 million. It eventually proved possible to cover 51% of this amount, thanks to the decision of the ACP-EEC Committee of Ambassadors,[1] acting on the authorization of the ACP-EEC Council of Ministers, to increase the resources ordinarily available under the system by ECU 70 million reallocated from Sysmin to Stabex, and also by the transfer of unused balances from funds for emergency aid and interest rate subsidies.[2] Table 12 gives a breakdown of operations by recipient country.

776.   On 28 February the Commission adopted for transmission to the ACP-EEC Council of Ministers a report on the financial difficulties encountered by Stabex in connection with the 1980, 1981, 1987 and 1988 trading years.[3]

Sysmin

777.   Two applications for assistance under Sysmin were presented in 1990, one from Senegal in respect of phosphates and the other from Papua New Guinea in respect of copper; both were declared admissible under Lomé III. Financing of ECU 15 million was approved for a scheme in Senegal.

Sugar Protocol

778.   On 18 June the Council adopted the Decision on the conclusion of an Agreement in the form of an exchange of letters between the Community and the ACP States on the guaranteed prices for sugar for the 1988/89 delivery period.[4] The agreed prices were ECU 44.92/100 kg for raw sugar and ECU 55.39/100 kg for white sugar. A similar Decision was adopted in July in respect of India.[5]

779.   On 24 September the Council adopted directives for the negotiation by the Commission of the guaranteed prices to apply during the 1990/91 delivery period.[6]

---

[1]   Bull. EC 7/8-1990, point 1.4.58.
[2]   Bull. EC 3-1990, point 1.2.43.
[3]   Bull. EC 1/2-1990, point 1.2.52.
[4]   Bull. EC 6-1990, point 1.4.35.
[5]   Bull. EC 7/8-1990, point 1.4.55.
[6]   Bull. EC 9-1990, point 1.3.35; Commission proposal: Bull. EC 7/8-1990, point 1.4.56.

Industrial cooperation

780. The development of enterprise in the ACP countries and cooperation between ACP and Community firms was the subject of special attention, notably in the programming of Community aid under the new Convention.[1] The Commission is endeavouring to make an active contribution to creating a favourable climate for the growth of private enterprise, by devising and implementing projects to encourage the development of enterprises and of investment flows. A joint ACP-EEC evaluation was made of the work of the Centre for the Development of Industry, and a study was also carried out on the Centre's activities under its cooperation agreements with European bodies. The Commission also helped organize the ninth Community-West Africa industrial forum, which was held in Dakar in December.

Financial and technical cooperation

781. The main feature of programmed aid in 1990 was the continuing drive to speed up the implementation of Community aid and of import programmes, notably under the special programme for low-income, highly indebted countries in sub-Saharan Africa,[2] in the second phase of which the Commission will take part according to procedures it established in December.[3] The trends to emerge, after just over four and a half years of implementation of the third Lomé Convention, were a continuing flow of commitments, albeit at a clearly lower rate than in previous years, and an increase in the rate of payments. By the end of the year the Commission had committed over ECU 3.6 billion, or 88.5% of programmable resources, from the sixth European Development Fund (EDF). There are two reasons for the slowdown in commitments: first, implementation of the third Convention was nearing its end and, second, most of the key programmes, requiring large amounts of finance, were committed between 1987 and 1989. Aid approved this year generally concerned operations on a more limited scale and requiring smaller amounts. Payments rose significantly, practically doubling to some 34% of programmable resources by the end of the year; the reason for this is the existence of large programmes with numerous components requiring certain decisions to be taken and contracts awarded in the course of implementation, and above all the speedy disbursement involved in import programmes, notably the debt programme. A total of 47 sectoral import programmes have so far been committed, including 22 under the debt programme; 35 countries have received support amounting in all to ECU 773 million, 66% has already been paid out. Of the 27 countries originally eligible, 24 are

---

[1]   Point 771 of this Report.
[2]   OJ C 348, 23.12.1987; Twenty-first General Report, point 857.
[3]   Bull. EC 12-1990.

now receiving support under the debt programme, which is administered in coordination with the World Bank's special assistance programme. Total commitments have now reached ECU 570 million. All the resources available had been committed by the middle of the year, which means that the Commission is the second-fastest donor in implementing its aid. Table 13 gives a sectoral breakdown.

Regional cooperation

782.   As in the previous year, 1990 saw a sharp increase in the implementation of various regional programmes under the third Lomé Convention, with the total level of commitments for regional cooperation rising from 60 to 85%. The funds available have virtually all been committed in some regions (East Africa, West Africa and the Caribbean), although the time-lag in implementing regional programmes by comparison with national programmes is still evident.

783.   Work also began during the year on putting into effect the guidelines for regional cooperation under the new Convention.

The main new features are as follows: the importance given to economic integration; 'transcendence' of purely geographical considerations (Article 156 of the Convention); the extension of regional cooperation to include the overseas territories and departments; extension of the scope of cooperation to cover operations encouraging the coordination of structural adjustment policies; clarification of the criteria for defining regional projects and also regional organizations, the importance of which was confirmed; and systematization of methods and procedures in the interests of greater effectiveness.

Institutional relations

784.   Following a preparatory meeting of the Committee of Ambassadors on 27 February,[1] the ACP-EEC Council of Ministers held its annual meeting in Suva, Fiji, on 28 and 29 March, concentrating largely on progress in implementing the third Lomé Convention, the transition between Lomé III and the new Convention, the Uruguay Round and a number of specific trade cooperation topics, the situation on commodity markets, ACP indebtedness to the Community and developments in southern Africa.[2]

---

[1]   Bull. EC 1/2-1990, point 1.2.56.
[2]   Bull. EC 3-1990, point 1.2.43.

TABLE 13

Lomé I, II and III financing decisions (EDF and EIB[1])
for ACP States, by sector, at 31 December

	Commitments (million ECU)						% of total commitments
	1976-86	1987	1988	1989	1990[3]	Total	
Development of production	4 200.96	1 378.52	1 268.47	563.26	257.34	7 668.57	47.49
Industrialization	2 362.32	492.41	373.91	262.11	145.17	3 635.93	22.52
Tourism	43.83	−0.61	13.96	9.07	22.48	88.73	0.55
Rural production	1 794.83	886.71	880.61	292.06	89.68	3 943.91	24.42
Economic infrastructure, transport and communications	1 583.66	521.89	206.54	275.18	150.89	2 738.17	16.96
Social development	1 093.23	176.30	273.15	179.48	70.08	1 792.23	11.10
Education and training	530.48	47.67	67.39	58.16	40.40	744.10	4.61
Health	152.53	78.18	60.69	50.55	6.68	348.63	2.16
Water engineering, urban infrastructure and housing	410.22	50.45	145.06	70.77	23.00	699.50	4.33
Trade promotion	90.59	27.51	20.13	14.23	31.70	184.17	1.14
Emergency aid	344.60	22.15	34.18	33.53	22.33	456.78	2.83
Stabex	1 117.75	289.03	553.49	274.03	141.47	2 355.78	14.59
RRP[1]	100.00	−0.05	0.07	0.13	−0.02	100.13	0.62
Refugee aid	0.00	0.86	18.63	31.98	17.48	68.95	0.43
Import programme	29.19	1.06	268.92	127.89	114.26	541.32	3.35
Other	187.59	9.20	20.88	11.94	12.81	242.41	1.50
Total	8 747.59	2 406.47	2 664.46	1 511.66	818.34	16 148.51	100.00

[1] For EIB operations, see the Bank's annual report.
[2] Rehabilitation and recovery plan.
[3] Forecast.

The general rules, conditions and arbitration procedures for EDF-financed contracts were approved, and also the Commission's proposal for setting up a joint working party with the ACP countries to identify the causes of delays and difficulties in the management of financial cooperation. At its meeting on 13 July the Committee of Ambassadors returned to a number of points discussed by the Council of Ministers and took the decisions on Stabex transfers for the 1989 trading year which were necessary because of the insufficiency of the resources available.[1]

---

[1] Bull. EC 7/8-1990, point 1.4.58.

785.   The ACP-EEC Joint Assembly held the first of its two annual sessions in Port Moresby, Papua New Guinea, from 19 to 22 March,[1] and the second in Luxembourg from 24 to 28 September.[2] The first session was dominated by examination of the specific problems of the South Pacific countries and completion of the task of assessing the impact of 1992 on the ACP countries. Both sessions also included discussion of the priorities adopted for implementing the ACP-EEC Convention, and also the situation in southern Africa. Other important points from the Luxembourg session were the following: ACP debt, with an appeal being made for cancellation of official debt; the effects of the Gulf crisis on the ACP countries and the consequent need for increased financial resources; a hearing on women in development; and progress reports from the groups set up to look into intra-ACP trade and transport issues.

Overseas countries and territories

786.   On 5 March the Council extended its Decision of 30 June 1986 on the association of the overseas countries and territories (OCTs) with the Community,[3] which was due to expire on 28 February, for one year until 28 February 1991,[4] and at the same time brought into effect for the OCTs the trade arrangements under the new ACP-EEC Convention.[5]

Following extensive prior consultation with the relevant OCT authorities, the Commission adopted on 19 September two proposals concerning the OCTs, one on a new phase of association with the Community and the other on ECSC products.[6] The first proposal broke new ground in many respects, and included a number of new features taken from the fourth Lomé Convention: extension of the period of validity from five to 10 years, except as regards financial arrangements, which are laid down for five years; improvements to the financing terms and the Stabex and Sysmin machinery; opportunities for decentralized cooperation involving local communities; importance given to respect for the environment, attention to the role of women and encouragement of enterprises and services; emphasis on regional cooperation between ACP States and OCTs in the same geographical area.

A number of legal improvements were also felt to be necessary to take account of the specific situation of the OCTs: more flexible procedures for derogations from the rules

---

[1]   Bull. EC 3-1990, point 1.2.42.
[2]   Bull. EC 9-1990, point 1.3.33.
[3]   OJ L 175, 1.7.1986; Twentieth General Report, point 943.
[4]   OJ L 84, 30.3.1990; Bull. EC 3-1990, point 1.2.46; Commission proposal: OJ C 44, 24.2.1990; Bull. EC 1/2-1990, point 1.2.49.
[5]   Point 766 of this Report.
[6]   Bull. EC 9-1990, point 1.3.32.

of origin applicable to products imported from the OCTs into the Community; inclusion of the OCTs in the Euro-Business Information Centre project;[1] clarification of the arrangements concerning establishment and the provision of services, and establishment of standing arrangements for a Commission-Member State-OCT partnership. The financial cooperation package for the OCTs under the seventh EDF was finalized at ECU 140 million, which represents a 40% increase; the figure for loans from the EIB's own resources is ECU 25 million, which is 25% more than under the sixth EDF.

On 5 October the Commission adopted two further proposals for Decisions to extend beyond 31 December the expiry date for the arrangements governing trade between Spain and Portugal and the OCTs.[2]

---

[1]   Point 235 of this Report.
[2]   Bull. EC 10-1990, point 1.4.30.

Section 8

General development cooperation

Cooperation through the United Nations

United Nations Conference on Trade and Development

787.   The Trade and Development Board met twice this year. The second part of the 36th session, held in the spring, was given over mainly to the trade problems linked with the GATT negotiations. During the first part of the 37th session, held at the beginning of October, the 1990 report on trade and development was examined; this report covered the changes in Central and Eastern Europe, the creation of the internal market and the probable changes in international trade rules following the Uruguay Round.

Unctad is preparing the eighth conference, which is to be held at the end of 1991. It also supervised the second United Nations Conference on the Least-developed Countries (LLDCs) which was held in Paris in September and the preparation of the programme adopted there. This Conference, for which the Council had approved the Community's position in July,[1] evaluated the progress made since the first meeting of this kind in 1981 in implementing the measures adopted at international and national level for the LLDCs, and drew up a new programme for the 1990s, which will be more realistic and operational than the previous one.[2]

The discussions held at the Conference reflected the outcome of the United Nations General Assembly's special session in April on international economic cooperation.[3]

788.   At its 17th meeting, held in May, the Special Committee on Preferences conducted the examination carried out every 10 years of the generalized system of preferences.[4]

789.   On 29 May[5] the Council adopted a decision on the conclusion of the agreement establishing the Common Fund for Commodities.[6]

---

[1]   Bull. EC 7/8-1990, point 1.4.72; Commission proposal: Bull. EC 6-1990, point 1.4.49.
[2]   Fifteenth General Report, point 658.
[3]   Point 854 of this Report.
[4]   Bull. EC 5-1990, point 1.3.57.
[5]   OJ L 182, 14.7.1990; Bull. EC 5-1990, point 1.3.45.
[6]   Fourteenth General Report, point 610.

United Nations Industrial Development Organization

790. The Commission took part in the sixth and seventh sessions of the Industrial Development Board, which were held in Vienna from 29 May to 1 June and from 5 to 9 November. The main topics discussed included examination of the activities of the United Nations Industrial Development Organization (Unido), in particular regional programmes and programmes for the least-developed countries; Unido's financial situation; the medium-term plan for 1992 to 1997 and the reorganization of the Secretariat, with the aim of giving it the optimum structure for carrying out Unido's work. During the sixth session, the Director-General of Unido was authorized by the International Development Board to conclude a new agreement with the Commission on relations between the Community and Unido.[1]

World Food Programme

791. The Community's total allocation to the World Food Programme (WFP), comprising foodstuffs and financial support for covering transport costs, amounted to ECU 110.6 million. This aid was used partly to meet the needs of 'food for work' projects, or free distribution projects managed by the WFP or the International Emergency Food Reserve. It was also channelled into programmes to help refugees, particularly Ethiopian refugees in Somalia and Afghan refugees in Pakistan. Mr Ingram, Executive Director of the WFP, met Mr Marín in September.[2]

World Food Council

792. The 16th ministerial session of the World Food Council (WFC), which was held in Bangkok in May,[3] was given over mainly to examining the implementation of the Cairo Declaration, adopted at the previous session.[4] The participants also held an exchange of views on how to improve coordination of the efforts of the international organizations responsible for agricultural development and food aid. The conclusions and recommendations adopted drew attention to the common perception of the most appropriate ways of improving food security. Emphasis was laid on the need to take account of environmental conservation and population growth, and to incorporate food security into economic adjustment programmes. The developed countries were called upon to ensure that their cooperation with the Central and Eastern European countries was not conducted to the detriment of the developing countries.

---

[1]   Twenty-third General Report, point 868.
[2]   Bull. EC 9-1990, point 1.3.47.
[3]   Bull. EC 5-1990, point 1.3.57.
[4]   Twenty-third General Report, point 870.

Food and Agriculture Organization of the United Nations

793.   The Commission continued its exploratory talks with the Food and Agriculture Organization of the United Nations (FAO) in order to work out membership status for the Community commensurate with its spheres of competence. On the basis of the outcome of these talks, in October the Council decided to initiate negotiations with the FAO with a view to amending the organization's Constitution to allow membership by a regional economic integration organization, since at present only States can be members.[1] At its 98th meeting the FAO Council expressed a favourable opinion on Community membership but felt that there were still some aspects which needed to be clarified. It will present its opinion in June 1991 in preparation for the biennial conference, which will meet in November 1991, and is the only body empowered to change the FAO Constitution.[2]

Generalized tariff preferences

794.   On 4 July the Commission adopted a memo on the broad lines of the Community's generalized preferences scheme for the 1990s.[3]

The Commission considers that a development-oriented commercial policy instrument such as the GSP that treats the Third World countries on a differential basis is still needed, but that it should be considerably improved in the light of developments since its inception. With this in view, it is drawing up a number of principles likely to contribute to the setting-up of an attractive new scheme, which would be simpler, more stable and more transparent. This approach requires coordination by the donor countries in order to achieve greater harmonization of their GSP policies, and also measures to take account of certain beneficiary countries' increasing ability to make their own contribution to trade liberalization. On the basis of the outcome of the Uruguay Round,[4] the Commission will propose specific measures based on these broad lines and will present the operational scheme which will enter into force on 1 January 1992. Parliament gave its opinion on these broad lines in December.[5]

795.   In December the Council adopted the Regulations and Decisions on the opening of the Community's generalized tariff preferences for 1991.[6] It is an interim scheme and

---

[1]   Bull. EC 10-1990, point 1.4.40; Commission proposal: Bull. EC 6-1990, point 1.4.50.
[2]   Bull. EC 11-1990, point 1.4.48.
[3]   Bull. EC 7/8-1990, point 1.4.59.
[4]   Point 817 *et seq.* of this Report.
[5]   OJ C 19, 28.1.1991; Bull. EC 12-1990.
[6]   OJ L 370, 31.12.1990; Bull. EC 12-1990; Commission proposals: Bull. EC 10-1990, point 1.4.32.

remains the same, in form and in substance, as in 1990,[1] with the exception of the amendments necessitated by external circumstances: the benefits of the scheme were extended to Czechoslovakia and Bulgaria and the arrangements for Romania were improved, and the GSP offer was increased following the rise in Community consumption resulting from German unification.

796.   In October the Council adopted the regulations giving Bolivia, Colombia, Ecuador and Peru special preferential treatment under the GSP, similar to the treatment accorded to the least-developed countries, as exceptional aid for their efforts to combat drug abuse.[2]

Commodities and world agreements

797.   Following the failure of negotiations on a new International Coffee Agreement in July 1989, the members of the Agreement endeavoured to establish the necessary basis for rapid resumption of the negotiating process.[3] Radical changes in market distribution combined with Brazil's inability to formulate its coffee policy proved a serious obstacle, however. As a result, the International Coffee Council decided at the end of September to extend the 1983 Agreement by one more year[4] until the end of September 1992 in order to give itself more time.[5]

798.   The Cocoa Council decided in March to extend the International Cocoa Agreement by two years until September 1992, without economic clauses.[6] This reflected the existing situation, in which serious problems had occurred as a result of non-payment of levies by certain producer countries, giving rise to difficulties in the management of the buffer stock. There has been no change in the fundamental problem of structural imbalance between supply and demand on the world market in cocoa.

799.   The work of the International Tropical Timber Organization, whose Council and technical committees met in November in Yokohama, gathered speed as regards the preparation of technical programmes and also the establishment of a number of standards for tropical forest exploitation in the producer countries.[7] This work has helped considerably to extend the scope of discussions on environmental protection in international forums.

---

[1]   OJ L 383, 30.12.1989; Twenty-third General Report, point 873.
[2]   Point 758 of this Report.
[3]   Twenty-third General Report, point 874.
[4]   Bull. EC 9-1990, point 1.3.39.
[5]   OJ L 308, 9.11.1983; Seventeenth General Report, point 732.
[6]   OJ L 69, 12.3.1987; Twentieth General Report, point 919.
[7]   Bull. EC 11-1990, point 1.4.45.

800. On 9 February the Commission adopted a proposal for a decision on the acceptance of the terms of reference of the international study group on copper,[1] adopted by the United Nations Conference in February 1989.[2]

801. The International Tin Council paid out UKL 182.5 million to its creditors, thereby ending disputes between the Council itself and/or its members and their creditors which had lasted since cessation of payments under the Agreement.[3]

802. The International Study Group on Nickel, for which the terms of reference had been negotiated in 1986, held its inaugural meeting in The Hague in June.[4]

803. At its meeting in Kuala Lumpur in July, the International Natural Rubber Council revised the price scale for buffer stock operations, and decided to conduct a study into the effectiveness of these operations.[5]

804. In December[6] the Council decided to sign the 1989 International Agreement on Jute and Jute Products.[7] The Council signature, and those of the Member States, took place before the end of the year, which had been set as the deadline by the Agreement. Meeting in Dacca from 29 November to 1 December, the International Council had stressed the need to obtain a sufficient number of signatures before 31 December, to avoid recourse to temporary implementation of the Agreement.[8]

Drugs

805. At its meeting in Dublin in June,[9] the European Council gave decisive impetus to the campaign against drug abuse and organized crime, at internal and external level.[10] Meeting in Rome in December,[8] it stressed that Community policies *vis-à-vis* non-member countries must take the combat against drug abuse as one of their objectives, and called on the European Committee for the fight against drug abuse (Celad) to drive and coordinate the Member States efforts at international level.

---

[1] Bull. EC 1/2-1990, point 1.2.62.
[2] Twenty-third General Report, point 878.
[3] Bull. EC 4-1990, point 1.2.34.
[4] Bull. EC 6-1990, point 1.4.42.
[5] Bull. EC 7/8-1990, point 1.4.61.
[6] Bull. EC 12-1990; Commission proposal: Bull. EC 7/8-1990, point 1.4.62.
[7] Twenty-third General Report, point 880.
[8] Bull. EC 12-1990.
[9] Bull. EC 6-1990, point I.16.
[10] Point 164 of this Report.

806.   The Community is playing an active part in the implementation of the world action programme adopted by the United Nations General Assembly at its February special session, and is in particular providing support for the restructuring of those UN bodies which are responsible for combating drug abuse. [1] On 22 October [2] the Council adopted the decision on the conclusion of the United Nations Convention on Illicit Traffic in Narcotic Drugs and Psychotropic Substances. [3] Under the North-South cooperation programme for combating drug abuse, with a budget this year of ECU 9.8 million, the Commission gave priority to Colombia and the other Andean Pact countries, while at the same time endeavouring to cope with other problems, such as that of heroin in Asia. The Community is to respond to the special plan to combat drug abuse proposed by Colombia by strengthening development aid, introducing temporary measures to facilitate access to the Community market for legal exports, and setting up machinery to coordinate the bilateral efforts of the Community and its Member States. [4]

AIDS

807.   Under the programme to combat AIDS in the ACP countries adopted in 1987, commitments reached 93% of the total of ECU 35 million earmarked for three years. [5] As in previous years, an appropriation of ECU 5 million was allocated under the special budget heading opened in 1988 to cover all the developing countries and to finance regional projects. [6] Unlike the two previous budgetary years, the programme received differentiated appropriations and therefore suffered less from the constraints arising from the budgetary time-limits inherent in non-differentiated appropriations.

Food aid

808.   On 19 March, the Commission adopted Decision 90/145/EEC concerning the establishment of overall quantities of food aid for 1990 and establishing a list of products to be supplied as food aid. [7] Preparing the preliminary draft budget for 1990, the only source of financing for food aid, the Commission adopted amounts which would make

---

[1]   Point 853 of this Report.
[2]   OJ L 326, 24.11.1990; Bull. EC 10-1990, point 1.4.39; Commission proposal: Twenty-third General Report, point 882; Bull. EC 7/8-1990, point 1.4.71.
[3]   Twenty-second General Report, point 986.
[4]   Point 758 of this Report.
[5]   Twenty-first General Report, point 843.
[6]   Twenty-second General Report, point 988.
[7]   OJ L 80, 27.3.1990; Bull. EC 3-1990, point 1.2.56.

it possible to supply the same overall quantities as in 1989, except for butteroil (reduced from 25 000 tonnes to 18 000 tonnes) and sugar (increased from 14 000 tonnes to 15 000 tonnes) and vegetable oil (increased from 40 000 tonnes to 50 000 tonnes).[1] The list of products remained the same, apart from the incorporation of pigmeat, cheese and fresh produce such as fruit and vegetables grown in the country itself.

809.   In January, the Commission ascertained that the allocations for transport were insufficient to cover the overall quantities set for 1990. It was therefore decided to cancel certain quantities and make an initial transfer of funds to help cover the costs of transporting the aid. This situation is partly a result of the increase in transport prices and the growing scale of operations within certain countries such as Ethiopia and Sudan and also the fact that appropriations for transport were, up to 1989, non-differentiated.

810.   On 29 June the Council adopted Regulation (EEC) No 1930/90[2] amending the three regulations on food-aid policy and management,[3] the implementation of storage programmes and early-warning systems,[4] and the cofinancing of the purchase of food products or seeds by international bodies or non-governmental organizations.[5] This new framework regulation has an unspecified period of validity and changes the nature of the Food Aid Committee, which becomes a Management Committee.

Standard food-aid programme

811.   In accordance with the rules in force on food-aid policy and management, the Commission set the overall quantities for food aid, a large proportion of which (94%) was programmed by country (direct aid) and by internal and non-governmental organizations (indirect aid). Proposals for the allocation of aid were put to the Food Aid Committee for its opinion before adoption by the Commission. Table 14 gives the breakdown of these operations.

812.   Within the limits of these quantities, the Commission decided to finance a new multiannual programme (1990-92) for Cape Verde (21 000 tonnes of cereals, and 1 600 tonnes of vegetable oil). This programme provides support for long-term development projects undertaken by Cape Verde and comes in addition to the three already in progress for Cape Verde, Kenya and China. Over and above these allocations, various operations have been undertaken for a total of ECU 10 million under storage and

---

[1]   OJ L 63, 7.3.1989; Twenty-third General Report, point 884.
[2]   OJ L 174, 7.7.1990; Bull. EC 6-1990, point 1.4.43; Commission proposal; OJ C 134, 1.6.1990; Bull. EC 5-1990, point 1.3.47.
[3]   OJ L 370, 30.12.1986; Twentieth General Report, point 934.
[4]   OJ L 220, 11.8.1988; Twenty-second General Report, point 995.
[5]   OJ L 220, 11.8.1988; Twentieth General Report, point 1003.

early-warning system programmes. They involve the financing of an early-warning system in Chad and storage facilities in Mozambique, Madagascar, Ethiopia, Bangladesh, and Eastern and Southern Africa, and for the International Red Cross Committee in Sudan and Jordan, the World Food Programme in Malawi and non-governmental organizations in Mozambique. The Commission also decided on alternative operations in place of food aid in India and Mali, for an amount of ECU 7.5 million. In addition, the sum of ECU 10 000 000 was allocated, as part of cofinancing, for operations to help the following countries: Ethiopia, Malawi, Madagascar, Nicaragua, Angola, Mozambique, Thailand, India, Pakistan, Algeria, Rwanda, Uganda, Philippines, Sudan, Côte d'Ivoire, Sierra Leone and Guinea.

TABLE 14

Region or organization	Cereals	Milk powder	Butter-oil	Vegetable oil	Sugar	Other products (million ECU)
			(tonnes)			
Africa	322 400	1 850	600	4 900	—	3 150
Indian and Pacific Ocean	17 000	100	—	100	—	—
Caribbean	240	140	—	—	—	—
Mediterranean	160 000	3 000	—	8 000	—	—
Latin America	77 251	5 927	600	6 150	1 000	1 075
Asia	180 000	10 800	3 600	2 200	—	—
Total direct aid	756 971	21 817	4 800	21 350	1 000	4 225
Total indirect aid	495 896	46 343	4 000	25 486	14 000	34 010
Grand total	1 252 867	68 160	8 800	46 836	15 000	38 235

Emergency food aid

813. The fact that such a large sum, ECU 12 725 000, was earmarked by the Commission for emergency aid during the year is explained largely by the Gulf crisis and the refugee situation in certain countries. This emergency aid was as follows:

Somalia (WFP): 2 400 tonnes of cereals

Lebanon (UNRWA): 2 400 tonnes of cereals

Rwanda (WFP): 2 500 tonnes of cereals

Peru: 1 600 tonnes of cereals in the form of seed

Jordan: 9 000 tonnes of cereals; 200 tonnes of milk powder; 500 tonnes of vegetable oil

Egypt: 24 000 tonnes of cereals; 1 440 tonnes of milk powder; 1 440 tonnes of vegetable oil; 480 tonnes of butteroil; approximately 2 400 tonnes of other products

Ethiopia: 25 000 tonnes of cereals; 1 244 tonnes of vegetable oil

Sudan (NGOs): 10 000 tonnes of cereals; ECU 20 000 for other products

Emergency aid

814. The Commission launched emergency aid operations for a total of ECU 67 055 000 for the victims of disasters in the developing countries and other non-Community countries, with the exception of emergency operations for people affected by the Gulf crisis. This sum includes ECU 41 620 000 from the European Development Fund (EDF) and ECU 250 435 000 from the Communities' general budget. Under the EDF, substantial assistance is still given to the victims of conflicts in Africa. The sum of ECU 9 975 000 was used to assist the population of Liberia and the neighbouring countries. Major sums were also committed for the victims of the fighting in Angola, Ethiopia, Sudan and Mozambique, the effects of which have been aggravated by the drought affecting wide areas of these countries. Under the general budget, major medical/food programmes were financed to the tune of ECU 11 120 000 for those affected by events in Romania at the end of 1989. Aid was granted to the victims of the fighting in Cambodia (ECU 2 670 000) and Lebanon (ECU 1 275 000). Aid was also made available to help the victims of the earthquakes in Iran (ECU 2 000 000), the Philippines and Peru.

The emergency aid funds were used to finance medical programmes, provide shelter, food, clothing, and transport and to meet some of the recipients' other essential requirements. The operations were carried out by specialized international and non-governmental organizations, the governments concerned and the Commission.

As regards the Gulf crisis, the Commission committed ECU 47 800 000 under the Community budget for emergency aid for refugees from Iraq and Kuwait. This sum was used mainly to finance transport to these people's countries of origin and to supply the refugee camps with basic essentials.

Cooperation with the non-associated developing countries

815.   In the fourth year of application of the system of compensation for loss of export earnings for least-developed countries (LLDCs) not signatory to the Lomé Convention, the Commission received six requests for transfers from two countries for losses incurred in 1989.[1] Two of these requests were held inadmissible following appraisal, whereas in the other four cases transfers were justified, as shown in Table 15. In July, following Haiti's accession to the Lomé Convention, the Commission proposed to the Council to withdraw Haiti from the list of eligible countries.[2]

TABLE 15

Recipient country	Product	Amount (ECU)
Bangladesh	Tea	2 344 746
	Jute	291 648
Nepal	Skins and hides	557 893
	Lentils	112 699
	Total	3 306 986

Cooperation through non-governmental organizations

816.   The funds earmarked for development cooperation with non-governmental organizations (NGOs) amounted for the year to ECU 90 million. At 31 December these funds had been fully committed for 349 development projects being cofinanced with the Member States of the Community in 85 African, Latin American and Asian countries.

This year block grants reached their highest level since operations began : 100 such grants totalling ECU 10.25 million were made.

At the end of the year the funds disbursed for operations aimed at increasing European public awareness of development issues totalled ECU 9 million. The funds available (ECU 5 million) to help the people of Chile under Article 992, inserted in the budget in 1986, were also fully committed.[3]

---

[1]   OJ L 43, 13.2.1987; Twenty-first General Report, point 861.
[2]   Bull. EC 7/8-1990, point 1.4.53.
[3]   Twentieth General Report, point 938.

Section 9

Multilateral trade negotiations — Uruguay Round

817. The Uruguay Round — the eighth round of multilateral trade negotiations conducted under the auspices of the GATT since it was set up in 1947 — brings together 107 countries from all over the world. In addition to the traditional subjects — market access and the rules and disciplines of the multilateral trading system — the Uruguay Round covers three areas not previously covered by the GATT: intellectual property rights, investment measures and trade in services. Planned to last four years when it was launched in Punta del Este in September 1986,[1] the Uruguay Round should have been concluded at the ministerial conference held in Brussels from 3 to 7 December. Although the conference was suspended on 7 December without reaching a conclusion, the December deadline dominated negotiations throughout the year.

818. The economic interests of the industrialized countries differ substantially from those of the developing countries — with regard, for instance, to textiles and the new subjects — and there are also major differences between the economic interests of the various industrialized countries themselves; from the outset, therefore, the Uruguay Round negotiators generally had to try to reconcile positions which were in some cases very divergent, if not diametrically opposed. This it took two years to agree — at the mid-term review, started in Montreal in December 1988[2] and completed in Geneva in April 1989[3] — on how the objectives of the negotiations should be approached. Even then fundamental conceptual differences persisted, and only in a few rare cases could substantial areas of agreement be reached between all participants during the first three years of the negotiations.

819. The first major deadline this year was the meeting at senior official level of the Trade Negotiations Committee at the end of July.[4] Called well in advance, this meeting of the highest negotiating body was to examine the first draft agreements reached in each of the 15 negotiating groups under the responsibility of their respective chairmen.

---

[1] Twentieth General Report, point 810.
[2] Twenty-second General Report, point 871.
[3] Twenty-third General Report, point 900.
[4] Bull. EC 7/8-1990, point 1.4.112.

Instead of agreements which left only the main political options to be decided, the delegations were faced with texts of very diverse quality, some of which were very controversial; in general they could do no more than take note of the various texts.

820.   On many subjects the substantive dialogue therefore really only started in the autumn. Conducted first of all by experts in negotiating groups on the basis of draft agreements and then, from the end of October, by senior officials across the board, very intensive discussions led to major progress in some areas. The United States abandoned its approach to textiles whereby the existing restrictions would be transformed into global quotas, thus enabling consensus to be reached on the automatic progressive integration into the GATT of trade in textiles. Likewise, most of the differences between the Community and the United States on intellectual property rights, the emergence of which in the final stage of the negotiations caused serious complications, were ironed out. On market access, however, US insistence on eliminating certain customs duties on a sectoral basis, while maintaining high duties in major sectors, ruled out any serious progress on the harmonization of duties. New difficulties arose regarding services, the United States throwing doubt on the binding nature of the most-favoured-nation clause, which all other participants accepted.

821.   This was an inauspicious backdrop for the final ministerial conference, which opened in Brussels on 3 December.[1] While the Chairman of the ministerial conference, the Uruguayan Minister, Mr Hector Gros Espiell, tried to preserve the overall balance of the negotiations, highlighting the need for a political breakthrough in all major areas — i.e. agriculture, textiles, GATT rules and disciplines, intellectual property rights and trade in services — the agricultural question rapidly monopolized attention. The Community had declared its readiness to reduce internal support by 30% over 10 years, to convert all internal protection into duties, provided it could restore the balance of protection by raising the bound duties on certain substitute products, and to strengthen disciplines on export competition. The United States and the other agricultural exporting countries immediately judged this position to be inadequate. In the face of the general impasse resulting from the impossibility of reaching a compromise on this aspect, in spite of a softening of the Community position and after the withdrawal of the United States and the Latin American countries from the other negotiating groups, the Chairman of the ministerial conference could only suspend the conference and ask the GATT Director-General, Mr Arthur Dunkel, to hold consultations with a view to enabling the negotiations to be resumed early in 1991.

---

[1]   Bull. EC 12-1990.

822.   Regretting the outcome of the negotiations, the European Council, at its meeting in Rome, reiterated the Community's attachment to a global approach based on balanced concessions enabling the multilateral trading system to be strengthened, and appealed to the political will of all parties to resolve the outstanding problems as soon as possible.

Section 10

Commercial policy

Implementing the common commercial policy

Commercial policy instruments and import and export arrangements

823.   On 16 May the GATT Council adopted the panel report on provisions in Community legislation to prevent circumvention of anti-dumping duties.[1] The report concluded that these provisions were incompatible with Articles III and XX(d) of the GATT. The Community did not object to the adoption of the report but indicated that it would reserve its position on the report's arguments and would retain and continue to apply its current anti-circumvention legislation until the Uruguay Round[2] produced an acceptable solution to the international issue of circumvention of anti-dumping duties.

824.   In accordance with UN Security Council resolutions and on the basis of Article 113 of the Treaty the Community adopted measures in respect of trade with Iraq and Kuwait.[3]

825.   The Council and the Commission adopted a set of measures in June in respect of trade with the German Democratic Republic, suspending customs duties and any charges having equivalent effect and also quantitative restrictions and any restrictive measures resulting from the instruments of the common commercial policy.[4] The anti-dumping measures thus suspended on products from the GDR became pointless on the date of German unification. As the former German Democratic Republic had introduced into its trade with third countries, with effect from 1 July, the Common Customs Tariff, Community customs legislation and other common commercial policy measures, duties on some imports originating in Bulgaria, Czechoslovakia, Hungary, Poland, Romania, the Soviet Union and Yugoslavia were suspended as part of the measures taken in the run-up to unification.

---

[1]   Bull. EC 5-1990, point 1.3.72.
[2]   Point 817 *et seq.* of this Report.
[3]   Point 734 of this Report.
[4]   Point 20 of this Report.

826.   During the year anti-dumping duties were imposed on imports of a number of products, including compact-disc players originating in Japan or South Korea, ferro-silicon originating in Iceland, Norway, Sweden, Venezuela or Yugoslavia, potassium permanganate originating in Czechoslovakia, certain types of welded tubes of iron or non-alloy steel originating in Yugoslavia or Romania, small-screen colour television receivers originating in South Korea, monosodium glutamate originating in Indonesia, South Korea, Taiwan or Thailand, certain types of electronic microcircuits known as DRAMS (dynamic random access memories) originating in Japan, ferroboron originating in Japan, silicon metal originating in China, certain kinds of ball-bearings originating in Japan, pure silk cloth for typewriter ribbons originating in China and audio-cassettes originating in Japan.[1]

827.   In some cases, the Commission accepted exporters' undertakings to increase their prices. The products covered by undertakings included ferro-silicon originating in Iceland, Norway, Sweden, Venezuela or Yugoslavia, welded tubes of iron or non-alloy steel originating in Yugoslavia or Romania, certain kinds of photograph albums originating in South Korea or Hong Kong, oxalic acid originating in Brazil and methenamine (hexamethylenetetramine) originating in Bulgaria, Poland, Romania or Czechoslovakia.[1]

The Commission also accepted the Thai Government's undertaking in connection with the anti-subsidy proceeding concerning imports of ball-bearings, with a greatest diameter not exceeding 30 mm, originating in Thailand.[2]

828.   In certain cases it was considered unnecessary to initiate protective measures, and investigations concerning a number of imports were terminated: plain paper photocopiers assembled or manufactured in the Community by Ricoh Industrie France SA, certain kinds of glass textile fibres originating in Czechoslovakia or the German Democratic Republic, ammonium paratungstate originating in China or South Korea, tungsten metal powder originating in China or South Korea, hardboard originating in Argentina, Finland, Switzerland or Yugoslavia, NPK fertilizer originating in Hungary, Poland, Romania or Yugoslavia, certain types of single phase two-speed electric motors originating in Bulgaria, Romania or Czechoslovakia, denim originating in Turkey, Indonesia, Hong Kong or Macao, sodium carbonate originating in the United States and propan-1-ol originating in the United States.[1]

829.   A number of anti-dumping measures expired under the provisions currently in force.[3] The products concerned included: plate glass originating in Czechoslovakia, the German Democratic Republic, Hungary, Poland, Romania or the Soviet Union; asbes-

---

[1]   For further details, see the monthly Bulletins.
[2]   OJ L 152, 16.6.1990.
[3]   Bull. EC 6-1990, point 1.4.52.

tos cement corrugated sheet originating in Czechoslovakia or the German Democratic Republic; plasterboard originating in Spain; certain kinds of glass mirrors originating in South Africa; glycine originating in Japan; certain types of polyester yarn (textured) originating in the United States; oxalic acid originating in Brazil; dense sodium carbonate originating in Yugoslavia; and roller chains for cycles originating in the Soviet Union.

830. In June the Commission presented to the Council and to Parliament its seventh annual report on the Community's anti-dumping and anti-subsidy activities in 1988.[1] The report gives a detailed review of proceedings initiated and investigations concluded or in progress and the provisional duties imposed. The report also contains comparisons covering the periods 1984-88 and, for certain data, 1980-88. It shows that less than 1% of imports into the Community are affected by anti-dumping duties. It also clearly shows that these measures are not concentrated on imports from a particular country or a particular geographical area. Nor has there been an increase in anti-dumping activity in recent years, and far from inhibiting trade, the countries whose products have been the subject of the greatest number of anti-dumping investigations have recorded the greatest relative increase, in value terms, in their exports to the Community.

In December Parliament adopted a resolution on the Community's anti-dumping policy.[2]

831. The Commission introduced retrospective Community surveillance of imports into the Community of footwear originating in any non-member country[3] and, following the introduction of voluntary restraint measures by South Korea and Taiwan, prior Community surveillance of imports of certain types of footwear originating in those two countries.[4] The implementing procedures for the latter were amended by the Council in order to avoid difficulties experienced in some Member States.[5]

832. In October the Council amended[6] Annex I to Regulation (EEC) No 288/82 on common rules for imports[7] with a view to removing a second set of national quantitative restrictions imposed by certain Member States on products originating in Japan.[8] This was the result of a partial compromise reached with Japan in 1989.[9]

833. In April the Council adopted negotiating directives for a trade agreement between the Community, the Government of Denmark and the Autonomous Government of the

---

[1] For further details, see the monthly Bulletins.
[2] OJ C 19, 28.1.1991; Bull. EC 12-1990.
[3] OJ L 30, 1.2.1990; Bull. EC 1/2-1990, point 1.2.86.
[4] OJ L 161, 27.6.1990; Bull. EC 6-1990, point 1.4.61.
[5] OJ L 292, 24.10.1990; Bull. EC 10-1990, point 1.4.52.
[6] OJ L 304, 1.11.1990; Bull. EC 10-1990, point 1.4.41; Commission proposal: Bull. EC 1/2-1990, point 1.2.70.
[7] OJ L 35, 9.2.1982; Sixteenth General Report, point 624.
[8] OJ L 230, 8.8.1989; Twenty-third General Report, point 732.
[9] Twenty-third General Report, point 732.

Faeroe Islands with a view to establishing uniform import arrangements for products originating in the Faeroes.[1]

834. In March the Commission adopted a proposal[2] amending Regulation (EEC) No 428/89 concerning the export of certain chemical products[3] in order to introduce certain administrative and technical details.

Trade agreements

835. The Council authorized the extension or automatic renewal for a further year of a number of trade agreements concluded between Member States and other countries, the agreements in question not consituting an obstacle to implementation of the common commercial policy.[4]

836. On 12 February it also authorized the automatic renewal or maintenance in force of a number of friendship, trade and navigation treaties and similar agreements concluded between Member States and other countries.[5]

Export credits

837. Negotiations continued in the OECD on guidelines for officially supported export credits (the 'Consensus') with a view to creating more transparency and discipline in the field of export credits, including aid credits. Amendments to the text of the understandings for aircraft and nuclear power stations were also discussed. The Commission also began examining the compatibility of the current export credit insurance system with the principles of the internal market, its effectiveness and ways of reducing distortions of competition. In November it proposed the creation of a credit reinsurance pool for exports to Central and Eastern European countries.[6]

838. In October the Council extended[7] the Decision of April 1978 concluding the Arrangement on guidelines for officially supported export credits[8] and also replaced the Annex by the consolidated text of the Arrangement.

---

[1]   Bull. EC 4-1990, point 1.2.54; Commission proposal: Bull. EC 1/2-1990, point 1.2.87.
[2]   Bull. EC 3-1990, point 1.2.63.
[3]   OJ L 50, 22.2.1989; Twenty-third General Report, point 727.
[4]   OJ L 21, 26.1.1990; Bull. EC 1/2-1990, point 1.2.88; OJ L 133, 24.5.1990; Bull. EC 5-1990, point 1.3.66.
[5]   OJ L 42, 16.2.1990; Bull. EC 1/2-1990, point 1.2.89.
[6]   OJ C 302, 1.12.1990; Bull. EC 11-1990, point 1.4.3.
[7]   Bull. EC 10-1990, point 1.4.53.
[8]   Twelfth General Report, point 452.

Export promotion

839. Export promotion activities focused on two priority areas — Asia and the Pacific, and Central and Eastern Europe.

Participation in major international conferences and exhibitions in Asia was particularly encouraged. In response to the strong interest shown by this part of the world in the single market, Community pavilions were organized jointly by European industry and the Commission. Community-run seminars of a scientific, sector-based or general nature held in parallel with the exhibitions put a very clear Community stamp on these activities and underlined the synergy between research and development and industry and the cooperation activities launched on the Commission's initiative. The choice of events, some of which were of prime regional importance, such as those held in Singapore and Hong Kong, also reflected sectoral priorities — principally those areas connected with Community research and technological development programmes and/or policies.

Another type of event, designed more for exploratory and information purposes, was organized for the countries of Central and Eastern Europe.

A trade forum held in Budapest and Warsaw from 19 to 23 November brought together over 100 potential partners to discuss three issues — modernizing of factories, energy conservation and environmental protection.

The seminar held in April in Amsterdam on opportunities for cooperation between small businesses and international trading houses rounded off a series of seminars organized since 1987 in all the Member States.[1]

Individual sectors

Steel

External element of the steel plan

840. The rules governing imports of ECSC steel products into the Community (formal arrangements for some suppliers, basic prices for the rest) are basically those dating from 1978[2] and there were no changes from 1989.[3] Imports for 1990 totalled about 12 million tonnes, as compared with the previous year's figure of 11.3 million tonnes.[3]

---

[1] Twenty-first General Report, point 734.
[2] OJ L 196, 13.5.1978; Twelfth General Report, points 125 and 953.
[3] Twenty-third General Report, point 737.

In March the Council adopted directives[1] for renewing[2] for 1990 the arrangements whereby six non-Community countries (Brazil, Bulgaria, Poland, Hungary, Czechoslovakia and Romania) propose to limit their exports to the Community market. Fewer countries than last year[3] were involved as the Community did not propose renewal for Venezuela or the Republic of Korea. Austria was offered the same system as Sweden and Finland, namely an exchange of letters with a consultation clause in the event of special difficulties. There are no longer any arrangements for Norway. The Republic of Korea was also given the chance to change over to the same system. The formal arrangements are marked by the process of liberalization begun several years ago. The range of products covered has been reduced with the removal of non-sensitive products while the quantities have been increased by 15%.

841. The Commission worked on preparing the guidelines for the external element of the 1991 steel plan, to be laid before the Council early in the new year.

Autonomous arrangements

842. The five Member States which maintained autonomous quotas for Central and Eastern European countries renewed them on 29 June.[4] The range of products covered was narrowed to take into account the liberalization of the arrangements[5] and the 15% increase in quantities covered by the arrangements was also applied to these quotas. On 12 February the Council authorized the Commission to negotiate trade and commercial and economic cooperation agreements with Poland and Hungary covering ECSC products.[6] These Agreements provide for the removal of autonomous quotas on the date of their entry into force and follow the same rules and principles as those adopted for products covered by general Agreements.[7] The Agreement with Poland was initialled in June and that with Hungary in October. The Commission also received a similar negotiating brief for Czechoslovakia and Bulgaria.

---

[1] Bull. EC 3-1990, point 1.2.82; Commission proposal: Bull. EC 1/2-1990, point 1.2.90.
[2] Bull. EC 7/8-1990, point 1.4.97.
[3] Twenty-third General Report, point 738.
[4] OJ L 199, 30.7.1990; Bull. EC 6-1990, point 1.4.62.
[5] Point 840 of this Report.
[6] Bull. EC 1/2-1990, point 1.2.10.
[7] OJ L 327, 30.11.1988; Twenty-second General Report, point 906; OJ L 339, 22.11.1989; Twenty-third General Report, point 790.

Relations with the USA

843. The agreement reached between the Community and the USA in November 1989,[1] under which Community exports of certain steel products to the US market are limited to 7% of US apparent consumption, worked smoothly in 1990. Since 1982 the main exporting countries' access to the US market has been restricted but in 1989, on the basis of a programme for the liberalization of trade in steel, the US authorities renewed the relevant quotas for the last time until March 1992.[2]

Shipbuilding

844. The exploratory talks undertaken in 1989 with the United States, Japan, the Republic of Korea and the northern European countries were continued actively.[3] The US authorities, which had expressed their firm intent to reach an agreement by May 1990 on re-establishsing normal competition in the industry, admitted that this deadline could not be met because of the complexity of the issues at stake. Discussions none the less continued beyond that date because of the considerable progress that had been made. In July the Council authorized the Commission to participate in negotiations under way within the OECD on an international agreement on adherence to normal and fair conditions of competition in the shipbuilding sector.[4]

Textiles

Bilateral agreements with non-member countries

845. The 26 bilateral agreements on trade in textiles renegotiated in 1986[5] or negotiated subsequently under the Multifibre Arrangement[6] generally operated satisfactorily throughout the year.

846. The Textile Committee, set up in 1978,[7] assisted the Commission in administering the agreements and contributed to the preparation of several consultations held during the year with various supplier countries. The consultations resulted in the introduction of 4 new quantitative limits, by comparison with eight in 1989, and the solution of other

[1] Twenty-third General Report, point 742.
[2] Sixteenth General Report, point 637; Twentieth General Report, point 821.
[3] Twenty-third General Report, point 743.
[4] Bull. EC 7/8-1990, point 1.4.111; Commission proposal: Bull. EC 5-1990, point 1.3.68.
[5] Twentieth General Report, point 804.
[6] OJ L 341, 4.12.1986; Twentieth General Report, points 815 to 817.
[7] OJ L 365, 27.12.1978; Twelfth General Report, point 454.

problems of administration, in particular those linked to the introduction of the Harmonized System.

847. With a view to implementing the agreement signed in 1989 and applied provisionally since 1 January,[1] the Council adopted a Regulation in June concerning the common rules applicable to imports of certain products originating in the Soviet Union.[2]

848. The agreements drawn up in 1986[3] with Bangladesh,[4] India,[5] Indonesia,[6] Malaysia,[7] Philippines,[8] Singapore,[9] Thailand,[10] Sri Lanka,[11] China,[12] Pakistan,[13] Uruguay,[14] Argentina,[14] Brazil[14] and Peru[14] were concluded this year. The Council also decided to apply provisionally the agreed minutes amending the agreements with Hong Kong,[15] China,[16] and Sri Lanka.[17]

The Commission decided to allocate additional quantities to the Federal Republic of Germany for the last three months of 1990 in order to take account of German unification.[18]

Under the Phare action plan,[19] the Council decided to adjust certain quantitative limits for Poland,[20] Hungary[21] and Czechoslovakia.[22] The Council authorized the Commission to open negotiations with the above three countries and Romania and Bulgaria with a view to aligning outward processing arrangements for these five countries on those provided for in agreements with other non-member countries.[23] The negotiations ended with the initialling of the agreed minutes provisionally applicable from 1 January 1991.

---

[1]   OJ L 397, 30.12.1989; Twenty-third General Report, point 746.
[2]   OJ L 177, 10.7.1990; Bull. EC 6-1990, point 1.4.64; Commission proposal: Bull. EC 4-1990, point 1.2.58.
[3]   Twentieth General Report, point 804.
[4]   OJ L 325, 23.11.1990; Bull. EC 7/8-1990, point 1.4.99.
[5]   OJ L 301, 30.10.1990; Bull. EC 7/8-1990, point 1.4.100.
[6]   OJ L 329, 28.11.1990; Bull. EC 7/8-1990, point 1.4.101.
[7]   OJ L 339, 5.12.1990; Bull. EC 7/8-1990, point 1.4.102.
[8]   OJ L 339, 5.12.1990; Bull. EC 7/8-1990, point 1.4.103.
[9]   OJ L 329, 28.11.1990; Bull. EC 7/8-1990, point 1.4.104.
[10]   OJ L 325, 23.11.1990; Bull. EC 7/8-1990, point 1.4.105.
[11]   OJ L 301, 30.10.1990; Bull. EC 7/8-1990, point 1.4.106.
[12]   OJ L 352, 15.12.1990; Bull. EC 9-1990, point 1.3.67.
[13]   OJ L 352, 15.12.1990; Bull. EC 9-1990, point 1.3.68.
[14]   Bull. EC 12-1990.
[15]   OJ L 96, 12.4.1990; Bull. EC 3-1990, point 1.2.83.
[16]   OJ L 96, 12.4.1990; Bull. EC 4-1990, point 1.2.56.
[17]   OJ L 281, 12.10.1990; Bull. EC 10-1990, point 1.4.56.
[18]   Point 24 of this Report.
[19]   Point 668 of this Report.
[20]   OJ L 285, 17.10.1990; Bull. EC 9-1990, point 1.3.70.
[21]   OJ L 285, 17.10.1990; Bull. EC 9-1990, point 1.3.71.
[22]   OJ L 13, 18.1.1991; Bull. EC 12-1990.
[23]   Bull. EC 11-1990, point 1.4.62; Commission proposal: Bull. EC 10-1990, point 1.4.57.

849. On 11 October Parliament adopted a resolution[1] on the possible renewal of the Multifibre Arrangement[2] or the system to take over after 1991.

Arrangements with preferential countries

850. Under its textile policy the Commission held consultations with Turkey and Malta with a view to extending the administrative cooperation arrangements. The arrangement with Malta covers both textiles and clothing products[3] and the arrangement with Turkey concerns clothing products.[4]

Other products

851. In October the Commission adopted a communication on directives for formal negotiations with the USA and subsequently with other parties to the GATT Agreement on trade in civil aircraft for the conclusion of new arrangements on international trade in this field.[5]

---

[1] OJ C 284, 12.11.1990; Bull. EC 10-1990, point 1.4.55.
[2] OJ L 341, 4.12.1986; Twentieth General Report, points 815 to 817.
[3] Twenty-second General Report, point 868.
[4] Twenty-first General Report, point 744.
[5] Bull. EC 10-1990, point 1.4.59.

Section 11

International organizations and conferences

United Nations

General Assembly

852.   The 45th regular session of the United Nations General Assembly opened in New York on 18 September[1] against the background of the Gulf crisis. In his speech Mr De Michelis, speaking as President of the Council on behalf of the Community and its Member States,[2] underlined the challenge the Iraqi aggression represented to international legality and to the political situation in the Middle East, and the adverse economic repercussions, actual and potential, for the world as a whole. He noted that the European Community considered it vital to continue efforts to find a political solution and ensure that the new order emerging thanks to the newly acquired influence of the United Nations was not jeopardized. In his view, moreover, a solution to the current crisis which was not followed up by the drafting of guidelines for future political and economic action in the Middle East would not be a lasting one, Mr De Michelis also spoke of the assistance rendered by the Community to the joint strategy being pursued under the aegis of the United Nations to control drugs and the use of profits from drug-related activities, and stressed that the Community would maintain its commitment to the Third World; this would not suffer as a result of greater cooperation with Central and Eastern Europe. In the course of the opening week of the 45th session, Mr Andriessen and Mr Matutes had a number of meetings at ministerial level with colleagues from the United States, Japan, the USSR and member countries of the Gulf Cooperation Council. Joint statements were issued at the end of the meetings with the USSR and the Gulf Cooperation Council.[3]

853.   At the special session on international cooperation to control drugs traffic, held in New York in February,[4] the General Assembly adopted a political declaration and a comprehensive action programme which bear witness to a greater international awareness of the problem and real political support for efforts to combat drug abuse.

---

[1]   Bull. EC 9-1990, point 1.3.80.
[2]   Bull. EC 9-1990, point 2.2.1.
[3]   Point 881 of this Report.
[4]   Bull. EC 1/2-1990, point 1.2.68.

854.   At the special session on international economic cooperation in New York in April[1] a well-balanced and measured final document was adopted, reflecting a growing convergence of views on economic problems and their causes and a profound change in the economic approach of Central and Eastern European countries. The Community's position had been decided by the Council on 2 April.[2] This new approach influenced the second Conference on the Least-developed Countries held in Paris in September at which an international development strategy for the 1990s was adopted.[3]

855.   Mr Pérez de Cuéllar, the UN Secretary-General, visited the Commission in April.[4] He outlined the areas in which the United Nations intended to concentrate its future work and the opportunities for cooperation between the United Nations and the Community.

Economic and Social Council

856.   The 45th session of the Economic Commission for Europe (ECE) took place in Geneva from 17 to 28 April. It was largely concerned with the consideration of practical measures in priority areas to assist the process of transition from planned to market economies in the countries of Central and Eastern Europe and the improved climate for cooperation following the recent political and economic changes in the ECE region. The ECE also approved its work programme for 1990/91 and adopted decisions on cooperation in various areas before adjourning until mid-December. The ECE agreed upon five priority areas, trade facilitation, statistics, environment,[5] transport and economic analysis, for its work programme when it resumed its session.

Convention on the Law of the Sea

857.   The 1982 Convention[6] will not enter into force until it has been ratified by 60 States. This has so far been done by only 42 States, all of which are developing countries except Yugoslavia and Iceland, and by the Council for Namibia. Within the Preparatory Commission, the industrialized countries, including the Community and its Member States, are striving to obtain improvements to the rules governing exploitation of the sea-bed so that the Convention can become universally acceptable.

---

[1]   Bull. EC 4-1990, point 1.2.46.
[2]   Bull. EC 4-1990, point 1.2.45.; Commission proposal: Bull. EC 1/2-1990, point 1.2.69.
[3]   Point 787 of this Report.
[4]   Bull. EC 4-1990, point 1.2.61.
[5]   Point 508 of this Report.
[6]   Eighteenth General Report, point 756.

United Nations Environment Programme

858.   The Community continued to play an active role in UNEP.[1] It attended the meeting in London in June at which the Montreal Protocol was amended and tightened up, and the special session of the Governing Council in August to draw up a blueprint for the Programme. The Community is also involved in preparations for the United Nations Conference on Environment and Development planned for 1992.

International Monetary Fund and World Bank

859.   The International Monetary Fund and the World Bank held their annual meetings in Washington from 25 to 27 September. The Community was represented by Mr Guido Carli, President of the Council, and Mr Henning Christophersen, Vice-President of the Commission. Commission representatives also took part in the proceedings of the Group of Ten, which met before the annual meetings, the Interim Committee of the IMF's Board of Governors, the Development Committee and the World Bank's Board of Governors.

General Agreement on Tariffs and Trade

860.   The Uruguay Round multilateral trade negotiations continued during the year, culminating with the December ministerial meeting.[2]

861.   The 46th session of the GATT Contracting Parties was held in Geneva on 12 and 13 December.[3] Since the Uruguay Round ministerial meeting in Brussels[2] had already given an opportunity to present general statements, and out of a concern to preserve the working climate, the majority of delegations preferred to abstain from taking part in the general debate.

Discussions on the report by the GATT Council since the last session were limited to matters demanding action by the Contracting Parties.[4] In particular, they granted a temporary derogation to the Community so that it could apply transitional measures to take account of the external economic impact of German unification.

---

[1]   Point 508 of this Report.
[2]   Point 821 of this Report.
[3]   Bull. EC 12-1990.
[4]   Twenty-third General Report.

862.   The Committee on Trade and Development continued its examination of the application of Part IV of the General Agreement. It also looked at trends in international trade, in particular regional integration in the Third World, progress in the Uruguay Round and the provision of technical assistance to developing countries to enable them to play an effective role in the negotiations.

863.   The GATT Council examined a number of disputes during the period under review. The United States amended its legislation on the 'superfund' tax[1] on petroleum products and customs user fees[1] in the light of the panel reports adopted by the Council in response to the Community's complaints. The Community continued to monitor the United States' implementation of the special panel report on the application of Section 337 (patents) of the 1930 Tariff Act.

The GATT Council also adopted the reports of the special panels which had examined the complaint lodged by the USA against the Community's use of subsidies to processors and producers of oilseeds[2] and Japan's complaint about the Community Regulation designed to prevent circumvention of anti-dumping duties.[3] The Community stated that it would implement both panels' recommendations under the Uruguay Round.

864.   The working party set up to examine the request by the People's Republic of China to rejoin the General Agreement met for a second time. Many of the Contracting Parties considered that the workings of China's external trade lacked transparency despite the explanations provided by the Chinese authorities. The government of Taiwan submitted a formal application for accession as an autonomous customs territory but had not yet received a reply. The terms of reference of the working party set up to examine Bulgaria's membership application were drawn up. Poland requested a renegotiation of its accession protocol.

The Council adopted decisions concerning the protocols on the accession of Costa Rica and Tunisia in April[4] and July[5] respectively.

It also authorized the Commission to institute tariff negotiations on processed sisal products under Article XXVIII of the Agreement.[6] In December the Commission forwarded to the Council a proposal for a Decision on the signing of the protocol of accession of Venezuela on behalf of the Community.[7]

---

[1]   Twenty-second General Report, point 1053; Twenty-third General Report, point 903.
[2]   Bull. EC 1/2-1990, point 1.2.100.
[3]   Bull. EC 5-1990, point 1.3.72; point 823 of this Report.
[4]   OJ L 219, 14.8.1990; Bull. EC 4-1990, point 1.2.67; Commission proposal: Bull. EC 1/2-1990, point 1.2.101.
[5]   OJ L 274, 4.10.1990; Bull. EC 7/8-1990, point 1.4.113; Commission proposal: OJ C 187, 27.7.1990; Bull. EC 6-1990, point 1.4.113.
[6]   Bull. EC 7/8-1990, point 1.4.114; Commission proposal: Bull. EC 6-1990, point 1.4.71.
[7]   Bull. EC 12-1990.

Organization for Economic Cooperation and Development

865.   In addition to its work on the industrialized economies the OECD looked more closely at ways of dovetailing economic and environmental policies through the use of economic instruments for pollution control. It also stepped up the dialogue both with the dynamic Asian economies and with the countries of Central and Eastern Europe now embarked upon a process of radical economic reform, and set up an office to handle cooperation with the latter. At the Western Economic Summit in Houston the OECD, the International Monetary Fund, the World Bank and the President-designate of the EBRD were asked to look at the problems of the Soviet economy and ways of assisting the Soviet Union in its reforms.[1]

866.   At the annual ministerial meeting on 30 and 31 May[2] the differing approaches to the liberalization of agriculture were acknowledged. The meeting did, however, underline its determination to combat protectionism and bring the Uruguay Round negotiations to a successful conclusion by the end of the year. Ministers viewed the economic situation in all OECD countries with some degree of optimism. They reiterated their desire to sustain and develop multilateralism in world trade and underlined the need to ensure that environmental protection was compatible with sustained economic growth and market mechanisms. Ministers also gave an assurance that their commitment to support the developing countries, in particular the least-developed countries, in their efforts to secure economic growth and social progress would not in any way be affected by the assistance given to the economies of Central and Eastern Europe undergoing reform.

Conference on Security and Cooperation in Europe

867.   The European Council has repeatedly underlined the leading role played by the CSCE in the reform process in Europe.[3] It confirmed the desire of the Community and its Member States to play a decisive role in this process and welcomed the decision to hold a summit meeting of Heads of State or Government to define the Conference's role in the future framework of Europe and to establish a new basis for relations between partners anchored in the principles of the Helsinki Final Act.[4]

---

[1]   Point 691 of this Report.
[2]   Bull. EC 5-1990, point 1.3.73.
[3]   Bull. EC 4-1990, points I.7 and I.14; Bull. EC 6-1990, point I.21; Bull. EC 10-1990, point I.17.
[4]   Ninth General Report, points 510 to 512.

868.   The Conference on Economic Cooperation in Europe, which the 1989 CSCE follow-up meeting in Vienna had decided to convene,[1] took place in Bonn from 19 March to 11 April.[2] This was the first intersessional meeting on areas falling within Basket II of the Helsinki Final Act.[3] The Conference considered practical measures to develop and diversify economic relations, industrial cooperation and the monetary and financial aspects of economic and industrial cooperation. The fundamental process of reform in Central and Eastern Europe created a climate of cooperation at the Conference hitherto unknown at such events. More generally, the Conference in Bonn gave the Community an opportunity to reaffirm its cohesion within the CSCE. In the Conference's conclusions, which to a great extent reflect the Community approach and the conclusions adopted by the Council in February,[4] the participants acknowledged the relationship between democracy and economic progress and stressed the importance of market economy for the current political and economic reforms.

869.   The second CSCE meeting on the human dimension in Copenhagen in June continued the discussions on human rights and fundamental freedoms,[5] human contacts and other related humanitarian issues which had begun in Paris in 1989.[1] The participants also stressed the need for complete implementation of the commitments entered into at the Conference. Albania attended a meeting of the CSCE for the first time as an observer. The final document covered acceptance of the rule of law, individual freedoms, the importance of democratic institutions, the rights of national minorities and development of the human dimension mechanism.

870.   The CSCE meeting on the Mediterranean took place in Palma de Majorca from 24 September to 19 October.[6] It examined various aspects of cooperation between Mediterranean countries and the protection of the Mediterranean ecosystems. In addition to the CSCE participating States the eight non-participating Mediterranean States (Israel, Egypt, Syria, Libya, Tunisia, Algeria, Morocco and Lebanon) were invited to the meeting. The Community contribution had been adopted by the Council on 17 September.[7] The Conference's results demonstrate that the participants are aware of the need for greater cooperation on environmental protection.

871.   The CSCE Heads of State or Government, the President of the Council, and the President and Vice-President of the Commission attended the Paris Summit from 19 to 21 November.[8] The meeting, for which a preparatory ministerial meeting had been held

---

[1]   Twenty-third General Report, point 908.
[2]   Bull. EC 4-1990, point 1.2.60.
[3]   Ninth General Report, points 510 to 512.
[4]   Bull. EC 1/2-1990, point 1.2.99.
[5]   Bull. EC 6-1990, point 1.4.66.
[6]   Bull. EC 10-1990, point 1.4.64.
[7]   Bull. EC 9-1990, point 1.3.79.
[8]   Bull. EC 11-1990, points I.1 and 2.2.1.

in New York in October,[1] ended with the adoption of the Paris Charter for a New Europe. The Charter, which to a large extent reflects the Community's contributions to the preparatory work, establishes a new code of conduct for relations between the European and the North American parties, and confirms their commitment to the principles of the Helsinki Final Act. The meeting reviewed the remarkable recent progress on cooperation and security in Europe and defined political guidelines clearly marking the end of the cold war and expressing the common resolve of the signatories to initiate a new era of peace and democracy on the continent. It was agreed to establish a number of CSCE institutions, including a Secretariat, a Conflict Prevention Centre, a Parliamentary Assembly and an Office for Free Elections. It was also decided to hold summits every two years and meetings of foreign ministers (the Council) regularly — at least once a year, with preparatory meetings of a Committee of Senior Officials. Parliament gave its view in October on the opportunities afforded by the Summit.[2]

Council of Europe

872. The year marked the revival of the Council of Europe's political fortunes and a consolidation of its relations with the Community. The President of the Commission participated at the special meeting of ministers in Lisbon on 23 and 24 March,[3] which mainly covered support by the Council of Europe for Central and Eastern European countries and its role in a future democratic Europe. Parallel to this meeting was held the second four-party meeting,[4] with Mr G. Collins, President of the Council, and Mr Delors, President of the Commission, Mr J. de Deus Pinheiro, Chairman of the Committee of Ministers, and Mrs C. Lalumière, Secretary-General of the Council of Europe, in attendance. The representatives of the two organizations discussed the political roles of the Community and the Council of Europe with regard to Central and Eastern Europe and, in particular, the future structures for cooperation in Europe.

The third four-party meeting was held in Venice on 7 October,[5] the chair being shared by Italy, for the Community, and San Marino, for the Council of Europe. The scope for integrating the countries of Central and Eastern Europe was studied in depth with a view to providing a political and economic framework allowing these countries to move towards democracy and the market economy. With regard in particular to the CSCE

---

[1]   Bull. EC 10-1990, point 1.4.65.
[2]   OJ C 284, 12.11.1990; Bull. EC 10-1990, point 1.4.66.
[3]   Bull. EC 3-1990, point 1.2.90.
[4]   Bull. EC 3-1990, point 1.2.91.
[5]   Bull. EC 10-1990, point 1.4.67.

process,[1] the participants were unanimous in agreeing that there was a need to strengthen their cooperation to ensure the complementarity and consistency of their activities.

On 8 November, the Commission was invited to attend the meeting of the Committee of Ministers in Rome to mark the accession of Hungary as the 24th member of the Council of Europe.[2]

873.   As regards sectoral policies and in accordance with the guidelines established at the four-party meetings, cooperation continued in all the Council of Europe's spheres of activity. The Community played an active part in the ministerial conference on human rights, which met in Rome for the 40th anniversary of the European Convention for the Protection of Human Rights and Fundamental Freedoms. At the conference the Commission informed the Council of Europe of its proposal on possible accession by the Community to the Convention.[3]

The two organizations took steps to coordinate their programmes of assistance to the countries of Central and Eastern Europe, taking the view that the priorities and guidelines for these programmes did not create any special difficulties and allowed the optimum use of resources. The Community, represented by the Commission, took part in most of the specialist ministerial conferences, in particular on combating drug abuse.

---

[1]   Point 871 of this Report.
[2]   Bull. EC 11-1990, point 1.4.65.
[3]   Point 899 of this Report.

Chapter V

Intergovernmental cooperation and human rights

Section 1

European political cooperation

874.   Political developments in Central and Eastern Europe were again of prime importance to the Community and its Member States, and German unification, which was described as a milestone along the road to the construction of a new framework for cooperation and stability in Europe,[1] was warmly welcomed. The crucial role of the Conference on Security and Cooperation in Europe was underlined at the CSCE Summit in November.[2] The situations in Romania, Albania and the Baltic States were also of particular concern to the Community.

875.   On 20 February[3] and 28 October[4] the Twelve issued statements underlining the fundamental role of the CSCE at a time of rapid and profound change in Europe. They recalled their earlier declaration at the Strasbourg European Council[5] and affirmed their determination to play a full part in the CSCE process. They also outlined the aims of the CSCE Summit scheduled for November. On 24 March the Community issued a statement on the situation in Lithuania,[6] calling on all parties to show maximum restraint and hoping for an open and fair dialogue between Moscow and Vilnius. This appeal for

---

[1]   Bull. EC 10-1990, point 1.5.2.
[2]   Point 871 of this Report.
[3]   Bull. EC 1/2-1990, point 1.3.9.
[4]   Bull. EC 10-1990, point I.17.
[5]   Twenty-third General Report, point 913.
[6]   Bull. EC 3-1990, point 1.3.5.

restraint was repeated in declarations on 4 and 21 April.[1] On 20 December the Community and its Member States voiced their regret upon learning the news of Mr Shevardnadze's resignation and hoped that it would not entail changes in Soviet policy.[2] At the 78th ministerial meeting on political cooperation matters in Luxembourg on 18 June, the Foreign Ministers of the Twelve issued a statement expressing their concern at the violence in Bucharest and recalled their willingness to support those countries which were working towards pluralist democracy based on the rule of law and respect for human rights.[3] On 5 July the Community and its Member States expressed deep concern about the human rights situation in Albania and called upon the Albanian authorities to adopt the reforms necessary to bring about the process of democratization.[4]

876.   On 22 and 23 November the Community and its Member States published comprehensive joint declarations with Canada and the USA, aimed at strengthening and expanding the transatlantic relationship.[5]

877.   Events in the Middle East were dominated by Iraq's invasion and subsequent annexation of Kuwait in early August. However, the Community and its Member States also remained deeply concerned about the situation in Israel and the Occupied Territories and in Lebanon.

878.   On 5 February the Twelve issued a statement on Lebanon deploring the latest fighting in the Christian areas, and calling on the protagonists to cease hostilities.[6] The Twelve affirmed their willingness to offer humanitarian aid to the people of Lebanon and reaffirmed the importance of the Ta'if agreement. On 5 September the Community and its Member States welcomed the Lebanese Parliament's ratification of the Ta'if accord.[7] The statement also deplored the continuing violence in the south of Lebanon and the Beqaa valley. In a general declaration on the Middle East made by the European Council in Rome on 28 October, the Community and its Member States expressed concern at the continuing violence in Lebanon, and at the lack of progress in the search for a peaceful settlement of the Arab-Israeli conflict.[8] The statement also welcomed the normalization of the Community's relations with Iran.[2] At its Rome meeting in December the European Council expressed its satisfaction at the implementation of the security plan in greater Beirut following the withdrawal of all militias from the Lebanese capital.[2]

---

[1]   Bull. EC 4-1990, points 1.3.1 and 1.3.7.
[2]   Bull. EC 12-1990.
[3]   Bull. EC 6-1990, point 1.5.4.
[4]   Bull. EC 7/8-1990, point 1.5.2.
[5]   Bull. EC 11-1990, points 1.5.3 and 1.5.4; points 693 and 712 of this Report.
[6]   Bull. EC 1/2-1990, point 1.3.5.
[7]   Bull. EC 9-1990, point 1.4.1.
[8]   Bull. EC 10-1990, point I.16.

879. On 31 January and 20 February the Twelve issued statements indicating their concern at proposals to settle Jewish immigrants from the USSR in the Occupied Territories.[1] On 5 February they issued a statement condemning the attack on a coach carrying Israeli tourists near Ismailiya in Egypt two days before.[2] Violence at Rishon le Zion in Israel and in the Occupied Territories prompted the Twelve to issue a statement on 22 May expressing their shock and sadness at the deaths of 18 Palestinians and the wounding of hundreds more.[3] They called on the Israeli authorities to show the utmost restraint and recalled the Venice,[4] Madrid[5] and Strasbourg[5] declarations on the Arab-Israeli dispute. In a further declaration on 2 June the Twelve reiterated the need for a rapid, peaceful settlement of the region's problems, through a peace conference under UN auspices, with the participation of the PLO.[6] They also restated their desire to contribute to the economic and social development of the Occupied Territories. On 26 June the Dublin European Council recalled its long-stated position on the Arab-Israeli conflict and its determination to encourage all efforts towards a dialogue.[7] It welcomed the commitment to pursue the peace process expressed in a letter from the Prime Minister of Israel to the President of the European Council, but voiced its fear that a territorial compromise could be made more difficult by the policy of Jewish settlement in the Occupied Territories. The European Council also recalled the obligation on all parties to conform to the Geneva Convention and the importance of the role of the United Nations in the settlement of the dispute. On 9 October the Community and its Member States issued a statement deploring the excessive use of force by the Israelis in repressing Palestinian demonstrations in Jerusalem.[8] On 15 December the Rome European Council adopted a further statement on the Middle East, in which the Community and its Member States called on Israel to cooperate with the United Nations and comply with Security Council Resolutions 672 and 673.[9]

880. On 15 March the Twelve condemned the execution by Iraq of the British journalist Farzad Bazoft.[10] On 20 April they deplored the statement by Iraq that it was prepared to use chemical weapons and stated that the acquisition of weapons of mass destruction by any State in the Middle East could only aggravate tensions.[11] The Twelve further

---

[1]   Bull. EC 1/2-1990, points 1.3.3 and 1.3.13.
[2]   Bull. EC 1/2-1990, point 1.3.6.
[3]   Bull. EC 5-1990, point 1.4.2.
[4]   Fourteenth General Report, point 707.
[5]   Twenty-third General Report, point 917.
[6]   Bull. EC 6-1990, point 1.5.1.
[7]   Bull. EC 6-1990, point I.39.
[8]   Bull. EC 10-1990, point 1.5.4.
[9]   Bull. EC 12-1990.
[10]   Bull. EC 3-1990, point 1.3.3.
[11]   Bull. EC 4-1990, point 1.3.6.

reaffirmed their support for a global, comprehensive convention banning chemical weapons.

881. The Community and its Member States adopted a number of declarations following the Iraqi invasion of Kuwait, unreservedly condemning the Iraqi action and expressing increasing concern over the plight of Community and other Western diplomats and citizens trapped in Kuwait and Iraq.

On 2 August the Community and its Member States expressed their condemnation of the invasion and demanded the withdrawal of Iraqi forces.[1] On 4 August they confirmed their full support for the UN Security Council resolutions.[2] A further declaration of 10 August rejected the annexation of Kuwait as contrary to international law and therefore null and void.[3] In the same statement they expressed grave concern for the situation of foreigners in Iraq and Kuwait and indicated that they would continue to coordinate their efforts aimed at guaranteeing the safety of Community citizens and would maintain close contact with Arab governments to try and reduce tensions and restore international legality. On 21 August another declaration was made condemning the Iraqi decision to detain foreigners against their will.[4] It expressed indignation at the heinous action and contempt for basic humanitarian principles shown by Iraq in grouping foreigners near military bases. They further reiterated that the Iraqi Government was fully responsible for the safety of foreign citizens. On 7 September a statement was made which, in addition to reaffirming the Community's condemnation of the measures taken by Iraq against foreign citizens and against embassies in Kuwait, deplored Iraq's non-compliance with Security Council Resolution 664 (requiring the Iraqi authorities to facilitate departure by foreigners).[5] The statement urged the early resumption of discussions between the Iraqi authorities and the International Committee of the Red Cross to protect and assist foreign citizens held in Iraq and Kuwait. In a separate statement on 7 September[6] the Community and its Member States reaffirmed their full support for the embargo against Iraq[7] as an essential condition for a peaceful solution to the crisis. They also indicated their willingness to extend short-term financial assistance to Egypt, Jordan and Turkey to offset the effects of the embargo.[8] The Community indicated its readiness to commit substantial extra amounts from its own budgetary resources for humanitarian aid.[9] In a third statement issued the same day, the Community and its Member States reaffirmed their determination to consolidate and re-

---

[1]   Bull. EC 7/8-1990, point 1.5.9.
[2]   Bull. EC 7/8-1990, point 1.5.11.
[3]   Bull. EC 7/8-1990, point 1.5.14.
[4]   Bull. EC 7/8-1990, point 1.5.16.
[5]   Bull. EC 9-1990, point 1.4.2.
[6]   Bull. EC 9-1990, point 1.4.4.
[7]   Point 734 of this Report.
[8]   Point 730 of this Report.
[9]   Point 814 of this Report.

inforce the historic ties of friendship which bind them to the Arab world and indicated that they remained committed to the Euro-Arab Dialogue.[1] They indicated that it was a further injustice to the Arab people that Iraq's aggression against Kuwait had delayed the search for a solution to other problems of the region. On 14 September the Community and its Member States denounced the very grave violations of the 1961 Vienna Convention by the Iraqi occupying forces in Kuwait when they broke into the premises of the French and Dutch embassies, taking away French nationals, one of them a diplomat.[2] On 17 September a statement was issued condemning the Iraqis' policy of brutal aggression, including the increasing persecution of Kuwaiti citizens and foreign nationals, taking of hostages and unacceptable violations of diplomatic premises in Kuwait.[3] The Twelve agreed that their embassies in Kuwait would collectively be responsible for the protection of nationals whose embassies had been forced to leave Kuwait as a consequence of the illegal actions of the Iraqi authorities.

On 26 September the Community and its Member States made a joint statement with the USSR on the Gulf crisis.[4] They noted the high degree of consensus that existed between all members of the UN Security Council and in the international community in condemning the invasion of Kuwait. They stressed the need to maintain that consensus for a political solution to be found. The two parties also indicated their commitment to a just, comprehensive and lasting peace in the Middle East. A joint communiqué of the Community and its Member States and the Gulf Cooperation Council and its Member States on 27 September reiterated their strong condemnation of the invasion of Kuwait and their categorical rejection of the purported annexation.[5] The two parties reaffirmed their total support for full implementation of all the UN Security Council resolutions on the Gulf crisis. They also agreed to implement actively their existing cooperation agreement and to start negotiations on a free trade agreement.[6] The Rome European Council of 28 October issued a further statement on the Gulf crisis reiterating the concerns of the Community and its Member States and expressing their satisfaction with the high degree of consensus among the members of the UN Security Council.[7] The statement also expressed the Community's determination to adhere to the embargo against Iraq and indicated that the Community and its Member States were prepared to consider additional steps consistent with the UN Charter. On 12 November the Twelve confirmed their complete solidarity for the purpose of securing the release of all foreign nationals held in Iraq and Kuwait and rejected any negotiation on that issue

---

[1]   Bull. EC 9-1990, point 1.4.3.
[2]   Bull. EC 9-1990, point 1.4.8.
[3]   Bull. EC 9-1990, point 1.4.9.
[4]   Bull. EC 9-1990, point 1.4.11.
[5]   Bull. EC 9-1990, point 1.4.12.
[6]   Point 733 of this Report.
[7]   Bull. EC 10-1990, point I.15.

between their governments and Iraq.[1] A further statement on the Gulf crisis was adopted by the Rome European Council in December.[2]

882.   In a declaration adopted on 26 June the European Council expressed its profound sympathy to the government and people of Iran following the terrible loss of human life in the earthquake of 21 June in the north-east of the country.[3] The Community and its Member States indicated their readiness to extend all possible assistance to the victims.

883.   On 26 June the European Council reaffirmed its previous declaration in favour of the unity, independence, sovereignty and territorial integrity of Cyprus in accordance with the relevant resolutions of the United Nations.[4] Recalling that this dispute affected relations between the Community and Turkey, it emphasized the necessity of eliminating obstacles to the pursuit of the intercommunity dialogue.

884.   The Community and its Member States expressed their concern at events in Africa, in particular the situations in Liberia, Senegal, Mauritania, the Horn of Africa, Nigeria and Angola. There were welcome developments, however, in Mozambique, Namibia and South Africa.

885.   On 23 January the Twelve issued a statement condemning attacks on merchant vessels in the Horn of Africa region.[5] This was followed on 20 February by a statement expressing disappointment at the lack of results in the different mediation efforts and outlining the Twelve's concern at the situations in Ethiopia, Somalia and Sudan.[6] On 15 March the Community and its Member States welcomed the agreement between the Ethiopian Government and the Tigre People's Liberation Front (TPLF) regarding food convoys and relief supplies for the north of the country.[7] The Foreign Ministers of the Twelve, meeting in Luxembourg on 18 June, issued a statement welcoming the decision of the Ethiopian authorities to accept in principle the use of the port of Massawa to deliver emergency aid.[8] They also welcomed the Ethiopian Government's acceptance of the participation of the UN as an observer. However, on 2 August the Community and its Member States expressed regret that a ship carrying relief aid to the port of Massawa was refused permission to dock.[9] On 14 September a further statement was issued indicating alarm at the continuation of the civil war and expressing regret at the interruption of the negotiations between the Government, the Eritrean People's Liber-

---

[1]   Bull. EC 11-1990, point 1.5.1.
[2]   Bull. EC 12-1990.
[3]   Bull. EC 6-1990, point I.41.
[4]   Bull. EC 6-1990, point I.42.
[5]   Bull. EC 1/2-1990, point 1.3.2.
[6]   Bull. EC 1/2-1990, point 1.3.12.
[7]   Bull. EC 3-1990, point 1.3.2.
[8]   Bull. EC 6-1990, point 1.5.5.
[9]   Bull. EC 7/8-1990, point 1.5.6.

ation Front (EPLF) and the TPLF.[1] Deep concern was also expressed regarding the deadlock in the talks on the use of the port of Massawa. In a statement issued on 24 December the Community and its Member States voiced their deep concern at the situation in Ethiopia and welcomed the recent agreement between the Ethiopian Government, the EPLF and the WFP.[2] They reaffirmed their commitment to continue their efforts to provide relief aid to those affected by famine. On 13 July the Community and its Member States expressed their concern about the human rights situation in Somalia.[3] On 13 September a further statement was made condemning the continuing human rights violations by Somali military forces and at the same time welcoming the plan to organize a round-table conference between the Government and the opposition.[4]

886.   On 19 February[5] and 5 April[6] the Twelve issued statements underlining their concern at the escalation of fighting in Angola and called on all parties to work towards a lasting negotiated political settlement. On 13 July the Community and its Member States noted the encouraging political developments in Angola and Mozambique,[7] and on 9 August they welcomed the statement made by President Chissano on the introduction of a multi-party system in Mozambique.[8] A further statement was made on 13 September welcoming the progress achieved in the peace negotiations under way in Angola and Mozambique and expressing the hope that this would lead to an early ceasefire in those countries.[9]

887.   On 26 April the Twelve announced that they had, on 14 April, made clear to the Liberian authorities their deep concern at the continued tragic situation in Nimba county.[10] The Twelve condemned the violence in Liberia and called upon the Liberian Government to follow a policy of reconciliation. On 25 July and 2 August the Community and its Member States again expressed deep concern about events in Liberia.[11] They reiterated their call for a ceasefire and respect for humanitarian principles. The Twelve issued a statement on 20 April expressing concern at the continuing dispute between Senegal and Mauritania and calling on the two sides to negotiate.[12] On 1 August the Community and its Member States stated that although they had no sympathy with the coup attempt in Nigeria on 22 April they regretted that this had led

---

[1]   Bull. EC 9-1990, point 1.4.7.
[2]   Bull. EC 12-1990.
[3]   Bull. EC 7/8-1990, point 1.5.3.
[4]   Bull. EC 9-1990, point 1.4.6.
[5]   Bull. EC 1/2-1990, point 1.3.8.
[6]   Bull. EC 4-1990, point 1.3.2.
[7]   Bull. EC 7/8-1990, point 1.5.4.
[8]   Bull. EC 7/8-1990, point 1.5.13.
[9]   Bull. EC 9-1990, point 1.4.5.
[10] Bull. EC 4-1990, point 1.3.9.
[11] Bull. EC 7/8-1990, points 1.5.5 and 1.5.7.
[12] Bull. EC 4-1990, point 1.3.5.

to executions on the scale announced by the authorities on 27 July.[1] On 19 October they expressed their concern at developments in Rwanda and hoped that joint consultations among all the parties concerned would take place without delay.[2] On 20 February the Twelve issued a statement welcoming the adoption of the new Namibian Constitution by the constituent assembly.[3] This was followed on 21 March by a message to the President of Namibia welcoming Namibian independence.[4]

888.   On 5 February the Twelve made a statement welcoming the reforms made by President de Klerk and looking forward to other measures which would lead to the abolition of apartheid.[5] Following the release of Nelson Mandela, the Twelve issued a statement on 13 February warmly welcoming this event and congratulating the South African Government on this very important contribution to the creation of a climate for negotiations with the black community.[6] On 20 February the Foreign Ministers of the Twelve approved the ninth report on the application of the code of conduct for Community companies with subsidiaries in South Africa.[7] On 9 June the Community and its Member States welcomed the announcement by the South African Government of the lifting of the state of emergency covering most of the country,[8] and on 9 August they expressed their satisfaction at the outcome of the meetings between the South African Government and the African National Congress.[9] They also welcomed the suspension of the armed struggle of the ANC and the decision to release political prisoners. However, on 20 August a further declaration was made expressing concern regarding the increase in violence in South Africa.[10]

In a declaration adopted on 26 June[11] the European Council welcomed the important changes which had taken place in southern Africa since its meeting in Strasbourg.[12] It warmly welcomed the independence of Namibia, the release of Nelson Mandela and other political prisoners and the positive roles of President de Klerk and Mr Mandela. It restated that the objective of the Community and its Member States was the complete dismantling of apartheid and the rapid, peaceful transition of South Africa to a non-racial democratic State. At the same time, the European Council fully recognized that the future prosperity of South Africa required access to economic resources. In the light of recent events, the Community therefore proposed an increase in its positive measures

---

[1]   Bull. EC 7/8-1990, point 1.5.8.
[2]   Bull. EC 10-1990, point 1.5.5.
[3]   Bull. EC 1/2-1990, point 1.3.11.
[4]   Bull. EC 3-1990, point 1.3.4.
[5]   Bull. EC 1/2-1990, point 1.3.4.
[6]   Bull. EC 1/2-1990, point 1.3.7.
[7]   Bull. EC 1/2-1990, point 1.3.10.
[8]   Bull. EC 6-1990, point 1.5.3.
[9]   Bull. EC 7/8-1990, point 1.5.12.
[10]   Bull. EC 7/8-1990, point 1.5.15.
[11]   Bull. EC 6-1990, point I.38.
[12]   Twenty-third General Report, point 921.

programme to alleviate the effects of apartheid.[1] At the Rome European Council in December,[2] the Community and its Member States announced their intention of relaxing the restrictive measures adopted in 1986[3] as soon as legislative steps to repeal the laws on separate residential areas and land ownership had been taken by the South African Government. They also decided to lift the ban on new investment with immediate effect.

889.   Human rights and regional tensions in Asia and the Far East also prompted statements by the Community.

890.   On 18 May the Twelve issued a statement on the human rights situation in Burma, calling on the Burmese Government to cease its repressive and undemocratic practices and to respect the wish of the Burmese people to establish a democratic society through free and fair elections.[4] Following the elections in Burma, the Twelve issued a further statement welcoming the outcome of the elections and calling on the Government to respect their results.[5] On 3 August they expressed the hope that the Burmese Government would effect a transfer of power to a civilian government without unreasonable delay.[6]

891.   On 18 January and 20 February the Twelve issued statements noting with concern the continuing conflict in Cambodia and welcoming the progress made on Cambodia by the five permanent members of the Security Council.[7] On 18 September the Community and its Member States welcomed the efforts of the permanent members towards a comprehensive political settlement as agreed on 27 and 28 August.[8]

892.   On 12 April the Twelve warmly welcomed the decision of the King of Nepal to remove the ban on political parties and to begin democratic reform.[9] On the same date the Twelve, recalling their good relations with both India and Pakistan, expressed their concern at the tension between these two countries.[10] They called on both parties to display restraint and moderation. On 23 October the Community and its Member States urged the Government of Sri Lanka to respect human rights and use only the minimum necessary force to restore peace and maintain order in the country.[11] On 9 March the Twelve announced a *démarche* to the Indonesian Government appealing for clemency

---

[1]   Nineteenth General Report, point 852.
[2]   Bull. EC 12-1990.
[3]   Twentieth General Report, point 995.
[4]   Bull. EC 5-1990, point 1.4.1.
[5]   Bull. EC 6-1990, point 1.5.2.
[6]   Bull. EC 7/8-1990, point 1.3.3.
[7]   Bull. EC 1/2-1990, points 1.3.1 and 1.3.14.
[8]   Bull. EC 9-1990, point 1.4.10.
[9]   Bull. EC 4-1990, point 1.3.3.
[10]   Bull. EC 4-1990, point 1.3.4.
[11]   Bull. EC 10-1990, point 1.5.6.

for prisoners condemned to death for their involvement in a coup attempt in 1965.[1] The Twelve published a declaration on 5 October which reaffirmed their support for the democratic process in the Philippines.[2] On 18 January the Community and its Member States issued a statement noting the lifting of martial law in Beijing and expressing the hope that this would lead to an improvement in the human rights situation in China.[3]

893.   Events in Central and Latin America were also of concern to the Community.

On 18 January the Twelve issued a statement condemning the assassination of opposition leaders in Guatemala which, they said, not only threatened dialogue and reconciliation in Guatemala and El Salvador but also imperilled the entire Central American peace process.[3] On 18 January[3] the Community and its Member States welcomed Colombia's announcement of the establishment of the special cooperation programme to combat drug trafficking.[4] On 26 March[5] and 27 April[6] the Twelve condemned the assassination of presidential candidates in Colombia. Following the holding of free elections in Nicaragua, the Twelve issued a statement on 27 February welcoming the election of the new President.[7] On 29 June the Twelve condemned the attempted assassination of members of the Conseil d'État in Haiti and called on all parties to refrain from actions which would disrupt progress towards democracy.[8] On 28 December they welcomed the fair and orderly manner in which the elections in Haiti had been conducted.[9] On 28 July the Community and its Member States conveyed their congratulations to the President-elect of Peru, Mr Alberto Fujimori. On 16 November the Community and its Member States expressed their concern at the lack of progress in the investigation into the murder of six Jesuit priests in El Salvador.[10] On 4 December a message of support was sent to the President of the Republic of Argentina, Mr Menem, following the attempted *coup d'état* in that country.[9] At the Rome Conference on 20 December between representatives of the Community and the Rio Group countries a declaration was adopted reaffirming the parties' determination to reinforce their relationship in a range of political and economic fields.[11]

894.   In the field of human rights, the Dublin European Council issued a declaration on anti-Semitism, racism and xenophobia on 26 June.[12] It expressed deep revulsion at

---

[1]   Bull. EC 3-1990, point 1.3.1.
[2]   Bull. EC 10-1990, point 1.5.3.
[3]   Bull. EC 1/2-1990, point 1.3.1.
[4]   Point 758 of this Report.
[5]   Bull. EC 3-1990, point 1.3.6.
[6]   Bull. EC 4-1990, point 1.3.8.
[7]   Bull. EC 1/2-1990, point 1.3.15.
[8]   Bull. EC 6-1990, point 1.5.6.
[9]   Bull. EC 12-1990.
[10]   Bull. EC 11-1990, point 1.4.66.
[11]   Point 750 of this Report.
[12]   Bull. EC 6-1990, point I.37.

the recent desecration of graves and declared that appropriate measures should be taken whenever similar outrages occurred in the Community. The European Council also recalled the declaration of the Community institutions and the Member States of 11 June 1986 on racism and xenophobia[1] and its support for action, notably in the context of the CSCE, to counter anti-Semitism, racism, incitement to hatred and xenophobia.

895.   In a declaration adopted on 26 June the European Council gave its full commitment to the objective of nuclear non-proliferation.[2] It expressed the view that the spread of nuclear arms endangered regional and global stability and recognized the essential role of the IAEA and its safeguards in the development of the peaceful uses of nuclear energy, this being inseparable from the problem of non-proliferation.

---

[1]   OJ C 158, 25.6.1986; Twenty-third General Report, point 464.
[2]   Bull. EC 6-1990, point I.40.

Section 2

Other intergovernmental cooperation

896.   The Ministers with responsibility for immigration, together with Mr Bangemann representing the Commission, met for the eighth time in Dublin on 15 June,[1] when 11 of the Member States signed the Convention determining the Member State responsible for examining an application for asylum.[2] The Convention, on which the United Nations High Commissioner for Refugees was consulted, is a significant step in the completion of the legislative programme on freedom of movement for persons. This contribution to international humanitarian law means that each request for asylum will now be examined by a single Member State. The Ministers adopted a public declaration, as they had after their previous meeting, in Paris,[3] taking stock of what they had done.[4] The Trevi Group of Ministers with responsibility for internal security matters met on the same day; the Commission was again not represented at the meeting.[5]

The ninth meeting took place in Rome on 7 December,[6] when Ministers took note of progress on the Draft Convention on the crossing of the Community's external borders, the negotiation of which they had hoped to see concluded by the end of 1990.[3] Ministers now asked that work should be completed during Luxembourg's term as President of the Council. They also said that the Twelve should adopt a common position at the Vienna Conference on population movements from Central and Eastern Europe (January 1991). A public declaration was adopted at the end of the meeting.[6] The Trevi Group of Ministers, which met the same day, raised the matter of the Commission's participation in the proceedings of the specialized group on measures relating to freedom of movement for persons (Trevi 1992).

897.   In Schengen, Luxembourg, on 19 June, Belgium, France, Germany, Luxembourg and the Netherlands signed an agreement to give effect to the agreement they had entered into at the same place on 14 June 1985.[7] The agreement provides for the total

---

[1]   Bull. EC 6-1990, point 1.5.7.
[2]   Bull. EC 6-1990, point 2.2.2.
[3]   Twenty-third General Report, point 932.
[4]   Bull. EC 6-1990, point 2.2.1.
[5]   Bull. EC 6-1990, point 1.5.8.
[6]   Bull. EC 12-1990.
[7]   Bull. EC 6-1990, point 1.5.9.

elimination of border checks between the parties and contains harmonized rules for the crossing of external borders, visa policy, the movement of foreigners, responsibility for examining asylum applications, drugs and arms. It provides for cooperation in police and security matters, including the setting-up of an information system coupled with guarantees concerning protection of personal data. The agreement represents an important first step towards the abolition of identity checks at intra-Community frontiers, serving as a precedent for measures to be introduced by the Member States. On 27 November Italy acceded to the Schengen Agreement, while Spain and Portugal were given observer status with a view to their accession at a later date.[1]

---

[1]   Bull. EC 11-1990, point 1.5.5.

Section 3

Human rights and fundamental freedoms

Inside the Community

898.   One of the themes of the intergovernmental conference on political union[1] is European citizenship, a concept which complements nationality and reflects the link between the Community and its citizens in the context of moves towards political union. Not only could it confer upon the nationals of Member States rights and duties which would have direct effect, but it could also embody constitutional principles which would be defined in Community legislation by reference to new or existing powers.

Parliament has played an active role in this area. On 11 July and 22 November it adopted resolutions concerning the conference and called for a common framework for protecting basic rights. This would be guaranteed by the Court of Justice, to which all Community citizens would have direct access after all domestic remedies had been exhausted. Parliament also asked for its Declaration of Fundamental Rights and Freedoms,[2] adopted on 12 April 1989, to be incorporated in the Treaties, together with the Declaration against racism and xenophobia adopted on 11 June 1986 by Parliament, the Council, the Commission and the Representatives of the Governments of the Member States.[3] In addition, Parliament again called on the Community to accede to the Council of Europe Convention for the Protection of Human Rights and Fundamental Freedoms (ECHR).

899.   Taking account of developments since its 1979 memorandum,[4] the Commission proposed that the Council agree to the Community applying to accede to the ECHR.[5] Although this would only affect the matters covered by Community law, it would mean that legal acts by Community institutions would be subject to the review mechanisms set up under the Convention and that citizens would enjoy greater protection *vis-à-vis* Community measures. Accession to the Convention is intended to complement, not replace, the preparation of a Community bill of rights.

---

[1]   Point 15 of this Report.
[2]   OJ C 120, 16.5.1989; Twenty-third General Report, point 934.
[3]   OJ C 158, 25.6.1986; Twentieth General Report, point 464.
[4]   Thirteenth General Report, point 537; Supplement 2/79 — Bull. EC.
[5]   Bull. EC 11-1990, point 1.3.203.

900. Now that citizens are exercising their right of petition more frequently, Parliament also looked into ways of improving the procedure.[1]

901. In line with its concern to protect the privacy of citizens once internal frontiers are removed, the Commission presented proposals to the Council on the protection of individuals in relation to the processing of personal data and the security of data systems.[2]

902. In June Parliament adopted a resolution[3] on the Schengen Agreement and on the Convention on the right of asylum and the status of refugees.[4] It stressed that the removal of border checks should not be accompanied by the introduction of new administrative checks which might constitute a violation of human rights.

903. The Council and the Representatives of the Member States meeting within the Council followed up the interinstitutional Declaration against racism and xenophobia of 11 June 1986[5] with a resolution adopted on 29 May.[6]

Following the desecration of the Jewish cemetery at Carpentras, near Avignon, the Dublin European Council expressed 'its deep revulsion at recent manifestations of anti-Semitism, racism and xenophobia'.[7] Parliament adopted a resolution on Carpentras[8] and also, on 15 March, voiced its opinion on racist attacks and crime in general and the handling of such incidents by the police and courts in the Member States.[9] On 10 October Parliament adopted a resolution in which it undertook to publish the report of its Committee of Inquiry into Racism and Xenophobia, to distribute it widely, and to follow up its recommendations.[10]

904. The protection of human rights and fundamental freedoms is relevant to immigration policy, a component of which — the integration of immigrants — was the subject of a report by independent experts which the Commission transmitted to the Council.[6] In a resolution passed on 14 June Parliament also stated its views on the situation of migrant workers from non-member countries.[11]

---

[1]   Point 171 of this Report.
[2]   Point 186 of this Report.
[3]   OJ C 175, 16.7.1990; Bull. EC 6-1990, point 1.3.268.
[4]   Point 896 of this Report.
[5]   OJ C 158, 25.6.1986; Twentieth General Report, point 464.
[6]   Point 339 of this Report.
[7]   Point 894 of this Report.
[8]   OJ C 149, 18.6.1990; Bull. EC 5-1990, point 1.2.248.
[9]   OJ C 96, 17.4.1990; Bull. EC 3-1990, point 1.1.199.
[10]   OJ C 284, 12.11.1990; Bull. EC 10-1990, point 1.3.222.
[11]   OJ C 175, 16.7.1990; Bull. EC 6-1990, point 1.3.76.

Outside the Community

905. The Community continued to affirm democratic principles and respect for the rule of law and human rights in its relations with non-member countries. In seeking to promote fundamental rights, it aims to ensure that individuals are able to enjoy all their economic, social, cultural, civil and political rights to the full. With many human rights situations still causing concern, the Community and its Member States frequently expressed their disquiet and declared their readiness to take a firm stand whenever serious violations occur.[1]

906. Other, more positive, developments in this area include the framework agreement for trade and economic cooperation between the Community and Argentina, signed on 2 April, Article 1 of which asserts that relations between the two parties and the agreement in its entirety are based on respect for democratic principles and human rights.[2] The agreement with Chile contains the same statement.[3] As regards future association agreements with Central and Eastern European countries,[4] the European Council, at a special meeting in Dublin in April, said that the Community would try to conclude the negotiations as soon as possible, 'on the understanding that the basic conditions with regard to democratic principles and transition towards a market economy are fulfilled'.[5]

907. Through the United Nations (General Assembly, Commission on Human Rights, and other bodies) and the Conference on Security and Cooperation in Europe (CSCE), the Community and its Member States have taken an active part in promoting human rights and democratic values. Community cohesion played an important role at the second meeting of the CSCE conference on the human dimension, which resulted in much firmer commitments concerning 'respect for all human rights and fundamental freedoms, human contacts and other issues of a related humanitarian character'.[6]

908. In the Charter of Paris for a New Europe adopted at the CSCE Summit on 21 November, the 34 Heads of State or Government restated their commitment to the 10 principles of the Helsinki Final Act, emphasizing in particular human rights, democracy and the rule of law.[7] They also voiced their determination to protect 'the ethnic, cultural, linguistic and religious identity of national minorities... without any discrimination and in full equality before the law'.

---

[1] Point 874 *et seq.* of this Report.
[2] Point 759 of this Report.
[3] Point 760 of this Report.
[4] Point 672 of this Report.
[5] Bull. EC 4-1990, point I.8.
[6] Point 869 of this Report.
[7] Point 871 of this Report.

909. On 12 July Parliament adopted a resolution[1] urging Member States to ratify as soon as possible the Convention on the Rights of the Child adopted by the United Nations General Assembly on 20 November 1989.[2]

910. On 17 January the Sakharov Prize for freedom of thought was presented by Mr E. Barón Crespo, President of the European Parliament, to Mr Alexander Dubcek, President of the Federal Assembly of Czechoslovakia.[3] Mr Nelson Mandela, Deputy President of the African National Congress and winner of the Prize in 1988, attended Parliament's June part-session.[4]

---

[1] OJ C 231, 17.9.1990; Bull. EC 7/8-1990, point 1.4.115.
[2] Twenty-third General Report, point 947.
[3] Bull. EC 1/2-1990, point 1.2.103.
[4] Bull. EC 6-1990, point 1.8.1.

Chapter VI

Community institutions and financing

Section 1

Institutions and other bodies

Relations between the institutions

Voting in the Council

911. The improvement in the Council's decision-making procedure which began with the signing of the Single European Act continued in 1990.

Wherever necessary, decisions have been taken by a qualified majority, either by means of a formal vote or by establishing that a majority exists without resorting to a formal vote. The possibility of majority voting has introduced an element of flexibility in the position of the Member States, which are forced to reach a consensus.

As in previous years, the dynamism generated by majority voting has not extended to those areas in which unanimity is still required.

Inclusion of Parliament in the decision-making process

912. The code of conduct which Mr Delors, President of the Commission, presented at Parliament's part-session in February[1] and which has been applicable since 3 April[2] lays down a number of reciprocal commitments in order to achieve more effective cooperation between the institutions in the decision-making process.

---

[1] Bull. 1/2-1990, point 1.6.6.
[2] Bull. EC 4-1990, point 1.6.1.

913.   The cooperation procedure has, in general, worked satisfactorily. Since the Single Act entered into force, 162 proposals have been adopted. More than 58% of the amendments requested by Parliament at first reading were accepted by the Commission and almost 46% by the Council. On second reading, 70 common positions of the Council were approved by Parliament and 92 were amended; of these, more than 50% were accepted by the Commission and almost 26% by the Council. The inclusion of Parliament in the decision-making process appears to have improved the texts and not disturbed the procedure. Relatively little use has been made of the possibility of extending the time-limits for examination allowed by the Single Act. Besides, Parliament has made progress under the internal market programme;[1] only five proposals are awaiting the delivery of Parliament's opinions or decisions at final reading.

Implementing powers conferred on the Commission

914.   The Council was still reluctant to grant the Commission implementing powers.[2]

Despite the request made by the intergovernmental conference[3] during the drafting of the Single European Act that the Council give priority to the advisory committee procedure for the exercise of implementing powers conferred on the Commission under Article 100a of the Treaty, the Council has accepted the advisory committee procedure only 9 times (while the Commission has proposed it 20 times). In all the internal market proposals, the Council has used this procedure only 12 times out of the 38 proposed by the Commission.

The Council has continued to use procedures which severely restrict the amount of delegation, with the attendant risk that no decision will be taken.

Finally, in some cases the Council has again kept the implementing powers for itself and not conferred them on the Commission. In a report[4] which it is drawing up for submission to the Council and Parliament in accordance with the 1987 decision laying down the procedures for the exercise of its implementing powers[5] the Commission confirms its deep concern on this matter:[2] it considers that developments in this sector run contrary to the spirit of the Single Act and are likely to compromise the effectiveness of Community activities with a view to achievement of the single market.

---

[1]   Twenty-third General Report, point 5.
[2]   Twenty-third General Report, point 6.
[3]   Twentieth General Report, point 4.
[4]   Bull. EC 12-1990.
[5]   OJ L 197, 18.7.1987; Twenty-first General Report, point 4.

Composition and functioning of the institutions

Parliament

915. The 518 seats in Parliament are distributed as follows:

Socialists	180
European People's Party	122
Liberal, Democratic and Reformist Group	49
European Democratic Group	34
Greens	29
European Unitarian Left	28
European Democratic Alliance	22
Technical Group of the European Right	17
Left Unity Group	14
Rainbow Group	14
Non-affiliated	9

The President, Vice-Presidents and Quaestors remained in office.[1]

916. German unification and progress towards European union, especially preparations for the two intergovernmental conferences on economic and monetary union and on political union, took up much of Parliament's time during the course of the year.

In February, following the debate on the Commission's programme, Parliament adopted a resolution on strengthening the political dimension of European integration.[2] In March Parliament specified the procedures and timetable to be followed in its strategy for European union.[3] An interinstitutional preparatory conference was held at the same time as Parliament's part-session in May,[4] and was followed by three others in October and December, dealing respectively with economic and monetary union[5] and political union.[6] In May Parliament also adopted a resolution on economic and monetary union,[7] the main lines of which were fleshed out in October.[8] Shortly after the special European Council meeting in Dublin,[9] Parliament expressed satisfaction that the scope of the forthcoming revision of the Treaties had been extended beyond economic and monetary

---

[1]   Twenty-third General Report, point 11.
[2]   OJ C 68, 19.3.1990; Bull. EC 1/2-1990, point 1.6.6.
[3]   OJ C 96, 17.4.1990; Bull. EC 3-1990, point 1.1.3.
[4]   Bull. EC 5-1990, point 1.1.2.
[5]   Bull. EC 10-1990, point 1.1.11.
[6]   Bull. EC 10-1990, point 1.1.6; Bull. EC 12-1990.
[7]   OJ C 149, 18.6.1990; Bull. EC 5-1990, point 1.2.1.
[8]   OJ C 284, 12.11.1990; Bull. EC 10-1990, point 1.1.12.
[9]   Point 922 of this Report.

union.[1] In a resolution adopted prior to the European Council meeting in June, Parliament reaffirmed the essential elements of European union.[2] In July it went on to spell out the precise institutional changes it was seeking in four separate resolutions,[3] one of which dealt specifically with preparations for the meeting with national parliaments to discuss the future of the Community which took place in November.[4] Also in November, Parliament, after having been consulted under the procedure provided for in Article 236 of the Treaty, gave a favourable opinon on the Council's acceptance of a number of commitments relating to the convening of the two intergovernmental conferences.[5] It stated its position on a number of subjects connected with the reform of the Treaties in resolutions it adopted in October,[6] November[7] and December.[8]

At the end of a debate in February, a consensus emerged on the need to speed up Community integration to keep in step with the gathering pace of the process of German unification, and Parliament accordingly passed a resolution in which it decided to set up a temporary comittee to study the question.[9] In a resolution adopted in April, Parliament took the view that the unification process had to be fitted into the Community context.[10] The following month, Parliament welcomed the support given by the Dublin European Council and the undertaking provided by the Federal Republic of Germany (reaffirmed by Chancellor Kohl in the House).[1] During the May part-session, a meeting with Mr de Maizière, Prime Minister of the German Democratic Republic, was also organized. The procedures to be applied to consideration of the German unification proposals were debated in July:[11] following the conclusion of an institutional agreement at the beginning of September involving an undertaking on timing and working methods, the proposals concerning both transitional and interim measures were dealt with within the very short deadlines imposed by the speed at which unification was proceeding: apart from the stages provided for by the legislative procedure, mainly September[12] for the provisional measures and October[13] and November[14] for the transitional measures, Parliament frequently stated its position in resolutions on those questions which attracted most of its attention.[15] In October Parliament amended its Rules of Procedure

---

[1] OJ C 149, 18.6.1990; Bull. EC 5-1990, point 1.7.1.
[2] OJ C 175, 16.7.1990; Bull. EC 6-1990, point 1.1.3.
[3] OJ C 231, 17.9.1990; Bull. EC 7/8-1990, points 1.1.1 to 1.1.4.
[4] Bull. EC 11-1990, points 1.1.1 and 2.3.1.
[5] OJ C 324, 24.12.1990; Bull. EC 11-1990, point 1.1.2.
[6] OJ C 284, 12.11.1990; OJ C 295, 26.11.1990; Bull. EC 10-1990, points 1.1.3, 1.1.7, 1.1.8, 1.1.12 and 1.1.13.
[7] OJ C 324, 24.12.1990; Bull. EC 11-1990, point 1.1.3.
[8] OJ C 19, 28.1.1991; Bull. EC 12-1990.
[9] OJ C 68, 19.3.1990; Bull. EC 1/2-1990, point 1.6.6.
[10] OJ C 113, 7.5.1990; Bull. EC 4-1990, point 1.6.1.
[11] OJ C 231, 17.9.1990; Bull. EC 7/8-1990, points 1.2.4 to 1.2.6.
[12] OJ C 260, 15.10.1990; Bull. EC 9-1990, point 1.1.2.
[13] OJ C 295, 26.11.1990; Bull. EC 10-1990, point 1.2.3.
[14] OJ C 324, 24.12.1990; Bull. EC 11-1990, point 1.2.1.
[15] OJ C 295, 26.11.1990; Bull. EC 10-1990, point 1.2.4; OJ C 324, 24.12.1990; Bull. EC 11-1990, point 1.2.3.

to allow observers from the former German Democratic Republic to be seated.[1] In November the number of observers was fixed at 18.

Other major issues were also considered during the year: the Social Charter and the Commission's action programme for implementing it were the subject of resolutions adopted in February[2] and September,[3] and in July Parliament adopted for the first time a resolution asking the Commission to make a proposal for a Directive on atypical employment contracts and terms of employment;[4] the free movement of persons in the internal market;[5] agricultural policy, especially the adoption of the opinion on prices for 1990-91 in March[6] and the resolution on the crisis in agriculture in September;[7] budgetary matters associated with the revision of the financial perspective and the adoption of the 1991 budget;[8] and environmental protection.[9]

In November Grand Duke Jean of Luxembourg addressed a formal sitting of the House.

The year also saw the introduction of the code of conduct presented by Mr Delors during the February part-session. The Commission and Parliament took note of the code, which is aimed at improving institutional relations, at the meeting of the enlarged Bureau during the April part-session.[10]

917. In external relations, developments in Central and Eastern European countries continued to claim Parliament's attention.[11] Two debates on the Community's relations with the EFTA countries were held,[12] and Parliament also expressed its position on the Uruguay Round of multilateral trade negotiations.[13]

---

[1]   OJ C 295, 26.11.1990; Bull. EC 10-1990, point 1.8.14.
[2]   OJ C 68, 19.3.1990; Bull. EC 1/2-1990, point 1.1.90.
[3]   OJ C 260, 15.10.1990; Bull. EC 9-1990, point 1.2.54.
[4]   OJ C 231, 17.9.1990; Bull. EC 7/8-1990, point 1.3.87.
[5]   OJ C 96, 17.4.1990; Bull. EC 3-1990, point 1.1.198.
[6]   OJ C 96, 17.4.1990; Bull. EC 3-1990, point 1.1.106.
[7]   OJ C 260, 15.10.1990; Bull. EC 9-1990, point 1.2.108.
[8]   OJ C 113, 7.5.1990; Bull. EC 4-1990, points 1.4.1, 1.4.4 and 1.4.6 to 1.4.8; OJ C 175, 16.7.1990; Bull. EC 6-1990, point 1.6.4; OJ C 231, 17.9.1990; Bull. EC 7/8-1990, point 1.6.2.
[9]   OJ C 68, 19.3.1990; Bull. EC 1/2-1990, points 1.1.131 and 1.1.133; OJ C 96, 17.4.1990; Bull. EC 3-1990, point 1.1.67; OJ C 113, 7.5.1990; Bull. EC 4-1990, point 1.1.75; OJ C 175, 16.7.1990; Bull. EC 6-1990, point 1.3.115; OJ C 231, 17.9.1990; Bull. EC 7/8-1990, point 1.3.145.
[10] Bull. EC 4-1990, point 1.6.1.
[11] OJ C 38, 3.2.1990; Bull. EC 1/2-1990, points 1.2.2 and 1.2.12; OJ C 68, 19.3.1990; Bull. EC 1/2-1990, points 1.2.15, 1.2.16, 1.2.18, 1.2.20 and 1.2.23; OJ C 96, 17.4.1990; Bull. EC 3-1990, point 1.2.10; OJ C 113, 7.5.1990; Bull. EC 4-1990, points 1.2.3 to 1.2.5; OJ C 231, 17.9.1990; Bull. EC 7/8-1990, points 1.3.129, 1.4.2, 1.4.9 and 1.4.13; OJ C 260, 15.10.1990; Bull. EC 9-1990, points 1.3.5, 1.3.7 and 1.3.9; OJ C 284, 12.11.1990; Bull. EC 10-1990, points 1.4.3, 1.4.4 and 1.4.66; OJ C 324, 24.12.1990; Bull. EC 11-1990, point 1.4.2.
[12] OJ C 113, 7.5.1990; Bull. EC 4-1990, point 1.2.15; OJ C 175, 16.7.1990; Bull. EC 6-1990, point 1.4.9.
[13] OJ C 284, 12.11.1990;; Bull. EC 10-1990, point 1.4.62; OJ C 19, 28.1.1991; Bull. EC 12-1990.

The September part-session was marked by an important debate on the Gulf crisis, with statements from Mr Andreotti, the Italian Prime Minister and President of the Council, and Mr Delors, President of the Commission. [1]

Mr Virgilio Barco, President of the Republic of Colombia, addressed Parliament at a formal sitting in May. [2]

918.   Two winners of the Sakharov Prize for freedom of thought were received by Parliament during the year. Mr Alexander Dubcek, President of the Federal Assembly of the Czech and Slovak Federal Republic, was presented with the prize in January, [3] and Mr Nelson Mandela, Deputy President of the African National Congress, who had been awarded the prize in 1988 but had been unable to receive it in person having been in prison at the time, addressed the House in June. [4] Parliament, faced by alarming situations involving human rights, continued to pass a large number of resolutions to draw attention to the most serious violations, irrespective of where and under what political system they were committed. Parliament also expressed its satisfaction as regards the restoration of democracy and freedoms in Central and Eastern Europe.

919.   Parliament held 12 part-sessions, during which it adopted 601 resolutions and decisions, including 159 embodying its opinion under the consultation procedure (single reading) and 119 under the cooperation procedure. On second reading, Parliament approved the Council's common position without amendment in 21 cases and after amendment in 28 cases.

The assent procedure (Articles 237 and 238 of the EEC Treaty as amended by the Single European Act) was applied in two cases. The House adopted 27 resolutions and decisions on budgetary matters.

Parliament adopted 282 own-initiative resolutions — 72 on the basis of reports, 155 by urgent procedure and 55 following an early vote to conclude debates on Commission or Council statements or on oral questions. It took 12 miscellaneous decisions concerning changes in the Rules of Procedure, requests to waive Members' immunity, etc.

A breakdown of Parliament's work in 1990 is shown in Table 16. A total of 3 075 written questions were tabled — 2 732 to the Commission, 217 to the Council and 126 to the Conference of Ministers for Foreign Affairs (political cooperation). Oral questions (Question Time) numbered 1 355 — 835 to the Commission, 280 to the Council and 240 to the Conference of Ministers for Foreign Affairs. There were also 411 oral questions with or without debate — 272 to the Commission, 88 to the Council and 51 to the Conference of Ministers for Foreign Affairs.

---

[1]   OJ C 260, 15.10.1990; Bull. EC 9-1990, point 1.3.81.
[2]   Bull. EC 5-1990, point 1.6.1.
[3]   Bull. EC 1/2-1990, point 1.2.103.
[4]   Bull. EC 6-1990, point 1.8.1.

TABLE 16

The year in Parliament

Part-session	Normal consultations (single reading)	Cooperation procedures (Article 149(2) of the EEC Treaty) I[1]	II[1]	Assents (Articles 237 and 238 of the EEC Treaty)	EP Rules 63 and 121 (own-initiative reports)	EP Rules 56 and 58 (resolutions following statements and oral questions)	EP Rule 64 (resolutions on urgent subjects)	Budget questions	Miscellaneous decisions and resolutions
January	10	2	6	—	2	5	18	—	2
February	6	3	7	1	3	6	10	2	1
March	15	4	4	—	3	2	24	1	1
April	17	3	3	—	8	—	9	7	—
May	11	6	6	1	2	7	20	1	1
June	13	7	3	—	8	6	9	1	—
July	12	4	1	—	12	4	11	1	1
September	13	3	7	—	2	2	15	—	2
October I	9	14	2	—	4	12	7	2	1
October II	9	2	4	—	7	3	—	2	3
November	20	11	4	—	7	6	19	5	—
December	24	11	2	—	14	2	13	5	—
Total	159[2]	70[3]	49[4]	2	72	55	155	27	12

[1] I: first reading; II: second reading.
[2] Including 101 where Parliament proposed amendments to and 4 where it rejected Commission proposals.
[3] Including 52 where Parliament proposed amendments to Commission proposals.
[4] Including 28 where Parliament proposed amendments to common positions by the Council.

920. At 31 December the establishment plan of the Secretariat comprised 3 007 permanent posts and 476 temporary posts.

Council

921. Ireland was in the chair for the first half of the year[1] and Italy for the second half.[2]

---

[1]   Bull. EC 1/2-1990, point 2.2.1; Bull. EC 6-1990, point 1.8.1.
[2]   Bull. EC 7/8-1990, point 1.8.1; Bull. EC 12-1990.

922.   The European Council met four times during the year — two ordinary meetings in Dublin in June[1] and in Rome in December,[2] and two special meetings in Dublin in April[3] and in Rome in October.[4]

At the April meeting unanimous agreement was reached on a common approach to German unification and relations with Central and Eastern Europe and to the CSCE process. The Heads of State or Government also agreed a procedure for preparing proposals on strengthening political union. In addition, they clearly restated their determination to see progress made in combating drugs and international organized crime. At its meeting in June the European Council unanimously decided that the two intergovernmental conferences, one on economic and monetary union and the other on political union, should both begin in December. The conferences should conclude their work rapidly, so that the results could be ratified by the end of 1992. The European Council also had an extensive exchange of views on possible assistance to the Soviet Union in support of the political and economic reforms it had undertaken. The European Council asked the Commission to assess the situation and prepare proposals for action in liaison with international financial agencies and in consultation with the Soviet authorities. In October the Council confirmed that it wanted a gradual transformation of the Community through the development of its political dimension, the strengthening of its capacity for action and the extension of its powers. It took note of the result of the preparatory work of the conference on economic and monetary union and 11 Member States agreed on the guidelines for EMU. It also adopted a very firm declaration on the Gulf crisis in which it unreservedly condemned the Iraqi attack and stressed the absolute priority which the Community and its Member States attached to a solution of this crisis on the basis of the UN Security Council's resolutions. In December, before the two intergovernmental conferences and after the CSCE Summit in Paris, the Heads of State or Government expressed their determination to complete the internal market within the time-limit laid down, to continue increasing economic and social cohesion and to lay down the stages of the process for transforming the Community into a political union which is designed to be a pole of stability in Europe. These intentions were reflected in particular in the active solidarity shown towards the Soviet Union and the countries of Central and Eastern Europe.

923.   Continuing the practice introduced in 1981, Mr Charles Haughey[5] and Mr Giulio Andreotti,[6] accompanied by Mr Delors, reported to Parliament on the conclusion of the European Council meetings.

---

[1]   Bull. EC 6-1990, points I.1 to I.42.
[2]   Bull. EC 12-1990.
[3]   Bull. EC 4-1990, points I.1 to I.16.
[4]   Bull. EC 10-1990, points I.1 to I.17.
[5]   Bull. EC 5-1990; point 1.7.1; Bull. EC 7/8-1990, point 1.8.1.
[6]   Bull. EC 11-1990; Bull. EC 12-1990.

924.   At its 86 meetings in 1990 the Council adopted 65 directives, 380 regulations and 169 decisions.

925.   There were 2 183 permanent posts and one temporary post on the Council's establishment plan at the end of the year.

Commission

926.   Following deliberations at the Dublin European Council,[1] the representatives of the Governments of the Member States decided on 4 December to reappoint Mr Jacques Delors President of the Commission and Mr Frans Andriessen, Mr Martin Bangemann, Sir Leon Brittan, Mr Henning Christophersen, Mr Manuel Marín González and Mr Filippo Maria Pandolfi Vice-Presidents for the period from 6 January 1991 to 5 January 1993.[2]

927.   On 21 February the Commission, which held 47 meetings in the course of the year, met for the 1 000th time since the three executives merged. It adopted 6 298 instruments (regulations, decisions, directives, recommendations, opinions) and sent the Council 726 proposals, recommendations or drafts and 237 communications, memoranda and reports. In August and October the Commission delivered the opinions provided for under Article 236 of the Treaty as part of the procedure for convening the intergovernmental conferences on political union and on economic and monetary union.[3] As the process of German unification speeded up, the Commission had to be delegated considerable powers to introduce provisional measures and it also managed to prepare, within a very short space of time, all the interim and transitional measures which followed.[4] It was also asked by the Dublin European Council to frame proposals on the support to be given to reforms in the Soviet Union.[5] In April the Commission received Mr Javier Pérez de Cúellar, Secretary-General of the United Nations.[6] The 40th anniversary of the Declaration of 9 May 1950 in which Robert Schuman proposed a European Coal and Steel Community was celebrated at a commemorative meeting organized by the Commission under the title 'Building a future together'.[7]

928.   The Commission's establishment plan for 1990 comprised 12 334 permanent posts (including 1 600 LA posts for the Language Service) and 553 temporary posts (including

---

[1]   Bull. EC 6-1990, point I.32.
[2]   OJ L 347, 12.12.1990; Bull. EC 12-1990.
[3]   Points 2 and 9 of this Report.
[4]   Point 21 of this Report.
[5]   Point 684 of this Report.
[6]   Bull. EC 4-1990, point 1.2.61.
[7]   Bull. EC 5-1990, points 2.2.1 to 2.2.5.

30 LA) paid out of administrative appropriations; 2 695 permanent and 590 temporary posts paid out of the research appropriations; 424 permanent posts in the Office for Official Publications; 65 at the European Centre for the Development of Vocational Training and 59 at the European Foundation for the Improvement of Living and Working Conditions.

929.   Under the secondment and exchange arrangements between the Commission and Member States' government departments, 39 Commission officials were seconded to national civil services and some 400 national experts came to work for Commission departments.

Court of Justice and Court of First Instance

930.   In accordance with Articles 32d of the ECSC Treaty, 168a of the EEC Treaty and 140a of the Euratom Treaty, the Council approved the Rules of Procedure of the Court of First Instance on 21 December.[1] It also approved a number of amendments to the Rules of Procedure of the Court of Justice[2] with a view to speeding up proceedings and clarifying the scope of some of the provisions in the light of experience.

931.   On 31 January Mr P.J.G. Kapteyn was appointed a member of the Court of Justice from 1 April 1990 to 6 October 1994, to replace Mr T. Koopmans, who had tendered his resignation.[3]

932.   The composition of the Chambers of the Court of Justice was determined as follows for a period of one year from 7 October:[4]

First Chamber: President: Mr G.C. Rodríguez Iglesias; Judges: Sir Gordon Slynn and Mr R. Joliet;
Second Chamber: President: Mr T.F. O'Higgins; Judges: Mr G.F. Mancini and Mr F.A. Schockweiler;
Third Chamber: President: Mr J.C. Moitinho de Almeida; Judges: Mr F. Grévisse and Mr M. Zuleeg;
Fourth Chamber: President: Mr M. Diéz de Velasco; Judges: Mr C.N. Kakouris and Mr P.J.G. Kapteyn;
Fifth Chamber: President: Mr J.C. Moitinho de Almeida; Judges: Sir Gordon Slynn, Mr G.C. Rodríguez Iglesias, Mr R. Joliet, Mr F. Grévisse and Mr M. Zuleeg;
Sixth Chamber: President: Mr G.F. Mancini; Judges: Mr T.F. O'Higgins, Mr M. Díez de Velasco, Mr C.N. Kakouris, Mr F.A. Schockweiler and Mr P.J.G. Kapteyn.

[1]   Bull. EC 12-1990.
[2]   OJ L 350, 28.12.1974.
[3]   OJ L 37, 9.2.1990; Bull. EC 1/2-1990, point 1.6.25.
[4]   OJ C 251, 5.10.1990; Bull. EC 7/8-1990, point 1.8.16.

Mr F.G. Jacobs was appointed First Advocate General for the year beginning 7 October.

933. The composition of the Chambers of the Court of First Instance was determined as follows for a period of one year from 1 September: [1]

First Chamber: President: Mr J.L. da Cruz Vilaça; Judges: Mr R. Schintgen, Mr D.A.O. Edward, Mr H. Kirschner, Mr R. García-Valdecasas y Fernández and Mr K. Lenaerts;
Second Chamber: President: Mr A. Saggio; Judges: Mr C.G. Yeraris, Mr C.P. Briët, Mr D.P.M. Barrington, Mr B. Vesterdorf and Mr J. Biancarelli;
Third Chamber: President: Mr G.C. Yeraris; Judges: Mr A. Saggio, Mr B. Vesterdorf and Mr K. Lenaerts;
Fourth Chamber: President: Mr R. Schintgen; Judges: Mr D.A.O. Edward and Mr R. García-Valdecasas y Fernández;
Fifth Chamber: President: Mr C.P. Briët; Judges: Mr D.P.M. Barrington, Mr H. Kirschner and Mr J. Biancarelli.

934. In 1990, 380 cases were brought (140 references for preliminary rulings, 15 staff cases and 225 others). Of the 225 judgments given by the Court, 133 were preliminary rulings, 9 were in staff cases and 83 were in other cases. [2] The Court of First Instance dealt with 52 cases and delivered 59 judgments.

935. There were 632 permanent and 84 temporary posts on the Court's establishment plan at 31 December. The corresponding figures for the Court of First Instance were 24 and 12.

Court of Auditors

936. Following the partial replacement of its members at the end of 1989, when Mr C. Androutsopoulos, Mr J. Carey, Mr B. Friedmann, Mr A. Middelhoek, Mr D. Strasser and Mr M. Thoss were appointed for the period 21 December 1989 to 20 December 1995, [3] Mr A. Angioi was elected President of the Court on 9 January 1990 for a term ending on 20 December 1992.

937. On 8 November the Court approved its annual report on the implementation of the general budget of the European Communities for 1989 and the operations of the European Development Funds in the same year. [4]

---

[1]   OJ C 199, 8.8.1990; Bull. EC 7/8-1990, point 1.8.17.
[2]   The Court's judgments are discussed in Chapter VII: Community law.
[3]   OJ L 382, 30.12.1989.
[4]   OJ C 313, 12.12.1990; Bull. EC 12-1990.

938.   The Court delivered an opinion on Council and Commission management of human resources.[1] On 26 July it published a report on the financial statements of the European Coal and Steel Community at 31 December 1989.[2] It also adopted a number of special reports on the management and control of export refunds,[3] ECSC, Euratom and NCI borrowing and lending operations[4] and the management of the integrated Mediterranean programmes.[5]

939.   There were 315 permanent and 64 temporary posts on the Court's establishment plan at 31 December.

Economic and Social Committee

940.   Following the partial replacement of its members for a term to run from 21 September 1990 to 20 September 1994,[6] the Economic and Social Committee elected Mr François Staedelin (Workers' Group, France) for a two-year term as its Chairman at its inaugural meeting on 17 and 18 October.[7] Mrs Susanne Tiemann (Various Interests, Germany) and Mr Filotas Kazazis (Employers' Group, Greece) were elected Vice-Chairmen for the same period.

941.   The January/February session[8] of the Committee was attended by Mr Delors, President of the Commission, who presented the Commission's programme for 1990. At the same session, Mr Gerard Collins outlined Ireland's programme for its term as President of the Council.

942.   During its plenary sessions the Committee adopted opinions on Commission proposals and communications on such subjects as the various aspects of the internal energy market,[9] Community transit,[10] the prices for agricultural products,[11] the Statute for a European company,[12] excise duties,[13] indirect taxation[14] and German unification.[15]

---

[1]   Bull. EC 5-1990, point 1.7.42.
[2]   Bull. EC 7/8-1990, point 1.8.34.
[3]   OJ C 133, 31.5.1990; Bull. EC 5-1990, point 1.7.43.
[4]   OJ C 160, 29.6.1990; Bull. EC 6-1990, point 1.8.27.
[5]   Bull. EC 12-1990.
[6]   OJ C 290, 23.10.1990; Bull. EC 9-1990, point 1.7.23.
[7]   Bull. EC 10-1990, point 1.8.37.
[8]   Bull. EC 1/2-1990, point 1.6.30.
[9]   OJ C 75, 26.3.1990; Bull. EC 1/2-1990, points 1.1.253, 1.1.260 and 1.1.268.
[10]   OJ C 112, 7.5.1990; Bull. EC 3-1990, point 1.1.5.
[11]   OJ C 112, 7.5.1990; Bull. EC 3-1990, point 1.1.106.
[12]   OJ C 124, 21.5.1990; Bull. EC 3-1990, point 1.1.100.
[13]   OJ C 225, 10.9.1990; Bull. EC 7/8-1990, points 1.3.40 to 1.3.43.
[14]   Bull. EC 9-1990, points 1.2.29 and 1.2.30.
[15]   Bull. EC 11-1990, point 1.2.1.

943.   The Committee also delivered own-initiative opinions on topics such as economic and commercial cooperation with Latin America,[1] the use of agricultural and forestry resources,[2] relations with the countries of Eastern Europe,[3] declining industrial areas,[4] Community-EFTA relations,[5] the economic situation in the Community in mid-1990,[6] social developments in the Community in 1989,[7] the GATT Uruguay Round negotiations[8] and the cooperative, mutual and non-profit sector.[9] On 20 November it also adopted a resolution on political union.[10]

944.   There were 501 permanent posts on the Committee's establishment plan at 31 December.

ECSC Consultative Committee

945.   At its opening meeting of the new business year on 17 December[11] the Committee, whose members had been renewed by the Council in November,[12] elected Mr J. Windisch (Germany — coal workers) Chairman and Mr Y.-P. Soule (France — steel producers) and Mr M. Cimenti (Italy — coal consumers and dealers) Vice-Chairmen.

946.   During its other meetings (four ordinary and two extraordinary), the Committee, having been formally consulted by the Commission, expressed its opinion on the general objectives for steel up to 1995,[13] the market for solid fuels in the Community in 1989 and the outlook for 1990,[14] the suspension of customs duties and quantitative restrictions for products falling within the ECSC Treaty coming from the German Democratic Republic,[15] the granting of ECSC loans for industrial projects in the German Democratic Republic,[16] the introduction of transitional tariff measures for products covered by the ECSC Treaty for Central and Eastern European countries to take account of German unification,[17] the amendent of Decision No 322/89/ECSC establishing Community rules

---

[1]   OJ C 75, 26.3.1990; Bull. EC 1/2-1990, point 1.2.46.
[2]   OJ C 124, 21.5.1990; Bull. EC 3-1990, point 1.1.70.
[3]   OJ C 124, 21.5.1990; Bull. EC 3-1990, point 1.2.1.
[4]   OJ C 124, 21.5.1990; Bull. EC 3-1990, point 1.1.61.
[5]   OJ C 182, 23.7.1990; Bull. EC 5-1990, point 1.3.18.
[6]   OJ C 225, 10.9.1990; Bull. EC 7/8-1990, point 1.3.3.
[7]   OJ C 225, 10.9.1990; Bull. EC 7/8-1990, point 1.3.81.
[8]   Bull. EC 9-1990, point 1.3.77.
[9]   Bull. EC 9-1990, point 1.2.104.
[10]   Bull. EC 11-1990, point 1.1.7.
[11]   Bull. EC 12-1990.
[12]   OJ C 300, 29.11.1990; Bull. EC 11-1990, point 1.8.37.
[13]   Bull. EC 3-1990, point 1.1.96.
[14]   Bull. EC 3-1990, point 1.1.186; Bull. EC 9-1990, point 1.2.184.
[15]   Bull. EC 6-1990, point 1.2.5.
[16]   Bull. EC 6-1990, point 1.2.9.
[17]   Bull. EC 9-1990, point 1.1.4.

unification,[1] the amendent of Decision No 322/89/ECSC establishing Community rules for aid to the steel industry,[2] the desirability of granting financial aid for various coal and steel research programmes[3] and the conclusion of protocols on trade and economic and commercial cooperation between the ECSC and Poland and Hungary.[4]

947.   On its own initiative the Committee also gave its opinion on the proposal for a negotiating brief concerning imports during 1990 of iron and steel products originating in certain non-Community countries,[5] the Commission communication on energy and the environment,[6] the Commission working paper on security of supply, the internal energy market and energy policy,[7] the Commission communication on the SAVE programme[7] and the first progress report on the internal energy market.[7]

948.   The Committee also discussed a Commission working paper on the future of the ECSC Treaty.[8] Its position was outlined in a memorandum adopted on 12 November[9] in the presence of Mr M. Bangemann, Vice-President of the Commission: the Committee stated that it preferred the Treaty to expire at its term in the year 2002 but accepted in principle that some of its provisions could be adapted in line with changes in the economic and political situation.

Administration and management of the institutions

Management, redeployment and information programme

949.   The Commission took specific action to give effect to the new guidelines set out in its management, redeployment and information programme.[10] Career management was decentralized and is now dealt with on a partnership basis with the operational departments. A number of new redeployment exercises were set in train in the course of the year which, combined with redeployments within Directorates-General, made it possible to achieve the target for 1989-90, namely the transfer of 7.5% of total staff, excluding the language service and staff paid from the research budget,[10] with their posts to priority areas. A new target of 4% has been set for 1991.

---

[1]   Bull. EC 9-1990, point 1.1.4.
[2]   Bull. EC 9-1990, point 1.1.5.
[3]   Bull. EC 6-1990, points 1.3.106 and 1.3.107; Bull. EC 9-1990, points 1.2.79 to 1.2.81.
[4]   Bull. EC 12-1990.
[5]   Bull. EC 1/2-1990, point 1.2.90.
[6]   Bull. EC 6-1990, point 1.3.255.
[7]   Bull. EC 12-1990.
[8]   Point 212 of this Report.
[9]   OJ C 302, 1.12.1990; Bull. EC 11-1990, point 1.3.101.
[10]   Twenty-third General Report, point 42.

The positive action programme for female staff at the Commission, which was launched in 1988 and came to an end on 31 December, has helped increase awareness of the problems existing in this area. There was also a significant rise in the number of women promoted to management posts during the reference period.

The Commission laid the foundations for a new staff-training policy. The aims of continuing training are to be reassessed with a view to making it an essential component of career policy. The main object of the exercise is to develop a coherent approach to the needs of the departments, the institution and the individual members of staff. The training programme for 1991 is the first fruit of the new policy.

The Commission also introduced two programmes designed to strengthen the ties between national civil services and the Community civil service: one sets out to familiarize Commission officials (A5) with government departments, and the other makes provision for an exchange scheme for national civil servants responsible for the application of directives geared to completion of the internal market.

Recruitment

950.   Having achieved its aim of speeding up recruitment procedures,[1] the Commission turned its attention to improving the quality of the selection procedure. First, in the interests of clarity, the notices of competition were entirely redrafted and a new guide for candidates produced. Second, the structure of the eliminatory tests was changed and a new test introduced to assess the candidates' knowledge of a second Community language. The Commission also advertised more widely in an attempt to attract a larger number of young students, especially university graduates, to a career on its staff.

Human resources management

951.   On 3 October the Commission adopted a number of measures in response to the recommendations contained in the Court of Auditors opinion on the management of human resources in the Council and the Commission, produced at the joint request of the two institutions.[2] The Commission decided first to ask each Directorate-General to produce a mission statement giving details of its objectives and the tasks and time-scale needed to attain them, and second to set up a departmental inspectorate reporting to the President. The Commission also proposes to set up a pilot scheme integrating and developing the various instruments used for planning the tasks of each administrative

---

[1]   Twenty-second General Report, point 43; Twenty-third General Report, point 43.
[2]   Bull. EC 5-1990, point 1.7.42.

unit and possibly even of each category A official. At the same time, aware that it is currently critically understaffed, the Commission forcefully underlined that it must be given adequate resources to cope with the increase in its workload. It confirmed its intention to continue to work in partnership with the national authorities and to explore the possibility of entrusting certain specific tasks to agencies or specialized offices, subject however to certain provisos, in particular the need to safeguard the powers of the Commission and preserve the integrity of the European public service.

Staff Regulations

Remuneration

952.   Early in October the Commission sent the Council a two-part proposal on the management of pay policy in the Community civil service. The first part of the proposal deals with the salary adjustment method as the present method is due to expire on 30 June 1991.[1] In general the proposed new method retains the elements contained in the previous one: the principle of parallel development designed to ensure that salaries in the Community civil service move in line with salaries in the national civil services; technical improvements in the method used to monitor application of the principle of the equivalence of purchasing power between the various places of employment in the Community; a safeguard clause coming into play in the event of a sudden and serious economic crisis, enabling the Commission to propose measures on the basis of objective data and the Council to adopt them. The second part of the proposal provides for the denomination and payment in ecus of the remuneration and pensions of Community officials and other servants, without affecting purchasing power.

Joint Sickness Insurance Scheme

953.   In a bid to remedy the difficulties encountered in maintaining the financial balance of the Joint Sickness Insurance Scheme, mainly as a result of the increase in the volume and cost of treatment, new provisions came into effect on 1 November which will make savings and also increase the contributions by the members and the institutions.

Data processing

954.   Growth in data processing has been balanced, greater attention being focused on improving the quality of services, training and user support. Over 60% of staff now use

---

[1]   Fifteenth General Report, point 32.

data-processing facilities and the total resources available increased considerably in 1990 in terms of local and central processing power, the capacity of shared and local networks and the number of processing tools. As far as the latter are concerned, substantial progress was made on infrastructure projects, backed up by the Insis[1] and Caddia[2] programmes, in particular the development of tools for the dissemination of Community information and the creation of standard gateways with the outside for electronic mail and file transfer.

The open systems policy has been continued, with a new invitation to tender for decentralized equipment and the adoption of protocols of agreement with all hardware suppliers for the computer centre, with a view to moving increasingly towards open systems. The new edition of the *Guidelines for an informatics architecture* specifies the technical and organizational frame of reference for the implementation of this policy: this paper was recognized as a major contribution by the public sector and industry.

955.   The reorganization of the Informatics Directorate carried out in 1989[3] has led to better cooperation between users and local and central data-processing departments, partly as a result of the introduction of consultation procedures for the selection of products. The Steering Committee on Data Processing in the Commission (CDIC) has been enlarged to make sure that the management of data processing reflects the Commission's needs. In addition the CDIC has initiated a far-reaching examination of data-processing strategy in the light of new organizational requirements and the greater experience of users, which enables them to play a larger part in the running of data processing.

Language services

956.   On account of the shortage of conference interpreters, the Joint Interpreting and Conference Service (JICS) continued its training efforts, maintaining the same standard for all languages. It organized 29 aptitude tests for young graduates (law, economics, science, etc.), in particular in Athens, Florence, Lisbon and Madrid. The Commission made a financial contribution to postgraduate training courses in Athens, Copenhagen, Florence and Lisbon. Thirteen interpreters from the established staff also received study grants to enable them to learn a further working language. Cooperation with non-member countries in the field of interpreter training continued, in particular with China and Turkey. Under the Tempus programme[4] the JICS was invited to Budapest to examine possibilities for cooperation in continuing training with the Hungarian authorities.

---

[1]   Point 315 of this Report.
[2]   Point 316 of this Report.
[3]   Twenty-third General Report, point 53.
[4]   Point 390 of this Report.

The project for the extension of the Borschette Conference Centre submitted to the Belgian authorities received a favourable opinion from the Consultation Committee.

957. The new Translation Service has been in operation since 1 March.[1] Reorganization was completed when the last of the Translation Units in Brussels were relocated under the same roof in September. During the year the Translation Service translated 805 000 pages. Since computerization in August of the translation of notices of tender, which have increased sharply in number, the workload involved has been substantially reduced.

958.   Under the Sysling project to provide the Translation Service with modern computer tools, more than 700 word-processing terminals have been installed over four years, which means that 45% of staff are now equipped. The Systran machine translation system now supplies 'raw' translations to 500 users in Commission departments; 25 000 pages were translated in the course of the year.

959.   The Eurodicautom terminology bank was extended further. It now contains some 495 000 entries with equivalents in other languages, broken down as follows: French 451 103, English 428 041, German 330 378, Danish 273 993, Dutch 266 807, Italian 252 564, Spanish 225 484, Greek 156 458, Portuguese 183 050. The bank also contains 140 926 abbreviations.

---

[1]   Twenty-third General Report, point 48.

Section 2

Information for the general public

Information activities

960.   Information and communication activities this year focused mainly on completion of the internal market, promotion of a people's Europe and the role of the Community in the world, particularly in the wake of events in Central and Eastern Europe. The drive to coordinate the various campaigns directed by the Commission at a wide range of audiences, to improve linkage and to make use of efficient information techniques continued under the priority information programme (PIP). The policy function of the PIP, the 1990 and 1991 guidelines for which were approved by the Commission in March[1] and July[2] respectively, is to ensure that the Commission's priorities in the field of information are consistent with the policy priorities set out in its annual programme. Also in the interests of consistency, particularly as regards the definition of priority subject areas, the priority publications programme has now been incorporated into the PIP.

Information activities relating to completion of the internal market were geared to a variety of target groups, but particular emphasis was placed on social aspects in anticipation of close cooperation on this front with the trade unions. The development of relay organizations providing information for the general public was stepped up, with the now well-established and expanded network of rural promotion and information forums[3] and citizens information centres being followed by the new and more comprehensive 'Symbiosis' project. The role of the Commission's Offices in the capitals and certain regions of the Community has also been strengthened as decided in 1989.[4] Information activities in non-member countries were the subject of a communication adopted by the Commission in May.[5] In view of the sweeping changes which have taken place on the international political scene and the increasing role now played by the Community, greater priority is to be given to providing information for the Community's traditional partners, both in the developing and in the industrialized countries, including

---

1   Bull. EC 3-1990, point 1.1.190.
2   Bull. EC 7/8-1990, point 1.3.304.
3   Bull. EC 6-1990, point 1.3.253; point 434 of this Report.
4   Twenty-third General Report, point 55.
5   Bull. EC 5-1990, point 1.2.231.

Central and Eastern Europe. Information is now seen as a major function of the Commission's Delegations in non-member countries. Special activities were also organized in the German Democratic Republic in the run-up to German unification. [1]

961. The Commission focused its attention on producing more substantial information better suited to young people, in the wider context of a people's Europe. The Commission also decided to review its policy on sport in an attempt to define the criteria for its action on this front. In particular, it wants to enhance the image of the Community at the 1992 Olympics in Albertville and Barcelona. [2] The Community image was projected through media coverage of this year's World Cup. The Community was also involved in the European Community Cycle Race, the European Swimming Championships and the special European Olympics for the mentally handicapped. [3] The 1990 Nike prize designed to encourage television programmes providing a new slant on the situation of women attracted contributions from a score of television companies. [4]

962. Fairs and exhibitions, campaigns on specific subjects, regional campaigns and large-scale public events are all popular instruments in the drive to increase public awareness. Geographically organized campaigns on the many aspects of 1992 were concentrated in the United Kingdom and Germany. European festivities were organized to coincide with the meetings of the European Council and Europe Day was celebrated in the Member States to mark 9 May. Special attention is being focused on Community participation in the 1992 Seville Universal Exposition, [2] where the Community will have its own pavilion designed by an architect selected by competition; [5] it will be built alongside those of the Member States. The Commission also gave the go-ahead for Community participation in the 1992 Genoa International Exhibition on the theme of 'Christopher Columbus: ships and sea'. [6]

963. In the sphere of cooperation between the Commission and institutions of higher education, 1990 saw the launching of the initial phase [7] of the multiannual Jean Monnet Project designed to promote European integration studies in universities, [2] an initiative which has aroused considerable interest in academic circles.

[1] Bull. EC 9-1990, point 1.2.189.
[2] Twenty-third General Report, point 57.
[3] Bull. EC 7/8-1990, point 1.3.305.
[4] Bull. EC 11-1990, point 1.4.190.
[5] Bull. EC 1/2-1990, point 1.1.271.
[6] Bull. EC 4-1990, point 1.1.159.
[7] Bull. EC 5-1990, point 1.2.232.

Press, radio and television

964. The number of journalists accredited to the Commission in Brussels remained high, at over 600 journalists from 50 countries, of whom around 453 were from the press and 130 from radio and television. This total includes 52 national and international press agencies.

965. The Spokesman's Service held 243 meetings with the press on Commission decisions, proposals and reactions, and Commission meetings were covered by 49 press conferences given by the Spokesman. The President and Members of the Commission gave 75 press conferences on key issues, several of which were given jointly with visitors to the Commission.

966. The Spokesman's Service also conveyed to the press the Commission's position on the occasion of Council and European Council meetings and part-sessions of Parliament. Special arrangements were made for international events such as the Houston Western Economic Summit.[1]

967. More than 2 600 information memos and papers were released to the accredited press, while the Offices in the Member States and the Delegations in non-member countries received over 800 telexed memos and commentaries drafted specially for their use in keeping their press contacts informed.

Office for Official Publications

968. On the grounds of its experience in the field of computer-assisted publishing the Publications Office has been entrusted by its Management Committee with the task of coordinating and advising the institutions on the introduction and use of this technology with a view to the rationalization and interinstitutional harmonization of working methods.

The Office has also been asked by the Committee to carry out a study on the consolidation of amended Community legislation. As it has at its disposal all the original legislation in all the Community languages and the facilities for storing data in optical and electronic form, it hopes to be able to produce consolidated texts on request to meet the requirements not only of the Community institutions but also of the European public and of private publishers.

---

[1]   Point 691 of this Report.

The Office also played its part in a major rationalization exercise by assuming responsibility for the stock management of publications previously distributed free of charge by the Commission. In addition, as part of a new project entitled 'Videopub', the Publications Office is making available to the public a range of video-cassettes produced by the various European institutions. A catalogue has been produced of the titles in question.

To keep pace with the political changes which have taken place in Central and Eastern Europe since 1989, the Office has embarked on the extension of its network for the distribution of Community publications in that region and on the setting-up of the machinery needed to meet the demand for publications in the languages of the countries concerned.

Historical archives

969.   The Commission released the historical archives of the ECSC High Authority, the EEC Commission and the Euratom Commission for 1959 for consultation.[1] Under the 30-year rule,[2] the Commission has so far made accessible to the public some 15 500 files covering the period 1952 to 1959 in the case of the ECSC High Authority and 1958 and 1959 in the case of the EEC and Euratom Commissions. The rate of historical analysis, which was relatively slow in respect of the first few years of ECSC activity, has increased considerably, particularly now that information is being released on EEC and Euratom activity. Each year, between 3 000 and 5 000 files on the three Communities now have to be processed. In the interests of ease and rationalization, the Commission has established the Archis databank, which provides facilities for electronic data retrieval and for producing and publishing a variety of research and consultation aids.

---

[1]   The historical archives are deposited at the European University Institute in Florence.
[2]   OJ L 43, 15.2.1983; Seventeenth General Report, point 54.

Section 3

Statistics

970. Implemention of the priority action plan adopted in 1989 (statistical programme of the European Communities 1989-92)[1] was the focus of statistical activities in 1990. In February the Commission adopted a document on the coordination of statistical work and the role of the Statistical Office.[2] A preliminary progress report on implementation of the action plan was presented to the Commission and the national statistical institutes. The Commission made proposals for establishing a European advisory committee on statistical information in the economic and social spheres[3] and a committee on monetary, financial and balance-of-payments statistics.[4] Both proposals, which, once adopted, will bring in important changes on the statistical front, were endorsed by the Economic and Social Committee in October[5] and by Parliament in November[6] and December.[7]

German unification also had important consequences for statistics, since technical adjustments and transitional measures proved necessary for the rapid incorporation of the system used in the former German Democratic Republic.[8]

971. Coordination with the EFTA countries was further improved as progress towards an integrated statistical system for the European economic area gathered momentum.[9]

After the upheaval that took place in the course of the year, cooperation with Central and Eastern European countries was stepped up considerably as part of the coordinated assistance from the Group of 24,[10] Operation Phare[11] and bilateral measures by Member States. Statistics are a key factor in the development of all the countries now in transition from a centrally planned to a market economy.

---

[1]   OJ C 161, 28.6.1989; Twenty-third General Report, point 65.
[2]   Bull. EC 1/2-1990, point 1.5.6.
[3]   OJ C 208, 21.8.1990; Bull. EC 7/8-1990, point 1.7.2.
[4]   OJ C 212, 25.8.1990; Bull. EC 7/8-1990, point 1.7.3.
[5]   Bull. EC 10-1990, points 1.7.2. and 1.7.3.
[6]   OJ C 324, 24.12.1990; Bull. EC 11-1990, point 1.7.3.
[7]   OJ C 23, 28.1.1991; Bull. EC 12-1990.
[8]   Point 23 of this Report.
[9]   Point 688 of this Report.
[10] Point 668 of this Report.
[11] Point 669 of this Report.

Statistical work associated with the Single Act

972.   A Regulation on the statistical classification of economic activities in the European Communities (NACE) was adopted on 9 October.[1] This classification may be regarded as a cornerstone of the Community statistical system, particularly since the members of EFTA and the countries of Central and Eastern Europe are now studying the possibility of adopting it for their own statistical purposes. Work continued on a revised common product classification and on the review of the European System of Integrated Economic Accounts (ESA) and accounts for trade in goods and services and capital movements. In June the Council also adopted a Regulation on the transmission of data subject to statistical confidentiality to the Statistical Office, under which Member States are authorized to transmit confidential statistics on condition that all the necessary steps are taken to ensure confidentiality.[2]

973.   In May the Commission amended for the first time[3] its proposal for a Regulation on the statistics relating to the trading of goods between Member States[4] — one of a number of measures proposed on indirect taxation with a view to the removal of tax frontiers.[5] This proposal, on which the Economic and Social Committee delivered a second opinon in September,[6] was amended a second time by the Commission[7] before being considered by Parliament.[8]

974.   As provided for in the Directive on the harmonization of the compilation of gross national product at market prices (GNPmp),[9] work began on improving the comparability and reliability of GNPmp data.

975.   The review of business statistics continued with work on the standardization of business registers in the Member States. The *Panorama of EC industry,* a publication revamped in 1990, now provides easily accessible business statistics for a wide range of users.[10]

976.   On 18 July the Commission approved a proposal for a Decision adopting a four-year programme (1990-93) to develop regular official statistics on the environ-

[1]   OJ L 293, 24.10.1990; Bull. EC 10-1990, point 1.7.1. Commission proposal: OJ C 58, 8.3.1990; Bull. EC 1/2-1990, point 1.5.1.
[2]   OJ L 151, 15.6.1990; EC 6-1990, point 1.7.1. Commission proposal: OJ C 86, 7.4.1989; Twenty-third General Report, point 66.
[3]   OJ C 177, 18.7.1990; Bull. EC 5-1990, point 1.2.5.
[4]   OJ C 41, 18.2.1989; Twenty-second General Report, point 69.
[5]   Point 156 of this Report.
[6]   Bull. EC 9-1990, point 1.6.3.
[7]   OJ C 254, 9.10.1990; Bull. EC 9-1990, point 1.6.3.
[8]   OJ C 324, 24.12.1990; Bull. EC 11-1990, point 1.7.2.
[9]   OJ L 49, 21.2.1989; Twenty-third General Report, point 68.
[10]   Point 212 of this Report.

ment.[1] This was endorsed by the Economic and Social Committee in September.[2]

Statistical support for common policies

977.   Eurostat continued its efforts both to improve coordination with the national statistical institutes by establishing efficient channels of communication and to support the measures taken by certain Member States to improve their statistical systems: the Council adopted a Decision[3] extending the current programme for the restructuring of the system of agricultural surveys in Greece[4] for a further three years; the corresponding support programmes for Italy and Ireland are still under way.[5]

The Commission made a contribution from the European Regional Development Fund to provide technical support for improving Portugal's regional statistics (Preder); this should bring about large-scale improvements in the entire Portuguese statistical system. Similar measures are being taken under the Phare programme to help restructure the statistical system in the former German Democratic Republic.[6]

978.   Against the background of the agricultural stabilizers[7] the Council adopted a Regulation concerning statistical information to be supplied by the Member States on cereals production.[8] The object of the exercise is to speed up the communication of harmonized data by the Member States and to increase their reliability. In April Parliament delivered a favourable opinion[9] on the proposal for a Regulation on the submission of data on the landings of fishery products.[10] In October the Commission amended[11] its 1973 Decision laying down detailed rules for statistical surveys of bovine livestock.[12] In the same month it also adopted its report on the surveys of the earnings of full-time and seasonal workers in the agricultural sector[13] as required by the 1988 Directive.[14]

---

[1]   OJ C 209, 22.8.1990; Bull. EC 7/8-1990, point 1.7.1.
[2]   Bull. EC 9-1990, point 1.6.2.
[3]   OJ L 190, 21.7.1990; Bull. EC 7/8-1990, point 1.7.4. Commission proposal: OJ C 135, 2.6.1990; Bull. EC 5-1990, point 1.6.2.
[4]   OJ L 191, 23.7.1985; Nineteenth General Report, point 71.
[5]   OJ L 359, 8.12.1989; Twenty-third General Report, point 72.
[6]   Bull. EC 9-1990, point 1.1.8.
[7]   OJ L 110, 29.4.1988; OJ L 132, 28.5.1988; Twenty-second General Report, point 625.
[8]   OJ L 88, 3.4.1990; Bull. EC 3-1990, point 1.5.2. Commission proposal: OJ C 8, 13.1.1990; Twenty-third General Report, point 72.
[9]   OJ C 113, 7.5.1990; Bull. EC 4-1990, point 1.5.1.
[10]   OJ C 214, 21.8.1989; Twenty-third General Report, point 72.
[11]   OJ L 278, 10.10.1990; Bull. EC 10-1990, point 1.7.4.
[12]   OJ L 253, 19.10.1973.
[13]   Bull. EC 10-1990, point 1.7.5.
[14]   OJ L 309, 15.11.1988; Twenty-second General Report, point 74.

979.   In December the Council decided to implement a multiannual programme for the development of Community statistics on tourism.[1]

980.   In December the Commission adopted a proposal for a Decision on the establishment of a European system for observing the markets for inland goods transport.[2]

981.   Pursuant to the Council Directive on energy prices[3] work began on the collection of data to improve the transparency of the electricity and gas markets. Preparatory work also began on similar statistics for coal and renewable forms of energy.

982.   The first database for steel statistics, which makes extensive use of modern telecommunications technology, is now fully operational. Work also continued on the improvement of several statistical questionnaires in line with the Decision adopted by the Commission in 1988.[4]

983.   In the field of external relations the Sectoral Production and Income Model for Agriculture (SPEL), as adapted for international trade, became fully operational and was used for the purposes of the Uruguay Round.[5] Under the technical cooperation programme with developing countries further assistance was provided not only to the ACP countries but also to the Mediterranean countries and Latin America.

---

[1]   OJ L 358, 21.12.1990; Bull. EC 12-1990; Commission proposal: OJ C 150, 19.6.1990; Bull. EC 5-1990, point 1.6.3.
[2]   Point 560 of this Report.
[3]   Point 601 of this Report.
[4]   OJ L 365, 30.12.1988; Twenty-second General Report, point 76.
[5]   Point 817 *et seq.* of this Report.

Section 4

Financing Community activities

Priority activities and objectives

984.   Community budgetary and financial policy faced a double challenge in 1990 since it has to cater for the development of the Community's internal policies and at the same time assume the responsibilities deriving from its growing international role. The budgetary procedure for 1991 was conducted in strict compliance with the provisions of the Interinstitutional Agreement of June 1988 although the changing international situation also had to be taken into account. The Community's budgetary options can therefore be analysed in two groups — the internal options and the external options.

The internal options mainly concern the priority given to the policies considered decisive for the establishment of a coherent Europe. First, agricultural expenditure has to be contained. Then, the development of structural operations must continue on course towards the doubling of the Funds by 1992 and various activities connected with the completion of the internal market, such as those in the transport, environment, energy, audiovisual and vocational training sectors, have to be given a boost.

The external options were enhanced by the revision of the financial perspective adopted in June, mainly to provide active support for the countries of Central and Eastern Europe as they progress towards a democratic system[1] and to boost cooperation with the Mediterranean countries[2] and with the developing countries of Asia and Latin America.[3] The Community also demonstrated that it was able to respond to the changes which occurred in the course of the year. The financial implications of German unification were incorporated into the financial and budget forecasts within a remarkably short period after the process gathered speed in the second half of the year.[4] The financial perspective was revised in December to raise the ceiling by a total of ECU 875 million in 1991 and ECU 1 150 million in 1992. The additional requirements were formally entered in the 1991 budget when letter of amendment No 1 was finally adopted on 13 December. The Community also reacted immediately to the Gulf crisis and granted the victims emergency

---

[1]   Point 669 of this Report.
[2]   Point 718 of this Report.
[3]   Point 763 of this Report.
[4]   Point 20 of this Report.

aid;[1] *in order to finance this aid in 1990 and from 1991 onwards, a complex budgetary package had to be put together, which the Community institutions completed in the final quarter with the adoption of an* ad hoc *revision of the financial perspective on 11 December. As a result financial aid of ECU 500 million can now be granted in 1991 to the countries most directly affected by the Gulf crisis and the ECU 30 million transferred from the appropriations intended for the countries of Latin America to provide this aid in 1990 can now be returned.*

Budgets

1990 financial year

985.   The budget for 1990 was finally adopted on 13 December 1989 following the trialogue meeting between the Council, Parliament and the Commission on 11 December.[2] It was decided to enter a negative reserve of ECU 38.4 million in respect of appropriations in heading 4 of the financial perspective in order to finance new policies; to cover this reserve a 2% freeze was imposed on all items coming under heading 4 with allocations in excess of ECU 1 million. Some of the frozen appropriations were released by the omnibus transfer in October in connection with the Notenboom procedure[3] and the remainder at the very end of the year.

986.   There were three supplementary and amending budgets to the 1990 budget:

(i) Supplementary and amending budget No 1, adopted by Parliament on 16 February,[4] provided the Community budget guarantee for the first tranche of a medium-term loan to Hungary[5] and for loans by the European Investment Bank to Poland and Hungary;[6]

(ii) Supplementary and amending budget No 2 enabled part of the 1989 surplus of ECU 2 517 million to be entered in the budget; it was finally adopted by Parliament on 11 July[7] despite the Council's objections.[8] In its resolution[9] Parliament argued that the supplementary and amending budget should reflect the own resources Decision[10] and in particular the provisions concerning application of a uniform VAT rate and that

[1]   Point 734 of this Report.
[2]   OJ L 24, 29.1.1990; Twenty-third General Report, point 88.
[3]   OJ C 284, 12.11.1990; Bull. EC 10-1990, point 1.6.2.
[4]   OJ L 62, 12.3.1990; Bull. EC 1/2-1990, point 1.4.2.
[5]   Point 50 of this Report.
[6]   Point 49 of this Report.
[7]   OJ L 239, 3.9.1990; Bull. EC 7/8-1990, point 1.6.4.
[8]   Bull. EC 5-1990, point 1.5.3.
[9]   OJ C 175, 16.7.1990; Bull. EC 6-1990, point 1.6.4; OJ C 231, 17.9.1990; Bull. EC 7/8-1990, point 1.6.2.
[10] OJ L 185, 15.7.1988; Twenty-second General Report, point 102.

Article 203 allowed it to amend the revenue section of the budget. The Council decided
to challenge Parliament's interpretation of these two points before the Court of Justice, [1]
claiming that the budget adopted did not comply with the provisions of the Financial
Regulation[2] as it did not take account of the whole of the balance carried over from
1989 and that the Treaty did not explicitly allow Parliament to amend the statement
of revenue in the budget. Two letters of amendment to this preliminary draft
supplementary and amending budget were presented, the first[3] increasing the Commission's administrative appropriations by ECU 15 million and those of the Court of
Auditors by ECU 340 800 and readjusting the final balance for 1989 to ECU 5 080
million, and the second[4] increasing the economic assistance to the countries of Central
and Eastern Europe by ECU 200 million in commitment appropriations and by
ECU 50 million in payment appropriations, in line with the revision of the financial
perspective for 1990 adopted in June;[5]

(iii) Supplementary and amending budget No 3 increased the Council's administrative
appropriations by ECU 3.8 million and covered payment of an additional ECU 160.7
million in refunds to Spain and Portugal resulting from the adjustment of the bases for
the calculation of GNP-based resources and VAT from previous years. Parliament
declared this budget finally adopted on 13 December.[6]

Implementation of the 1990 budget

987.   The rates of utilization of appropriations in 1990 are shown in Tables 17 and 18.
With an average of 92.3 for commitment appropriations and 91.4 for payment appropriations, overall performance is satisfactory. This year again there is a surplus of ECU
1 387 million for agricultural expenditure (heading 1) after major internal adjustments.
However, in contrast with previous years, actual expenditure has moved much closer
to the ceiling for the heading as the international market situation has deteriorated.[7]
Implementation of administrative expenditure, on the other hand, has been subject to
particularly tight constraints: to offset the decline in the value of the ecu against the
Belgian franc and Luxembourg franc, the administrative appropriations for the Commission, the Court of Justice and the Council had to be increased in supplementary and
amending budgets No 2 and No 3,[8] and the margin available within the ceiling for
heading 5 to finance refunds to Spain and Portugal was used up.[8]

---

[1]   Bull. EC 7/8-1990, point 1.6.4.
[2]   Point 1003 of this Report.
[3]   Bull. EC 6-1990, point 1.6.5. Commission proposal: Bull. EC 5-1990, point 1.5.4.
[4]   Bull. EC 6-1990, point 1.6.6.
[5]   Point 988 of this Report.
[6]   OJ C 19, 28.1.1991; Bull. EC 12-1990. Commission's preliminary draft: Bull. EC 10-1990, point 1.6.3.
[7]   Points 463 and 468 of this Report.
[8]   Point 986 of this Report.

1991 financial year

Preliminary draft budget for 1991

988.   The Commission adopted the preliminary draft budget for 1991 on 13 June for transmission to the budgetary authority.[1] The breakdown of appropriations between the various headings of the financial perspective is shown in Table 19.

Political presentation of the budget

989.   The budgetary procedure for 1991 was marked by the decision in June to revise and adjust the financial perspective for 1990-92.[2] In adopting this revision, the Community institutions showed their determination to adjust political priorities to changes inside and outside the Community, in full compliance with the principles of budgetary discipline and the Interinstitutional Agreement.[3] This revision had three objectives which were reflected in the preliminary draft budget: to provide active support for the political and economic changes in Central and Eastern Europe; to increase cooperation with the Mediterranean countries and the countries of Asia and Latin America; to promote the completion of the internal market by stepping up certain policies accompanying implementation of the Single Act. The changes in the financial perspective increased the ceiling for heading 4 by over 50% from ECU 2 180 million to ECU 3 355 million for 1991.

Apart from the ECU 820 million earmarked for Central and Eastern Europe, this increase provided a considerable boost for the Commission's priority policies. The ceiling for heading 2 was raised by ECU 247 million, of which ECU 90 million related to the difference between the original forecasts and the current estimates of the rate of inflation. The ceiling for heading 5 was reduced by ECU 40 million, thereby further restricting the already limited margin of manoeuvre for administrative expenditure.

Revenue

990.   The preliminary draft budget was drawn up in accordance with the Decision on the own resources system.[4] Own resources came to ECU 52 970 million (as against ECU 46 767 million in 1990), around 1.06% of Community GNP compared with the

---

[1]   Bull. EC 6-1990, point 1.6.1.
[2]   Point 992 of this Report.
[3]   OJ L 185, 15.7.1988; Twenty-second General Report, point 84.
[4]   OJ L 185, 15.7.1988; Twenty-second General Report, point 102.

1.19% ceiling of own resources which may be called in for 1991. The uniform VAT call-in rate was 1.2179%, i.e. a little lower than the 1990 rate of 1.2465%. The uniform call-in rate for the GNP-based resource was 0.1574%.

Expenditure

991.   Compared with the general budget for 1990,[1] the appropriations for commitments in the preliminary draft budget for 1991 increased by around 13% from ECU 49 047 million to ECU 55 472 million. The proportion accounted for by agricultural expenditure remained roughly the same (54.7% in 1991 as against 54.08% in 1990) and at ECU 30 356 million the amount was well within the agricultural guideline of ECU 32 511 million for 1991 despite the appreciable increase (14.5%) on 1990. The allocation for structural operations was 20.5% higher than in 1990, reflecting the special political priority the Commission attaches to this field. In 1991 the appropriations allocated to the structural Funds will, for the first time, account for over a quarter of the Community budget: the cohesion effort behind the reform[2] is to continue and at the same time the objective of doubling the Funds by 1992-93 will be respected. Appropriations for the integrated Mediterranean programmes amount to ECU 330 million; this leaves a further ECU 350 million in 1992 to reach the total of ECU 1.6 billion planned for 1985-92.[3] The high rate of increase in research expenditure (up by 17.2%) reflects the importance of this activity for the Community's future development. The overall budget for other policies (heading 4) was raised by 28.2%, to permit a substantial increase for policies to which the Commission attaches particular importance, such as cooperation with the countries of Central and Eastern Europe, the Mediterranean countries and the countries of Asia and Latin America and the policies in support of the Single European Act. Finally, despite a 10% increase which at first sight seems generous, the allocation for administrative expenditure will impose severe constraints on the functioning of the institutions.

Five-year financial perspective

992.   The turbulent international situation in which the 1991 budgetary procedure took place had various repercussions on the financial perspective for 1988-92 contained in the 1988 Interinstitutional Agreement.[4]

---

[1]   OJ L 24, 29.1.1990; Twenty-third General Report, point 82.
[2]   OJ L 185, 15.7.1988; OJ L 374, 31.12.1988; Twenty-second General Report, points 533 and 534.
[3]   OJ L 197, 27.7.1985; Nineteenth General Report, points 465 to 468.
[4]   OJ L 185, 15.7.1988; Twenty-second General Report, point 84.

A first revision, adopted by Parliament on 7 June,[1] was intended to accommodate the Community's major policy guidelines resulting from its growing role on the international stage and the need to boost certain policies linked with the implementation of the Single Act.[2] On the same date Parliament also adopted an adjustment to the financial perspective[3] so that appropriations for policies with multiannual allocations in headings 2 and 3 could be transferred to 1991 and 1992 in accordance with points 10 and 11 of the Interinstitutional Agreement. The preliminary draft budget for 1991[4] was based on this revision and adjustment, which affect headings 2, 3, 4 and 5 in 1991 and 1992. As part of this revision, the aid for the economic restructuring of the countries of Central and Eastern Europe was also increased by ECU 200 million. Letter of amendment No 2 to supplementary and amending budget No 2 put this into effect.[5]

Because of the speed with which the process of German unification was completed and the consequences of the Gulf crisis, the Commission proposed two further changes to the financial perspective on 19 September. The first change,[6] based on point 4 of the Interinstitutional Agreement, was to provide financial cover for the enlargement of Community territory resulting from German unification. It concerns the final two years of the agreement (1991 and 1992) and provides for an increase in headings 2, 4 and 5 totalling ECU 875 million in 1991 and ECU 1 150 million in 1992. The second change,[7] based on point 12 of the Interinstitutional Agreement, is designed to allow financial assistance to be provided in 1991 to countries affected by the Gulf crisis (ECU 500 million) and to restore to the appropriations for cooperation with the countries of Latin America the ECU 30 million taken from there in 1990 to grant emergency aid. A third change[8] added ECU 180 million to heading 5 to finance the balance of the refunds to Spain and Portugal not covered by supplementary and amending budget No 3. These three revisions formed part of an overall package negotiated at two meetings of the trialogue on 15 and 28 November.

The decision to revise the financial perspective finally adopted on 11 December[9] thus involves the following changes: the ceiling for heading 2 is raised by ECU 750 million for 1991 and by ECU 100 million for 1992; the ceiling for heading 3 is lowered by ECU 50 million for 1991; the ceiling for heading 4 is raised by ECU 665 million for 1991 and by ECU 110 million for 1992. This allows ECU 40 million to be entered for 1991 to set up a Community initiative programme (Perifra) within the Regional Fund and ECU 30 million is entered for a new financial instrument for the environment (LIFE).

---

[1]   Bull. EC 6-1990, point 1.6.3. Commission proposal: Bull. EC 1/2-1990, point 1.4.1.
[2]   Point 989 of this Report.
[3]   Bull. EC 6-1990, point 1.6.2.
[4]   Point 988 of this Report.
[5]   Point 986 of this Report.
[6]   Bull. EC 9-1990, point 1.5.1.
[7]   Bull. EC 9-1990, point 1.5.2.
[8]   Bull. EC 12-1990.

The ceiling for heading 5 remains the same — the increase of ECU 40 million for administrative expenditure in 1991 and 1992 and ECU 180 million in 1991 for expenditure on refunds to Spain and Portugal is offset by a corresponding reduction for the stock disposal subheading.

Table 20 shows the financial perspective as adjusted and revised.

TABLE 20

Financial perspective 1988-92
(Appropriations for commitments)

million ECU

	1988	1989	1990	1991	1992
	Current prices				Constant 1991 prices
1. EAGGF Guarantee[1]	27 500	28 613	30 700	33 000	33 750
2. Structural operations	7 790	9 522	11 555	14 804	16 598
3. Policies with multiannual allocations[2]	1 210	1 708	2 071	2 466	2 820
4. Other policies[1]	2 103	2 468	3 229	4 920	4 933
of which: non-compulsory	1 646	1 864	2 523	4 010	3 976
5. Repayments and administration	5 700	5 153	4 930	4 559	3 936
of which: stock disposal	1 240	1 449	1 523	1 378	1 108
6. Monetary reserve[3]	1 000	1 000	1 000	1 000	1 000
Total	45 303	48 464	53 485	60 749	63 036
of which:[4] compulsory	33 698	33 764	35 454	37 579	37 771
non-compulsory	11 605	14 700	18 031	23 170	25 265
Appropriations for payments required	43 779	46 885	51 291	58 035	60 181
of which: compulsory	33 640	33 745	35 372	37 506	37 546
non-compulsory	10 139	13 140	15 919	20 529	22 635
Appropriations for payments required as % of GNP	1.12	1.07	1.09	1.12	1.13

[1] In accordance with the joint declaration by the three institutions on the adoption of the revision of the Financial Regulation and to ensure the proper financing of food aid without having to revise the financial perspective, compliance with the ceilings for headings 1 and 4 in 1990 and heading 5 in 1991 and 1992 will not prevent a transfer between the headings in Article 292 of the budget (Refunds in connection with Community food aid) and Chapter 92 (Food aid). This means that these transfers will not be included with the total appropriations to be taken into consideration for complying with the ceilings of the financial perspective. The criteria for examining these transfers are those agreed by the Council, Parliament and the Commission in their declaration of 12 February 1990.
[2] Chapter F on budget estimates of the European Council indicates a figure of ECU 2 400 million (1988 prices) for policies with multiannual allocations in 1992. The policies in question are research and development and integrated Mediterranean programmes. Only expenditure for which a legal basis exists may be financed under this heading. The present framework programme provides a legal basis for research expenditure of ECU 863 million (current prices) for 1992. The Regulation on integrated Mediterranean programmes provides a legal basis for an estimated amount of ECU 300 million in 1992 (current prices). The two arms of the budgetary authority undertake to respect the principle that further budget appropriations within this ceiling for 1990, 1991 and 1992 will require a revision of the existing framework programme or, before the end of 1991, a decision on a new framework programme based on a proposal from the Commission in accordance with the legislative provisions in Article 130q of the Single European Act.
[3] At current prices.
[4] Based on the classification in the preliminary draft budget for 1990. The amendments resulting from decisions by the budgetary authority to change classification will be implemented as a technical adjustment under point 9 of the Agreement.

Budget procedure

993. On 27 July the Council adopted the draft budget for 1991 on first reading.[1] It granted all the appropriations requested by the Commission for aid for the economic restructuring of Central and Eastern Europe and the appropriations proposed for the structural Funds. However, it made severe cuts in areas which the Commission considered to be priorities such as transport, the environment, completion of the internal market and the development of cooperation with Latin America.

994. At its first reading on 25 October[2] Parliament stressed that the 1991 budget should incorporate the requirements resulting from the integration of the new German *Länder* in the Community. It entered in the draft a new heading relating to a financial instrument for the environment (LIFE). Parliament's draft also contained the Perifra programme for the remote regions most affected by the exceptional events of 1990. In the research sector, Parliament made substantial increases for the second framework programme and activities outside the programme. Overall, Parliament's draft allowed an increase of appropriations of around 2.2% in relation to the Commission's preliminary draft and of 3.5% in relation to the Council's draft (in commitment appropriations).

995. On 19 November the Council accepted the increase which Parliament requested for various appropriations for transport, the environment, training and development aid.[3] It also accepted token entries for the two new headings for LIFE and Perifra.

996. It was only after the decision to revise the financial perspective was adopted on 11 December[4] that Parliament was able to declare the 1991 budget finally adopted on 13 December.[5] With the changes made by letter of amendment No 1,[6] this budget covers the additional requirements linked with German unification (ECU 1 315 million for agricultural expenditure, ECU 900 million for the structural Funds and ECU 100 million for other policies in commitment appropriations) and those for the countries affected by the Gulf crisis (ECU 500 million). The 1991 budget thus comes to ECU 58 535.3 million in commitment appropriations and ECU 55 556 million in payment appropriations.

---

[1] Bull. EC 7/8-1990, point 1.6.1.
[2] OJ C 295, 26.11.1990; Bull. EC 10-1990, point 1.6.1.
[3] Bull. EC 11-1990, point 1.6.3.
[4] Point 992 of this Report.
[5] OJ C 19, 28.1.1991; Bull. EC 12-1990.
[6] Bull. EC 12-1990.

ECSC budget

997.   After taking note of Parliament's opinion[1] and after informing the ECSC Consultative Committee, the Commission decided on 18 December to reduce the ECSC levy rate for 1991 from 0.31 to 0.29% and adopted the ECSC operating budget for 1991 on this basis.[2] The foreseeable resources (levy, net balance from previous years, fines, cancellations and budgetary resources not used the previous year), estimated at ECU 482 million, should cover the ECSC's requirements, which break down as follows (million ECU):

Administrative expenditure	5
Redeployment aid	145
Aid for research	135
Interest subsidies on ECSC loans (Articles 54 and 56)	127
Social measures (steel)	20
Social measures (coal)	50

Own resources

1990 financial year

998.   Since Parliament did not enter the entire balance from 1989 in the second of the three supplementary and amending budgets adopted in the course of the year on the grounds that this would have resulted in a lower VAT rate than that provided for in the 1988 Decision on own resources, the Council referred this budget to the Court of Justice with a request that it be declared null and void.[3]

999.   In 1990 own resources assigned to the Community totalled ECU 42 290.9 million, the equivalent of 1.01% of GNP. The revenue for 1990 is shown in Table 21.

---

[1]   OJ C 19, 28.1.1991; Bull. EC 12-1990.
[2]   OJ L 357, 20.12.1990; Bull. EC 12-1990; Commission *aide-mémoire*: Bull. EC 7/8-1990, point 1.6.9; Bull. EC 10-1990, point 1.6.5; Bull. EC 11-1990, point 1.6.5.
[3]   Point 986 of this Report.

1991 financial year

1000.   The 1991 budget will be financed in accordance with Council Decision 88/376/EEC, Euratom on the system of the Communities' own resources.[1] An estimate of the additional revenue in the Community budget resulting from German unification was incorporated in the 1991 budget by means of letter of amendment No 1.[2] Foreseeable revenue for 1991 is shown in Table 21.

TABLE 21

Budget revenue

million ECU

	1990 Outturn	1991 Estimates
Agricultural levies	1 173.4	1 260.8
Sugar and isoglucose levies	910.6	1 288.2
Customs duties	11 427.9	13 277.6
Own resources collection costs	(−)1 351.2	(−)1 582.7
VAT own resources	27 440.1	30 522.2
Financial contributions	—	—
GNP-based own resources	94.3	8 471.8
Balance of VAT and GNP-based own resources from previous years	1 720.0	token entry
Budget balance from previous year	4 464.2	1 986.6
Other revenue	411.0	331.6
Total	46 290.9	55 556.1
	% of GNP	
Maximum own resources which may be assigned to the budget	1.18	1.19
Own resources actually assigned to the budget	1.01	1.07

---

[1]   OJ L 185, 15.7.1988; Twenty-second General Report, point 102.
[2]   Point 996 of this Report.

Budgetary powers

Discharge procedure for previous years

1001. On 3 April Parliament adopted a package of decisions[1] and resolutions[2] completing the procedure for giving discharge to the Community institutions and other bodies (general budget, ECSC management, EDF, the Centre for the Development of Vocational Training and the Foundation for the Improvement of Living and Working Conditions) for 1988. In a resolution accompanying the decision giving the Commission discharge in respect of the implementation of the budget, Parliament underlined the role which the Commission had played in preparing the decisions taken by the Brussels European Council in February 1988.[3]

1002. On 31 May the Commission sent the budgetary authority and the Court of Auditors the revenue and expenditure account and balance sheet for 1989 together with the report on action taken in response to the observations contained in Parliament's resolution accompanying the decision on the discharge in respect of the implementation of the 1987 budget.[4]

Changes to financial regulations

General Financial Regulation

1003. On 13 March the Council adopted Regulation (Euratom, ECSC, EEC) No 619/90[5] amending the Financial Regulation of 21 December 1977 applicable to the general budget of the Communities.[6] This general revision is an essential adjunct to the reform of the Community's finances laid down by the European Council of February 1988[7] as it improves the conditions under which the general budget is drawn up and implemented: a number of provisions have been updated, additions have been made to the old text because of the development of certain policies and appropriate measures have been provided for to improve relations between the institutions and modernize

---

[1] OJ L 174, 7.7.1990; Bull. EC 4-1990, points 1.4.6 to 1.4.10. Council recommendations: OJ L 73, 20.3.1990; Bull. EC 3-1990, points 1.4.2 to 1.4.5.
[2] OJ C 113, 7.5.1990; Bull. EC 4-1990, points 1.4.6 and 1.4.8.
[3] Twenty-second General Report, point 80 to 84.
[4] OJ C 120, 16.5.1989; Twenty-third General Report, point 97.
[5] OJ L 70, 16.3.1990; Bull. EC 3-1990, point 1.4.6; Commission proposal: OJ C 115, 8.5.1989; Twenty-second General Report, point 117.
[6] OJ L 356, 31.12.1977; Eleventh General Report, point 62 to 64.
[7] Twenty-second General Report, point 82 to 84.

financial management. On 29 November the Commission adopted a package of proposals to bring the rules on the Centre for the Development of Vocational Training and the European Foundation for the Improvement of Living and Working Conditions into line with the new provisions of the Financial Regulation. [1]

Budgetary nomenclature

1004.   The preliminary draft budget for 1991 [2] applies the new budgetary nomenclature deriving from the revised Financial Regulation. [3] It increases transparency and makes the budget easier to read. It also brings budget headings more closely into line with the headings of the financial perspective. The budgetary authority had a subsection set aside for budget headings making up mini-budgets for operations contained in the other subsections of Part B.

Sectoral rules

1005.   The Commission adopted two regulations laying down detailed rules for the use of the ecu and rules concerning the interest to be paid when undue amounts are recovered as part of the budgetary implementation of the structural Funds. [4]

Financial Control

1006.   Following the reform of the structural Funds [5] and taking account of the Commission's guidelines, Financial Control stepped up its audit of the management and control systems operated by each Member State, and the organization of on-the-spot inspections during and after operations to check that the arrangements are being applied correctly, detect any shortcomings, propose remedies and assess the cost/benefit trade-off or cost-effectiveness of the programmes financed. The seminars organized in a number of Member States (Italy, Portugal, Spain, France) on the management, financing and control of the Funds made a substantial contribution to better mutual understanding concerning application of the principles of subsidiarity and partnership and to the identification of possible improvements.

---

[1]   Bull. EC 11-1990, point 1.6.4.
[2]   Point 989 of this Report.
[3]   Point 1008 of this Report.
[4]   Point 323 of this Report.
[5]   OJ L 185, 15.7.1988; OJ L 374, 31.12.1988; Twenty-second General Report, points 533 and 534.

1007.   In accordance with the Commission decision of 7 June on the financial controller's role as an internal auditor, Financial Control started its activities in this sector; its audit programme will be stepped up in the years ahead. The purpose of this internal audit is to assure the Commission that the systems and methods of financial management available within its departments function properly.

1008.   Following the latest revision of the Financial Regulation,[1] a great deal of attention has been given to developing the application of the concepts of cost-benefit and cost-effectiveness; this included a seminar on the subject and an internal training programme.

Action to combat fraud

1009.   In 1990 the Commission stepped up its anti-fraud activities.

On 31 January it presented its first annual report on the progress made in this field in 1989.[2] The Council again demonstrated its support for the Commission's actions in a positive and encouraging statement on the need to continue these efforts and reinforce current measures.[3] This report was favourably received by Parliament and discussed at length with the Member States. The Member States were also informed of the progress made within the Community Committee for the Coordination of Fraud Prevention, which met in February and July.

1010.   The work programme[4] drawn up by the Commission ensures that this progress can be measured and continues to serve as a reference for the Community's fraud prevention policy. The developments which will be set out in the second annual report covering 1990 include the establishment of a group of experts to examine agricultural legislation with a view to possible simplification,[5] the adoption of a communication laying down rules of procedure and internal rules on fraud prevention at legislative level as part of the improvement of internal coordination,[6] the drafting of a code of conduct for the notification of fraud and irregularities under the structural Funds,[7] which has been accepted by all the Member States after discussions within the Community Committee for the Coordination of Fraud Prevention, and the stepping-up of investigations by the Commission's fraud prevention departments in high-risk CAP sectors.

---

[1]   Point 1003 of this Report.
[2]   Bull. EC 1/2-1990, point 1.4.16.
[3]   Bull. EC 3-1990, point 1.4.9.
[4]   Twenty-third General Report, point 104.
[5]   Bull. EC 4-1990, point 1.4.10.
[6]   Bull. EC 4-1990, point 1.4.17.
[7]   Bull. EC 7/8-1990, point 1.6.17.

On 8 May the Commission also adopted a communication[1] on the judgment by the Court of Justice in Case 68/88,[2] in which it draws attention to the Court's new case-law, which obliges Member States to ensure that infringements of Community law are penalized in the same way as infringements of national law in similar cases.

Borrowing and lending operations

1011. Table 22 shows the loans granted each year from 1988 to 1990.

Borrowing operations during the year totalled ECU 12 455.1 million, of which ECU 31.3 million was to refinance earlier operations.

TABLE 22

Loans granted

million ECU

Instrument	1988	1989	1990
New Community Instrument[1]	356.5	78.3	23.6
EEC balance-of-payments loans[1]	—	—	350
ECSC[1]	907.8	700.1	993.8
Euratom[1]	—	—	—
EIB (from the Bank's own resources)	9 638.4	12 041.8	13 325.9
of which: loans to Community countries[2]	9 118.3	11 555.9	12 656.9
loans to ACP countries and overseas territories	(129.1)	(155.1)	117.5
loans to Mediterranean countries[1]	(391.0)	(330.8)	336.5
loans to Eastern Europe	—	—	215
Total	10 902.7	13 306.1	14 693.3

[1] With partial or total guarantee from the general budget.

[2] With no guarantee from the general budget.

[1] Bull. EC 5-1990, point 1.5.10.
[2] Judgment of 21 September 1989 in Case 68/88 *Commission* v *Greece* (OJ C 266, 18.10.1989; Twenty-third General Report, point 956).

Operations concerning the New Community Instrument

New Community Instrument

1012. In 1990 the EIB, acting on behalf of the Community, granted loans totalling ECU 23.6 million under the New Community Instrument.[1] The loans were in the form of global loans to intermediary financial institutions for on-lending to small and medium-sized firms to promote investment. Since 1979 loans totalling ECU 6 347.2 million have been made under the NCI.

1013. During the year NCI borrowing operations totalled ECU 23.6 million (as against ECU 521.5 million in 1989, including ECU 353.9 million for refinancing).

EEC — Balance of payments

1014. Following the Council's decision to grant Hungary medium-term financial assistance up to a maximum of ECU 870 million in a number of tranches,[2] the Commission raised ECU 350 million for the first tranche. An interest-rate swap arrangement was concluded so that the loan finally granted carries a variable rate of interest.

Financing ECSC activities

1015. Eligibility for ECSC loans was extended to Poland and Hungary and a further extension to Czechoslovakia, Bulgaria and Yugoslavia was also proposed.[3]

1016. During 1990 the Commission continued to support coal and steel industry investment through ECSC financial loans totalling ECU 398.3 million.

ECSC loans paid out in 1990 totalled ECU 993.8 million, compared with ECU 700.1 million in 1989.

Loans for the steel industry rose from ECU 152.4 million in 1989 to ECU 213 million in 1990. Loans for the coal industry totalled ECU 30.1 million, while loans for investments to promote the consumption of Community steel under the second paragraph of Article 54 of the ECSC Treaty amounted to ECU 155.2 million.

1017. The ECSC continued to look to the capital market for funds, raising a total of ECU 1 058.9 million, including ECU 31.3 million to refinance earlier operations (com-

---

[1]   OJ L 71, 14.3.1987; Twenty-first General Report, point 141.
[2]   Point 50 of this Report.
[3]   Point 51 of this Report.

pared with ECU 913.3 million in 1989, including ECU 186.4 million to refinance earlier operations).

Financing Euratom activities

1018. In view of the unfavourable situation in the industry, there were no loan operations in 1990 despite the fact that the Council raised the authorized ceiling by ECU 1 billion.[1]

The grand total of loans since such operations began in 1977 is now ECU 2 753.1 million (at the exchange rates obtaining when contracts were signed).

European Investment Bank

1019. Since the activities of the European Investment Bank — an autonomous Community institution — in 1990 are described in its annual report, only the main figures are set out here.[2]

Financing operations by the Bank in 1990 both inside and outside the Community amounted to ECU 13 325.9 million from its own resources and ECU 67.5 million from resources supplied by the Community, a total of ECU 13 393.4 million compared with ECU 12 246.1 million in 1989.

1020. In 1990 the first operations took place in the new German *Länder*,[3] Poland and Hungary.[4] The EIB also took part as a founder member in the creation of the European Bank for Reconstruction and Development.[5]

At its annual meeting on 11 June the Board of Governors decided to increase the Bank's subscribed capital from ECU 28.8 billion to ECU 57.6 billion on 1 January 1991. This doubling of its capital will enable the EIB to continue to develop its activities to promote Community policies and at the same time keep its top-class credit rating.

1021. Loans granted for projects in the Community totalled ECU 12 656.9 million from the Bank's own resources and ECU 23.6 million from NCI resources, a total of

---

[1]   Point 48 of this Report.
[2]   Copies of the report and of other publications relating to the Bank's work and its operations can be obtained from the main office (100 boulevard Konrad Adenauer, L-2950 Luxembourg, tel. 43 79-1) or from its offices in Belgium (rue de la Loi 227, B-1040 Brussels, tel. 230 98 90), Italy (Via Sardegna 38, I-00187 Rome, tel. 47 19-1), the United Kingdom (68 Pall Mall, London SW1Y 5ES, tel. 839 3351), Greece (Amalias 12, GR-10557 Athens, tel. 32 20 773, 32 20 774 or 32 20 775), Spain (Calle J. Ortega y Gasset 29, E-28006 Madrid, tel. 431 1340) and Portugal (144-156 Avenida de Liberdade, 8°, P-1200 Lisbon, tel. 342 89 89).
[3]   Point 20 of this Report.
[4]   Twenty-third General Report, points 118 and 145.
[5]   Point 54 of this Report.

ECU 12 680.5 million compared with ECU 11 634.2 million in 1989 and ECU 9 474.8 million in 1988. The breakdown by country is shown in Table 23.

TABLE 23

EIB loans in the Community in 1990

	From own resources (million ECU)	From NCI resources (million ECU)	Total	
			(million ECU)	%
Belgium	182.8	23.6	206.4	1.6
Denmark	564.7	0.0	564.7	4.5
Germany	863.5	0.0	863.5	6.8
Greece	176.3	0.0	176.3	1.4
Spain	1 942.0	0.0	1 942.0	15.3
France	1 684.6	0.0	1 684.6	13.3
Ireland	217.7	0.0	217.7	1.7
Italy	3 855.7	0.0	3 855.7	30.4
Luxembourg	11.8	0.0	11.8	0.1
Netherlands	245.3	0.0	245.3	1.9
Portugal	794.7	0.0	794.7	6.3
United Kingdom	1 892.8	0.0	1 892.8	14.9
Miscellaneous (Article 18)	225.1	0.0	225.1	1.8
(of which: guarantees)	(52.5)	0.0		
Total	12 656.9	23.6	12 680.5	100.0

Loans for regional development projects account for almost 61% of loans in the Community, most of them in regions on which activities under the structural Funds are focused.

Loans for environmental protection (ECU 2 196 million), transport infrastructures and, in particular, telecommunications (ECU 4 509 million) are on the increase. Assistance to promote the Community's energy objectives remains high (ECU 1 477 million).

Individual loans for industry and services totalled ECU 2 279 million, mainly for projects designed to increase international competitiveness or promote European integration. A further ECU 3 295.5 million was granted in the form of global loans to intermediaries; 7 500 credits totalling around ECU 2 000 million were on-lent to small and medium-sized businesses from global loans.

1022.   Operations outside the Community totalled ECU 712.9 million, as against ECU 612 million in 1989, of which ECU 669 million was from the Bank's own resources.

Mediterranean countries received ECU 344.5 million, of which ECU 182 million went to Yugoslavia. In the ACP countries loans totalled ECU 153.4 million, of which ECU 117.5 million was from the Bank's own resources. The first loans, totalling ECU 215 million, were granted in Poland and Hungary for priority projects.

1023.   The Bank raised a total of ECU 10 996 million on the capital markets to provide itself with the funds it requires to grant loans from its own resources. Most of this amount was raised in Community currencies and in ecus in the form of public issues and private placings.

1024.   The Bank's Board of Governors appointed Hans Duborg Vice-President to replace Mr Erling Jørgensen, who died in February.

General budget guarantee
for borrowing and lending operations

1025.   The guarantee by the Community budget can cover both borrowing and lending operations. For borrowing operations the Community provides the budget guarantee to its own lenders when floating an issue under one of its financial instruments — balance-of-payments facility, Euratom loans, New Community Instrument. For loans granted, the guarantee is given to the European Investment Bank for the loans it makes from its own resources under the Mediterranean protocols. In February the Council provided its guarantee for loans which the Bank was to grant from its own resources to Hungary and Poland; in August the Commission proposed that this guarantee be extended to loans for Czechoslovakia, Bulgaria and Romania. [1]

In 1990 authorized borrowing and lending operations guaranteed by the general budget totalled ECU 30 129 million; at 31 December the guarantee was in operation for ECU 8 547.5 million of Community borrowings and for loans of ECU 2 077 million granted out of the EIB's own resources.

1026.   In 1990 the budget guarantee was again activated for loans granted by the EIB to Lebanon. [2] When Lebanon failed to make certain repayments, the Community paid the EIB ECU 3.828 million at the beginning of March and a further ECU 3.199 million at the beginning of August. These were the sixth and seventh occasions on which the guarantee was activated in respect of Lebanon. At the end of 1990 Lebanon had still not repaid ECU 15.327 million of the amount guaranteed. The guarantee was also

---

[1]   Point 49 of this Report.
[2]   Twenty-second General Report, point 134; Twenty-third General Report, point 120.

activated four times in respect of EIB loans to Syria, for which the Community paid the Bank ECU 6 280 million. On 31 December Syria had still not repaid ECU 5 716 million of the amount guaranteed.

Chapter VII

Community law

Section 1[1]

General matters

Powers

1027. In the *Nashua* cases the Court held that the rejection by the Commission of a proposed undertaking in the course of an anti-dumping proceeding was not a measure having binding legal effects of such a kind as to affect the interests of the applicant, since the Commission could revoke its decision or the Council could decide not to introduce an anti-dumping duty. Such a rejection was an intermediate measure whose purpose was to prepare for the final decision and was not therefore a measure which could be challenged under the second paragraph of Article 173 of the EEC Treaty. The Court also pointed out that a regulation imposing different anti-dumping duties on a number of traders was of direct concern to any one of them only in respect of those provisions which imposed on that trader a specific anti-dumping duty and determined the amount thereof, and not in respect of those provisions which imposed anti-dumping duties on other traders. Consequently, the claim for the annulment of the contested regulation in its entirety had to be rejected.[2]

1028. In *ECSC* v *Busseni* the Court declared itself competent to give a preliminary ruling on the interpretation of the ECSC Treaty and of legislation enacted under it. The ECSC Treaty contains no express provision governing the exercise by the Court of an interpretative jurisdiction. Article 41 simply states that 'the Court shall have sole

---

[1] This section and Section 2 (p. 418) cover the main judgments given by the Court of Justice and the Court of First Instance in 1990

[2] Case C-156/87 *Gestetner Holding* v *Council and Commission* and Joined Cases C-133/87 and C-150/87 *Nashua and Others* v *Commission and Council* (OJ C 92, 11.4.1990).

jurisdiction to give preliminary rulings on the validity of acts of the High Authority and of the Council.' Stressing the link between the interpretation of law and the assessment of its validity, the Court held that it would be contrary to the objectives and the cohesion of the Treaties if it had no power to ensure the uniform interpretation of rules derived from the ECSC Treaty, whereas Article 177 of the EEC Treaty and Article 150 of the Euratom Treaty allowed it to determine the meaning and scope of rules derived from those Treaties.[1]

1029. In Case C-62/88 *Greece* v *Council* the Court rejected Greece's application for the annulment of Regulation No 3955/87 on the conditions governing imports of agricultural products originating in third countries following the accident at the Chernobyl nuclear power station.[2] Mindful of the need for full and consistent verification of the Regulation's legality, the Court declared itself competent to examine, in the context of an application for the annulment of an act based on a provision of the EEC Treaty, a complaint alleging an infringement of a rule in the Euratom or ECSC Treaty. In this specific case the Court considered the Council's choise of legal basis, namely Article 113 of the EEC Treaty, appropriate, since the Regulation, according to its stated purpose and content, was intended to regulate trade between the Community and other countries and thus fell within the scope of the common commercial policy within the meaning of Article 113. The fact that it took account of environmental or health-protection requirements was not in itself sufficient to remove it from the scope of the common commercial policy and place it in the specific fields covered by Article 30 of the Euratom Treaty (protection of the health of the general public against the dangers arising from ionizing radiations) or Articles 130r and 130s of the EEC Treaty (protection of the environment).[3]

1030. In its judgment in Case C-70/88 *Parliament* v *Council* the Court established a clear distinction from earlier case law.[4] While confirming its reading of Articles 173 of the EEC Treaty and 146 of the Euratom Treaty (which are identical) — to the effect that Parliament is not normally entitled to bring an action for annulment when other legal remedies are available not only to parliament but also to Member States, individuals and the Commission, whose responsibility it is to ensure that Parliament's prerogatives are respected and to bring actions for annulment if necessary to ensure the legality of acts of the institutions — the Court found in this case that the various remedies available under the Euratom and EEC Treaties, however effective and varied they might generally be, could prove to be ineffective or unreliable in certain circumstances, particularly where the Commission considered an action for annulment to be ill-founded.

---

[1]   Case C-221/88 *ECSC* v *Acciaierie e Ferriere Busseni* (OJ C 92, 11.4.1990); point 1033 of this Report.
[2]   OJ L 371, 30.12.1987; Twenty-first General Report, point 694.
[3]   OJ C 105, 27.4.1990.
[4]   Case 302/87 *Parliament* v *Council* [1988] ECR 5615.

The Court went on to point out that Parliament's prerogatives were one of the elements of the system of institutional balance created by the Treaties and that there must be provision for challenging any act which disregarded them. Accordingly, it was for the Court to ensure that the provisions of the Treaties creating this institutional balance were applied in full and to ensure that Parliament's prerogatives, like those of the other institutions, were protected by access to a remedy under the Treaties which could be exercised in a reliable and effective manner. Having contrasted the 'procedural gap' — the absence of relief specifically recognized in the Treaties — and the 'fundamental interest' which attached to the maintenance of the institutional balance established in the Treaties, the Court concluded that an action for annulment brought by Parliament against an act of the Council or of the Commission was admissible provided that the action sought only to safeguard its prerogatives and that it was founded only on submissions based on the infringement of those prerogatives. Provided these conditions were met, Parliament's right to bring an action for annulment was governed by the rules laid down by the Treaties for actions for annulment by other institutions. [1]

General principles of Community law

1031.   In considering the various grounds for invalidity alleged against Council directive 88/146/EEC prohibiting the use in livestock farming of certain substances having a hormonal action, [2] the Court clarified, in its *Fedesa* judgment, the scope in Community law of the fundamental principles of legal certainty, proportionality, equal treatment and the non-retroactive nature of legislation. The principle of legal certainty required the courts to assume that any measure taken by the Community institutions was enacted on a rational and objective basis, so that judicial review had to be confined, in the light of the Council's recognized discretionary power concerning the implementation of the common agricultural policy, to ascertaining whether or not the measure challenged was obviously mistaken or involved misuse of power or whether or not the institution in question had manifestly exceeded the bound of its discretionary power. The principle of proportionality meant that the lawfulness of prohibiting a particular economic activity was conditional upon the prohibition measures being appropriate and essential to the achievement of their legitimate objectives, bearing in mind that, where a choice had to be made between a number of appropriate measures, the least onerous should be selected and the resultant disadvantages should not be disproportionate to the aims in view. [3]

---

[1]   OJ C 146, 15.6.1990.
[2]   OJ L 70, 16.3.1988.
[3]   Case C-331/88 *The Queen* v *the Minister for Agriculture, Fisheries and Food and the Secretary of State for Health,* ex parte *Fédération européenne de la santé animale and Others* (OJ C 306, 6.12.1990).

Judicial review and fulfilment by the Member States of their obligations

1032.   In *Triveneta Zuccheri* the Court restated the point that, except when considering an application for a declaration in infringement proceedings, it was not for the Court to rule on the compatibility of a national provision with Community law. That fell within the jurisdiction of the national courts, which could first, if need be, refer to the Court for a preliminary ruling to settle any questions concerning the scope and interpretation of Community law.[1]

1033.   In its *Busseni* judgment the Court also recalled its rulings on the effects of a directive which has not been transposed into national law. The Court held that the same rules also applied to recommendations under the ECSC Treaty, which are acts of the same kind, placing the Member State to which they are adressed under an obligation as to the result to be achieved but allowing it to choose the appropriate means of achieving that result. If the relevant provisions of the recommendation were unconditional and sufficiently precise, then, they could be relied on before national courts if no implementing measures had been adopted within the period prescribed. On the other hand, such a possibility could only exist as against the Member State concerned and public authorities (a directive or recommendation which had not been implemented would have no 'horizontal effect' between individuals).[2]

1034.   The judgment given in *Factortame* is of major institutional importance, particularly for the United Kingdom. To put a stop to the practice known as 'quota hopping', the Merchant Shipping Act 1988 established a new register in which all British fishing vessels which met the nationality conditions laid down in Section 14 of the Act had to be registered. Since their vessels failed to meet one or more of the new conditions of registration and therefore faced the prospect of being no longer allowed to engage in fishing from 1 April 1989, a number of fishing companies challenged the compatibility of Part II of the 1988 Act with Community law in the British courts; they also applied for interim relief to be granted until such time as judgment was given on their application for judicial review. The case eventually reached the House of Lords, which asked the Court of Justice whether a national court which, in a case before it involving a question of interpretation of Community law, considered that the sole obstacle precluding it from granting interim relief was a rule of national law must set aside that rule. The rule in question was the old common law rule that no interim injunction can be granted against the Crown, i.e. against the Government, and there was in addition the presumption that national laws are consistent with Community law as long as they have not been declared inconsistent. In its judgment, the Court of Justice, having pointed out the implications for the national courts of the direct applicability and primacy of Community law, found

---

[1]   Case C-347/87 *Triveneta Zuccheri and Others* v *Commission* (OJ C 105, 27.4.1990).
[2]   Case C-221/88 *ECSC* v *Acciaierie e Ferriere Busseni* (OJ C 92, 11.4.1990); point 1028 of this Report.

that, in these circumstances, the national court must set aside the national rule precluding it from granting interim relief. The full effectiveness of Community law could be just as much impaired if a rule of national law could prevent a court seized of a dispute governed by Community law from granting interim relief in order to ensure the full effectiveness of the judgment to be given on the existence of the rights claimed under Community law.[1]

1035.   Again in the matter of interim measures, note should be taken of Case C-217/88, which raised the question of the suspensory effect of actions brought by individuals in the national courts against administrative acts based on Community law. The Court held that the failure of the Federal Republic of Germany to use the coercive measures available under German law (immediate enforcement) against producers who had refused to deliver table wine for compulsory distillation was contrary to Article 5 of the EEC Treaty and Article 64(1) of regulation No 337/79 on the common organization of the market in wine.[2] The objective of the compulsory distillation measures could only be attained if they were implemented within a specific time-scale (which, in the case in point, had been determined by the Commission) and it was therefore incumbent on Member States to take whatever measures were necessary to ensure that producers delivered their wine for distillation within the period prescribed, even where the producers concerned had successfully brought an action in the national courts to suspend the enforcement of notices of liability for compulsory distillation.[3]

1036.   The order made by the Court in *Zwartveld* recalled that Article 5 of the EEC Treaty placed the Community institutions too under an obligation of reasonable cooperation with the national authorities, requiring them to make documents available and to authorize the examination of officials as witnesses before the national courts. Departures from this principle could only be allowed where there were imperative reasons arising from the need to avoid any hindrance to the functioning and independence of the Communities, which it was the specific purpose of Article 1 of the Protocol on Privileges and Immunities to protect.[4]

1037.   In *Gmurzynska-Bscher* the Court found that it has jurisdiction under Article 177 of the EEC Treaty to rule on the interpretation of a provision of Community law even where the provision in question is applied in the law of a Member State in an area outside that defined by Community law. The Court held that in such a case it was necessary to ensure that Community law had the same effect in all the Member States in order to prevent disparities in the interpretation of Community law in cases in which its

---

[1]   Case C-213/89 *The Queen* v *Secretary of State for Transport,* ex parte *Factortame and Others* (OJ C 169, 11.7.1990).
[2]   OJ L 54, 5.3.1979.
[3]   Case C-217/88 *Commission* v *Germany* (OJ C 193, 2.8.1990).
[4]   Case C-2/88 Imm. *Criminal proceedings against Zwartveld and Others* (OJ C 199, 8.8.1990).

application was directly at issue. It did not follow from the terms of Article 177 or from the purpose of the procedure laid down in that article that the authors of the Treaty had intended to exclude from the Court's jurisdiction preliminary references on a provision of Community law in the particular case in which the national law of a Member State referred to the content of that provision in order to determine the rules applicable to a situation which related solely to that State.[1]

1038. In *Marleasing* the Court ruled that a national court called on to determine a dispute in a matter falling within the sphere of application of Council Directive 68/151/EEC[2] is obliged to interpret its national law in the light of the wording and purpose of that Directive in order to prevent the nullity of a limited liability company from being declared on a ground other than those listed in Article 11 thereof. The Court pointed out that Member States are under an obligation to achieve the results provided for in directives and are required by Article 5 of the Treaty to take all appropriate measures, whether general or particular, to ensure the performance of this obligation. The obligation was incumbent on all the authorities of the Member States, including — within the bounds of their jurisdiction — the courts.[3]

1039. In monitoring the application of Community law the Commission initiated the infringement procedure in 1 322 cases (704 in 1989 and 569 in 1988) and sent 259 reasoned opinions (199 in 1989). Proceedings were brought before the Court in 73 cases (108 in 1989).

Infringements of Articles 9, 30 or 95 of the EEC Treaty, the basic provisions relating to free movement of goods, an essential element in the completion of the internal market, gave rise to 103 letters of formal notice and 42 reasoned opinions.

To take each country separately, the Commission brought proceedings before the Court against Belgium on 13 occasions (10 concerning directives), against Denmark on 3 occasions (2 concerning directives), against the Federal Republic of Germany on 5 occasions (2 concerning directives), against Greece on 10 occasions (6 concerning directives), against Spain on 3 occasions (3 concerning directives), against France on 6 occasions (5 concerning directives) against Ireland on 3 occasions (3 concerning directives), against Italy on 20 occasions (17 concerning directives), against Luxembourg on 4 occasions (3 concerning directives), against The Netherlands on 2 occasions (1 concerning directives), against Portugal on 2 occasions (0 concerning directives), and against the United Kingdom on 2 occasions (1 concerning directives).

The Court delivered 39 judgments in cases brought under Article 169, censuring Member States for failure to fulfil their obligations under Community law in 36 cases. In the

---

[1]   Case C-231/89 *Gmurzynska-Bscher* v *Oberfinanzdirektion Köln* (OJ C 307, 7.12.1990).
[2]   OJ L 65, 14.3.1968.
[3]   Case C-106/89 *Marleasing* v *La Comercial International de Alimentación* (OJ C 306, 6.12.1990).

course of the year 25 cases were removed from the Court Register because the Member States concerned had conformed to Community legislation in the mean time.

Fuller information is given in the eighth annual report to Parliament on Commission monitoring of the application of Community law (to be published in 1991).

Section 2

Interpretation and application of the substantive rules of Community law

Free movement of goods and Customs Union

1040. In *Du Pont de Nemours Italiana* v *Unità Sanitaria Locale No 2 di Carraca*[1] the Court found against the Italian system of regional preferences, which reserves 30% of public supply contracts to firms in the Mezzogiorno. Asked for a preliminary ruling, the Court held that products originating in other Member States were discriminated against in relation to products manufactured in Italy and there was thus an obstacle to the normal pattern of intra-Community trade, contrary to Article 30 of the EEC Treaty. This conclusion was not invalidated by the fact that the restrictive effects of the system affected to the same extent products manufactured by Italian firms which were not situated in the Mezzogiorno and products manufactured by firms established in other Member States. Although all Italian products were not favoured in relation to foreign products, nevertheless the products enjoying preferential treatment were national products, and the fact that the restrictive effect of a government measure on imports did not favour all national products but only some of them did not exempt the measure from the prohibition of Article 30.

1041. In *GB Inno BM* v *Confédération du Commerce Luxembourgeois*[2] the Court held, for the first time, that legislation prohibiting a method of advertising that applied without distinction to domestic and imported products was incompatible with Article 30. In the *Oosthoek* case[3] the Court had already established the principle that legislation prohibiting certain forms of advertising could constitute an obstacle to imports by obliging a producer to alter or abandon a particular sales promotion scheme but had finally decided that in that specific case the legislation was justified by the imperative need to protect the consumer. In this instance the Court held that legislation prohibiting the supply of certain information to the consumer could not be regarded as justified on grounds of consumer protection since the provision of information was itself a paramount requirement.

---

[1]   Case C-21/88 (OJ C 105, 27.4.1990).
[2]   Case C-362/88 (OJ C 92, 11.4.1990).
[3]   Case 286/81 *Criminal proceedings* v *Oosthoek's Uitgeversmaatschappij* [1982] ECR 4575.

1042. In *Gourmetterie Van den Burg*[1] the Court reaffirmed its view that if a directive provides for the full harmonization of national provisions (as does Directive 79/409/EEC on the conservation of wild birds[2]), a Member State cannot rely on Article 36 of the EEC Treaty to justify restrictions on the free movement of goods on the ground that it is protecting the health and life of animals. Reference should be made solely to the powers conferred on Member States by the provisions of the directive in question, in this case by Article 14 of Directive 79/409/EEC.

1043. In Case C-128/89 *Commission* v *Italy*[3] the Court reviewed its past rulings on the relationship between Articles 30 and 36 of the EEC Treaty, on the one hand, and harmonization directives, on the other. Having found that Italy's prohibition on imports of grapefruit through its inland borders had the effect of making imports from other Member States difficult if not impossible, in contravention of Article 30, the Court went on to consider whether the measures at issue nevertheless fell within the Member States' powers to regulate trade on grounds of plant health protection. Where a Community directive provides, pursuant to Article 100, for the harmonization of health protection measures and lays down Community procedures for its enforcement, Member States are entitled to adopt protective measures only within the limits specified in the directive. The purpose of such directives is to promote the free movement of goods by eliminating or at least reducing any obstacles resulting from national health protection measures taken under Article 36.[4] Any national rules or practices adopted for a purpose specified in Article 36 are therefore incompatible with the Treaty if they go beyond the limits of what is appropriate and necessary to achieve the desired result.[5] In this particular case the Court held that the legislation in question went beyond the permissible limits since the Italian authorities had been unable to show that it was impossible to carry out health checks on the grapefruit at inland borders.

1044. The judgment handed down by the Court in *CNL-Sucal* v *Hag GF*[6] completely reversed that given on the same matter in 1974.[7] The Court justified this about-turn by reference to the case-law which had gradually developed on the relationship between industrial and commercial property and the general rules of the Treaty, particularly in the area of free movement of goods. The central issue was whether Articles 30 and 36 of the Treaty precluded national legislation from allowing a firm which held a trade mark in one Member States (in this case Hag GF) from opposing the importation from another Member State of similar products lawfully bearing an identical trade mark in the latter

---

[1]   Case C-169/89 (OJ C 151, 20.6.1990).
[2]   OJ L 103, 25.4.1979; Thirteenth General Report, point 281.
[3]   OJ C 198, 7.8.1990.
[4]   Case 45/76 *Bauhuis* v *Netherlands State* [1977] ECR 5.
[5]   Case 104/75 *Criminal proceedings* v *de Peijper* [1976] ECR 613.
[6]   Case C-10/89 (OJ C 285, 13.11.1990).
[7]   Case 192/73 *Van Zuylen* v *Hag* [1974] ECR 731.

State even though the trade mark had originally belonged to a subsidiary (Café Hag) of the firm opposing the imports in question and had been acquired by a third firm (now CNL-Sucal), the subsidiary having been sequestrated as enemy property by the Belgian authorities in 1944. The Court concluded that the essential function of the trade mark would be compromised if the holder could not avail himself of the possibility offered to him under national law of opposing the importation of a similar product under a name that could be confused with its own trade mark, because consumers would no longer be able to identify with any certainty the origin of the product bearing the trade mark and the holder could find that a poor-quality product for which he was in no way responsible was attributed to him.

1045.   In *Bonfait*[1] the Court was asked for a preliminary ruling on whether national rules which reserved the appellation 'prepared meat products' to products conforming to the conditions prescribed by such rules and which represented an obstacle to the importation of products lawfully marketed under that appellation in their country of origin could be justified by the need to protect the consumer, public health or fair trading. The Court held that national rules could not be justified on these grounds since the necessary protection could be afforded if the nature of the products for sale was indicated by appropriate labelling and if mutual respect was shown for the practices lawfully and traditionally followed in the various Member States.

Competition

1046.   In *Sandoz Prodotti Farmaceutici* v *Commission*[2] the Court held that the regular inclusion of the words 'not to be exported' on all the invoices dispatched by a company to its consumers was not of a purely unilateral nature but amounted to an agreement within the meaning of Article 85(1) of the EEC Treaty by virtue of the customers' tacit acquiescence.

1047.   In Case C-301/87 *France* v *Commission*[3] the Court clarified competition law concerning the monitoring of State aid schemes in several important respects — notably as regards (i) the procedural rules in Article 93(3), whereby Member States must notify aid measures at the draft stage so that they are not implemented before the Commission has approved them as compatible with the Treaty, and (ii) the obligation laid upon Member States to recover any aid which does not qualify for exemption under Article 92 and is therefore incompatible with the common market.

---

[1]   Case C-269/89 (OJ C 307, 7.12.1990).
[2]   Case C-277/87 (OJ C 28, 7.2.1990).
[3]   OJ C 61, 10.3.1990.

1048.   In Case C-142/87 *Belgium* v *Commission*[1] the Court rejected Belgium's application for the annulment of Decision 87/418/EEC,[2] in which the Commission found that the various forms of assistance which the Belgian Government had granted to Tubemeuse were unlawful because the procedure laid down in Article 93(3) of the Treaty had not been observed and because the aid was incompatible with the common market within the meaning of Article 92 and should therefore be recovered. To determine whether the Government's measures to boost the capital of Tubemeuse constituted State aid, the Court considered that it was appropriate to apply the test of the firm's ability to obtain the sums in question on the market. Of this there was 'little likelihood', given Tubemeuse's lack of profit-making capacity. The aid in question could affect competition between Community businesses in the relevant market even if Tubemeuse did export almost its entire output to non-member countries, given the interdependence of the markets on which Community businesses operated and the general context of crisis and recession (and, therefore, keener competition) on the world market for seamless tubes at the material time. In the Court's opinion, the fact that the aid was relatively insignificant or that the recipient was a relatively small firm did not necessarily preclude the possibility that trade between Member States might be affected.

1049.   In *Tetra Pak Rausing* v *Commission*[3] the Court of First Instance was asked to rule on whether the Commission could still decide that there had been abuse of a dominant position within the meaning of Article 86 of the EEC Treaty when the conduct in question involved the use of an exclusive patent licence for which the Commission had already granted block exemption. Tetra Pak's main argument was that it was a manifest contradiction for the Commission to prohibit under Article 86 conduct which it had declared compatible with Article 85 and that this constituted an improper assessment of the relationship between Articles 85 and 86. The Court of First Instance held, however, that the applicant's position was tantamount to claiming exemption under Article 86 whereas the wording of Article 86 made it clear that the prohibition on the abuse of dominance was unconditional; Articles 85 and 86 were independent and complementary provisions designed, in general, to regulate distinct situations by different rules.

1050.   The judgment given by the Court in Case C-5/89 *Commission* v *Germany*[4] sets out the conditions under which a firm may rely on the argument of legitimate expectations to contest a Commission decision ordering the recovery of illegal State aid. According to the Court, firms should assume that, as a rule, any aid which has not been notified to the Commission will have to be repaid. Firms cannot claim, as an argument

---

[1]   OJ C 101, 21.4.1990.
[2]   OJ L 227, 14.8.1987; Twenty-first General Report, point 483.
[3]   Case T-51/89 (OJ C 193, 2.8.1990).
[4]   OJ C 261, 16.10.1990.

against a decision ordering repayment, that they were entitled to presume that aid granted was lawful since they are usually in a position to ascertain whether the Article 93 procedure has been duly observed. Only in exceptional cases may firms contest the repayment order on grounds of legitimate expectations. Member States, in any event, are never entitled to invoke the legitimate expectations of the recipients of aid as grounds for non-compliance with a Commission decision ordering its repayment, irrespective of any national rules concerning such matters. In this particular case the German Government, having infringed Article 93(3) of the Treaty, was not entitled to rely on Baden-Württemberg legislation on the protection of acquired rights in order to free itself from its obligation.

Free movement of persons, social provisions and capital movements

1051. In *Rush Portuguesa* v *Office national d'immigration*[1] the Court held that, where workers employed by a firm providing services are temporarily moved to the Member State in which the services are to be provided and then return to their country of origin on completion of their duties, the provisions of the Act of Accession of Spain and Portugal[2] whereby the other Member States may make access to employment and immigration subject to prior authorization are not applicable. When workers are temporarily relocated in this way, it is the rules on freedom to provide services which must apply. The freedom to provide services (in this case, in the building and public works industry) must be fully operative in the case of Portugal from the time of accession to the Community. Nevertheless, the host Member State must be able to check whether a Portuguese construction firm is not availing itself of the freedom to provide services for another purpose — for example, to enable its staff to travel for the purpose of being taken on as workers in breach of Article 216 of the Act of Accession. Finally, the Court held that Community law did not preclude Member States from extending their legislation or the collective bargaining agreements concluded by labour and employers to any person in paid employment, even of a temporary nature, on their territory, irrespective of the country in which the employer was established; Community law did not prohibit Member States from requiring observance of these rules by appropriate means.

1052. Although the Court has given a large number of consistent rulings on equality of treatment between Community nationals, *Biehl* v *Administration des Contributions du Grand-Duché de Luxembourg*[3] was of particular interest in that it related to a case of concealed discrimination in the taxation field, which is prohibited under Article 7 of

---

[1]   Case C-113/89 (OJ C 118, 12.5.1990).
[2]   OJ L 302, 15.11.1985; Nineteenth General Report, points 720 to 724.
[3]   Case C-175/89 (OJ C 135, 2.6.1990).

Regulation (EEC) No 1612/68[1] and, in more general terms, by Article 48(2) of the EEC Treaty. Even though it applied irrespective of nationality, the condition that the taxpayer must be permanently resident in Luxembourg in order to obtain any refund of an overpayment of tax was liable to penalize taxpayers who are not Luxembourg nationals; it was often they who would leave the country during the year, or who would take up residence there. To justify the national provision in question, the tax authorities had stated that its purpose was to ensure that taxation was progressive since income and, consequently, tax liability arose in at least two Member States if there was a change of residence during the tax year. This reasoning was rejected by the Court, which ruled that if taxpayers who are temporarily resident have received no income during the tax year in the country which they have left or in the country in which they take up residence, they will be at a disadvantage as compared with permanently resident taxpayers since they are deprived of their entitlement to the refund of any overpayment of tax, whereas the permanent resident is entitled to such a refund at all times.

1053. In *Di Leo* v *Land Berlin*[2] the Court held that the right to equality of treatment, as provided for in Article 12 of Regulation No 1612/68 on freedom of movement for workers within the Community,[1] must also be extended to a child who follows a training course outside the host country — in particular, in the Member State of which he or she is a national. The Court based its ruling mainly on the purpose of the Regulation — freedom of movement for workers. If this was to be guaranteed without any infringement of individual liberty or dignity, the families of Community workers had to be integrated as fully as possible into the society of the host country. And this in turn required that the children of Community workers living with their family in a Member State other than their own had to be able to choose their course of studies on the same terms as children who were nationals of that Member State.

1054. In *Yáñez-Campoy* v *Bundesanstalt für Arbeit,* [3] which related to the payment of family allowances to workers moving from one Community country to another, the Court ruled on the interpretation of Article 99 of Regulation No 1408/71,[4] as amended by Regulation No 2001/83[5] and by Article 60 of the Act of Accession of Spain and Portugal.[6] The issue arose from the fact that the Court's judgment in *Pinna* v *Caisse d'allocations familiales de la Savoie*[7] had invalidated Article 73(2) of Regulation No 1408/71. The Court held that the uniform solution for all Member States, as referred to in Article 99 of Regulation No 1408/71 and in Article 60 of the Act of Accession (on

[1]   OJ L 257, 19.10.1968.
[2]   Case C-308/89 (OJ C 306, 6.12.1990).
[3]   Case C-99/89 (OJ C 306, 6.12.1990).
[4]   OJ L 149, 5.7.1971.
[5]   OJ L 230, 22.8.1983; Seventeenth General Report, point 326.
[6]   OJ L 302, 15.11.1985.
[7]   Case 41/84 [1986] ECR 1.

the termination of the transitional arrangements governing the payment of family allowances to Spanish workers who are employed in a Member State other than Spain but whose family resides in Spain), came into force on 15 January 1986, the date on which the *Pinna* judgment was given. Once Article 73(2) of Regulation No 1408/71 had been declared void, the system laid down in Article 73(1) for the payment of family allowances became generally applicable, the Council having failed to adopt new rules under Article 51 of the EEC Treaty.

Taxation

1055.   In Case C-30/89 *Commission* v *France*[1] the Court had to decide whether France was obliged to make available to the Commission, as own resources, the VAT on that part of the transport service between mainland France and Corsica which is provided in or above international waters. The Court held that the only obligation which the sixth Directive[2] placed on the Member States as regards the taxation of transport services was that they should subject to taxation the services provided within their territorial limits. The Directive does not, then, oblige Member States to tax those parts of the journey which occur in international waters or airspace, even if transport is provided between two points of the same national territory without any place of call in another country and without any encroachment on the tax jurisdiction of other States. The only consequence which may be inferred from the general objective of the sixth Directive is that Member States which make use of the freedom to extend the scope of their tax legislation beyond their strict territorial limits must observe the common rules laid down by the Directive as regards subjecting transactions to tax.

Equal treatment for men and women

1056.   In *Barber* v *Guardian Royal Exchange Assurance Group*[3] the Court resolved a long-standing dispute by ruling that benefits payable under contracted-out occupational schemes constituted consideration paid by the employer to the worker in respect of his employment and consequently fell within the scope of Article 119 of the EEC Treaty, with all the consequences which this entailed (direct 'horizontal' effect; full application of the principle of equal treatment, with no possibility of derogation). It was contrary to Article 119 for a man made compulsorily redundant to be entitled to only a deferred

---

[1]   OJ C 92, 11.4.1990.
[2]   OJ L 145, 13.6.1977; OJ L 149, 17.6.1977; Eleventh General Report, point 219.
[3]   Case C-262/89 (OJ C 146, 15.6.1990).

pension payable at the normal retirement age when a woman in the same position received an immediate retirement pension as a result of the application of an age condition that varied according to sex in the same way as was provided by the national statutory pension scheme.

In *Kowalska* v *Freie und Hansestadt Hamburg*[1] the Court was asked by the Hamburg Arbeitsgericht to rule whether a collective agreement whereby a temporary severance grant could be paid only to full-time workers was compatible with Article 119 of the EEC Treaty. The Court held that an agreement which enabled employers to maintain different overall pay levels for two categories of workers, namely those who worked the minimum number of hours per week or per month and those who, although doing the same job, did not work that minimum number of hours, amounted to *de facto* discrimination between men and women workers, since 'a considerably lower percentage of men than of women work part-time.' Normally, therefore, such an agreement must be considered to be contrary to Article 119 (unless the employer shows that it is based on objectively justified factors unrelated to any discrimination on grounds of sex, and that is a matter for the national courts since only they are competent to assess the relevant facts).

1057.   In *Dekker* v *VJV-Centrum Plus*[2] the Court held that, under Directive 76/207/EEC on the implementation of the principle of equal treatment for men and women as regards access to employment, vocational training and promotion, and working conditions,[3] the refusal to engage a female worker because of her pregnancy constituted direct discrimination on grounds of sex, in the same way as the dismissal of a pregnant woman. A refusal to engage a woman because of the financial consequences which would follow from her absence during pregnancy must be considered as motivated essentially by the fact of her pregnancy, even if the public authorities have laid down rules on inability to work which treat pregnancy on the same basis as illness.

1058.   In *Handels- of Kontorfunktionaerernes Forbund i Danmark* v *Dansk Arbejdsgiverforening,*[4] on the other hand, the Court ruled that the dismissal of a female worker because of repeated absences resulting not simply from pregnancy or confinement but from an illness due to pregnancy or confinement did not constitute direct discrimination on grounds of sex. A pathological condition of that kind, if it developed after maternity leave, was covered by the general rules applicable to any illness. The only question was whether the woman had been dismissed on the grounds of absence due to illness in the same way as a man would have been dismissed.

---

[1]   Case C-33/89 (OJ C 179, 19.7.1990).
[2]   Case C-177/88 (OJ C 304, 4.12.1990).
[3]   OJ L 39, 14.2.1976; Ninth General Report, point 204; Twelfth General Report, point 202.
[4]   Case C-179/88 (OJ C 301, 30.11.1990).

Common agricultural policy and fisheries

1059. In *Wuidart and Others* v *Laiterie coopérative Eupenoise and Others*[1] the Court gave its first ruling on the legal validity of the option which Member States have, under the milk quota system, of collecting the additional levy on deliveries in excess of reference quantities either from producers (formula A) or from purchasers (i.e. dairies) (formula B). The Court held that the principle underlying the option was justified by the need to ensure that the system was fully effective throughout the Community, with due regard for the diversity of milk-production and milk-collection structures in the various parts of the Community. The Court was also asked to specify the conditions under which a Member State could apply, in one part of its territory, a formula (A or B) which differed from that applicable elsewhere, bearing in mind the geographical structure of the territory, natural conditions, production structures and average herd yields. In the *Klensch* case[2] the Court had already ruled that Member States exercising an option available under Community rules must observe the principle of non-discrimination. In this instance the Court kept within the same judicial constraints as it imposes on itself in cases where the institutions enjoy wide powers of discretion, restricting itself to verifying that no manifest error had been committed.

1060. In Case C-62/89 *Commission* v *France*[3] the Court held that the obligation on Member States to place a temporary prohibition on fishing from the date on which the quota concerned was considered exhausted constituted a general rule which was needed to ensure the effectiveness of any system for the conservation and management of fishery resources where the total quantities available were shared out among the Member States. A decision by the national authorities to prohibit fishing must be binding and must be taken before the quotas are exhausted. The Court thus reaffirmed the preventive role of this obligation, pointing out that the pattern followed by catches of one of the species in question was sufficiently regular to enable the national authorities to forecast the exact time when the quota would be exhausted. Although exchanges of quotas between Member States made it possible to increase a Member State's quota in the course of the year, such exchanges had to be negotiated either before the exhaustion of the original quota or after the provisional ban on fishing. Since the outcome of such negotiations was uncertain, the mere prospect of an exchange was no reason for the relaxation of a formal ban on fishing.

1061. In *Scarpe* v *ONIC*[4] the Court had to decide on the validity of the price set by the Commission for intervention purchases of common wheat of bread-making quality,

---

[1]   Joined Cases C-267/88 to 285/88 (OJ C 92, 11.4.1990).
[2]   Joined Cases 201/85 and 202/85 *Klensch and Others* v *Secrétaire d'Etat* [1986] ECR 3503.
[3]   OJ C 105, 11.4.1990.
[4]   Case C-27/89 (OJ C 132, 31.5.1990).

having already ruled in *AGPB* v *ONIC*[1] that the setting of different quantitative limits for intervention buying in the various Member States did not constitute discrimination. Since the Council had failed to adopt cereal prices for 1985/86 the Community had been forced to do so in order to ensure the continued operation of the market organization. The Court accepted the Commission's argument that its power to set these prices did not derive from the Council's failure to do so (although this did threaten to bring the common agricultural policy to a halt) but from the existing provisions of Regulation (EEC) No 2727/75,[2] whereby the Council had delegated to the Commission the power to introduce special intervention measures on the market for common wheat of bread-making quality and, consequently, to set the buying-in price for the wheat when such measures were adopted and to lower the price as compared with that for the previous marketing year, in line with the surplus-reduction policy announced by the Council in 1984.

1062.   In *Sofrimport* v *Commission*[3] the Court ruled that Regulations Nos 962/88 and 984/88 suspending the issue of import licences for dessert apples originating in Chile[4] and Regulation No 1040/88,[5] which set maximum limits for imports of dessert apples from non-member countries, were void in so far as they related to products in transit, on the grounds that in this particular case the Commission had not shown that it was in the overriding public interest to suspend imports of the products in question. Only if the overriding public interest was jeopardized could there be any justification for measures contrary to the legitimate expectations of businesses importing into the Community goods (fruit and vegetables) specified in Regulation No 2707/72,[6] Article 3(3) of which protects importers from the ill effects of any protective measures taken by the Community institutions. The interest of the case lies in the fact that the Court ordered the Community to make good the damage suffered by the applicant as a result of Community legislation. The Court held that, by failing completely to take account of the position of traders such as Sofrimport, without showing any overriding public interest, the Commission committed a serious breach of Article 3(3) of Regulation No 2707/72 and that the damage claimed by Sofrimport went beyond the limits of the economic risks inherent in the business in issue inasmuch as the purpose of that provision was precisely to minimize those risks with regard to goods in transit. These circumstances met the very strict requirements laid down by the Court's earlier rulings on non-contractual liability, particularly as regards legislative measures which involve economic policy choices.

---

[1]   Case C-167/88 (OJ C 175, 11.7.1989).
[2]   OJ L 281, 1.11.1975.
[3]   Case C-152/88 (OJ C 179, 19.7.1990).
[4]   OJ L 95, 13.4.1988; OJ L 98, 15.4.1988; Twenty-second General Report, point 651.
[5]   OJ L 102, 21.4.1988; Twenty-second General Report, point 651.
[6]   OJ L 291, 28.12.1972; Sixth General Report, point 242.

1063.   By its judgment in Case C-366/88 *France* v *Commission* [1] the Court declared void, on grounds of lack of competence, the Commission's internal instructions entitling its staff to take and analyse samples independently of the Member States for EAGGF management and control purposes and laying down the procedures to be followed in this context. The Court held that no such powers had been conferred on the Commission by Regulation No 729/70 on the financing of the CAP [2] and that only the Council was competent, under Article 9(3) of the Regulation, to lay down general rules for verifying whether the operations financed by the EAGGF had in fact been carried out in the proper manner.

1064.   In *The Queen* v *IBAP,* [3] which concerned the question of penalties proportional to infringements of the common fisheries policy, the Court found that, given the importance of quality standards in the market organization for fishery products, any significant failure by a producers' organization to comply with these standards (in respect of fish put up for sale and not withdrawn from the market where such fish is of the same species as other fish which was withdrawn during the same period) should rule out the payment of any financial compensation to the organization for the fish withdrawn. The Court rejected the argument that the financial compensation should merely be reduced in proportion to the quantities which failed to meet the standards.

Commercial policy

1065.   The Court's judgment in *Cartorobica* v *Ministerio delle Finanze dello Stato,* [4] which related to anti-dumping measures, made some interesting points as regards the setting of threshold prices in US dollars rather than ecus. The Court remarked that there was no provision of Community law which required the value of the threshold price used in the calculation of the anti-dumping duty to be expressed in ecus. Nor had the Council exceeded its discretion in the matter in deciding to express the threshold price in US dollars so as to take account of the fact that the price in question reflected the normal value of the dumped goods on the United States market. Any anti-dumping duty, regardless of its type and the currency in which it was stated or to which it referred, could be affected by exchange-rate fluctuations, and in the current state of Community law the Community institutions could not control the fluctuations of the ecu any more than those of any other currency.

---

[1]   OJ C 274, 31.10.1990.
[2]   OJ L 94, 28.4.1970.
[3]   Case C-301/88 *The Queen* v *Intervention Board for Agricultural Produce,* ex parte *the Fish Producers' Organization and the Grimsby Fish Producers' Organization* (OJ C 288, 16.11.1990).
[4]   Case C-189/88 (OJ C 109, 3.5.1990).

External policy

1066. In *Sevince* v *Staatssecretaris van Justitie*[1] the Court clarified the meaning of 'direct effect' in the context of association agreements, ruling that the interpretation of Decisions 2/76 and 1/80 of the Association Council set up by the EEC-Turkey Association Agreement signed in Ankara on 12 September 1963[2] fell within the scope of Article 177 of the EEC Treaty. The Court had consistently held that the provisions of any agreement concluded by the Council under Articles 228 and 238 of the Treaty formed an integral part of Community law. The same had to apply to the decisions of an Association Council since they followed direct from the Agreement which they implemented. Since the Court had jurisdiction to give a preliminary ruling on the Agreement as an act of a Community institution, it was also competent to rule on the interpretation of decisions taken by an executive body set up by the Agreement. The Court concluded that Articles 2(1)(b) and 7 of Decision 2/76 and Articles 6(1) and 13 of Decision 1/80 had direct effect in the Member States, thus guaranteeing that Turkish workers who had been in legal employment in a Member State for a certain number of years would have free access to any paid employment of their choice in that State and requiring Member States not to introduce any new restrictions on access to employment. This conclusion was based on an examination of the clear, precise and unconditional terms in which the provisions in question were couched and took account of the nature and purpose of both the decisions and the Agreement. In this connection the Court made the point that although Article 12 of the Agreement and Article 36 of the Additional Protocol[3] served essentially to set out a programme, this did not preclude Decisions 2/76 and 1/80, which were intended to implement the said Articles in particular respects, from having direct effect, even where national legislation laid down detailed rules concerning the rights enjoyed by Turkish workers.

Staff

1067. In *Weiser* v *CNBF*[4] the Court ruled that a person pursuing an activity as a self-employed person, such as that of a lawyer, who abandons his practice in order to become an official of the European Communities is not entitled, as Community law now stands, to claim the application for his benefit of Article 11(2) of Annex VIII to the Staff Regulations, which provides for the possibility of transferring pension rights from a national scheme to the Community scheme. The Court went on, however, to declare

---

[1]   Case C-192/89 (OJ C 261, 16.10.1990).
[2]   OJ 217, 29.12.1964.
[3]   Case 12/86 *Demirel* v *Schwäbisch Gmünd* [1987] ECR 3719.
[4]   Case C-37/89 (OJ C 169, 11.7.1990).

this provision invalid in so far as it provides for a difference in treatment, as regards the transfer of pension rights from a national scheme to the Community scheme, between officials who have acquired pension rights as employed persons and those who have acquired them as self-employed persons.

Institutional and budgetary questions

1068.   In *Le Pen and Front National* v *Puhl and Others*[1] the Court was asked by the Colmar Court of Appeal to give a preliminary ruling on an action for libel brought by Mr J.M. Le Pen and the Front National, a French political party, against the authors and printers of a leaflet deploring the resurgence of racism and Fascism in Europe and the Chairman of the Socialist Group in the European Parliament. The Court held that it had no jurisdiction with respect to acts committed inside the premises occupied by Community institutions. Article 1 of the Protocol on the Privileges and Immunities of the European Communities, on which the Socialist Group sought to rely, contained no express or implied provision to this effect, its sole purpose being to protect the premises in question against any national measure of constraint designed to impede the deliberations of Parliament. The Court's ruling means, essentially, that Parliament is not liable for the actions of political groups, for whom it cannot be held responsible. No provision of Parliament's Rules of Procedure empowers a political group to act in the name of Parliament *vis-à-vis* other institutions or third parties. And no rule of Community law implies that the acts of a political group may be attributed to Parliament as a Community institution.

1069.   In Case C-6/89 *Commission* v *Belgium*[2] the matter at issue was the 50% reduction, under Article 2 of Royal Decree No 471 of 24 October 1986, in the salary allowance granted to Belgian teachers seconded to the European Schools, with the result that an additional burden was placed on the Community budget. To finance the European Schools, Member States pay a contribution equal to the national salaries of the teachers seconded by them and the Commission pays a contribution which covers the remainder of expenditure under the Schools' budget (the 'European supplement'). The Court confirmed the scope, as defined in *Hurd* v *Jones,*[3] of the duty of genuine cooperation and assistance which Member States owe the Community, as expressed in Article 5 of the EEC Treaty. A Member State would be repudiating that Article if it unilaterally adopted rationalization measures in the field of public expenditure which jeopardized the Community's system of financing and distributing the financial burden

---

[1]   Case C-201/89 (OJ C 101, 21.4.1990).
[2]   OJ C 118, 12.5.1990.
[3]   Case 44/84 [1986] ECR 29.

among the Member States. It is interesting to note that in this particular case the measures in question were introduced in the context of a series of intergovernmental agreements (concerning the establishment and operation of the European Schools) which do not form an integral part of Community law, though they do relate to the Community and the operation of its institutions.

1070.   In Case C-251/88 *Commission* v *Germany*[1] the Court had to rule on the method used by the German authorities, pursuant to Article 9(2) of Regulation (EEC) No 2892/77,[2] to calculate the notional VAT resources base for the transactions of the Deutsche Bundespost in the telecommunications sector, such transactions being exempted from VAT as is permitted by the sixth VAT Directive.[3] It pointed out that the purpose of Article 9(2) was to neutralize the effects of the temporary exemption of the transactions listed in Annex F to the sixth Directive in order to enable a uniform base to be determined for the calculation of VAT own resources, by including in that base the value of the exempt transactions. Unlike the other Member States, the German authorities deduct from the Bundespost's turnover the amount of VAT paid to its suppliers. The Court held that where the value added at each production stage was taxed, this had no effect, whatever the rate of VAT applied, on the base calculated as the sum of the net purchase value and the value added by the Bundespost. The Court concluded that since the second indent of Article 9(2) of the Regulation was not sufficiently precise and left room for more than one method of calculation, the Commission had failed to show that the method used by Germany was contrary to that provision.

---

[1]   OJ C 151, 20.6.1990.
[2]   OJ L 336, 27.12.1977; Eleventh General Report, point 64.
[3]   OJ L 145, 13.6.1977; Eleventh General Report, point 219.

Section 3

Computerization of Community law

1071. At the end of the year the interinstitutional computerized documentation system for Community law (Celex) contained nearly 135 000 documents. Celex is available in Danish, German, English, French, Italian and Dutch, and there is a pilot Greek version. Loading of the Spanish base has been going on since May, and the Portuguese base will be launched in the course of 1991.

There were nearly 3 000 users of the system at the end of 1990, including over 1 500 external subscribers and around 20 commercial hosts. Demand rose even more sharply than in 1989. Most subscribers are private or public bodies in Member States, though a number of users are from outside the Community — mainly in the United States and EFTA countries.

Work on modernizing the system — with a view to making the bases more accessible to non-specialists, adding to them, and updating them more rapidly — continued in 1990, though progress was slowed by overall budgetary constraints.

1072. The 14th and 15th editions of the *Directory of Community legislation* were published in February and August in the nine Community languages. The titles and references of legislation in force at 1 June and 1 December each year are selected using Celex, and the directory is then published by the Office for Official Publications of the European Communities.

The year in brief[1]

1990

European Tourism Year
Glasgow, European City of Culture

January

5 January

At Italy's request, fluctuation margin for the lira reduced within the European Monetary System.

Point 38 of this Report

16 January

New Council President, Mr Collins, presents Parliament with programme for Ireland's six-month term in Council chair.

Bull. EC 1/2-1990, point 1.6.1

17 January

Mr Delors, President of the Commission, presents Commission's programme for 1990 to Parliament.

Bull. EC 1/2-1990, Point 1.6.19; Supplement 1/90 — Bull. EC

February

5 February

On basis of Commission's guidelines, Council defines action programme for development of relations between Community and countries of Central and Eastern Europe.

Point 668 of this Report

---

[1] This chronological summary does not claim to be exhaustive. For further details, see the passages of this Report and the Bulletin cited in the margin.

21 February

Commission holds its 1 000th meeting.

Point 927 of
this Report

Commission adopts communication on audiovisual policy, setting
out broad lines of Community strategy.

Point 178 of
this Report

March

5 March

Council adopts transitional measures to apply to ACP-EEC
cooperation and to OCT-EEC Association between end of Lomé
III and entry into force of Lomé IV.

Point 766 of
this Report

28 March

Commission adopts three-year action plan (1990-92) for consumer
protection policy in Community.

Point 541 of
this Report

April

2 April

Framework Agreement for Trade and Economic Cooperation
with Argentina signed in Luxembourg.

Point 759 of
this Report

6 April

1 000 days to 31 December 1992.

8 April

General elections in Greece.

10 April

Commission proposes action programme to promote development
of European audiovisual industry — Media (1991-95).

Point 179 of
this Report

18 April

Commission puts forward new approach to company taxation.

Point 154 of
this Report

23 April

Council formally adopts new framework programme (1990-94) for research and technological development.

Point 247 of this Report

28 April

Extraordinary meeting of European Council in Dublin frames common approach to German unification, relations with countries of Central and Eastern Europe, and the CSCE process. Defines procedure for preparing proposals for strengthening political union.

Bull. EC 4-1990, points I.1 to I.16

May

2 May

Commission sets general objectives for steel up to 1995.

Point 215 of this Report

Commission adopts action plan to extend coordinated assistance from 24 Western countries (G-24).

Point 668 of this Report

7 May

Council adopts provisions establishing Tempus programme and European Training Foundation.

Points 390 and 391 of this Report

Council adopts Regulation on establishment of European Environment Agency and European environment monitoring and information network.

Point 502 of this Report

8 May

Commission proposes guidelines for cooperation with developing countries of Latin America and Asia.

Point 763 of this Report

9 May

Fortieth anniversary of Schuman Declaration.

Point 927 of this Report

17 May

1990-94 'Europe against cancer' action plan and Directive on maximum tar yield of cigarettes adopted.

Point 174 of this Report

22 May

Commission adopts communication on 'Redirecting the Community's Mediterranean policy' (1992-96).

Point 718 of this Report

23 May

Commission formally adopts 13 out of 15 specific research and technological development programme proposals in connection with new framework programme.

Point 247 of this Report

29 May

Agreement establishing European Bank for Reconstruction and Development signed in Paris.

Point 54 of this Report

Council adopts action programme for development of continuing vocational training (Force).

Point 386 of this Report

30 May

Commission adopts communication on relations between Community and Yugoslavia.

Point 728 of this Report

June

6 June

Commission presents Green Paper on urban environment.

Point 536 of this Report

Commission proposes package of measures to strengthen relations between Community and Turkey.

Point 719 of this Report

13 June

Commission adopts three proposals for Directives on atypical work.

Point 337 of this Report

Commission presents Community response to special cooperation plan drawn up by Colombia in fight against drugs.	Point 758 of this Report

25 and 26 June

Dublin European Council convenes for December two intergovernmental conferences on economic and monetary union and on political union. Commission is instructed to prepare proposals for supporting reforms in Soviet Union.	Bull. EC 6-1990, points I.1 to I.42

28 June

Council adopts three Directives on right of residence.	Point 168 of this Report
Council adopts Directive on open network provision (ONP) for telecommunications.	Point 312 of this Report
Council formally adopts promotion of energy technologies programme (Thermie).	Point 608 of this Report

29 June

Council issues negotiating directives for agreement with EFTA countries on establishing European economic area.	Point 688 of this Report

July

1 July

Stage I of economic and monetary union begins.	Point 32 of this Report

4 July

Commission proposes guidelines for Community's generalized preferences scheme for 1990s.	Point 794 of this Report
Cyprus applies to join European Communities.	Point 722 of the Report

9, 10 and 11 July

Western Economic Summit in Houston.	Point 691 of this Report

12 July

New Council President, Mr De Michelis, presents Parliament with programme for Italy's six-month term in Council chair.

Bull. EC 7/8-1990, point 1.8.1

16 July

Malta applies to join Communities.

Point 724 of this Report

18 July

Commission proposes package of measures for protection of personal data and information security.

Point 186 of this Report

23 July

Council adopts two Directives adjusting system of taxation applicable between parent companies and subsidiaries of different Member States.
Simultaneously the Member States sign convention on eliminating double taxation.

Point 155 of this Report

24 July

Council formally adopts three Regulations constituting second stage of air transport liberalization policy.

Point 584 of this Report

25 July

Commission adopts proposal for Directive on certain aspects of adaption of working time.

Point 371 of this Report

August

2 August

Iraq invades Kuwait.

Point 734 of this Report

8 August

Measures instituting an embargo on trade with Iraq adopted.

Point 734 of this Report

21 August

Commission adopts communication on Community and German unification, backed by package of proposals for interim measures — allowing early application of essential transitional measures and technical derogations — and for those transitional measures and derogations.

Point 21 of this Report

Commission presents comprehensive paper on economic and monetary union.

Point 2 of this Report

27 August

Commission specifies, in a communication, objectives and content of Association Agreements to be negotiated with countries of Central and Eastern Europe.

Point 673 of this Report

September

17 September

Council adopts interim measures in connection with German unification.

Point 22 of this Report

Council adopts Directive on procurement procedures of entities operating in the excluded sectors.

Point 121 of this Report

19 September

Commission presents package of proposals on general system and structure of excises within internal market.

Point 159 of this Report

21 September

Merger Control Regulation comes into force.

Point 188 of this Report

October

3 October

Germany unified.

Point 17 of this Report

6 October

Sterling joins EMS exchange-rate mechanism.

Point 39 of
this Report

27 and 28 October

At extraordinary meeting in Rome, European Council continues and, for economic and monetary union, completes preparation for intergovernmental conferences. Reaffirms total condemnation of Iraq, stressing Community and Member States accord top priority to resolving Gulf crisis on basis of United Nations resolutions.

29 October

Council strengthens embargo against Iraq.

Point 734 of
this Report

30 October

Commission approves communication on industrial policy in an open and competitive environment.

Point 212 of
this Report

November

7 November

Commission proposes to Council Directives authorizing it to negotiate European Agreements with Czechoslovakia, Hungary and Poland.

Point 672 of
this Report

8 November

Council adopts second Directive on direct life assurance and Directive relating to freedom to offer services in insurance against civil liability in respect of use of motor vehicles.

Points 133 and 134 of
this Report

14 November

Commission proposes Council relieve indebtedness of ACP countries to Community.

Point 769 of
this Report

19, 20 and 21 November

CSCE meeting in Paris of 34 Heads of State or Government, who signed a Charter for a New Europe.

Point 871 of
this Report

22 November

Community and its Member States adopt two joint declarations with United States and Canada expressing a common resolve to strengthen their partnership and develop closer cooperation.

Points 692 and 712 of this Report

28 November

Commission adopts communication setting out a number of general guidelines for future of common fisheries policy.

Point 471 of this Report

December

2 December

General elections in the Federal Republic of Germany.

3 to 7 December

Uruguay Round — ministerial conference in Brussels.

Point 821 of this Report

4 December

Council adopts transitional measures in connection with German unification.

Point 23 of this Report

Council adopts Regulation on financial aid for countries most directly affected by Gulf crisis.

Point 734 of this Report

5 December

Commission adopts proposal for Directive on European works councils in companies or groups of companies operating Community-wide.

Point 363 of this Report

12 December

General elections in Denmark.

14 and 15 December

Rome European Council commends preparations for political union and identifies aspects for special consideration by intergovernmental conference.

Decides to grant Community aid to help Soviet Union meet urgent needs and sets number of guidelines for support for reforms.

Bull. EC 12-1990

15 December

Opening of intergovernmental conferences on political union and on economic and monetary union.

Points 4 and 16 of this Report

Annexes

Annex to Chapter III, Section 2

**Directives and proposals on the removal
of technical barriers to trade in industrial products**

I. Directives adopted by the Council

Reference	Subject	Date adopted	OJ No and page ref.	OJ date
90/384/EEC	Non-automatic weighing machines	20.6.1990	L 189/1	20.7.1990
90/385/EEC	Active implantable medical devices	20.6.1990	L 189/17	20.7.1990
90/396/EEC	Appliances burning gaseous fuels	29.6.1990	L 196/15	26.7.1990
90/486/EEC	Electrically operated lifts (amendment of Directive 84/529/EEC)	17.9.1990	L 270/21	2.10.1990
90/487/EEC	Electrical equipment for use in potentially explosive atmospheres employing certain types of protection (amendment of Directive 79/196/EEC)	17.9.1990	L 270/23	2.10.1990
90/488/EEC	Simple pressure vessels (amendment of Directive 87/404/EEC)	17.9.1990	L 270/25	2.10.1990
90/517/EEC	Classification, packaging and labelling of dangerous substances (11th adaptation to technical progress)	9.10.1990	L 287/37	19.10.1990
90/683/EEC	Modules for the various phases of the conformity assessment procedures which are intended to be used in the technical harmonization Directives	13.12.1990	L 380/13	31.12.1990

II. Directives adopted by the Commission

Reference	Subject	Date adopted	OJ No and page ref.	OJ date
90/121/EEC	Cosmetic products (adaptation to technical progress of Annexes II, III, IV, V and VI to Council Directive 76/768/EEC)	20.2.1990	L 71/40	17.3.1990
90/128/EEC	Plastics materials and articles intended to come into contact with foodstuffs	23.2.1990	L 75/19	21.3.1990
90/207/EEC	Methods of analysis necessary for checking the composition of cosmetic products (amendment of Directive 82/434/EEC)	4.4.1990	L 108/92	28.4.1990
90/335/EEC	Prohibition of the placing on the market and use of plant protection products containing certain active substances (fourth amendment of the Annex to Council Directive 79/117/EEC)	7.6.1990	L 162/37	28.6.1990
90/492/EEC	Classification, packaging and labelling of dangerous preparations (second adaptation to technical progress of Council Directive 88/379/EEC)	5.9.1990	L 275/35	5.10.1990
90/612/EEC	Specific purity criteria for emulsifiers, stabilizers, thickeners and gelling agents for use in foodstuffs (amendment of Directive 78/663/EEC)	26.10.1990	L 326/58	24.11.1990
90/628/EEC	Safety belts and restraint systems of motor vehicles	30.10.1990	L 341/1	6.12.1990
90/629/EEC	Anchorages for motor-vehicle safety belts	30.10.1990	L 341/14	6.12.1990
90/630/EEC	Field of vision of motor vehicle drivers	30.10.1990	L 341/20	6.12.1990

III. Proposals sent to the Council but not yet adopted

Reference	Subject	Date sent	OJ No and page ref.	OJ date
COM(89) 607 final	Wholesale distribution of medicinal products for human use	26.1.1990	C 58/16	8.3.1990
COM(89) 607 final	Legal status for the supply of medicinal products for human use	26.1.1990	C 58/19	8.3.1990
COM(89) 607 final	Labelling of medicinal products for human use and on package leaflets	26.1.1990	C 58/21	8.3.1990
COM(89) 662 final	Measures to be taken against air pollution by emissions from motor vehicles (amendment of Directive 70/220/EEC)	5.1.1990	C 81/1	30.3.1990
COM(89) 665 final	Restrictions on the marketing and use of certain dangerous substances and preparations	22.1.1990	C 24/20	1.2.1990
COM(89) 653 final	Safety glazing and glazing materials on motor vehicles and their trailers	12.2.1990	C 95/1	12.4.1990
COM(89) 653 final	Masses and dimensions of motor vehicles of catergory M_1	12.2.1990	C 95/92	12.4.1990
COM(89) 653 final	Pneumatic tyres for motor vehicles and their trailers	12.2.1990	C 95/101	12.4.1990
COM(90) 72 final	Medicinal products and homeopathic medicinal products (widening of the scope of Directives 65/65/EEC and 75/319/EEC)	23.3.1990	C 108/10	1.5.1990
COM(90) 72 final	Veterinary medicinal products and homeopathic veterinary medicinal products (widening of the scope of Directive 81/851/EEC)	23.3.1990	C 108/13	1.5.1990
COM(90) 174 final	Measures to be taken against the emission of gaseous pollutants from diesel engines for use in vehicles (amendment of Directive 88/77/EEC)	21.5.1990	C 187/6	27.7.1990
COM(90) 212 final	Advertising of medicinal products for human use	12.6.1990	C 163/10	4.7.1990

COM(90) 381 final	Sweeteners for use in foodstuffs	18.9.1990	C 242/4	27.9.1990
COM(90) 408 final	Flavourings for use in foodstuffs and source materials for their production (supplementing Directive 88/388/EEC)	12.10.1990		
COM(90) 440 final	Indications or marks identifying the lot to which a foodstuff belongs	5.10.1990	C 267/15	23.10.1990
COM(90) 458 final	Designation of flavourings in the list of ingredients on the label of foodstuffs	12.10.1990		

Annex to Chapter VII

Activities of the Court of Justice and of the Court of First Instance, in figures

TABLE 1

Cases since 1953 analysed by subject-matter [1]

Situation at 31 December 1990

	ECSC				EEC													Total
	Scrap compensation	Transport	Competition [5]	Other [2]	Free movement of goods and Customs Union	Right of establishment and freedom to supply services	Taxation	Competition and State aid [3]	Social security and free movement of workers	Agriculture	Transport	Article 220 Conventions	Other [4]	Euratom	Privileges and immunities	Proceedings by staff of institutions [3]	Total
Actions brought	167	35	67 [5] (1)	266 [6] (1)	784 (39)	160 (27)	285 (26)	498 [7] (36)	498 (37)	1 310 (155)	71 (16)	74 (3)	395 (32)	15 (1)	16 (2)	2 444 [8] (56)	7 085 [9] (432)
Cases not resulting in a judgment	25	6	24	123	180 (27)	30 —	57 (1)	53 [5] (5)	45 (4)	115 (8)	13 (2)	5 —	102 (9)	1 —	4 (1)	1 378 [10] (17)	2 161 [11] (74)
Cases decided	142	29	43 (1)	139 (1)	507 (39)	87 (8)	178 (12)	338 [5] (19)	385 (28)	992 (75)	37 (2)	62 (3)	234 (31)	13 (1)	12 (2)	1 002 [12] (61)	4 200 [13] (283)
Cases pending	—	—	—	4	97	43	50	107	68	203	21	7	59	1	—	64	724

The figures in brackets represent the cases dealt with by the Court in 1990.

1 Cases concerning more than one subject are classified under the most important heading.
2 Levies, investment declarations, tax charges, miners' bonuses, production quotas.
3 Including appeals against decisions by the Court of First Instance.
4 Contentious proceedings, Staff Regulations, Community terminology, Lomé Convention, short-term economic policy, commercial policy, relations between Community law and national law and environment.
5 Including 1 case before the Court of First Instance
6 Including 3 cases before the Court of First Instance.

7 Including 83 cases before the Court of First Instance.
8 Including 119 cases before the Court of First Instance.
9 Including 205 cases before the Court of First Instance.
10 Including 15 cases before the Court of First Instance.
11 Including 16 cases before the Court of First Instance.
12 Including 53 cases before the Court of First Instance.
13 Including 60 cases before the Court of First Instance.

TABLE 2

Cases analysed by type (EEC Treaty)[1]
Situation at 31 December 1990

	Arts 169, 93 and 171	Art. 170	Art. 173				Art. 175	Art. 177			Art. 181	Art. 215	Protocols to Art. 220 Conventions	Appeals	Grand total[2]
			By governments	By Community institutions	By individuals	Total		Validity	Interpretation	Total					
Actions brought	800	2	180	31	590[5]	801[5]	42[6]	275	1 841	2 057	11	329	73	1	4 116[7]
Cases not resulting in a judgment	288	1	25	8	80	113[8]	5	41	134	145	4	48	6	—	610[8]
Cases decided	361	1	116	17	383[9]	520[9]	30[8]	263	1 462	1 699	7	177	64	—	2 856[10]
In favour of applicant[3]	322	1	49	—	92	150	3	—	—	—	5	13	—	—	492
Dismissed on the merits[4]	35	—	61	7	185[8]	257[8]	3	—	—	—	—	145	—	—	439[8]
Rejected as inadmissible	4	—	6	1	105[6]	112[6]	23[8]	—	—	—	—	20[8]	—	—	152[9]
Cases pending	151	—	39	6	127	168	7	29	245	213	—	104	3	1	650

Proceedings brought under

1 Excluding proceedings by staff and cases concerning the interpretation of the Protocol on Privileges and Immunities and of the Staff Regulations (see Table 1).
2 Total may be smaller than the sum of individual items because some cases are based on more than one Treaty article.
3 In respect of at least one of the applicant's main claims.
4 This also covers proceedings rejected partly as inadmissible and partly on the merits.
5 Including 77 cases before the Court of First Instance.
6 Including 5 cases before the Court of First Instance.
7 Including 10 cases before the Court of First Instance.
8 Including 1 case before the Court of First Instance.
9 Including 6 cases before the Court of First Instance.
10 Including 7 cases before the Court of First Instance.

TABLE 3

Cases analysed by type (ECSC and Euratom Treaties)[1]
Situation at 31 December 1990

	By governments		By Community institutions		By natural or legal persons		Art. 41 ECSC Questions of validity	Art. 150 Euratom Questions of interpretation	Art. 153 Euratom	Total	
	ECSC	Euratom	ECSC	Euratom	ECSC	Euratom				ECSC	Euratom
Actions brought	32	—	—	1	502[4]	11	5	4	2	539[4]	18
Cases not resulting in a judgment	14	—	—	—	163	—	—	—	1	177	1
Cases decided	17	—	1	1	333	10	5	3	1	355	15
In favour of applicant[2]	6	—	—	—	81	3	—	—	—	87	4
Dismissed on the merits[3]	10	—	—	—	188	7	—	—	1	198	8
Rejected as inadmissible	1	—	—	—	64	—	—	—	—	65	—
Cases pending	1	—	—	—	6	1	—	1	—	7	2

Number of proceedings instituted

[1] Excluding proceedings by staff and cases concerning the interpretation of the Protocol on Privileges and Immunities and of the Staff Regulations (see Table 1).
[2] In respect of at least one of the applicant's main claims.
[3] This also covers proceedings rejected partly as inadmissible and partly on the merits.
[4] Including 3 cases before the Court of First Instance.

Institutions and other bodies

European Parliament
Secretariat
Centre européen, Plateau du Kirchberg
L-2929 Luxembourg
Tel.: 43001

Council of the European Communities
General Secretariat
Rue de la Loi 170
B-1048 Brussels
Tel.: 234 61 11

Commission of the European Communities
Rue de la Loi 200
B-1049 Brussels
Tel.: 235 11 11

Court of Justice
Plateau du Kirchberg
L-2925 Luxembourg
Tel.: 43031

Court of Auditors
12 rue Alcide de Gasperi
L-1615 Luxembourg
Tel.: 43981

Economic and Social Committee
Rue Ravenstein 2
B-1000 Brussels
Tel.: 512 39 20

List of abbreviations

ACE	Action by the Community on the environment
Acnat	Action by the Community relating to nature conservation
ACP	African, Caribbean and Pacific countries party to the Lomé Convention
AIM	Advanced informatics in medicine
ANC	African National Congress
Asean	Association of South-East Asian Nations
BAP	Biotechnology action programme
BC-Net	Business Cooperation Network
BCR	Community Bureau of References
Bridge	Biotechnology research for innovation, development and growth in Europe
Brite/Euram	Basic research in industrial technologies for Europe/raw materials and advanced materials
Caddia	Cooperation in automation of data and documentation for imports/exports and agriculture
CAP	Common agricultural policy
CEN	European Committee for Standardization
Cenelec	European Committee for Electrotechnical Standardization
CEPT	European Conference of Postal and Telecommunications Administrations
CMEA	Council for Mutual Economic Assistance
Comett	Community programme in education and training for technology
Cordis	Community research and development information service
Corinne	Coordination of information on the environment in Europe
CSCE	Conference on Security and Cooperation in Europe

CSF	Community support framework
Delta	Development of European learning through technological advance
Drive	Dedicated road infrastructure for vehicle safety in Europe
EAGGF	European Agricultural Guidance and Guarantee Fund
EBRD	European Bank for Reconstruction and Development
ECCD	European Committee to Combat Drugs
ECHO	European Commission host organization
Eclair	European collaborative linkage of agriculture and industry through research
Ecu	European currency unit
EDF	European Development Fund
EEA	European economic area
EFTA	European Free Trade Association
Ehlass	European home and leisure accident surveillance system
EIB	European Investment Bank
EMS	European Monetary System
EMU	Economic and monetary union
Envireg	Community initiative concerning the environment in the regions
Epoch	European programme on climatology and natural hazards
Erasmus	European Community action scheme for the mobility of university students
ERDF	European Regional Development Fund
Ermes	European radio messaging system
Esprit	European strategic programme for research and development in information technology
ETSI	European Telecommunications Standards Institute
Euret	European research for transport
Euroform	Community initiative for the development of new qualifications, new skills and new employment opportunities
FADN	EEC farm accountancy data network
FAO	Food and Agriculture Organization of the United Nations

Force	Action programme for the development of continuing vocational training
GATT	General Agreement on Tariffs and Trade (UN)
GCC	Gulf Cooperation Council
Horizon	Community initiative on handicapped persons and certain other disadvantaged groups
IAEA	International Atomic Energy Agency (UN)
IBRD	International Bank for Reconstruction and Development (World Bank) (UN)
IEA	International Energy Agency (OECD)
IMF	International Monetary Fund (UN)
IMP	Integrated Mediterranean programme
Impact	Information market policy actions
Insis	Interinstitutional system of integrated services
Interreg	Community initiative concerning border areas
IRCC	International Radio Consultative Committee
ISDN	Integrated Services Digital Network
ITER	International thermonuclear experimental reactor
JET	Joint European Torus
Joule	Joint opportunities for unconventional or long-term energy supply
JRC	Joint Research Centre
Leader	Links between actions for the development of the rural economy
Lingua	Action programme to promote foreign-language competence in the Community
MAST	Marine science and technology
MCA	Monetary compensatory amount
Media	Measures to encourage the development of the audiovisual industry
MFA	Multifibre Arrangement (Arrangement regarding International Trade in Textiles)
Miriam	Model scheme for information on rural development initiatives and agricultural markets
Monitor	Research programme on strategic analysis, forecasting and assessment in research and technology

NACE	General industrial classification of economic activities within the European Communities
NCI	New Community Instrument
NET	Next European Torus
NGO	Non-governmental organization
NOW	Community initiative for the promotion of equal opportunities for women in the field of employment and vocational training
OCTs	Overseas countries and territories
OECD	Organization for Economic Cooperation and Development
ONP	Open network provision
Pedip	Programme to modernize Portuguese industry
Petra	Action programme for the vocational training of young people and their preparation for adult and working life
Phare	Poland and Hungary — Aid for economic restructuring
PINC	Community's illustrative nuclear programme
PIP	Priority information programme
Poseican	Programme of options specific to the remote and insular nature of the Canary Islands
Poseidom	Programme of options specific to the remote and insular nature of the overseas departments
Poseima	Programme of options specific to the remote and insular nature of Madeira and the Azores
Prisma	Preparation of industries situated in the regions for the single market
RACE	Research and development in advanced communications technologies for Europe
R&TD	Research and technological development
Rechar	Programme to assist the conversion of coalmining areas
Regen	Community initiative on energy networks
Regis	Community initiative concerning the most remote regions
Renaval	Programme to assist the conversion of shipbuilding areas
Resider	Programme to assist the conversion of steel areas
Reward	Recycling of waste R&D
SAVE	Specific actions for vigorous energy efficiency

SMEs	Small and medium-sized enterprises
Spear	Support programme for a European assessment of research
SPES	Stimulation plan for economic science
Sprint	Strategic programme for innovation and technology transfer
STAR	Community programme for the development of certain less-favoured regions of the Community by improving access to advanced telecommunications services
STEP	Science and technology for environmental protection
Stride	Science and technology for regional innovation and development in Europe
TAC	Total allowable catch
Taric	Integrated Community tariff
Tedis	Trade electronic data interchange system
Télématique	Community initiative for regional development concerning services and networks related to data communication
Tempus	Trans-European mobility scheme for university studies
Thermie	Programme for the promotion of energy technology
UN	United Nations
Unctad	United Nations Conference on Trade and Development
UNEP	United Nations Environment Programme
Unido	United Nations Industrial Development Organization
Valoren	Community programme for the development of certain less-favoured regions of the Community by exploiting endogenous energy potential
Value	Programme for the dissemination and utilization of research results
WFC	World Food Council (UN)
WFP	World Food Programme (UN)

Publications cited in this Report

General Report on the Activities of the European Communities
(abbr.: General Report), published annually by the Commission

— *the Agricultural Situation in the Community*
(Published in conjunction with the General Report)
(abbr.: Agricultural Report), published annually

— *Report on Social Developments*
(Published in conjunction with the General Report)
(abbr.: Social Report), published annually

— *Report on Competition Policy*
(Published in conjunction with the General Report)
(abbr.: Competition Report), published annually

Bulletin of the European Communities
(abbr.: Bull. EC), published monthly by the Commission

Supplement to the Bulletin of the European Communities
(abbr.: Supplement ... — Bull. EC), published at irregular intervals by the Commission

1/89 Statement on the broad lines of Commission policy and reply to the ensuing Parliamentary debate

2/89 Programme of the Commission for 1989

3/89 Takeover and other general bids

4/89 Medium-term Community action programme to foster the economic and social integration of the least-privileged groups

5/89 Statute for a European company

1/90 Commission's programme for 1990

2/90 Community merger control law

3/90 Public procurement in the excluded sectors (II)

4/90 The European Community and German unification

Official Journal of the European Communities
Legislation series (abbr.: OJ L)
Information and notices series (abbr.: OJ C)
Supplement on public works and supply contracts (abbr.: OJ S)

Reports of Cases before the Court
(abbr.: ECR), published by the Court of Justice in annual series, parts appearing at irregular intervals throughout the year

**All the above publications are printed and distributed through
the Office for Official Publications of the European Communities,
L-2985 Luxembourg**

Annual Report of the European Investment Bank
published and distributed by the EIB,
100, boulevard Konrad Adenauer
L-2950 Luxembourg

European Communities—Commission

Twenty-fourth General Report on the Activities of the European Communities—1990

Luxembourg: Office for Official Publications of the European Communities

1991 — 460 pp. — 16.2 × 22.9 cm

ISBN 92-826-2176-6

Catalogue number: CM-60-90-086-EN-C

Price (excluding VAT) in Luxembourg: ECU 12.50

The General Report on the Activities of the European Communities is published annually by the Commission as required by Article 18 of the Treaty of 8 April 1965 establishing a Single Council and a Single Commission of the European Communities.

The Report is presented to the European Parliament and provides a general picture of Community activities over the past year.